Roadmap to Reality

*Consciousness, Worldviews, and
the Blossoming of Human Spirit*

Thomas J. Elpel
Illustrated by Bonnie Andrich

*Dedicated to my children—
Felicia, Cassie, Donny, and Edwin.
You are the magic and inspiration in my life.*

HOPS Press, LLC
12 Quartz Street
Pony, MT 59747
www.hopspress.com

Roadmap to Reality
Consciousness, Worldviews, and the Blossoming of Human Spirit
© Thomas J. Elpel, 2008

First Edition. May 2008. ISBN: 978-1-892784-29-2. 5,000 copies printed.

Publisher's Cataloging-in-Publication Data
    Elpel, Thomas J. 1967-
    Roadmap to Reality: Consciousness, Worldviews, and the Blossoming of Human
Spirit / Thomas J. Elpel.

    Includes bibliographical references and index.
    ISBN: 978-1-892784-29-2 $30.00 Pbk. (alk. paper)

    1. Social History—Cultural Evolution. 2. Consciousness—Worldviews.
3. Philosophy—Enlightenment. 4. Reality.

    I. Elpel, Thomas J. II. Title.
    HN13.D5 2008   304.2'8

 Printed on 100% recycled paper.

Table of Contents

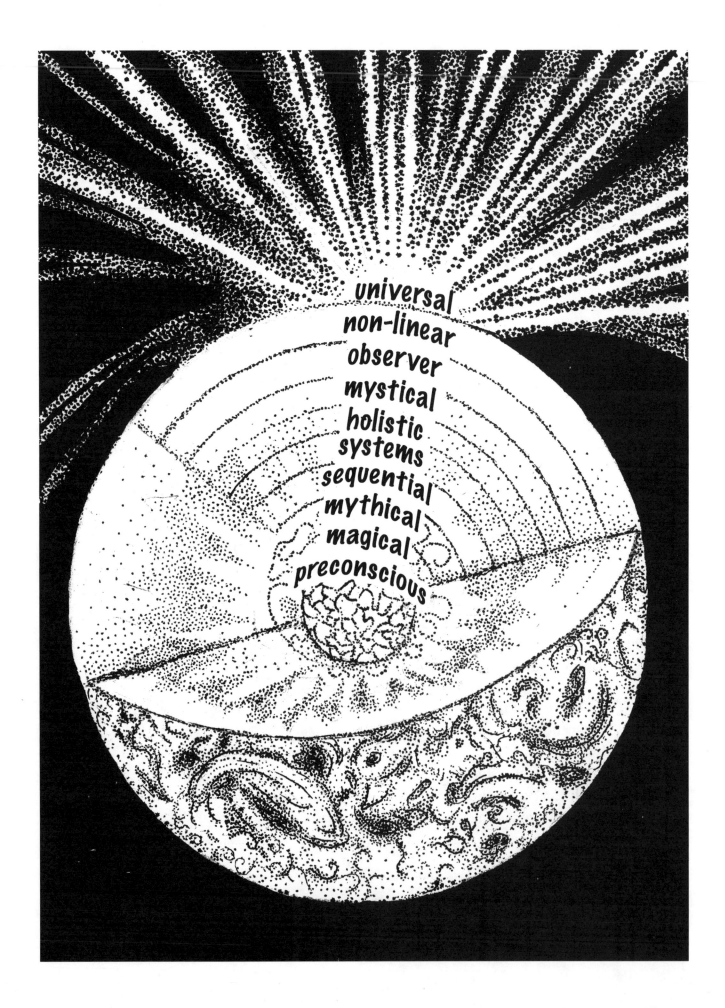

Introduction

Two people can share the experience of walking a dog, riding in a car, or watching a movie together, yet perceptions of those experiences may differ greatly. Children's movies, for example, often include humor intended for the parents. Kids are oblivious to the puns and cultural references that are not part of their world.

In the journey ahead we find that the reality experienced by children is defined by predictable patterns of behavior and perception. We explore the world as children see it and discover how perceptions of reality change as we mature. Each of these generalized perceptions of reality can be thought of as a worldview.

Infants start out with a *preconscious* worldview, unaware of their existence. As they mature into childhood they discover a *magical* worldview, like the stories of Harry Potter, where anything is possible. Older children acquire a *mythical* worldview, obsessed with role-playing and understanding the rules of society in black-and-white terms. Adolescents and young adults begin to perceive a *sequential* worldview, characterized by critical thinking and an understanding of linear cause and effect. Most adults mature to a blend of the mythical and sequential worldviews.

Perceptions of reality are not hardwired into the human brain. Children mature through each worldview until they acquire a similar perspective as their culture. However, not all cultures perceive reality in the same way. In studying past cultures, we discover that hunter-gatherer societies perceived reality in magical terms, agricultural societies perceived reality in mythical terms, and industrial societies perceive reality in sequential terms. In other words, perceptions of reality are linked to technology.

Two new worldviews arose with computer networking and global environmental monitoring. Linear cause and effect is being succeeded by interconnected systems processing, leading to a *systems* worldview. Global environmental awareness is leading towards a *holistic* worldview, the recognition that we are all in this world together like strands in a great web. These viewpoints are beginning to percolate through our culture. Meanwhile, microbiology, genetics, nanotechnology, and quantum physics are enabling entirely new perceptions of reality, leading to the emergence of *mystical, observer, and nonlinear* worldviews.

Given that the definition of reality changes with each worldview, we must wonder if there is some *universal* reality that encompasses all others. Through the pages of this book we explore all these realities in depth, building a roadmap to navigate through them in search of the real reality.

In the quest to determine what reality is, we must acknowledge that reality itself probably doesn't change from one worldview to another. It is our perceptions of reality that constantly evolve. Therefore, the quest to define reality is the quest to understand ourselves and why we perceive reality the way we do. Along the way we discover unexpected insights about humanity, including: 1) we may not qualify as self-aware or sentient beings, 2) free will is an illusion, 3) the mind and our self-identity are illusions, 4) the illusions are generated by the structure of language, and 5) the structure of language is linked to technological innovation.

The ultimate goal of this quest is freedom. We cannot be free as long as we are deluded by illusions of sentience, free will, and self-identity. We must shatter those illusions to discover our true nature. As a bonus to the journey, we discover answers to the challenge of achieving environmental sustainability, global peace, and prosperity for all. The answers are staring us in the face already. We only need to open our eyes to see what reality really is.

Part I

Testing
Assumptions

Roadmap to Reality

–One–

Quest for the Real Reality

Poking Holes in the Illusion

"A belief system may be defined as open to the extent that new data can enter and affect existing beliefs. A person will be open to information insofar as possible, but will unconsciously reject it, screen it out, or alter it insofar as is necessary to ward off threat and anxiety. The closed mind can distort the world and narrow it down to whatever extent is needed to serve these protective goals and still preserve the illusion of understanding it."

—*William Harmon, Global Mind Change*[1]

Oxana was raised by dogs since she was three years old. Her home was crowded with older siblings, so Oxana crawled into the doghouse and lived there. Her alcoholic, neglectful parents eventually disappeared, so Oxana lived with stray dogs. She ate raw meat and carrion and learned to walk on all fours and bark like a dog. She lapped at her food, bit at fleas, and scratched behind her ear with her foot. She had acute senses for hearing, sight, and smell. Authorities in Ukraine discovered Oxana in 1991 when she was eight years old. With intensive speech therapy she was able to acquire basic language skills. However, at age twenty-two she remained developmentally a six year-old.[2] When she showed her boyfriend her ability to run on all fours and bark like a dog, he "bolted like a terrified postman." In times of stress she still reverts to dog-like behaviors.[3]

Oxana is not so different from the rest of us. She mimicked what she was exposed to as a child and that defined her reality. We also mimicked what we were exposed to, and that defines our reality. Her reality was normal to her. Our reality seems normal to us. She didn't question her reality. We rarely question ours. Yet, our behaviors might seem as bizarre to an outside observer as Oxana's behavior seems to us.

Whether we are five years old or fifty, each of us has a mental model of how the world works. It is our map of reality. We accumulate new information and perspectives as we mature, updating our model as we go along until the reality we know at fifty is radically different than the one we understood at five. The funny thing is that we live every day in between as if our map of reality is complete. No matter how old we are, we assume that today's version of reality is the correct one. We update our map only when new evidence forces us to make corrections. It is exceedingly rare that we assume the map is incomplete or flawed and ask what we might be missing.

We are blind to our blindness. We assume we know what counts because we are oblivious to what we don't know. We go through our lives believing we can see, while remaining blind to that which we have not seen. We assume our beliefs, values, and decisions are correct. We charge ahead on the assumption that we are right until evidence to the contrary smacks us in the face. And yet, what would happen if we questioned everything? What would happen if we questioned our likes and our dislikes, our beliefs, our values, and our motivations in everything that we do? Instead of assuming that we are right, what would happen if we assumed that we are wrong? In this book we will test our most basic assumptions about reality to separate ourselves from that which we mimicked growing up. We will detach from preconceived notions in the hope of discovering what reality really is.

The results of this quest may be unsettling. Along the way we will find compelling evidence to suggest that 1) we do not qualify as a self-aware species, 2) our perception of free will is largely an illusion, 3) our sense of self and mind are not hardwired but emerge from language, 4) our definition of reality, or worldview, changes in predictable ways as we mature, 5) entire cultures evolve through similar stages, 6) these worldviews are dictated by technology, and 7) these worldviews determine our morals and values, how we perceive cause and effect, how we solve problems, how we raise and educate our children, and how we govern ourselves.

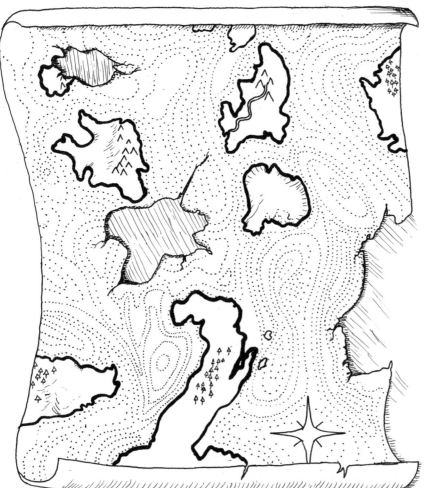

This book is the quest to become less blind. It is a quest to see what has been staring us in the face all along. It is a quest to define reality, a journey that will take us to the ends of the universe and back in reflections of self-discovery. It is only by stepping beyond these worldviews that we can discover the true nature of reality. It is only as outside observers that we can see a clear path forward to build an abundant and sustainable society, achieve world peace, and find contentment in our lives.

Beliefs about Reality

Stepping out on the front porch one bright, warm morning, we see a familiar scene of houses, cars, lawns, trees, pets, and people. Like the neighbors, we are preparing for the daily commute, or perhaps getting ready to send the kids off to school. As we pick up the paper to see what is happening in the world, we note the next door neighbor doing the same thing. It is a familiar routine. This is reality as we know it.

Some days we enjoy visiting with the neighbors. We talk about the weather, the latest headlines, sports, politics, the opposite sex, or any number of possible subjects. We may differ in opinions on certain issues, such as which is the better football or baseball team, but we can talk about the strengths and weaknesses of each. We could have similar conversations with almost anyone else we see on the street because we share a common reality. Aside from cultural variations, this reality seems to stretch from coast to coast, around the world, and encompasses the entire universe. Because we share a common reality, we can predict what would happen if we tossed a ceramic coffee cup onto the concrete sidewalk. And because reality is consistent, we would expect the same results anywhere else in the world. Thus, we seem to agree on the fundamental parameters, and our opinions differ only over the minor details, such as which is the better political party. Right?

Maybe not. Among people we visit with every day, viewpoints about reality may vary widely. Obvious differences revolve around our views of creation or evolution. Looking out the window, we may see a world that was created in six days by a God who lives in heaven above, or we may see a world that was a big accident: first there was nothing, and then "BANG"—the universe materialized itself into stars, planets, dinosaurs, apes, people, soap operas and cell phones. These are substantial discrepancies in beliefs about the nature of reality. We may be surprised at the diversity of viewpoints among people we interact with daily.

Including nonreligious people as a group, there are more than twenty broadly defined religions with their own beliefs about reality, each with a following of at least half a million people.[4] Each group claims to represent the correct version of reality. Several thousand smaller religions have also been documented.[5] Variations *within* many of these broadly defined groups, including Christianity, are so great that some factions don't recognize the others as sharing a common religion at all. For example, Mormons consider themselves Christians, but many Christians of other denominations would argue otherwise. Frequently, people are willing to kill each other to prove that their version of reality is the right one, such as in the Sunni versus Shia schism over Islam. Ultimately, it must lead us to wonder: How we can determine which reality is really real? If we declare that our reality is the one and only correct version, then how can we be certain of it?

Most of us assume that the correct version of reality is the set of beliefs we were most exposed to as children, typically influenced by our parents. After all, we trusted them since childhood, and they always seemed to know everything about the universe—things like how to make macaroni and cheese, how to tie shoes, and how to cross the street without being hit by a car. We absorbed similar beliefs through exposure, the same way we learned language. However, if we think about it in purely statistical terms, with all the different belief systems in circulation, there is a very low probability of being born into a family that has figured out which one is the real reality. Perhaps the only reason any of us question reality now is due to the realization that so many of our fellow human beings grew up with a different version than we did.

A Mind Game

The quest to determine the real reality may be the ultimate mind game. Imagine a virtual reality scenario in which we put on a headset to go into a simulation. Our mission is to find our way back to the real reality. However, as part of the game, we enter this virtual world as newborn children. We lose all prior memories. We lose all prior knowledge, language, and personal identity. We don't even remember that we have a mission, or that we are playing a virtual reality game. To accomplish this mission we are no longer aware of, we are born to some virtual parents who will take care of us until we can stand on our own.

How do we proceed to achieve such a mission? Is it achievable at all? How can we be certain that we are not already in a simulation, playing this game already? To discover the real reality, we have to probe around and poke holes in the illusion that now seems so real, until we can find a doorway beyond it. When we have successfully broken through one reality, we might reasonably assume that we are closer to the truth, but we should not assume that we have actually found it yet. We must poke around in whatever new reality we find ourselves in, searching for inconsistencies until we can break through that one as well. We must break through reality after reality to see what remains. Only then, when we have nothing left to poke and prod, can we assume that we have either discovered the real reality, or at least discovered a less distorted version of it.

As we begin this game, we Americans can be thankful that we have been born into a melting pot of diverse cultures. After all, if we were born into a culture that was largely isolated from all the others, then we would grow up with only the local version of reality, never having the opportunity to mingle with people who perceive reality differently. For example, an inner city child might perceive a raven as a noisy, garbage-eating bird, while a rural Native American child might perceive a raven as a spiritual messenger with something to say. If circumstances bring these two children together to play, and they see a raven, then each child will notice the other's reaction to the bird.[6] It is only by realizing that other people have a different version of reality that we are able to begin questioning and poking holes in our own.

The Tool Shed

The first step in our quest is to take stock of the available tools to probe and poke at our reality in search of answers. Let's start with our basic senses: Can we accurately define reality through direct examination with our eyes, ears, nose, taste, and touch? As we continue standing on the front porch in our imaginations, we look around at the sky above and the grass in the yard and the cars going by in the street. It is easy to assume that we are seeing reality as it really is. However, keep in mind that what we see is limited to the visible spectrum of light. The "visible spectrum" is not a property of light itself but rather a property of our eyes and what our eyes are adapted to seeing. Thus, if we could see the world through the eyes of certain insects or animals, then the "visible spectrum" might include infrared light, which makes the world look dramatically different. If we look at a person in infrared we would see a bright spot where the head and heart are, since those parts of the body are warmer and radiate more heat. It would be darker in the coolest parts of the body, such as the fingers and toes, which tend to have a cooler body temperature. The world appears greatly different in infrared, and it is important to acknowledge that this version of reality is equally as valid as the reality we experience.

Also consider the human nose. Our noses are pathetic sensory organs compared to dog noses, which are a hundred times more sensitive. A dog going across the yard with its nose to the ground can read the soil the way we might read a book, gathering volumes of information about who has been there and what they did in the yard. This sensory experience is dramatically different from ours and almost completely inaccessible to us as we stand on the front doorstep sniffing the air. This quick evaluation of two of our basic senses demonstrates that we cannot trust our senses alone to give us an objective perception of the reality we experience. When we acknowledge the limitations of our basic senses, then we have to acknowledge that, at best, we have a skewed perception of reality.

As noted by Jim Baggott, author of *A Beginner's Guide to Reality*, there is no evolutionary reason why we should be wired to perceive reality as it is: *"Just because I cannot understand what reality might be like for a bat does not mean that the bat's perceptions and experiences of that reality are any less legitimate than mine. What this implies is that evolutionary pressures lead to the selection of sensory apparatus that delivers a finely tuned* representation *of reality. What kind of representation depends on what kind of ecological niche a living creature is competing in. All that matters is that this is a representation that creates survival advantages. There is no evolutionary pressure to select a mind to represent reality as it really is."*[7]

While we cannot know what reality is like to a bat, we can at least understand that a bat navigates through reality with sonar. Similarly, with infrared imaging we can simulate how reality might be perceived by a snake. While we cannot hope to fully know what reality is like to other species, at least we can extrapolate from our accumulated knowledge to imagine the possibilities.

While recognizing that each creature experiences reality in a dramatically different way, we can reasonably argue that it is the same reality, just a different perception of it. In other words, our perceptions may be limited by our senses, or lack of them, but we can still probe the fabric of reality with the senses we have. The results will be perceived differently by our senses than by the senses of a dog or a bat, but it is apparently the same reality. It is sufficient for our quest to merely acknowledge that these different perceptions exist. If need be, we can conceptually build crude models of reality from these different perspectives, if only to remind ourselves that our senses don't give us the whole story.

Complicating matters is the issue of virtual reality. We acknowledged the limitations of our senses, but can we trust that *anything* we experience is actually real? For example, most humans enjoy the feeling of physical intimacy. But it isn't touching or being touched that we experience as pleasurable; it is the electrical impulses running through the nerves to the brain that signals the brain to decide it is experiencing pleasure. Likewise, we never actually see the world we live in, because our brains process electrical impulses, not light waves. Photons that strike the nerve cells in our retinas are converted to electrical impulses and passed along to the brain for processing. The world we see is created inside our brains.

If you and I exist as mere brains in a laboratory, or if we are hooked up to a virtual reality machine, then our entire experience of reality could be generated by the careful manipulation of electrical signals. For example, stimulation to specific areas of the brain can induce wild emotional swings in patients, from laughter to sobbing. Patients have no idea where the emotions come from. When one woman was asked what she was laughing about she replied, *"You guys are just so funny… just standing around."*[8] While it seems improbable that we are experiencing some kind of artificial reality, it is challenging to prove that we are not. We might exist as brains in a laboratory or software in some kind of reality simulation. We will attempt to tackle these issues before the end of our quest.

Parameters

Besides being limited in our sensory organs, another obstacle to defining reality is that our perceptions are distorted by our survival needs. For example, in the human experience of reality, the deadly amanita mushroom is toxic and aptly named. However, from the perspective of squirrels, it might be more correctly called the "delicious amanita," which they eat and thrive upon.[9] In a truly objective sense, an amanita is neither good nor bad, but from a human-centric perspective, it is definitely bad to eat. Similarly, we could not at this point declare that either murder or war are "bad" since that would be a judgment based on assumptions about reality. Nevertheless, I have no desire to eat a deadly amanita, nor to be stabbed or bombed. Dying might be a viable shortcut to get outside of this reality, but we may not find the answers we seek. We might also lose the chance to try again. There may be a better path to determining the real reality, and we can always resort to dying some other time, so let's start with a more inspired strategy and reserve death as a future possibility.

Thus, our quest is not objective in an absolute sense. It is undeniably biased towards the assumption that there is value in living, if only to have more time to ponder what that value might be. This bias is evident especially in regards to tackling the issues that threaten the future of humanity. If we are to survive as a species, then we must find a way to live harmoniously and sustainably with each other and the planet. Implicit in that statement is the judgment that our species is worth saving, at least for now.

We began this quest by acknowledging that our senses and survival needs provide us with a perception of reality that is both limited and distorted, and could be entirely illusory anyway. By this initial assessment of our situation, the task of determining the real reality would seem to be utterly hopeless. But let's consider the resources we do have at our disposal: We have the ability to compare different theories of reality, and to the extent that we can detach from our own cultural biases, we can reason through the differences between them in search of supporting or refuting evidence. We may not be able to prove any particular version of reality correct, but we might at least be able to dismiss some versions based on inconsistencies within them, which is equally helpful. By process of elimination, we can see what's left.

To ensure an objective playing field in this quest to define reality, I propose the following methodology: 1) we distinguish cultural realities from universal reality, 2) we assume that *everything* is true—at least within the proper context, 3) we proceed with unbounded open-mindedness tempered by equally unhindered skepticism, and 4) we look for consistency to test the probability or improbability of any particular version of reality.

Cultural Reality versus Universal Reality

Different cultures and religions often have very different viewpoints about what is right and wrong or how the universe works. In terms of food, for example, we may be horrified at the thought of eating a cat or a dog, but other people in the world are equally repulsed at the idea of eating beef or pork. Some cultures eat horses, rats, and insects, while others don't. Some ethnic groups avoid foods for legitimate physiological reasons, such as lactose intolerance. And in starvation situations, people have eaten almost anything, including other people. The point here is that food preferences often have little physical or nutritional basis; they are cultural biases—true within the context of the culture, but not universally true. Whether or not we personally decide to partake of new foods like cats or dogs or sushi, the quest to define reality requires that we recognize cultural realities for what they are—localized truths. Once we realize that, then we can seek out the greater universal truths. By detaching from our own conditioned sentiments about how things should and should not be, we can be open to discovering the universe as it really is.

Everything Is True within the Proper Context

In the quest to determine the nature of reality, all events and statements must be true—at least *within the proper context*, simply because they are generated by this reality and thus reflect something about it. In other words, no statements, anecdotes, or mysterious events can be dismissed as absolute fiction, because at some level there is truth about the nature of the reality that generated them.

For example, Renee and I adopted three of our four children. After living as a family for a couple years, my oldest daughter, Felicia, expressed how much she liked living in our sturdy stone and log house. She described how her birth family once lived in a house on the beach that was battered by a big storm, and they didn't know if the house would hold up through it. I listened to her story, knowing she never lived in a house on the beach and had never been in an awful storm. However, I also knew she wasn't lying. The symbolic nature of the story was obvious. She described in metaphor the stormy situation in her birth family and how much she liked being in a stable family. Lacking the tools to express herself directly, she was nevertheless able to communicate what she felt. Understanding the truth is just a matter of determining the proper context.

Similarly, we must acknowledge that all religions are true, at least within the proper context, since every religion generated by reality ultimately says something about the nature of reality. Interpretation of the truth of each religion may be debatable, yet the mere existence of each religion is itself a contribution to the reality we live in. The same could be said for alien abductions, out-of-body experiences, miraculous healings, fairy tales, and highly improbable good or bad luck. Whether real or imagined, the discussion of such phenomena is inherently part of our reality.

Open Minded and Skeptical

If we are to discover the true nature of reality, we must be open to even the most outrageous possibilities and yet be skeptical of everything, especially our own assumptions and convictions. Consider how outrageous it must have seemed when it was proposed that the earth was round instead of flat. We know the earth is round because we are told that since childhood. We have pictures of earth from space for proof. Pythagoras proposed that the

earth was round in the sixth century B.C., an idea that was tested and debated by scholars for hundreds of years until it gradually became common knowledge. Yet today there are still people in tribal cultures who *know* the world is flat.[10] How preposterous to think that the earth is round like a ball with land and water and people all the way around! It doesn't make any rational sense. How could people be walking around upside down on the other side of the planet without falling off?

The idea that the earth moves around the sun was equally preposterous, since anyone could see that the sun rose in the east and moved westward across the sky each day. But by observing the phases of Venus (like our phases of the moon), Galileo found evidence to support a theory articulated by Copernicus that the earth orbits the sun. His published works contradicted Church dogma that the earth was the center of the universe. Galileo was tried for heresy in 1633 and placed under house arrest for the last nine years of his life. Confinement had little or no effect on the nature of reality. The earth continued to revolve around the sun, regardless of the position of the Church, as it has for billions of years.

Scientists can be equally blind. While scientists could be perceived as open minded, curious explorers of natural phenomena, it is nearly impossible for scientists to discover anything that doesn't fit established preconceptions about the nature of reality. For instance, a scientific committee was appointed by the French Academy in 1772 to investigate meteorites. The scientists concluded that hot stones could not fall from the sky on the basis that there were no such stones in the Newtonian model of the solar system. The committee dismissed the idea of rocks from space and "explained" the phenomena in terms that fit existing models: the rocks must have been heated by lightning, or they were sent aloft by volcanic eruptions or whirlwinds, or the observers who witnessed them fall from space were delusional. The committee was so prestigious and their arguments so convincing that museums across Western Europe discarded their meteorite specimens.[11]

If we hope to discover the true nature of reality, then we must be open to the possibility that reality isn't what we expected it to be. We must be prepared to openly investigate ideas as outrageous as the notion that the earth is round and orbits the sun. If, for example, we hear about animals talking to people, or of people hearing the voice of God, we should not dismiss these stories without being open to the possibility that these people experienced *something*. In other words we should neither believe nor disbelieve anything, but rather, we should suspend judgment and allow the available facts to speak for themselves.

Any phenomena lacking a satisfactory explanation should not be dismissed simply because it does not fit into present worldviews. In questioning the validity of such a phenomena we must be equally open to the possibility that, like the scientists who dismissed the notion of meteorites, our inability to explain it could be due to the limitations of how we presently define reality. Rather than either accepting or dismissing unfamiliar phenomena, we should instead suspend judgment and let it float along in an indeterminate state, in the hope of finding an acceptable explanation later on. Even if claims of unusual events are proven false, we may learn something about reality through the process of investigation.

Being open minded to the most outlandish possibilities ensures that we won't dismiss something that might be important, while being equally skeptical ensures that we won't embrace a literal interpretation of an idea or belief that lacks substance upon investigation. However, the question remains: How can we determine whether or not we have found something true?

Consistency

It might be ideal to approach this quest for reality with the scientific method, to generate a hypothesis and to test it by controlling all the variables, arriving at consistent results whenever and wherever each experiment is performed. With a proper laboratory and an infinite amount of time to learn and tinker, I could conduct all previous scientific experiments to verify their authenticity and run additional tests of my own. However, even if I had such a lab at my disposal, then you as the reader would be stuck accepting my results on *faith*, unless you had a similar lab and an infinite amount of time to verify my work.

Thus, the reality of this quest for reality is that we are constrained by the tools at our disposal, which for most of us consists of little more than books and media, a keyboard and mouse, and personal experience. It is impossible to verify every fact, but we can look for consistency. For example, science might be unable to describe that which remains unknown, but it has established some consistent facts about reality to provide us with a suitable foundation to start from. Consider consistency within the scientific timeline of the universe compared to consistency within the literal biblical timeline.

Scientists have been able to measure the speed of light at 186,282.397 miles per second, and we know that it takes light eight minutes to traverse the ninety-three million miles from the sun to the earth. If the sun were suddenly yanked out of existence, we wouldn't notice it for another eight minutes. Similarly, when we look at stars in the sky, we are looking back in time. Our nearest neighboring star is Proxima Centauri, 4.22 light years away. A light year is the distance light travels in one year, or nearly 5.9 trillion miles. When we see Proxima Centauri, we are looking more than four years back in time. When we look at other stars, we look even farther back in time. If the universe is only six thousand years old, as suggested by the Bible, then we would see only six percent of our galaxy, which is about a hundred thousand light years across. New stars would seem to pop into existence every night as their light reached us for the very first time, but that's not what we see.

If the universe were only a few thousand years old, then we could not hope to see much of our own galaxy, let alone any other galaxies beyond it. Thus, we have reasonably established that the earth isn't the center of either the universe or the solar system, and the beginning of creation occurred much longer than six thousand years ago. The Bible may be full of many great truths, but the history of the universe doesn't seem to be one of them.

While scientific facts are constantly the subject of debate and revision, the revisions lead towards greater resolution, like piecing together a photograph from individual pixels. Without the benefit of knowing what the final image looks like, scientists have painstakingly fitted pixels of information together to form a fuzzy image of the universe. Researchers debate every detail and agree or disagree, or change their conclusions based on new evidence, but the big picture doesn't change much anymore. It becomes clearer with each passing year. Each discovery brings greater resolution, as events and dates are clarified back through time. It is this consistency that we will use as a reasonable guide to steer us along in the quest for the real reality.

A Fish in the Ocean

With unbounded open-mindedness tempered by equally unbounded skepticism we can proceed to explore the universe. We will seek the proper context behind every truth in the hope of distinguishing universal reality from cultural realities. Like fish trying to define the ocean, we will attempt to build a model of the reality we live in. Using consistency as evidence, we can then determine if we are on the right track.

Our model of reality must be representational, in the sense that a map is representational of the land. On a map, the roads or topography may be exaggerated to see them more clearly, or the curvature of the earth may be distorted to fit on a flat page. It is impossible to eliminate all the distortions, but cartographers do the best they can to minimize them to provide functional maps. In our own quest, it may be similarly impossible to define reality precisely, but as in mapmaking, we will seek to minimize the distortions to provide a functional roadmap to reality.

We may not see in infrared like a snake, read the ground with our noses like a dog, or see in the dark by listening to our own high-pitched screams like a bat, but—conceptually at least—we can understand that these perceptions of reality are as legitimate as our own. The bigger problem is to sort through human perceptions of reality. Although we all share the same basic senses, we perceive many different versions of reality. Thus, the quest for reality immediately becomes a study of human thought and perception. In order to figure out what reality is, we must understand how different people can look at the same thing and come up with such vastly different conclusions about it. In the process, we will explore many different versions of reality and assemble a sort of roadmap to navigate through them.

Roadmap to Reality

The reach of this book is necessarily as expansive as reality. The remainder of Part I is oriented towards "emptying one's cup" by testing familiar assumptions and deconstructing preconceived notions about reality. In short, we think we are a self-aware species and possess free will, but individually and collectively our behaviors suggest otherwise. We react to circumstances without consciously thinking, based on behaviors that were acquired subconsciously through mimicry and accumulated experience. As we will see, self-awareness—

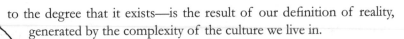

to the degree that it exists—is the result of our definition of reality, generated by the complexity of the culture we live in.

In Part II we explore relationships between common worldviews and the structure of the societies that generate them. These worldviews can be loosely defined and navigated like a map to retrace our history as a species, to understand our present experience of reality, and to explore the future.

In Part III we explore the frontiers of human potential, free from past assumptions, to see where reality might take us. Each level of reality can be thought of as a new layer that encompasses those that came before it. We can accept the good and shatter the illusions within each version of reality to move to the next layer. In the quest for the real reality, we will navigate through the layers, shattering illusions along the way, and see what is left over when we have stepped outside all other realities.

A fair warning is in order here. The journey ahead is not for the faint of heart. The quest for the real reality requires deconstructing one's existing beliefs about reality. If you are significantly attached to the illusion of reality you exist in now, then you may find the process jarringly uncomfortable at times. It is supposed to be. The path ahead requires questioning your most basic convictions. You may not like what you find. On the other hand, if you are ready to experience reality in ways you never imagined possible then you will find the adventure worth your time to explore. To begin this journey, we must start by questioning one of our most firmly entrenched assumptions: do we qualify as a self-aware or sentient species?

Two

Are we a Sentient Species?

Testing the Most Basic Assumption

"There is little conscious training of children, and thus no real discipline. Boys play with small bows and arrows and spears, gradually learning to track and hunt as they grow up. Girls learn to gather plants and berries along with their mothers, to cook, to make bark cloth and houses. As the years go by they find themselves doing these things in earnest instead of in play. And what else does a Pygmy child need to learn?"

—Lewis Cotlow, In Search of the Primitive[1]

What if our entire experience of reality were based on a false assumption? The assumption that we are self-aware is the cornerstone of our definition of reality. We invent tests and debate whether or not other species are self-aware, which impacts whether or not we decide to use them for medical experiments, food, or trophies. While the debate rages on about which species are self-aware, we have never tested ourselves to see if we qualify.

We think we are self-aware, yet our behaviors suggest we are not. Like sleepwalkers, human beings are capable of operating entirely without self-awareness. We think we are self-aware, yet we impulsively react to circumstances without thinking about why we do the things we do. There may be glimmers of self-awareness, but if we were tested by an impartial outside observer, our species would flunk any reasonable test for self-awareness.

Ironically, the first step to becoming self-aware is to awaken to the realization that we are not. It is only by acknowledging that we exist and function as automatons that we can begin to investigate the programming that defines our reality. It is only by defining and detaching from this programming that we can move beyond it to see what reality really is.

Language Clues

Imagine belonging to a tribe living in a tropical region where it never snows. If your people had never seen snow before, and never heard of it from neighboring tribes, how many words would your language have for snow? Why would you have any? How could you have a word for something you were not aware existed?

Inuit peoples, on the other hand, living in the frozen expanse of the Arctic Circle have at least fifteen words for snow—words that convey precise meanings about different types and textures of snow. Snow is a dominant part of their day-to-day lives, an essential aspect to their reality, so they describe it extensively.

By comparison, how many words does the English language have to convey the concept of self-awareness? The words *intelligent, cognizant, conscious,* and *consciousness* all have ambiguous meanings that do not necessarily imply self-awareness. For example, when we use the word "conscious" we must ask, *"Conscious of what?"* As we will see, there is a difference between being conscious of food or pain, versus being truly conscious of self. That leaves us with self-awareness, which doesn't really qualify as a word, since it is two words cobbled together with a hyphen to convey a concept that is otherwise alien to our language. It is the equivalent of saying "cold-white-fluffy-rain" in a language that has no word for snow.

The only other word in the English language that comes close to conveying the concept of self-awareness is *sentient.* According to Webster's College Dictionary, sentient means *"having the power of perception by the senses, conscious."*[2]

In essence, a sentient being is something that is able to sense and feel things—not exactly a very demanding standard. The word doesn't imply anything more than the ability to sense or feel, but for lack of any other word, *sentient* has been expanded through science fiction genre to serve as a synonym for self-awareness. In science fiction, notably *Star Trek,* space-faring humans visit other worlds and recognize the rights of any sentient beings they encounter, whether those beings are humanoid in form, self-aware machines, or some kind of highly intelligent space blobs.

The utter paucity of words in our language to describe self-awareness is a clue to our lack of it. Perhaps we got ahead of ourselves when we started conducting tests to determine whether or not dogs, chimpanzees, or parrots are self-aware. We have not yet proved that we qualify for that status ourselves.

Animal Intelligence and Awareness

As science has investigated and tested the intelligence and self-awareness of other species on our own planet, it has been interesting to witness the old assumptions crumble away. It was once assumed that the differences between humans and other animals were so vast that only our species had the mental capacity to manufacture and use tools. No other species could creatively solve new and unfamiliar problems. Only humans could share knowledge and pass a cultural heritage down from generation to generation. Only we could execute a strategy to achieve a goal. Only we could look in the mirror and recognize ourselves. Only we could understand symbolic language, and only we could recognize that the same symbols in a different order have a different meaning. Many native peoples, who are keen observers of nature, could have refuted most such assumptions long ago, but science required empirical data to quell erroneous beliefs.

In 1960 a chimpanzee was observed trimming a blade of grass to make a tool to probe a termite nest. Other chimps have since been observed using twigs for sandals to protect their feet from thorns. They have also used rocks to break open nuts, banged empty metal cans together to intimidate larger

12

chimps, and they've sought out medicinal plants to treat stomachaches.[3] [4] Chimpanzees in Senegal have even been witnessed making and hunting with spears. Numerous other species have since been observed using—and in many cases manufacturing—tools. Some dolphins pick up sponges and use them to protect their noses from stings when foraging on the sea floor, a skill that is taught from mother to daughter dolphins.[5]

Acts of intelligence are hardly limited to primates and dolphins. Beach-nesting water birds called plovers can strategize to achieve a goal. Plovers fake a broken wing to draw predators and people away from their nests. Studies reveal that the birds gauge the level of threat based on how close a person's direction of travel brings them towards the nest, whether or not the person looks toward or away from the nest when passing, and whether or not that person was a threat in the past. The plovers vary their strategies, apparently triangulating the subject's movements with their own. They position themselves between the nest and the approaching danger, feign the broken wing, and lead the threat away at an angle. The behavior might be instinctive, but it is goal-oriented rather than mechanically repetitive, since the birds have an objective and vary their behavior to achieve it.[1]

In terms of social cooperation and coordination, lions and wolves have been observed executing complex hunting strategies. In one instance, two lionesses perched themselves conspicuously on mounds where a herd of wildebeests could see they posed no threat. A third lioness slunk down in a ditch near the wildebeests, while a fourth circled around through the trees and erupted from the woods at the optimal point to panic the herd across the ditch where the hidden lioness made the kill. All four lions gorged in leisure. Such hunting strategies are common among predators, although not always of such complexity.[7]

Some species have also passed the basic self-awareness test: being able to recognize themselves in the mirror. Biologists tranquilized chimpanzees and orangutans and marked an ear or brow with paint, without the animals knowing. And yet, when the animals saw the paint in a mirror, most investigated and groomed these otherwise out-of-sight places. Dolphins and some elephants have passed similar tests. Interestingly, when three-year-old children are shown a video of someone placing a large, brightly colored sticker on their heads moments earlier, most recognize themselves, but fail to realize the sticker is still on their heads. Four-year-old children usually make the connection and reach up to remove the sticker, suggesting that four-year-olds are at least as self-aware as chimps, but three-years-olds are not.[8] The gap between humans and animals shrinks with each passing test.

Moreover, numerous species have proven somewhat adept at understanding and using symbolic language to communicate with people. Bonobos have proven especially adept at communicating using lexicon boards with symbols that can be arranged in unique sequences to mean different things. One bonobo named Kanzi has learned nearly four hundred symbols, which he can assemble into phrases to describe complex ideas, such as the desire to go to Dairy Queen for ice cream. Bonobos can learn to understand complex human speech if they are exposed to it from an early age, and Kanzi recognizes thousands of human words. In one demonstration, Kanzi followed instructions to do several tasks such as "pour salt on the ball," "put pine needles in the refrigerator," and "carry the TV outside." These were intentionally nonsensical suggestions to demonstrate that Kanzi could understand the syntax of a unique string of words. The researcher wore a welding mask to avoid giving social cues, such as looking at the objects being described.[9]

Meanwhile, other studies have revealed the intricacies of animal communication. For example, vervet monkeys learn and use different alarm calls for leopards, snakes, and eagles.[10] Even prairie dogs, a type of rodent, seem to have an extensive vocabulary. Based on computer-analyzed voice recordings, researchers have identified more than twenty "words" for things like coyotes, deer, cows, red-tailed hawks, and humans.[11] Dolphins have been shown to identify each other by specific whistles, much as we call each other by name.[12]

In addition to these demonstrations of intelligence, communication, cooperation, and apparent self-recognition, primates have been observed engaging in less-angelic human-like behavior—deceiving others about the availability of food, engaging in warfare[13], lying about doing bad deeds (such as crapping on the carpet), or disguising their feelings by using a hand to wipe away a grimace of fear.[14] Dolphins apparently have the ability to talk about other dolphins in their absence, though it is unknown what they say about them.

Animals were once viewed as biological machines without consciousness by Western cultures, but evidence of animal intelligence has narrowed the gap, making animals seem increasingly human-like. However, it would be erroneous to jump to the conclusion that animals are self-aware when we have not yet proven that we are. Humans are capable of performing complex tasks without any awareness at all. By examining the behavior of sleepwalkers, we can see that it might be possible to live an entire lifetime without waking up.

Sleepwalking

It is easy to determine you are aware of your existence, but how do you determine someone else is self-aware? It is surprisingly difficult to tell from the outside. For example, you could potentially interact with a sleepwalker without realizing that he is asleep unless you noticed a glassy-eyed look. Sleepwalkers do not lumber around like zombies with their arms out in front of them in a stupor, as we might see on television, although they may be confused and anxious. They can be highly agile and capable, getting dressed, cooking, eating, and even driving without any conscious recollection of the experience.[15] A sleepwalker could potentially look at himself in the mirror without being aware of the experience.

Sleepwalking is the result of sleep disorders, often associated with sleep deprivation such as might be caused by breathing problems at night. While sleep waking is caused by sleep disorders, it is instructive to understand how capable people are while conscious awareness is turned off.

Without the benefit of any conscious restraint, sleepwalkers are driven by any impulse that bubbles up out of the subconscious, often mixing dream material with their interactions in the physical world. One twenty-five-year-old man with a history of sleepwalking and night terrors bolted out of bed in his underwear, walked right through the screen door, and drove several miles to his parents' house to pound on their door. He woke up when they started talking to him.[16] A Canadian man drove twenty-three kilometers in his sleep and stabbed his father-in-law to death and nearly killed his mother-in-law.[17] An Australian woman reportedly left her home and had sex with complete strangers, returning home with no conscious recollection of the experience.[18]

Sleepwalking is a form of hypnosis, and sleepwalkers are highly suggestible, so anything they see or hear may lead to another behavior, provided it is something they are familiar with already. Sleepwalking behavior is most prevalent in kids, peaking between the ages of eight and twelve (about 17 percent of all kids of this age exhibit some sleepwalking behavior), usually decreasing as they mature into adults.[19] Approximately 4 percent of adults continue sleepwalking; they are usually easier to hypnotize than the average person.

Interestingly, young children exist in intermittent states of hypnosis even while awake, and according to psychologists they have little sense of the passage of time before the age of two.[20] Look at the eyes of young children and you will often notice a soft, unfocused look, or a glassy-eyed stare. In this hypnotic state children sometimes engage in odd behavior. As the youngest of six children in my family, I vaguely recall incidents where I was accused of doing things that I obviously must have done, but had no recollection of actually doing them, such as hiding my messy underwear behind the toilet.

For the purpose of our quest, sleepwalking and other subconscious behavior demonstrates that it is possible for human beings to function without awareness of their actions. Interestingly, most of us have experienced this lack of awareness many times in our normal lives. For example, have you ever found yourself driving down the road with no recollection of where you are or how much time has passed? It is amazing, if you think about it. Here you are driving a lethal weapon, cruising down the road in traffic at high speed, and yet you have no recollection of it whatsoever. You slip into a hypnotic state and run entirely on autopilot, completely unaware of the experience.

Now imagine living a lifetime in a hypnotic state like this, operating entirely on impulse and subject to suggestion. Paradoxically, there is nothing to imagine, because there is no conscious recollection. A person could exist without knowing they existed.

Conscious versus Subconscious

Learning to type requires conscious attention. You look at a page of letter sequences and peck them out very slowly. Trying not to look at your fingers, you consciously direct them to the proper keys from memory. You lift up each finger, reach out, and press down this key and that one. With practice you are able to do it faster. The more typing you do the more automated the process becomes, until you can type without thinking about each letter or where it is on the keyboard. You get to the point where you can delegate typing to your subconscious mind and bang out sixty or more words a minute. But whatever you do, don't look down at your fingers!

If you look at your fingers while typing, you will immediately come to a crashing halt. You will be a tangle of fingers in all the wrong places. Your conscious mind cannot keep up with the action on the keyboard the way the subconscious mind can. The conscious mind excels at handling complex tasks that require recalling specific steps from short-term memory, while the subconscious mind excels at repeating preprogrammed behaviors wired into long-term memory. Typing isn't an intuitive process. You cannot learn to type by putting on a subliminal tape that tells you how to type in your sleep. It's something you have to consciously attend to, but once you've got it down, then you can let your subconscious mind take over and do what it does best, operating without you having to consciously think about it.

There is a similar concept in sports. An athlete might be very good at the high jump to begin with, but she might be able to improve with the aid of a video camera to analyze her performance frame by frame. With the coach, she can evaluate where there is room for improvement, then consciously work to modify her moves, practicing the new moves over and over again until they are wired into her subconscious. In competition she has to let go and allow the subconscious mind to take over. Athletes often let their bodies take over to do what needs to be done. The subconscious mind takes over and enables them to excel in what they are doing without thinking about it.

Similarly, you have to pay attention to the entire process when learning to drive a car. You focus on operating the vehicle, particularly if it is a manual and you are using the clutch and switching gears, while keeping traffic laws in mind and trying not to crash into anyone. It requires your full conscious attention while learning, but the more you drive the less you have to think about it and the more automatic it becomes. Your subconscious mind learns the routine until you achieve the ability to drive down the road without any conscious recollection of the experience at all. However, most of what we learn in life is not acquired consciously, the way we learn typing or driving, but subconsciously through mimicry and experience.

Mimicry and Accumulated Experience

At school we attend classes and memorize many facts and figures or concentrate on deciphering the order of operations in word problems. But it is astonishing to realize how much we learn through mimicry and accumulated experience without ever becoming consciously aware of it. For example, a newborn baby doesn't have much programming. It doesn't know how to walk, or talk, or feed itself, or anything. It can't do much. But we don't send infants to school. We don't manually move their lips and force them to make our language sounds, nor do we go around pointing to things and saying "couch," "window," "ceiling fan," "curtains," and so forth. We might do that with some words but most language is acquired through mimicry and accumulated experience. The grey matter in our heads wires itself to understand the complexities of whatever language is spoken in the household, which is a truly astounding task.

Science fiction stories sometimes feature life forms called "shape shifters" that can transform their appearance to look like other beings. That's basically what the human brain is, a shape shifter that can mimic whatever it is exposed to. It doesn't matter whether we grow up in an English or a Chinese household; the brain wires itself according to the sounds of that language. The brain builds neural connections around sounds that are heard repeatedly, and it gradually pays less attention to sounds that are not as common. Over time it becomes increasingly difficult for a person to hear or speak unfamiliar languages.

Thus, a baby is born without language, but wires itself to hear and speak any language it is repeatedly exposed to. In a bilingual family, a baby will wire itself for two separate languages, switching back and forth between them more easily than most of us switch to using a fork in the other hand at the dinner table. That is very different from the experience of trying to learn a foreign language in high school or as adults, when we take classes to consciously memorize words, verb forms, and syntax. Two-year-olds don't study textbooks on verb conjugation. They learn through mimicry and experience with little or no instruction at all.

Most of our physical skills, such as learning to use a hammer, are acquired in the same way. When a baby or young child sees Mom or Dad use a hammer, she will automatically copy the behavior, using a stick or whatever she can find to start hammering on something. She may not be good at hammering, and it looks like mere child's play, but practice brings accumulated experience, so the more she hammers while growing up, the better she gets. If she is building forts and pounding a lot of nails, she will bend many of them at first, but over time she will learn to pound nails in straight.

If you grew up building things all your life then you might not realize how much of a learning curve is involved in using a hammer. One of the funniest things I've ever seen was Bill

Clinton and Al Gore volunteering for Habitat for Humanity while on the campaign trail for president and vice-president back in 1992. It was evident that they had not spend much time hammering nails when they were growing up. They tried to position themselves so that the cameras couldn't show how poorly they were doing it.

Hammering is actually a complicated skill that requires adjusting each swing to the current status of the nail, a skill my kids struggle with. I found myself giving them instructions to consciously evaluate the angle of the nail, to mentally adjust the angle and speed of the hammer with each stroke to keep the nail straight. I was amazed to discover how much I knew about pounding nails, because I never thought about the process before. Nobody ever taught me how to hammer nails, and I certainly didn't read a book on it or consciously think about it. It was only through mimicry and experience that I learned to pound nails in straight.

It is hard to appreciate just how much our lives are shaped by mimicry and accumulated experience. We might assume that something as basic as our sleep cycle is hardwired into our biology, but it too is acquired through mimicry. In many primitive cultures, for example, sleep is intermittent and communal, often with groups of people snuggled together while others remain awake visiting around a central fire. As much as a quarter of the population may be active at any time of night, and it is normal to nap during the day. Similarly, in Cairo, Egypt, people typically doze off by open windows listening to a deafening roar of traffic, sleeping about six hours at night and two in the afternoon. The most unusual sleep pattern in the world is our Western preference for eight continuous hours in a dark, quiet room on a padded "sleep machine," usually alone or with only one partner.[21] As any parent knows, infants do not have a fixed sleep cycle at first. In this case, we actively encourage mimicry, so babies will learn to sleep all the way through the night for our own sake.

Suicide is also learned through mimicry. In Micronesia, for example, suicide was virtually unknown until 1966. Then a popular and charismatic young man killed himself in despair over a love triangle. That suicide led to others, gradually evolving into a suicide culture with its own set of rules and symbols. By the 1980s, Micronesia had the highest suicide rate in the world, seven times the U.S. rate, with young people leaving notes and hanging themselves for trivial reasons. Teenage boys killed themselves after seeing a girlfriend with another guy, or because their parents wouldn't give them a few dollars spending money, or because someone reprimanded them for being loud. Younger kids mimicked the behavior, successfully or unsuccessfully hanging themselves to find out what suicide is like, not necessarily because they desired to die.[22]

In this way, children subconsciously acquire the mannerisms and beliefs of family members, friends, and television characters. We don't recall learning these things, but most of our behaviors as adults are driven by these deeply embedded programs. We assume we are self-aware, but human behavior suggests that we live like automatons reacting to circumstances according to preprogrammed scripts.

Self-awareness, as it is conventionally defined, is the ability to recognize one's own existence, to look in the mirror and say, "Yep. That's me. I exist." It is not exactly the most demanding standard. Any species that passes this test could be aware of its existence, but not in control of—or even aware of—its behavior. Given that we can look in a mirror and recognize our existence, we are at least as sentient as chimpanzees and orangutans. But we are far from being a truly sentient species.

The Sentience Test

Suppose we had the technology to fly around the galaxy exploring distant solar systems. What would happen if we discovered a planet inhabited by an apparently self-aware species with primitive technology?

How would we be greeted if we landed upon this alien world? Would the natives recognize us as equals? Or would they greet us with fear and hostility? Would they comprehend the technology that enabled us to travel between star systems, and would they believe that we are benevolent? Would they recognize us for what we are, or would they believe us to be some kind of supernatural beings?

When British explorer John Ross made first contact with the Inuit on the northwest coast of Greenland in the 1800s, the Inuit hesitantly advanced toward his wooden ships with trembling limbs and a look of terror. They asked about the ships through an interpreter. They saw the sails billowing in the wind and believed the ships to be alive. What kind of creatures were they? Were they from the sun or from the moon? After finally coming onboard, the Inuit again asked whether their visitors were from the sun or the moon.[23] Although the Inuit were as human as we are, they were unable to comprehend the nature of their visitors, and these explorers didn't even have electricity, lightbulbs, radios, or the ability to fly.

If we were to fly across the galaxy and visit a pre-industrial culture with our starship technology, it is easy to imagine the confusion that might ensue. Even if the natives concluded we were benevolent, how could they possibly understand what we were if they didn't understand their own relationship with the universe? They might perceive us as angels from heaven riding chariots through the sky. Interestingly, some people interpret passages from the Bible that way; they believe extraterrestrials visited in biblical times. While this scenario seems improbable, it is easy to imagine how such a visit could be misinterpreted, forever altering the natural development of a culture. We do not know the whole story from biblical times, but whatever happened, people have been killing each other over it ever since.

Thus, if we were to visit a distant planet with a technological culture, it would be essential to determine that the natives were fully sentient—fully aware of themselves and their relationship to the universe—in order to correctly understand what we were. Only then could we safely consider introducing ourselves.

Coming back to the present, we have not yet proved that we are self-aware. If there are extraterrestrials touring the galaxy, they would be wise to avoid Earth until we demonstrate sentient behavior. After all, while we like to imagine we are sentient, it is possible that someone merely recognized himself in the mirror and said, "Hey, I am self-aware." and everyone else mimicked him, saying, "Yeah, I'm self-aware too." without really thinking about what it means. Thus, it seems reasonable to put our species to the test. Do we qualify as a sentient species?

Test Number 1: Food Culture

Suppose we have a roommate—a spouse, partner, friend, or apartment buddy—and they happen to be a good cook. We've been thinking that they might make a yummy cheese omelet for breakfast, but we walk into the kitchen to find—surprise—a plate of fried mealworms. How do we respond? Do we look at the mealworms and think, "Oh, this looks new and interesting. I wonder if it is any good?" Or do we react to it? Do we contort our faces in disgust and say, "What is this, a joke?!?" Would we declare that there is no way in the world we would try this substance—that it doesn't even qualify as food? While we are sniffing this plate of mealworms, some guy on the other side of the world is in a parallel test, sniffing our cheese omelet and wondering what happened to his usual breakfast of mealworms. He is wondering whether or not this new substance constitutes food.

Food culture is a particularly easy way to test for sentience due to the potential to elicit a strong response. If the subject happens to be sentient, then he or she might respond rationally and say, "This is different than my usual fare, but I recognize that mealworms are a common food source, even a delicacy in other parts of the world." At the very least they might say, "These worms are highly nutritious, so it wouldn't hurt to at least try them, even if it is different from the food I am accustomed to."

On the other hand, if the subject is nonsentient—someone who has merely mimicked responses from people they grew up with—then their reaction may be more intense. If people around them gagged at the thought of worms and bugs as food when they were young, then they would likely mimic that response and copy it when faced with a plate of mealworms. In other words, they would react based on subconscious programming, rather than by rationally evaluating the situation and acting accordingly.

However, by any objective assessment, a plate of mealworms is more edible than a cheese omelet. People are far more likely to be allergic to eggs or dairy products than mealworms. In fact, some population groups are lactose intolerant and do not consume dairy products at all. And since cheese is made from milk that has soured *and* turned rancid, it is entirely reasonable that people in other lands should make a face in disgust at the thought of eating it. On the other hand, when we sit down to a plate of mealworms, there is really no rational reason to be disgusted by it.

The value of an experiment like this is to see if the test subject is aware of their behaviors. Do they think through a situation and determine how best to respond? Or do they react in a way that has been copied from generation to generation without consciously evaluating the behavior? A pre-programmed reaction would suggest that the test subjects had no real minds of their own. How would you respond to the mealworm test?

Test Number 2: Provocation

It might not be fair to use food culture as the sole measure of sentience, since some people might fare poorly in that test, while demonstrating other signs of sentient behavior. Suppose, for example, we are tested by a man who is rude and belligerent. He chews his food loudly in a restaurant then belches repeatedly while we are trying to have a conversation. He walks down the street bumping into people and yelling obscenities. He lays on the horn in traffic to see how people respond.

To all of these situations, do we act or do we react? Do we respond rationally and work to diffuse the situation, or do we get all huffed up, red in the face, and start yelling obscenities back? In the case of traffic, does someone pull out a gun and start shooting, as has been known to happen in certain cities? Do we have sufficient self-awareness and free will to modify our behaviors, or are we slaves to our impulsive emotions of the moment?

How would you score when provoked? If someone yells in your face, do you generate a menu of possible choices and choose the action that will most likely bring the best possible outcome? Or do you merely react without thinking, getting as bent out of shape as the provoker? How does our species score in situations like this? Individually and collectively, how do we deal with provocation? Do we think through our actions or merely react? Do we strive for positive international solutions, or do we attempt to solve problems with brute force?

Test Number 3: Shopping

The next part of the test evaluates shopping behavior. How do we determine what to spend our money on? Do we generate clearly defined goals and shop for specific products and services to meet the stated needs? Every purchase we make has some impact, good or bad, in our immediate lives and to the rest of the world. Do we consider where the material resources came from, or wonder if workers were treated fairly during the manufacturing process? Or are our shopping habits the result of mimicking other people and celebrities, copying the latest fashions in everything from clothes and cars to houses, buying what the commercials tell us to get? Do we buy a car merely because it is the popular style, or do we consider gas mileage, price, safety, and storage needs? Do we delay purchases as long as possible to ensure that we are making sensible choices, or do we get an idea for something we "need" and act on it immediately? These questions help reveal whether we make decisions cognitively as a species that is self-aware enough to think through multiple perspectives on an issue, versus a species that operates primarily on autopilot, motivated by mimicked responses.

Suppose we have to choose one of two new houses of equal size and cost. One is a Victorian-style home, while the other is a dome. The dome house will probably be more energy efficient, require less maintenance, and be more resistant to earthquakes, hurricanes, and tornadoes, but the Victorian house is quaint and "house-like" with its square walls and peaked roof. Which one would you choose? Dome-shaped dwellings are common and "normal" in many primitive cultures, but they don't look "house-like" to Americans, so we usually choose houses that are more expensive to maintain and less safe in disasters. If people demanded dome homes, then builders would make more of them.

Consider house size in relation to wealth. With the rising affluence of the middle class between 1950 and 2005, the average American house more than doubled in size to 2,414 square feet[24], while average family size dropped from 3.38 to 2.59 people over the same time period.[25] None of that is particularly surprising in itself, but it doesn't stop there. In communities across the nation, millionaires are building 10,000 square-foot houses, often demolishing perfectly good homes to make room for them. Meanwhile, billionaire Bill Gates of Microsoft built a 40,000 square-foot house, which is conservative compared to the 50,000 square-foot houses built by other billionaires. For reference, the White House encompasses 55,000 square feet. Where does it all end? Imagine being a couple with one child rattling around in a house with a dozen bathrooms. Is there any logic to it, or is it a petty game of status, some deeply embedded program to demonstrate superiority compared to less-wealthy people? What happens when the middle class becomes millionaires, the millionaires become billionaires and the billionaires become trillionaires? Is there any point to this game of status? Is it sentient behavior?

Would you pass the shopping test? Do you delay purchases by days, weeks, or months to consider the best possible alternatives, or do you impulsively hand over the credit card to buy something you didn't know you needed? Do you consider the ethics and environmental impact of everything you buy?

Test Number 4: Values and Beliefs

We must also investigate the procedures we use to determine our values, our beliefs about right and wrong, and our political and religious leanings. Do we actually think about these things, or do we merely mimic them from generation to generation or across peer groups? If we do reflect on our values, is it through any truly objective process, or is the evaluation based on our cultural upbringing, which is similarly mimicked?

When it comes time to vote, do we seriously consider the policies advocated by the political candidates, or do we merely vote for whichever candidate is funniest on late-night TV or most popular in the polls? As we will see in the following chapter, votes can be swayed by subtle expressions on a television newscaster's face, regardless of whether the news coverage about the candidates is good or bad. If we do evaluate the issues, do we use objective criteria, or do we evaluate them according to biases we have previously mimicked? Are the beliefs and values we use to make decisions truly our own, or are they merely beliefs and values we mimicked growing up?

When it comes to choosing a religion, do we systematically explore them all and select the one that best fits the available facts, or are we drawn to something familiar, something similar to what we have been around all our lives? Can we call ourselves self-aware if we acquired our beliefs the same way we acquired language: by absorbing it without ever really thinking about it?

Test Number 5: Environmental Stewardship

Any self-aware species can reasonably be expected to have a sense of self-preservation, avoiding behaviors that obviously threaten its existence or that of its progeny. However, self-preservation doesn't qualify as sentient behavior by itself, given that even a worm has basic instincts for survival. A worm will avoid hot, dry soil, choosing to move downward in search of cooler, moister earth to sustain itself. But any species that is truly sentient, truly aware of its own behavior, could reasonably be expected to take steps to change its behavior if there were foreseeable dangers ahead that could potentially lead to its harm or destruction.

Imagine a carrot sitting on a table, with a string tied from to the trigger of a gun. In the layout of this room, there is no possible way to grab the carrot without shooting oneself. As a supposedly sentient species, we can see the danger and recognize that it would be foolish to get the carrot. A nonsentient species probably wouldn't make this association between cause and effect, even if they had witnessed guns in action before. Surely we can pass this test! And yet, if we examine environmental issues and evaluate the way our species consumes resources, it is difficult to argue that we are doing anything but committing suicide.

Consider our ocean fisheries. We have systematically gone through the food chain to catch the easiest, most abundant species first, then the next species, on down the list, such that at present we have wiped out most of the common fisheries and are down to species that require long life spans to reach productive maturity. Fishermen once caught three-hundred-pound halibut in the oceans, but now they are down to catching juvenile fish. Many restaurant menus have replaced halibut with codfish, and then replaced the codfish with haddock, and then the haddock with scrod, which are juvenile codfish or haddock.[26] Two-thirds of our planet's surface is ocean, and yet, if trends continue, it is estimated that there will be virtually nothing left to take from the sea by the middle of this century.[27] Huge ships with gargantuan nets literally scrape the bottom of the ocean, scooping up all kinds of life, taking even the coral off the bottom, leaving behind a swath of destruction. We are literally to the end of the ocean food chain, and there simply isn't anything else to consume.

Suppose there was a pride of lions along with a declining herd of zebras. Would there ever be a time when the lions would notice the diminishing resource and think, "There used to be more zebras. The population seems to be dwindling. Maybe we should conserve our zebra supply and find a way to help boost the population." No. If the lions were hungry and they saw a zebra, then they would kill it, even if it were the last one on earth. Lions, as far as we can tell, lack the foresight to speculate about zebra population dynamics and sustainability. Lions apparently lack the ability to even imagine a future without zebras. This lack of foresight among predators contributes to the fact that 99.9 percent of everything that ever lived is now extinct. But we imagine ourselves to be different. Surely, we would not fall victim to the same trap and wipe out our own resource supply!

21

Unfortunately, the cumulative human impact on earth threatens to wipe out half of all life on earth this century, with unique plants, animals, insects, and fungi currently disappearing at an estimated rate of 17,500 species per year.[28] The cumulative impact of our species is approximately equivalent to the earth being hit by an asteroid like the one linked to the extinction of the dinosaurs sixty-five million years ago.

In the words of author Thomas Campbell, *"It is an obvious fact that the easiest way to get some quick cash to support an immediate higher standard of living is to mug Mother Nature as she walks through her park. Fortunately, she is an exceptionally hardy and charitable sort and gracefully tolerates our abuse up to a point. However, to pass that point is to trade an endless supply of golden eggs for a single goose dinner. Even if you are extraordinarily hungry, that is a stupid trade."*[29] We might think that habitat loss and species extinctions are somebody else's fault on the other side of the world. But most of us have no clue about what life forms are vanishing within fifty miles of our homes, or what our actions do to increase species loss here and abroad. Most people are not aware enough of the local ecosystem to notice when a native species disappears from the front yard.

The danger in addressing environmental issues is that once we admit there is a problem, then it is easy to slide off into the depths of despair due to the sheer magnitude of the crisis. It may be for this reason that so many people avoid acknowledging environmental issues, as if the problems will go away if they ignore them long enough. Some readers may comfort themselves with the belief that either the universe or God will provide for us, or that human ingenuity will engineer a way out of the problem. That may be a correct assumption, but the irreversibility of species extinction, along with scores of previously collapsed civilizations, suggests that it might be wise to develop a Plan B.

As we will discover later in this quest, none of our environmental problems are excessively difficult to deal with, and we can solve most of them at a profit. However, achieving sustainable prosperity requires a high level of self-awareness, which the sentience test indicates we are seriously lacking. While it is unlikely that aliens have visited our solar system, it is even more improbable that they would reveal their existence if they did come. Who knows what kind of horrible misunderstandings could arise through interactions with such a primitive and volatile race of barely sentient beings as these Earthlings? We barely get along with each other.

With our status as sentient beings in jeopardy, how might that affect everything else? Our history books are written on the assumption that we are a sentient species and have been all along. Our religions, our philosophies, the way we connect or don't connect with the world around us, are all based on the assumption that we are sentient. Yet, if this assumption is false, and we are not yet sentient beings, then we need to go back and consider how this realization could alter our entire perception of reality. Fortunately, the situation is not as bad as it seems.

A Light in the Darkness

We tested the assumption that we are a sentient species and fared poorly. Most of what we like or dislike, believe or don't believe, is dictated by our subconscious programming. We subconsciously mimicked the values and biases of other people until our brains were wired to react to situations without the need for conscious thought. There are, however, glimmers of sentient behavior among our species, as if we have the potential to awaken for the first time. We do not yet qualify as sentient beings, but at least there are more moments when we are being sentient.

We live like a mutant species with two brains inhabiting a single body. We go through life consciously searching for things that we unconsciously set down somewhere along the way. The subconscious mind knows exactly where the keys and remote control are, and a million other things, but doesn't share this knowledge with the conscious mind. Our conscious experience is like a pinpoint of light in a vast cavern of darkness. In the darkness we are consciously aware of anything we shine our light on, and we can point the flashlight in any direction, seeming to be aware of everything. However, it is only an illusion that we are aware,

because as soon as we swing the flashlight towards a new target, that which was illuminated falls back into darkness.[30] The scope of our awareness is shockingly limited.

While focusing clearly on one thing we may be doing scores of other things we are completely unaware of.[31] As I am focused on these thoughts, for example, I am completely oblivious to my fingers typing out the letters on the keyboard—until this example calls my attention to it. And while I might put on some music to facilitate my writing, I hear only the first few seconds of an entire album. I find myself snacking in the kitchen while mulling over my thoughts; it is a wonder I don't weigh four hundred pounds. In short, the conscious mind believes it is aware of everything and deserves all the credit, while the subconscious mind quietly handles the other 99.9 percent.

The Dawn of Consciousness

There is a tendency to assume that self-awareness, to the degree that it exists, is a property of the hardware we are born with. At some point in the past there was an evolutionary tweak that allowed our reptilian, mammalian, or primate ancestors to first recognize that they existed. However, what if self-awareness isn't merely biological, but also cultural—a mental program that developed over time and was mimicked and passed down from generation to generation ever since?

As we have seen, most of what we know we acquire subconsciously through mimicry and accumulated experience. At times we are capable of operating entirely on autopilot without any conscious awareness of our experience at all. And even when we believe ourselves to be self-aware, we are really just reacting to circumstances based on deeply embedded programming from our childhood. Based on this line of reasoning, we must wonder: Could our distant ancestors have learned everything they needed to know through mimicry and accumulated experience, without ever experiencing a moment of self-awareness?

Imagine growing up surrounded by people who are tanning hides, starting fires by rubbing sticks together, and hunting with bows and arrows. You are surrounded every day with all of the skills you will ever need to live your life, and you learn them the same way you learn to speak—through mimicry and accumulated experience. As a child you might not be particularly efficient at rubbing sticks together to start a fire, but over time you continue to mimic the behavior and accumulate experience until you are ultimately able to start a fire that way. The same goes for shooting a bow and arrow, or tanning hides and making clothes. As suggested by the quote at the beginning of this chapter, you could learn everything you need to know about life purely through mimicry and accumulated experience. You may not need conscious awareness at all.

Theories vary widely regarding the origin of consciousness, that moment when our ancestors recognized their existence for the first time. Some people believe that most or all mammals, as well as many other species, are conscious beings, but as we have seen, it is possible to be conscious of external things without becoming self-aware. Other people believe that consciousness arose only within the genus *Homo*, either with ancestors like *Homo habilis* or *Homo erectus*, or more recently with the beginnings of *Homo sapiens*. Some researchers think consciousness is even more recent, tied to the rise of language, possibly 50,000 to 100,000 years ago. Debates about the origin of language are equally contentious.

In his 1976 book, *The Origin of Consciousness in the Breakdown of the Bicameral Mind*, Dr. Julian Jaynes of Princeton University theorized that our ancestors existed as automatons in a hypnotic state as recently as 3,000 years ago. According to Dr. Jaynes (1920–1997), consciousness emerged as a result of complex languages that evolved to cope with problems created by early civilizations. Thirty years of research since publication of Jaynes' book has revealed more evidence to support his theory than to refute it. However, one glaring problem with his theory is that it implies that modern hunter-gatherer cultures must *still* exist as automatons, at least until sufficiently influenced by outside cultures. That assertion is hard to imagine or accept.

Most of us don't live next door to hunter-gatherers, so we cannot ask them if they are aware of their existence. However, there is no shortage of documentation about encounters between hunter-gatherer societies and explorers, missionaries, anthropologists, and other Westerners. The challenge in determining whether or not these primitive cultures were and are self-aware is that, similar to interacting with a sleepwalker, we wouldn't necessarily notice if they weren't.

Consider the various "cargo cults" that formed among indigenous groups after first contact with the outside world, most prominently in New Guinea after World War II. Western powers set up military bases there and brought in supplies by sea and by air. Clothing, canned food, tents, weapons, and other manufactured goods were delivered in great quantity for the soldiers and their native hosts and guides. The bases were abandoned after the war, but the natives wanted more. Sometimes they believed the goods were sent by their ancestors but the white men stole them away. They felt that their ancestors' spirits were angry and would stop the stealing, so all they had to do was to wait until the goods were delivered. Tribes living by the sea were literally waiting for their ship to come in.[32][33]

The problem was that they typically stopped tending their gardens and ate all the pigs or cut down the banana trees, believing that better goods would be delivered. They were not merely sitting around either. The natives mimicked the behavior of the soldiers to help bring in the ships and planes. They built their own communications antennas out of branches and strung vines for wires. People sat at desks and pretended to read and write all day. Men carried sticks that looked like rifles and marched back and forth like soldiers. They painted military insignia and "USA" on their bodies to mimic military uniforms. Inland, the natives cleared flat runways for the planes to land on. They carved headphones from wood and wore them in fabricated control towers. People stood on the runways waving the landing signals used by the white men to guide in the planes. They lit signal fires and used torches to light up the runways. Many even built life-size mock-ups of airplanes out of straw.[34][35]

If you read through this passage too quickly to process it fully, then try this: unplug the telephone and spend the rest of the day pretending to talk on it. Pick up a book in a language that is completely alien to you and spend hours pretending to read it. It doesn't matter whether you hold it right side up or upside down. Imagine doing this for days or weeks or months in the belief that you can make a ship come in or a plane land. Is this sentient behavior? As was the custom since the dawn of time, these people saw a behavior that worked and mimicked it in the belief they could produce the same results.

Stories such as this seem to lend credibility to the theory that our ancestors could have lived as automatons within an entirely subconscious experience of reality until shockingly recent times. Yet, we will examine contradictory evidence that suggests conscious awareness may have originated much farther back in time. In the end we will reconcile the contradictions, arriving at a modified version of the theory with a more precise definition of consciousness, which will better fit the available facts. Keep in mind that people from primitive cultures were not dumb or inferior in any way. If we were transplanted to a hunter-gatherer society, we would quickly discover that they had an encyclopedic knowledge of their reality, and they might be puzzled by our inability to see the most basic information in front of our faces.

For example, the !Kung people of the Kalahari Desert in Africa can look at a track and determine how old it is to within about fifteen minutes of when the animal passed by. The more obvious signs include tracks that zig-zag from tree to tree for shade, indicating the animal passed through during the heat of the day. If the tracks pass by the west side of the tree, then the animal was seeking shade in the morning, and vice versa for tracks on the east side. Other signs are not so obvious. A fresh track presses into the soil, revealing a slight dampness that gradually dries out. The !Kung are intimately familiar with the moisture content of the top layers of soil and the rate it dries under all conditions, so they can read a track almost like a clock to tell how old it is. Furthermore, a fresh track is crisp, but it begins to collect a fine dusting of windblown sand after an hour or so. Twigs and leaves might fall into the track over time, or insects may walk across it. After shooting game with a poison arrow, the !Kung simply go home. They let the poison do its work and track the animal down the next day, following the tracks through sand, grass, thickets, rocks, and forest debris. While the tracks might be invisible to most of us, they read them as easily as we read a book.[36] If we asked the !Kung if they are aware of their existence, they would almost certainly answer yes, if they could contain their laughter at such a ridiculous question.

25

While the behavior of the cargo cults might seem bizarre, it isn't necessarily that much different from our own behavior at times, as we will see in the next chapter. The bottom line is that we operate under the illusion that we are self-aware when we are mostly not. Furthermore, if we do not qualify as sentient beings, then by definition, we must not possess free will either. Our sense of free will is an illusion of our own making.

—Three—

The Illusion of Free Will

Biological, Psychological, and Cultural Programming

"The conscious mind is like a monkey riding a tiger of subconscious decisions and actions in progress, frantically making up stories about being in control. As a result, physicists, neuroscientists and computer scientists have joined the heirs of Plato and Aristotle in arguing about what free will is, whether we have it, and if not, why we ever thought we did in the first place."

—*Dennis Overbye, New York Times*[1]

In the previous chapter we discovered that we could fail a reasonable test for sentience. If that insight isn't disturbing enough, then consider that any species that lacks self-awareness must also lack free will.

Our perceptions and decisions are dictated by deeply embedded scripts mimicked from parents, peers, and culture, as suggested by anthropologist Edward T. Hall in his 1959 book, *The Silent Language: "The idea that man as a cultural being is bound by hidden rules and is not master of his fate may come as a shock to some—it has always been hard to accept. The one thing that is quite clear, however, is that man is bound as long as he remains ignorant of the nature of the hidden pathways culture provides for him. To the traditional questions about free will, determinism, and his unique individuality which the ordinary citizen is apt to bring up when he meets the concept of a world of hidden rules, the anthropologist can give a convincing answer. Of course there are impulses that appear to have independent origins from within, but even these are radically altered by culture so that they are brought into play under controlled circumstances."[2]*

Our choices in life are not necessarily ours, and the perception of free will is an illusion. In this chapter we investigate the illusion of free will in greater depth, starting with individuals in history who were commanded to action by unseen voices. Next, we investigate our

27

daily experiences in depth, exploring the sequence we use to delude ourselves into thinking we have conscious control over our actions. Then we search for and identify the biological, psychological, and cultural programming that ultimately determines our choices before we make them.

Commanded by Voices

People who hear voices or see visions in our society are often diagnosed as mentally ill, and if the problem is persistent, they might be medicated or institutionalized. How odd that is, considering that much of human history was shaped by individuals who were commanded to action by unseen voices.

For example, Joan of Arc (1412–1431) had visions in which God instructed her to take back her French homeland from English occupation.[3] Joseph Smith, Jr. (1805–1844) started experiencing visual and auditory hallucinations at age fourteen, when God and Jesus appeared to him in person. He later wrote the book of Mormon and founded the Church of Latter Day Saints.[4] Muhammad (570–632 AD) began hearing revelations from God at age forty through the angel Gabriel, and he wrote the Koran, which today forms the core of Islamic faiths.[5] Socrates (470–399 BC) is credited with the reasoning that led to the scientific method, yet he listened to and obeyed the voice of an unseen daemon.[6]

Similarly, medieval scholars recorded numerous accounts of visions, which have been found to be similar to the religious hallucinations experienced by modern mental health patients.[7] Apparently, they either had it wrong in the past, praising and canonizing mental health patients, or we have it wrong in the present, medicating or confining the new prophets of God. Even if we explain away voices and visions as mental health issues, we must not dismiss the possibility that there may be great truths in some of the revelations and prophecies.

The impact of these voices can be quite commandeering. One man, relaxing on a deck chair at Coney Island, New York, described hearing a voice loud and clear—as if everyone around him should have heard it—that admonished him that he wasn't any good. He walked down to the beach and the voice commanded him to walk into the ocean and just keep on walking, which is what he did, until lifeguards rescued him against his will.[8]

In *The Origin of Consciousness*, Dr. Julian Jaynes theorized that our ancestors were commanded by unseen voices similar to those experienced by schizophrenics today. In a nutshell, Jaynes theorized that prior to the rise of language, subconscious impulses originating in the right side of the brain were transmitted to the left side of the brain as instructions to be acted upon (typically opposite in left-handed people). With the development of language, these instructions were sometimes experienced in the form of voices, *especially in moments of uncertainty and stress*. The voices instructed individuals what to do in an unfamiliar situation. Jaynes called it the "bicameral" mind, meaning "two houses."

In comparing the bicameral mind and schizophrenia, Jaynes wrote, *"The voices in schizophrenia take any and every relationship to the individual. They converse, threaten, curse, criticize, consult, often in short sentences. They admonish, console, mock, command, or sometimes simply announce everything that's happening. They yell, whine, sneer, and vary from the slightest whisper to a thunderous shout. Often the voices take on some special peculiarity, such as speaking very slowly, scanning, rhyming, or in rhythms, or even in foreign languages. There may be one particular voice, more often a few voices, and occasionally many, As in bicameral civilizations, they are recognized as gods, angels, devils, enemies, or a particular person or relative."*[9]

Jaynes believed that all people were directed by voices of command up until the rise of increasingly complex civilizations about three thousand years ago. For example, in the *Iliad*, the actions of men seem to be dictated by the voices of gods. When Agamemnon, the king of men, takes Achilles' mistress, a god warns Achilles not to strike him. Another god consoles him. Gods start the quarrels among men that cause the fighting; then the gods lead the armies into battle, speak to each soldier at critical points along the way, and urge the soldiers into defeats or victories by casting spells and visual hallucinations over them. Gods debate and teach Hector, whisper to Helen, and instruct Glaucus. One god makes Achilles promise not to go into battle, while another urges him on. Another god screams through his throat at the Trojans, rousing them in panic. When Achilles confronts Agamemnon about taking his mistress, Agamemnon replies that it was not his doing. It was the gods that commanded him to do it, an explanation that was fully accepted by Achilles.[10]

Human history is full of similarly suggestive material, which led Jaynes to conclude that our ancestors existed as automatons without self-awareness or free will, doing whatever the voices commanded them to. In their book *Voices of Reason, Voices of Insanity*, authors Ivan Leudar and Phillip Thomas concurred with Jaynes that the behavior described in the *Iliad* is consistent with people hearing voices, but they also noted evidence of self-awareness and free will among the characters.[11] Leudar and Thomas systematically compared modern and historical reports and found that voice hearers only felt *impelled* against their will a fraction of the time. More often they felt *compelled* to follow the advice of the voices, but chose to do so of their own free will. In many cases the individuals conversed with their unseen voices, reasoning through problems as if dialoguing with another person.[12]

In reviewing human history, it is apparent that events were shaped by these voices as if our ancestors either had no free will of their own, or didn't exercise it. When people heard voices of command they usually did as they were instructed, or they did as they were instructed by other people who heard those voices. For example, in the Old Testament, Moses had a private channel with God and served as a conduit to the children of Israel, instructing them to do as God commanded. In one revealing passage, God reminds Moses to tell the people to observe the Passover. Due to a death, however, some men responded that they could not observe rites on that day, as recorded in Numbers:

> *9.8: And Moses said unto them, Stand still, and I will hear what the LORD will command concerning you.*
>
> *9.9: And the LORD spake unto Moses, saying,*
>
> *9.10: Speak unto the children of Israel, saying, If any man of you or of your posterity shall be unclean by reason of a dead body, or be in a journey afar off, yet he shall keep the passover unto the LORD.*[13]

The Old Testament is filled with similar commands from unseen voices telling people how to live their lives. It is clear that people tended to obey the commands, whether they received them directly or indirectly. What may be more surprising, however, is that people today obey similar commands; most of us just don't hear the voices. At least voice hearers recognize that they are hearing a voice. The rest of us simply obey the commands, then make up a story to go along with our actions, as if we were in control all along.

Free Will in the Laboratory

In the 1970s Dr. Benjamin Libet wired the brains of volunteers to an electroencephalogram and instructed them to make random motions, like pressing a button or flicking a finger, while he noted the time on a clock. Libet found that brain signals associated with these actions occurred half a second *before* the subject was conscious of deciding to make them. Similar studies have repeatedly produced the same results.[14]

In essence, if we decide to have a cookie, the brain initiates the process of either reaching for it or asking for it a full half-second before we arrive at the decision to do so. We seem to consciously choose to have a cookie, but the "decision" is more correctly described as agreeing to do what has already been determined and initiated in the subconscious mind. In other words, the action is initiated before we become aware of it, and the mind is trying to take credit for the decision to project the illusion of control. Thus, our conscious existence is the equivalent of being a passenger on a train. We can narrate what we see out the window, but we are really just along for the ride.

This tendency to make up stories to explain behavior is also evident from research with split-brain epileptic patients. In the 1960s it was common to cut part or all of the corpus callosum that connects the right and left hemispheres of the brain to treat severe cases of epilepsy. The patients were then able to lead relatively normal lives. However, research revealed some unusual behaviors when sensory input was restricted to one eye or the other.

Information from the right eye is processed by the left hemisphere and vice versa. The left side excels at language skills and reasoning, while the right side excels at skills like pattern recognition and creativity. Patients could easily name an object if they saw it with their right eye/left hemisphere, but not with their left eye/right hemisphere, because the sensory input couldn't cross over to the language center. If a dollar sign were flashed to the right and a question mark to the left, patients would draw a question mark with their left hand, while insisting that they had drawn a dollar sign.

If a patient were shown an emotionally evocative picture to the right hemisphere they would react appropriately with blushing, anxiety, or fear. When asked why, the uninformed left hemisphere would always make up a plausible excuse. Similarly, if the right brain were commanded to laugh or walk, the body would carry out the command, while the left brain would invent its own reason why the person was "choosing" this particular behavior. The patients didn't know they were following commands.[15]

Fortunately for most of us, sensory information is shared between the hemispheres, so the left brain can consciously communicate the whole story. However, as we saw with Libet's half-second delay, our decisions are not necessarily conscious choices. We only narrate the story that is already happening. The perception of free will is an illusion, and our choices are ultimately driven by deeply embedded programming. Our actions are subconsciously generated before the conscious mind wakes up and tries to take credit by making a "decision."

In essence, we have to question the logic behind every decision we make. For example, I am contemplating purchasing a new laptop computer. The logic is simple: I need to be able to work away from the distractions of home. I will need a laptop anyway for an extended trip to Australia. Thus, there is a defined need, and the laptop is a logical decision to meet that need. However, it is also possible that the laptop purchase is an impulse, a decision that has already been made, and the logic for purchasing it is merely my conscious mind's effort to make up a story as if it were in control. Realistically, that is probably how most shopping decisions are made.

In actuality, I rarely have an impulsive moment in my life, and I typically delay purchasing decisions for days, weeks, or months to ensure that I am making a sensible choice. However, in struggling with some of my personal issues, I was once shocked to find myself at the mercy of impulses and anxieties that I could not control, hurting some of the people I care about most. In moments of seemingly lucid logic I could determine a clear plan to resolve my crisis, then reach for the telephone to act upon it. Yet, looking back on my actions a few hours or days later was like watching a mad man. My choices were anything but logical. As if controlled by some other entity, I could not recognize my behaviors as my own.

This loss of control was both fascinating and terrifying. In the rear view mirror I could see that I was operating without free will, and the evidence suggests that we function like that most of the time, but never distinguish the difference. We are little more than automatons mechanically reacting to stimuli in our environment under the delusion that we are in control. By acknowledging our delusions, we take the first step towards becoming self-aware and gaining free will. We are no longer blind to our blindness but can begin to openly investigate the sources of our biological, psychological, and cultural programming and reconsider our values. As we will see, it is possible to consciously moderate or "veto" our choices before carrying them out, but we seldom do.

Biological Programming

We like to imagine that we control our actions, but much of our behavior is driven by our biology. For example, without knowing anything else about humanity, a biologist would recognize that we are a mildly polygamous species based on the size difference between men and women. The average harem size among polygamous mammals increases with the ratio between male and female body sizes. Tree-dwelling apes called gibbons are monogamous and nearly identical in size. Male gorillas, on the other hand, have a harem of three to six females and are nearly twice as large. Among elephant seals there are an average of forty-eight females in a harem. The males weigh about three tons, compared to seven hundred pounds for the females. Thus, a biologist looks at the size difference between males and females of our species and correctly predicts that we are mildly polygamous. Monogamous relationships are the norm, but polygamous relationships are common. Polygamous marriages are legal in some cultures, while affairs are common in other societies where polygamy is illegal.[16] We are biologically programmed as polygamous primates, no matter what else we may pretend.

Similarly, individual temperament, such as a calm or easily agitated personality, is influenced by our genetic make-up. For example, variations in the TPH gene apparently contribute towards anger, aggressiveness, and impulsivity by depriving the brain of serotonin.[17] Our individual dispositions are significantly driven by our genetic makeup, which may lead one to believe that we should not be held accountable for our actions. We seem to be victims of our genetic programming.

We are also enormously susceptible to suggestion, almost as if we live in a perpetual state of hypnosis. For example, in his book *The Tipping Point*, author Malcom Gladwell tells of a study where college students were recruited under the pretense that they were doing market research on high-tech headphones. One group of students listened to the headphones with their heads still, a second group shook their heads side-to-side, and the third group shook their heads up and down. They listened to music, followed by an editorial about raising college tuition. Afterwards, the students were queried about the quality of the sound, as if they were actually testing the headphones. The final question was regarding the appropriate cost for a year of undergraduate tuition. The group who kept their heads still picked dollar amounts close to the existing level. Those who shook their heads side-to-side suggested lower dollar amounts, while the students who shook their heads up and down suggested higher dollar amounts, even at their own expense. Their opinions corresponded to nodding or shaking their heads in the experiment.[18]

Similarly, television newscasters can sway voters with subtle facial expressions as they speak about presidential candidates. Even if a network's coverage of a candidate is more negative than other networks, viewers are more likely to vote for the candidate if the newscaster measurably brightens up while talking about him or her.[19] Seeing how decisions, big and small, are made, it is astonishing that we are able to function as a society at all.

Psychological Programming

In addition to biological programming, we are driven by many forms of psychological programming. For example, a traumatic childhood experience can physically impact the developing brain. In cases of abandonment, a child who doesn't bond with his mother may struggle with attachment issues for life. Many kids in foster care and adoptive families act out in ways that push family members away. A child will subconsciously try to recreate the abandonment situation by being mean and aggressive towards family members to make them abandon him as well. Sometimes the issue can be resolved when the child sees that his parents won't abandon him no matter how awful he treats them. The process can take years, or it may never resolve itself; the grown child may continue testing and pushing people away.

Even minor traumas can affect a child for life, such as being forced to give a presentation in front of class before he ready. Great or small, every person grows up with some kind of psychological baggage from childhood that affects how they interact with the world in adult life.

Adults can also be permanently traumatized. For example, women who have been raped may never relate to men in the same way again—even men they have always been close to. The programming we acquire dictates our behaviors, determining how we react to circumstances. It can take a tremendous amount of determination, introspection, or therapy to overcome our psychological programming to give us more options in life. One of the biggest sources of our programming, however, is neither biological nor psychological, but cultural.

Cultural Programming

In the sentience test we were offered the opportunity to indulge in a breakfast of mealworms. Depending on our cultural heritage, we may react to this offering with either delight or disgust. Our reaction has nothing to do with the food itself. We like to imagine that we possess free will to decide what we like or don't like to eat, but our choices are the result of our cultural programming.

Many people around the world eat rats and cockroaches while most Americans nearly retch at the thought. Similarly, Americans disdain the thought of eating dogs, cats, or horses. The Hindu must think we are like cannibals to eat beef, while Muslims believe we sin by eating pork. The basis of such beliefs, according to Marvin Harris (1927–2001), author of *The Sacred Cow and the Abominable Pig*, is not in the quality of the food itself or in the religion, but in practical economics.

For example, most Americans are opposed to the idea of eating horses, but horsemeat has gone through many surges of popularity in America and Europe based on economic trends. Horsemeat becomes popular when other sources of protein are more expensive but falls out of favor again when the economics swing the other way.

Similarly, Harris points out that while the Hindu people abhor the idea of eating beef, that was not always the case. The Indian people regularly consumed beef up until a few centuries BC, at which time the rising population created more need for cropland, since crops can produce more calories and protein per acre than livestock. Stock needed to be kept to plow the fields and to produce milk to drink and dung for fuel. Beef consumption dropped over the centuries until only the wealthy priests consumed it. The disparity between the rich and poor created an opportunity for the rise of a new religion among the peasant masses. Cows became sacred and it was considered wrong to kill them. The upper classes were eventually overthrown and Hinduism dominated the culture. Hinduism flourished and became an effective means for a largely illiterate society to pass along cultural wisdom. Thus, the faith-based practice of abstaining from beef originated from economic necessity.

Likewise, Marvin Harris suggests that we think of mice, rats, and cockroaches as filthy not because of their habits but because they are uneconomical sources of protein. We could get meat by skinning and butchering rats or by catching cockroaches, but we have more economical choices. We scorn the uneconomical choices as "bad" or "filthy," even while people in other countries consider the same foods as delicacies.[20]

Poor economic policies in Zimbabwe, once considered the breadbasket of Africa, crashed the national economy in 2006 and sent people foraging for traditional foods. Western journalists sensationalized stories of people being reduced to eating rats as a sign of how desperate they were. While the situation was clearly desperate, eating rats is not by itself a bad thing, as Zimbabwe's ambassador to the United States tried unsuccessfully to communicate to the media, *"The eating of the field mice—Zimbabweans do that. It is a delicacy. It is misleading to portray the eating of field mice as an act of desperation. It is not."*[21] I agree. I've eaten rat on wilderness survival treks. It is a delicacy. It is only our cultural conditioning that makes us think it disgusting.

In *The Silent Language*, anthropologist Edward T. Hall observed, *"Culture hides much more than it reveals, and strangely enough what it hides, it hides most effectively from its own participants."*[22] We mimic the likes and dislikes of our culture until we are programmed to react in a similar way. Our sense of free choice is an illusion, our choices dictated by patterns of behavior mimicked from our heritage. Everything about our lives, from the way we interact with other people to purchasing decisions, voting choices, and the way that we deal with—or don't deal with—environmental issues, can all be executed without true introspection. We are functionally automatons, reacting to the circumstances of our lives while wrapped up in the illusion that we are self-aware and making decisions.

Subconscious Adaptation

According to evolutionary theory, we evolved through millions of years and innumerable mutations. There was never any plan to make us what we are. Our journey from amino acids to tool-using primates was, and continues to be, a journey of accidents that worked. Our ancestors did not have a goal to become *Homo sapiens*, only to survive. Being here is the result of one mutation band-aided over another. There was never any conscious goal behind the process.

Likewise, the evolution of our customs and beliefs occurred without any plan beyond day-to-day survival. Cultural evolution has been a haphazard process of mutations and adaptations, or reactions to problems and circumstances along the way. Our ancestors who traded furs for tools did not plan to develop the New York Stock Exchange any more than their ancestors planned to develop an opposable thumb or to stand up straight.

In the examples of food culture, societies adapted to their circumstances subconsciously, based on behaviors that seemed to work. Cultural preferences—espoused through likes and dislikes, popular opinion and religion—grew out of economic choices to become cultural realities. In his 1968 book *Man's Rise To Civilization*, author Peter Farb (1929–1980) wrote: *"Adaptation is not a conscious choice, and the people who make up a society do not quite understand what they are doing; they know only that a particular choice works, even though it may appear bizarre to an outsider."*[23] In other words, entire cultures subconsciously adapt or react to circumstances, oblivious to why they make the collective choices they do.

Farb illustrates this point with an example of the Koryak of Siberia, who depended on dogs for hunting and herding reindeer until recent times. Yet, their religion required them to slaughter all of their dogs every year. Such a move seems entirely illogical from a survival standpoint, but it makes sense in the broader context. After killing the dogs, they traded meat and furs for new dogs from neighboring tribes that specialized in breeding dogs. If the Koryak stopped killing their dogs, then the neighboring tribes would be in direct competition with the Koryak for hunting and herding, jeopardizing a peaceful trade relationship. Nobody planned the relationship that way, but they unconsciously adapted to circumstances over time until it formed the basis of their religion.[24]

We might like to imagine our own culture to be advanced enough that we wouldn't unconsciously fall into a similar pattern of behavior. Yet, a quick examination of our economy reveals behaviors that would seem even more bizarre to an outside observer than the Koryak killing their dogs. As Henry David Thoreau noted in *Life Without Principle*, *"Most men would feel insulted if it were proposed to employ them in throwing stones over a wall, and then in throwing them back, merely that they might earn their wages. But many are no more worthily employed now."*[25] Consider that land is typically free in primitive cultures, yet we expend many years of our lives working to earn the money to buy a piece of land we can call our own. Few hunter-gatherers could conceive of owning land at all, let alone working for years to pay for something that would exist whether we paid for it or not.

Similarly, consider income taxes, which are so bizarre that fifty professional tax accountants arrived at fifty different answers for a hypothetical family's tax returns.[26] Try to imagine the cumulative amount of paper and ink consumed in income tax accounting throughout the year, plus the cost of accounting for tax purposes, plus the cost of related software, plus the value of every person's time spent filing taxes, plus the expense paid to private tax-preparation firms, plus the number of IRS employees required to process the tax forms and conduct audits. In 2002, Americans spent 6.6 billion hours filling out tax forms and $194 billion on tax compliance, or 20¢ for every dollar collected by the IRS.[27] We imagine ourselves to be productively employed while cutting down trees to make paper that will ultimately be shredded and disposed of. We write software that will be obsolete and often punch buttons on computers for no constructive purpose. We have unconsciously evolved an economy that employs people to pretend they are working while either producing nothing at all or producing goods that will be disposed of.

Consider that insurance companies seem to provide an important service, but they do not produce houses, cars, clothes, or food. Insurers punch numbers and consume resources, while other people produce the goods that sustain them. If we distinguish those who produce from those who consume, we would find that only a fraction of the workforce supports the entire economy, while everyone else consumes resources in the illusion that they are doing something useful. Perhaps we are not so different from the cargo cults where tribal peoples pretended to read books, talk over the radios, and march like soldiers with stick guns. None of it is real.

To discover what reality really is, we have to learn to see our culture from the outside. We must be skeptical of every thought, every belief, every emotion that we have, and realize that these might not actually be our own thoughts, just part of the cultural baggage passed down to us through generations. We have to go back and ask, "Where did these thoughts and values come from, and are there broader truths?" Individually and collectively, we need to challenge our most basic assumptions about the world we live in. We have to set aside our cultural beliefs and familiar background and be willing to step beyond our comfort zones. We have to consciously challenge our own impulsive reactions as we go through our daily lives.

Veto Power

If you looked at the plate of mealworms and reacted to it in disgust, was that really your own reaction—your own thoughts and feelings—or was it simply a behavior that has been mimicked and passed down through our culture? Is it possible that you have lived your life on autopilot, as an automaton operating on a script copied from parents, peers, and popular culture? As Anthony deMellow (1931–1987) wrote in his book *Awareness, "People go through life with fixed ideas; they never change. They're just not aware of what's going on. They might as well be a block of wood, or a rock, a talking, walking, thinking machine. That's not human. They are puppets, jerked around by all kinds of things. Press a button and you get a reaction.'*[28] How can you distinguish between thoughts that are legitimately your own and those that are the result of cultural programming? Your reaction to the mealworms, positive or negative, is probably part of your cultural heritage, a cultural reality that is true within itself, but isn't the whole, universal truth.

Although our choices originate in the subconscious mind prior to our "conscious decisions," we are able to "veto" those choices, to avoid following through with our impulses. For example, even if our initial reaction to the mealworms was disgust, our brains can veto the behavior before it happens, choosing another course of action. We can put on a brave front and step outside of our cultural reality to explore ethnic foods that are otherwise completely alien to our programming. Similarly, when we "need" to buy something, we can delay the decision by weeks or months to determine whether the need is real or whether our rationalization is merely an illusion to justify a subconscious impulse. Unfortunately, while we have the ability to act instead of react, we rarely exercise it. The subconscious mind is powerful. It is difficult to change our ingrained patterns, so we are driven by subconscious impulses according to our biological, psychological, and cultural programming. We rarely make conscious decisions. In essence, we don't drive the train, but we can control the brakes; most of the time we don't choose to apply them.

Ultimately, we have to make a choice. We have to choose between existing as automatons enshrouded in the illusion of cultural reality or consciously applying the brakes, questioning everything and seeking a more universal reality. We have to test our most basic assumptions about the world we live in. Only then are we ready to begin discovering reality for the first time.

In that spirit we must debunk another assumption: that words and language are neutral. We assume we can define reality with words, pointing out rocks, trees, birds, and airplanes without changing what reality is. But paradoxically, the invention of language is what makes it so difficult to recognize what is right in front of us. To understand the relationship between language, consciousness, and reality, we must retrace the journey of human evolution.

—Four—

Language and Metaphor
Generating Maps of Reality

"Subjective conscious mind is an analog of what is called the real world. It is built up with a vocabulary or lexical field whose terms are all metaphors or analogs of behavior in the physical world. Its reality is of the same order as mathematics. It allows us to shortcut behavioral processes and arrive at more adequate decisions. Like mathematics, it is an operator rather than a thing or repository. And it is intimately bound up with volition and decision."

—Julian Jaynes, *The Origin of Consciousness*[1]

According to anthropologists, the last ancestor we share in common with the chimpanzees lived six or seven million years ago. Since then we have followed separate paths, with our lineage becoming increasingly human while the other lineage became increasingly chimpanzee. Our ancestors adapted to walking upright shortly after the split. The first crude stone tools were manufactured about 2.6 million years ago, followed by the rise of the genus *Homo*, a doubling in brain size over half a million years, and divergence into at least a dozen different species of humans.[2]

Although some human species had cranial capacities as large as modern people, there is little evidence of additional technological advancement in the archaeological record. Nor was there technological advancement with the emergence of our species approximately 200,000 years ago, as noted by William H. Calvin in *The Birth of the Mind: "Anatomically modern Homo sapiens of Africa were not conspicuously successful like the behaviorally modern Africans that followed. They certainly didn't leave much evidence for a life of the mind."*[3] A trickle of artifacts started showing up about 90,000 years ago, which finally blossomed into recognizable human behavior with the Cultural Revolution 50,000 to 40,000 years ago. For the first time in history, humans acted human, leaving all kinds of tools, artifacts, and artwork behind for us descendents to ponder.[4] While earlier humans were equally human, they apparently did not use their brains the way we do. The critical factor that enabled people to act like people was a shift in the structure of language. In other words, self-awareness, the experience of consciousness as we know it, is an emergent property of language.

In this chapter we explore the evolution of language and metaphor and how they influence our perception of reality. Language is a powerful tool for describing the world we live in, and we cannot define reality without words. However, language also distorts our perceptions, altering what we see and hear in the world around us as well as our interpretation of it. Thus, language allows us to become self-aware and define reality, but at the risk that our definition may be so distorted that it bears little resemblance to reality after all.

Wired for Language

Language among social animals deals with threats, social dynamics, and foraging. Various grunts and calls express immediate concerns such as "Lion!" or "She's mine!" or "I found food!" Animal calls and alarms don't necessarily translate as specific words, and according to Terrence W. Deacon in *The Symbolic Species*, even well-defined calls do not qualify as true language, since the calls are "involuntary and contagious." For example, when a vervet monkey sounds the alarm call for a leopard, all the monkeys run for cover and repeat the call. Deacon compares these alarm calls to human laughter, noting that laughing is contagious. Join a group of laughing people and it is compelling to laugh with them, even when we have no idea what is so funny. Deacon wrote, *"This involuntary power of laughter is shared by many other innate social signals as well, including sobbing, smiling, grimacing, etc., and contrasts sharply with the absence of such echoic tendency in normal language communication."*[5]

The human brain is wired for language in a way that is not found among other species, and part of that uniqueness is in our ability to assign function. If we pick up a stick and throw it at a rabbit, then it is no longer just a stick; it is a special kind of a stick, which we might call a "throwing stick" or a "rabbit stick." Besides assigning function to the stick, we can make up an arbitrary name for it. Instead of a "rabbit stick" we could call it a "zathfrop." We could even make up a gesture for it, such as a flick of the wrist to symbolize throwing a stick, or a completely arbitrary sign that means nothing in itself unless we agree that it represents a "throwing stick."

In addition to describing things and actions in the present moment, we can talk about them in absentia. It does not appear that other creatures, except potentially chimps, bonobos, and dolphins, can talk about someone that is absent. Humans, however, are able to talk about lions that came around in the past, or might come around in the future. We can talk about tame lions or mean-spirited lions, pink lions or flying lions, even two-headed lions from space. While the human brain might be a virtual blank slate that can acquire any language it is exposed to, it is definitely prewired to learn language in a way that no other species can. Indeed, when people are deprived of a common language, they quickly invent a new one.

In New Guinea, for example, there are seven hundred indigenous languages that evolved in isolation from each other. No native language is spoken by more than 3 percent of the population. However, beginning with English colonialism in the 1820s, people from diverse tribes were thrown together to work at sugar plantations. Lacking a common language of their own, the people started talking in pidgin, using a limited number of mostly English words without grammar. Workers spoke their native languages among their own people, but they communicated cross-culturally through pidgin. This pidgin quickly evolved into a complete mixed language known today as Neo-Melanesian. The language consists of about 80 percent English, 15 percent Tolai (one of the major labor groups at the plantations), with the remaining 5 percent of the language borrowed from Malay and other languages. Neo-Melanesian became the national language as New Guinea modernized from hundreds of separate tribes into a functional nation in the last half of the twentieth century.[6]

Language is wired into our brains more deeply than mere speech and interpretation, and even deaf people quickly invent language where none exists. For example, deaf children in Nicaragua were brought together for the first time in special schools in the late 1970s. Wanting to communicate with each other, the children invented a new sign language, which acquired the rich communicative power and grammatical complexities of any other language within a few decades.[7] However, while younger children in the program acquired fully expressive language, those who started learning language as teenagers never did.[8]

People may be born wired to acquire language, but there is a limited window in which to do so. For example, a deaf child named Joseph was mistakenly labeled retarded, so he didn't have the opportunity to learn speech or sign language until he was ten years old. Joseph acquired a limited vocabulary with instruction, and had no trouble categorizing or generalizing, but he had no imagination. Deprived of language, he never learned to introspect, plan, or hold abstract ideas in mind. He was stuck in the present moment like an infant, apparently unable to ponder the past or future or to reflect in any other way.[9]

The limited window for language acquisition is especially problematic for autistic children. Many autistics acquire language normally at first but regress between eighteen months and two years of age. With the aid of intensive speech therapy by the age of three, continuing until at least four or five years old, autistic children usually acquire some linguistic ability and about half can enter first grade at a normal school. Without speech therapy, however, a child may retreat into an isolated world of his own sensations, permanently unable to communicate normally with other people.[10]

The problem of acquiring language among our earliest ancestors is analogous to the chicken-and-egg situation: How could our ancestors acquire a complex language before such languages existed? Language did not magically appear out of a vacuum but had to start from somewhere, with a rudimentary vocabulary that could be built upon over time. Our ancestors had the ability to mimic and rapidly acquire any skill, language, or behavior they were exposed to, and yet, if we travel far enough back in time, there was little or nothing to copy. Imagine growing up in a culture glued to the present moment, where everyone talked about things and events that were happening around them, such as, "Deer cross river," or "Johnny throw rock." If this were the only language a child was ever exposed to, then how could he learn to converse about the past or future, or about complex ideas and philosophy?

Theory of Mind

Theory of mind refers to the ability to recognize that another person thinks somewhat like we do. It is so much a part of our existence that it is hard to imagine not being capable of it. While the phrase "theory of mind" suggests a complex ability to imagine getting inside someone else's head, it is really very simple. The difference between not having, versus having a theory of mind is the difference between "here" and "there."

For example, when a rooster discovers a tasty morsel, he cackles excitedly, which might be translated as, "Food, *here!*" The nearby hens run over to see what the rooster has found. That is very different from either saying or pointing, "Look by that tree over *there!*" Even chimpanzees, some of whom can recognize their own faces in a mirror, apparently have little grasp of theory of mind. Like vervet monkeys, they can look at a predator and throw a fit, which calls the rest of the group's attention to the threat, but the threat is still effectively something that is "here," which the chimp is excited about. That behavior is very different from me looking at you, then pointing towards the tree *over there*. Without words, I would expect you to turn your head and understand.

It has long been debated whether the higher intelligence of people over chimps is the result of brain size alone, or if it is also a factor of specific wiring in the brain that favors social learning. To help answer this question, a team of anthropologists conducted a series of learning tests with 106 chimpanzees, 32 orangutans, and 105 children, age 2 ½. It was known that children that age perform similarly to chimps in *physical* learning, such as locating food or a toy hidden behind a box. Children and chimps equally proved that they understood that an object didn't cease to exist when hidden from view.

In terms of *social* learning, however, the children greatly outperformed their primate cousins, indicating that the human brain is wired specifically for learning by watching and copying other people. When researchers demonstrated how to open a plastic tube to get a treat, the children copied the behavior, while the chimps and orangutans tried to chew their way into the tube. Researchers also hid objects while the test subjects watched, then hinted at the hiding spot by looking in that direction. Only the children excelled at figuring out the clue. The study indicates that social learning is hardwired into our brains.[11] Our species is unique in our exceptional ability to copy behavior and grasp theory of mind.

It seems probable that this grasp of theory of mind was pivotal to the rise of the human genus. Our ancestors gained a survival advantage by copying behaviors from each other, including the ability to look in the same direction. With a rudimentary grasp of theory of mind, our ancestors could have pointed to objects, animals, or people, either nearby or far away, that were potentially significant to the group. Theory of mind virtually necessitates social coordination and language. Our ancestors evolved communities of social beings, requiring larger and larger brains to communicate and keep track of social relationships.

In the same way that prairie dogs have calls or alarms for coyotes, hawks, and other critical aspects of their reality, we can suppose that our early ancestors had an extensive vocabulary. We can imagine an early conversation running something like this: Sam points and says "Deer." Bill says, "Huh?" Sam points again, "Deer." Bill looks but doesn't see anything. "Huh?" Sam points again, "Deer" and clarifies with gestures and sounds, in an attempt to communicate "tree." Bill looks by the tree. "Ahhh." With a limited vocabulary and a few gestures, Sam has communicated a complex, three-component message to Bill: 1) a deer, 2) is out "there" (not "here"), and 3) it is by the tree. Not only would language facilitate the identification of something that is far away on the savannah, it would facilitate group decision making regarding what to do about it. The use of calls for objects with established names, combined with crude gesturing and pantomiming for things that didn't have names, could have evolved into the hardwired ability that enabled people to learn language either as sound or as signs. However, while theory of mind may have precipitated a *biological* rise of linguistic capability, the rise of complex languages was *cultural*. In other words, early humans could have evolved linguistic ability and used it to describe the immediate present without any incentive to develop language into more complex concepts, theories, or discussions about the past and future.

Necessity is the Mother of All Language

A limiting factor in the pace of biological and cultural evolution is *need*. Why evolve bigger brains, more complex languages, or new technologies if one can survive without them? Perhaps the most remarkable part of the human story is that we evolved in spite of a tendency for life forms to *devolve* into the simplest form that can survive within any given niche.

Many early biologists assumed that organisms evolved in one direction only, towards greater complexity, as if the ultimate goal of evolution was for all living beings to become more like us. They were unable to reconcile this assumption with the fact that many parasites seemed to devolve into simpler forms, discarding limbs, sensory organs, and intelligence to latch onto and feed off of something else. The most successful reproducers don't waste resources on extraneous body parts. This is the reason we have evolved only average capabilities, without great strength or speed, and without the superior vision, smell, and hearing that many other species have. Natural selection ensures that we have only what we need to be successful in our niche and no more. The same phenomenon is largely true of cultural evolution.

The island of Tasmania was populated by Aborigines 10,000 years ago via a dry land bridge from Australia. Sea levels rose and left the people isolated on Tasmania until

Europeans first encountered them in 1642. Unlike Aborigines on the mainland 130 miles away, the islanders had no boomerangs, spear throwers, shields, or bone tools. Their stone tools were crude and none had handles attached. Despite snowy winters, they didn't know how to sew or make clothing, nor could they cut down a tree and hollow out a canoe. They didn't even know how to make fire, and although they lived along the seacoast, they didn't catch or eat fish. Several of these technologies were invented on the mainland after the islanders were isolated, yet the islanders never invented anything comparable. Instead, the archaeological record shows that the Tasmanians arrived with, but later abandoned, bone tools and fishing equipment.[12] The reason for the lack of technology is simple: Why waste time making tools and clothing if one can survive well enough without them? The next time you see a herd of deer, slow down and watch how they live: They graze, wander, play, mate, and rest. That's life. Aside from hunting season, there isn't much work or stress in the lifestyle of a deer.

We believe technology provides us with wonderful labor-saving devices, but the reality is that technological advances have consistently created more work for our species, not less. Stone-age technology required more effort than wandering and grazing but still only a few hours work per day to survive. By the 1950s, amid rapid technological progress, it was believed that the future promised shorter work weeks and more leisure time. However, the reality is that today both parents often have to work to survive, even though families are smaller.

Our ancestors had the aptitude but not the need for more advanced technologies. Technology and complex language became necessary only as a result of natural selection through competition for resources, as detailed in Jared Diamond's Pulitzer-prize winning book *Guns, Germs, and Steel*. Groups of people that found new ways to eke out a living in competitive situations were better able to survive and pass along their traditions. Competing groups either adapted similarly or lost their niche and went extinct.

The Cultural Revolution

It is one thing to develop a language that consists of nouns, verbs, and adjectives, such as *lions*, *tigers*, and *bears*; *run*, *walk*, *chase*, and *kill*; or *blue*, *red*, *fast*, *big*, and *mean*. It is entirely another matter to develop a language of metaphor. A metaphor uses existing words or new combinations of words to convey new meanings. The word *arrowhead*, for example, is a metaphorical label for the point on the front of an arrow. It is a simple descriptive metaphor, relying on the universal recognition that the head is the front of an animal, and thus the arrowhead is the front of the arrow.

Similarly, plumbing parts and garden hoses have "male" and "female" ends, a simple metaphor based on which one fits inside the other. Look around and you will quickly see how common such metaphors are: a hammer has a *head*, as does the nail it hits, while open-ended tools like pliers might be described as having *jaws*. A needle has an *eye*, while a shoe has a *tongue*, and a comb has *teeth*. A soda bottle has a *neck* and a *mouth*, while a table and chair have *legs*. Animals apparently lack the ability to make such associations.

These are elementary metaphors, but they are instrumental in discussing millions of manufactured items that make up our day-to-day reality. Most of the time we speak or hear these metaphors without thinking about them at all. We refer to the "mouth of the bottle" without actually visualizing a mouth there. Similarly, it is comical to imagine plugging a rodent into a computer, but we accept a "mouse" as standard office equipment.

All modern languages are built upon metaphor, and it is fascinating to see a young language blossom from simple roots, such as Neo-Melanesian from pidgin vocabulary. For example, the term *banis pik* is a linguistic corruption of the English "fence pig," indicating a fence or pigpen to keep the pigs in. The word *susu* is taken from the Malay word for "milk" and is extended to indicate "breast" as well, while *bilong* translates as our preposition "of."

41

These words are combined metaphorically as *banis bilong susu*, which literally translates to "fence of breasts" to indicate a bra.[13] Neo-Melanesian includes thousands of metaphorical phrases like this, which become shortened over time, just as "bra" is an abbreviated version of "brassiere."

If we trace the etymology of our vocabulary far enough back in time, we find similar metaphors and extensions. For example, "bras" means "arm" in French. Brassiere is derived from *bracière*, an Old French word meaning "arm protector," in reference to military uniforms. The word was later extended to describe a military breastplate, then a type of women's corset, before evolving into its present use and spelling.[14]

Our ancestors invented new tools, artwork, and trade networks during the Cultural Revolution 40,000 to 50,000 years ago, which required new language, which in turn facilitated more tools, artwork, and trade. While the ability to manufacture an arrowhead could be mimicked from generation to generation without words, language made it possible to refer to items while telling a story, trading goods, or describing a place to find raw materials. More importantly, the act of describing objects in metaphorical terms wired the neural pathways to envision or innovate other things metaphorically. It is probably not accurate to say technological advances caused metaphorical thinking, or to say that metaphorical thinking led to technological advances, but rather that the two coevolved, each advance contributing to the other.

Try to imagine a world that consists solely of objective terms, such as *deer*, *rocks*, and *sticks*. Now imagine a world that is more symbolic, where inanimate objects have mouths, legs, or heads, or might be named after totally unrelated objects that they superficially resemble. When we start making these associations, perhaps looking up to see the shape of a horse with wings in the clouds, then the world is a vastly different and much more creative place. We can begin to innovate new ideas because we have the means to imagine them. *Imagination* was the Cultural Revolution. The ability to think and talk in metaphor made our ancestors human for the first time, with linguistic ability and self-recognition similar to any surviving hunter-gatherer peoples today. In other words, the mind was an emergent property of language. Without language we would not know we existed.

Interestingly, Kanzi, the bonobo who understands basic human speech, once requested marshmallows and fire while on an outing in the forest. After being presented with a bag of marshmallows and a box of matches, he broke twigs, started a fire and roasted marshmallows. More significantly, a visitor once demonstrated a Maori war dance, which sent all the other bonobos into a frenzy—baring their teeth, screaming, and pounding the walls and floor. Kanzi waved his handler over to him and apparently expressed that he understood the demonstration was not meant to be threatening. He asked for, and received, a private demonstration where it wouldn't upset the other bonobos.[15] In the same way that language made our ancestors human for the first time, it would seem that language made Kanzi bonobo. He seems aware of the world in a way that the others of his species are not. However, the depth of his self-awareness, as well as that of our hunter-gatherer ancestors, remains difficult to gauge, based on the material covered so far.

Julian Jaynes proposed that our ancestors lived a perpetually subconscious existence, without awareness of their own experiences. However, hunter-gatherer societies also engaged in activities like chanting to work themselves into hypnotic states, which would seem to indicate that they were *not* in a subconscious state already. It may be more accurate to say that they experienced a largely first-person existence, aware of themselves, but not in a deeply introspective way. As we will see in later chapters, it worked well for the way they lived. However, more complex societies required the ability to get outside of a problem, to see it and ourselves from a third-person perspective.

Seeing Oneself from the Outside

Take a moment to remember the last time you went swimming. Do you recall the event in first person as if you were reliving it, seeing it through your own eyes? Do you recall it in second person, as if you were seeing events through the eyes of someone else who was with you? Or do you remember it in third person as if you were watching a movie or looking at photos of yourself? Some individuals store memories exclusively from one perspective, while other people store memories from a variety of viewpoints. Interview your family and friends to find out how they store their memories. Probably half or more of the respondents will say they recall most of memories from a third person perspective.

Shift into this third-person perspective now, and imagine that you are looking at yourself from across the room. Isn't it a bit strange that you have the ability to see yourself this way at all? Isn't it bizarre that this third-person perspective is the *normal* mode of retrieving memories for many people? We are not followed by a detached set of eyeballs or a video camera. It is a trick of the mind that generates a fabricated version of our experiences. How often that external camera is turned on varies from person to person, and no one keeps it turned on all the time, but one thing for certain is that you are much less likely to act impulsively while you are watching your behavior from an outside perspective.

How did our species acquire the ability to imagine the self from an outside perspective as if it were a real observation? The image we create of ourselves in the mind's eye is a model of the real thing, just as a map is a model of the real world. A map is not the same as reality; it is a symbolic representation or metaphor of the original. As we shall see, our mental maps of reality are built upon metaphors.

Symbolic Representations

There is something dazzling about looking up at a twinkling sky on a dark night, seeing thousands of distant stars dotting the sky. As a child I saw the sky as a sea of stars without specific patterns, but then I learned a number of constellations, including Leo, the Twins, Cassiopeia, Orion, and the Big and Little Dippers. These are Western constellations, passed down through our culture. I enjoy looking at the night sky and seeing familiar constellations. I can quickly orient myself to the directions with a glance at the sky. Unfortunately, however, now that I have learned these constellations, I am unable to *not* see them.

Indigenous people looked up at the stars and created their own unique constellations. I am blind to their constellations and unable to see the sky without the constellations of our culture. When I look at the sky, my focus is drawn to the symbols I know. I have defined this aspect of reality and therefore changed my experience of it. Language has a similar effect on our perceptions of reality. When we acquire language, we cease to see reality as it really is, and we see our symbols of it instead. For example, when you use the word "tree," do you recall a photographic image of a specific tree, or do you imagine a more generalized, symbolic tree? Many people are so disconnected from nature that all trees tend to look alike. Consequently, few people ever really see a tree.

In war it is common practice to dehumanize the enemy. Instead of talking about mothers, fathers, children, and friends, we lump them together with symbolic labels. They become heathen savages, an inferior race, Jews, communists, Muslims, or terrorists. Our ancestors didn't commit genocide in the conquest of the Americas, they were merely clearing the wilderness of heathen savages. Hitler wasn't indiscriminately murdering people, he was purging the Arian nation of an inferior race. Communists were not compassionate like us; they wanted to nuke us, and the only reason they didn't was because we had more nuclear weapons. America doesn't bomb families; we only kill terrorists. We conjure a symbolic image of a terrorist and hold it in mind every time we attack. As long as we can avoid seeing pictures of the children we have killed, maimed, or left parentless, then we can go on purging the world of terrorists.

Likewise, with the aid of symbols and labels we can reduce a richly abundant ecosystem of thousands of unique plant and animal species down to mere commodities such as "trees" or "forest." We simplify the real world into "resources" and perceive development as "progress." However, to a person intimately connected with nature, resource extraction and real estate development are destructive experiences like war, and the victims are personal friends. Without labels we could not organize and build a civilization, nor could we describe reality. But the labels change our relationship to the world, and we no longer see reality without judging it to be one thing or another.

Many autistic people struggle to grasp symbolic language, and their experiences offer clues to what reality might be like without it. For example, Temple Grandin is an autistic who overcame her disabilities to build a successful life and career in the modern world. Her experience of reality is unique and remarkable in that she was able to attain self-awareness in spite of the linguistic obstacles. Through Grandin we can get a sense of what reality might be like if we didn't process it into symbolic language. For example, when we hear the word "dog," we typically recall a generalized symbol, not an actual dog. But Grandin recalls a photographic image of the first dog she knew when she learned to associate the word with the animal. From that point she can scroll through a photographic collection of other dogs she has known. In a forest, Grandin sees every tree and they are all unique and different.

Since she is unobstructed by symbols, Grandin has an essentially photographic memory. She can look at a page of text and read it later in her mind. On the other hand, she is unable to generalize the way other people do. For example, as we drive by a barn we mentally fill in the other side and recognize the landmark on the return trip. We build a symbolic map of reality as we go. Grandin is unable to fill in her mental map with symbols, so she must see the other side of the barn to recognize it later. Grandin apparently sees reality as it is, while the rest of us see and navigate a symbolized version of it.

Advanced Metaphors

As we saw earlier, descriptive metaphors enable us to describe something new in terms of something familiar. For example, a "dental bridge" is a descriptive metaphor for a dental procedure. Nothing walks or drives across a dental bridge, but the bridge does cover the gap of a missing tooth. Descriptive metaphors like this apparently enabled the rise of human culture 40,000 to 50,000 years ago. However, there is a big difference between describing a new object in terms of that which is already familiar, and describing intangible concepts as if they had physical properties.

Modern language is full of metaphorical phrases such as "building a bridge between our differences," or "thinking outside the box." We use rich metaphorical language every day and depend on it to communicate effectively. In the same way that we refer to the mouth of a bottle without imagining a mouth, we can imagine building a bridge between our differences without imagining a crane moving steel girders into place. The use of metaphors is so common to our language that we use them without thinking about it. Indeed, metaphors are so thoroughly embedded in the structure of our language that you may not recognize most of them. Consider the phrase, *"I ran in a race."* In linguistics this phrase is considered a container metaphor. The race is perceived as being something we can get *into.*

In the book *Metaphors We Live By*, authors George Lakoff and Mark Johnson demonstrate how we use metaphor to structure the world we live in. For instance, orientational metaphors are related to basic physiology. If we feel bad, either physically ill or emotionally depressed, then we tend to be down physiologically as well. We lay around until we get better, or may sit or stand in a slouched position. On the other hand, feeling good is associated with being up and about. These physiological realities are reflected metaphorically in our language: We say things like, "She is at the *peak* of health." "His health is *falling.*" "My heart is *sinking.*" "He came *down* with the flu." "He *dropped* dead."[16]

Ontological metaphors transform things that lack physical substance, such as ideas, events, and emotions, into entities we can describe in physical terms. For example, we can say that a person lacks *moral fiber*, or has a *fragile ego.* We could describe him as having an ego that is *easily crushed*, or say that he was *shattered* by a traumatic event. A container metaphor, such as the notion of being *in a race* is a common type of ontological metaphor. We can talk about our *field of vision*, and describe things as *coming into* our field of vision or *going out* of it. Owing a friend a favor can become a container as well, such as when we become *indebted* to them.[17]

It is nearly impossible to open one's mouth without invoking metaphors. Metaphors allow us to communicate concepts that are difficult or impossible to convey without them. If you tell me to *pack my thoughts into fewer words*, you imply that my thoughts are objects and the words are containers to put them into. In addition to communicating, metaphors allow us to think thoughts we could not have without them. Common expressions such as *thinking outside the box* help wire our brains to imagine such things. We are exposed to complex metaphorical language throughout childhood, and we gradually form the neurocircuitry to process information in a similar way. We learn to talk about intangible concepts as if they had real substance. We can imagine thinking inside or outside of a box. We can imagine a thousand other things that are equally intangible.

In essence, we can hypothesize that hunter-gatherer languages should be rich with descriptive metaphors, while lacking the intangible, increasingly abstract metaphors of modern languages. I'm not aware that anyone has analyzed hunter-gatherer languages with that question in mind. However, it is known that some cultures do not have words to count past ten or to refer to the passage of time. For example, the Pirahã tribe of Brazil has only three words for numbers: "one," "two," and "many." Besides lacking words for higher numbers, matching tests reveal that adults have trouble conceptualizing larger numbers. Pirahã children, however, grasp number concepts very easily.[18]

Similarly, many tribal languages lack words to distinguish the past or future. In Hopi there are no words for time, and no words that imply the passage of time, such as the idea that something might last or endure.[19] In Hopi, people talk about long-dead friends and relatives as if they just walked out the door, as if all time runs together in a perpetual present moment.[20] Where we describe summer as a season, implying a span of time, the Hopi describe it as a phenomenon where conditions are hot.[21] It should be noted, however, that the Hopi do not lack a concept of the past, since they have a rich oral history that is linked to past generations, rather than to a numerical calendar.[22] Instead of talking about the past in past tense, stories are retold or re-enacted vividly in present tense regarding individuals who passed on generations ago.

Interestingly, autistics struggle with the complexities and abstractions of modern language, providing additional clues to the structure of languages prior to the rise of complex metaphors. For example, in his autobiography, *Born on a Blue Day*, Daniel Tammet describes his life as an autistic savant. Like most autistics, he struggled with idiomatic language as a child, such as describing a sick person as "under the weather." To him, it seemed like everyone was "under the weather," because the weather was in the sky.[23] As an adult, Tammet still struggles to connect the bits and pieces of a multipart sentence into a complete mental movie. For example, someone might say, *"I was writing an essay on my computer when I accidentally hit the wrong button and deleted everything."* Tammet hears the words and understands that the person was writing an essay and hit the wrong button, but doesn't connect the different statements together to get the end result that the essay was lost.[24] Temple Grandin still struggles with abstract words. When she hears a word like "macroeconomics," she pictures a woven macramé flowerpot holder.[25]

Reality by Metaphor

A map of the world is not the world. It is a model built with symbols arranged to metaphorically represent the world. The relationship between the symbols tells us something about the relationship between the original objects. Similarly, a map of reality is not reality. It is a mental map built with symbolic excerpts arranged to metaphorically represent reality. If I say "San Francisco," one person might recall an image of the Golden Gate Bridge while another hears a clip of the song *San Francisco: "Be sure to wear flowers in your hair."* The real world does not exist in our heads, and we don't recall reality itself but merely symbolic excerpts of it. We recall snippets of images, sounds, smells, and feelings that symbolize the original experience. We also make excerpts about the people we know, events in the news, past recollections, ideas, proposals, and our own self-identity.

Excerpts are unique to each person. A dozen people on a fishing trip will create a dozen different excerpts of the trip. Reminisce about the trip a year later, and each person will initially recall a different excerpt of it. One person might recall a snapshot and emotion relating to the big catch. Someone else may store a snippet of tripping on the way out of the boat, or saying something incredibly stupid, or perhaps falling in love. No two excerpts of the same event will look and feel the same. From the initial snippets we can open up other snippets and assemble the bits and pieces into an accelerated movie of the experience. We navigate symbolic excerpts in our minds, scrolling through them in our memories, making comparisons between different thoughts and experiences, regrouping them to consider new possibilities. As Julian Jaynes observed, *"language is an organ of perception, not simply a means of communication."*[26]

It is easy to assume that we see reality with our eyes, but our perceptions are distorted by language. The reality we see is dictated by our mental map of the world, and that map is based on metaphor. We make excerpts and assemble them as a map to navigate by, but we may never know reality itself. As anthropologist Edward T. Hall observed, *"No two languages are alike; each has to be approached afresh. Some are so dissimilar, English and Navajo, for example, that they force the speaker into two different images of reality."*[27] Our lives are shaped by our metaphors, our experiences colored by our map of reality. The best we can do is to question our representation of reality and seek to minimize the distortions in our map.

Consider how our map of reality might influence our experience of an illness. In hunter-gatherer societies, illnesses were typically perceived as being caused by evil spirits or magic spells. In a deeply religious civilization an illness might be perceived as a guilty conscience, the work of the devil, or "bad humors." The rise of germ theory led to a map of reality in which illness is caused by microorganisms. These are dramatically different maps of reality, resulting in significantly different methods of treatment. The symptoms may be identical, but the prescription could vary from shamanic magic to religious fervor or blood purging to a prescription for antibiotics, each with its own successes and failures. The metaphors we use to describe reality become the maps we use for navigation.

Excerpts of Self and Time

Through our minds we can see ourselves from a third-person perspective. The image we see is not our actual self, but a symbolic representation of our self-identity. We watch animated symbols of ourselves in mental movies to recall the past or visualize the future. We can make this symbolized version of ourselves act out various scenarios until we come up with a satisfactory course of action.

In our minds we can make a movie of hiking up a mountain trail and decide whether or not the experience would be enjoyable. We might build a movie based on excerpts from previous experiences on the trail, or assemble excerpts from experiences on nearby trails. We can look at a map of a trail hundreds of miles away and create a movie of our possible experience based on our limited knowledge about the topography, weather, and wildlife. These movies are not real, but we make decisions as if they are.

Whether or not these are good decisions depends on the accuracy of the scenarios we create. The danger is that we tend to live vicariously. We hike up a trail in our imaginations and finding the experience too boring to do in life. As noted by Jim Baggott in *A Beginner's Guide to Reality*, *"We construct a reality based on models of how we would like that reality to be, not on reality itself."*[28] We go golfing instead, never knowing that something exciting could have happened on the hike, such as seeing a bobcat.

Our sensation of time is also directly connected to the ability to make symbolic excerpts. For example, recalling the significant events of our lives, most of us imagine something like frames of a movie stretched out from left to right in front of us. We can scroll back through symbolic excerpts of events such as graduation, the birth of our children, our wedding day, or a skiing accident, and zoom in on any excerpt we wish to explore in greater depth. In effect, we symbolize the passage of time as the spatial distance between events, which is revealed in our language through metaphors such as *a stretch in time* or *a long day*.[29] It is apparently impossible to imagine the passage of time except in spatial terms. The use of metaphor enables us to step outside of time to compare past and future side-by-side in chronological order. However, the negative side of this skill is that it separates us from the natural world. We no longer flow along with the perpetual present moment. We have stepped outside of time to recognize its existence. We dwell in the past or worry about the future, neglecting to fully experience the present moment.

Previously we might have assumed that language is neutral, that we could use words to define reality. But language shapes our perceptions. We label the world with symbolic representations and no longer recognize reality itself. We navigate according to our symbolic map of reality, blind to the errors in our mapmaking. On the positive side, the structure of language enabled the emergence of the mind. The rise of metaphorical language unleashed human creativity, while complex metaphors made it possible to discuss abstract concepts as if they were tangible things. Language and metaphor made it possible to construct mental models of our selves, to imagine seeing ourselves from an outside perspective for the first time. Without language we would lack conscious minds and a sense of self-identity. We would not know we existed.

In the next chapter we explore stages of human development, discovering that children must retrace our evolutionary history as they mature. Children's perception and experience of reality changes in predictable ways as they grow up and acquire language skills.

Suggested Reading

The Symbolic Species by Terrence W. Deacon. Structural consistencies between diverse languages have led some researchers to argue that the human brain evolved a hard-wired "universal grammar." Deacon suggests the opposite, that languages consistently evolve to fit the wiring of the brain, especially the wiring of children's brains. Chimpanzees, for example, can acquire a versatile grasp of symbolic language even though it is not part of their evolutionary history.

Five

Growing Up

Stages of Human Development

"The human brain is a complex matrix of superimposed and interwoven systems corresponding to the various stages of evolution, and the self that arises from it is something like a city built across the ages. Its archaeology includes a prehistoric layer, a medieval layer, and some modern buildings... Each of us carries within his own nervous system the whole history of biological life on the planet, at least that belonging to the animal kingdom."

—Danah Zohar, The Quantum Self

The perception and experience of reality of adults is vastly different from that of children. We begin exploring and defining the world around us as infants and gradually refine our understanding of reality as we mature.

The differences between our perceptions as children and as adults stems from a combination of physiological, psychological, and cultural factors. Physiologically and psychologically, our brains continue developing long after we are born. Culturally, we mimic behaviors we are exposed to at home, in public, and on television, growing the neural circuitry required to behave like a member of our society. In this chapter we consider the reptilian and mammalian evolutionary heritage of our brains, then explore psychological stages of human development and how these relate to our assimilation of culture and perceptions of reality.

A Brief History of the Brain

The human brain is highly complex, with parts grouped into three distinct layers representing various stages of our evolutionary history from reptiles to mammals to primates. Based on fifty years of research by neuroscientist Paul MacLean, these layers are popularly known as the R-complex, limbic, and neocortex. The layers of the brain are highly interconnected, but still separate enough that we functionally have three different brains, each with a will of its own.

R-complex (reptillian): The brainstem is the oldest part of the brain, consisting of the medulla, pons, cerebellum, mesencephalon, olfactory bulbs, and the oldest basal nuclei, called the globus pallidus. These parts of the brain dominated the mechanical or reflexive behavior of our reptilian ancestors. Think of it as hardwired programming; the reflexive brain controls bodily functions such as muscles, balance, temperature control, breathing, and heartbeat, as well as the drive to eat and reproduce. These instincts are hardwired to the extent that a reptile may repeat the same behaviors over and over again without learning from past mistakes. We can imagine a reptile as a sort of biomechanical device that operates according to a preprogrammed set of instructions. In humans, this ancient part of our brain is active at all times, even during deep sleep. However, our reflexive tendencies are usually moderated by connections from more recently evolved parts of the brain.

Limbic (old mammalian): The limbic system formed around the reptilian brain and consists of the hypothalamus, hippocampus, and amygdala. This part of the brain arose with the early mammals and is associated with emotions and instincts regarding feeding, fighting, fleeing, and sexual desire. Stimulating the limbic system with a mild electrical current triggers various emotional responses, such as fear, joy, rage, pleasure, or pain. Emotionally charged memories are also stored in this part of the brain. When driven by this emotional system, everything is either agreeable or disagreeable, and survival depends on seeking pleasure and avoiding pain. A mouse can apparently function adequately if its higher brain functions are removed, as long as its limbic system and r-complex are in tact.

Humans are more dependent on our higher brain functions for social interactions, but we tend to fall back on our limbic system for decision-making. Studies show that people use logic to make small decisions, such as determining which can of tuna is the most economical purchase. Larger decisions, like buying a new car, are often determined emotionally, according to what feels right. The limbic system also asserts itself in stressful or traumatic situations, dampening our ability to reason.

Neocortex (primates): The neocortex or cerebrum wraps around the limbic system and consists of the familiar left and right sides of the brain that are referred to in popular culture. While all mammals have a neocortex, it is most developed among the primates, enabling complex social interactions and planning, far beyond the abilities of dogs, cats, or horses. The neocortex is largest among humans, accounting for two-thirds of our brain capacity. This enlarged size and capacity probably arose in conjunction with rudimentary language and social complexity among our distant ancestors.

The right side of the neocortex controls the left side of the body and vice versa. The right side is greatly interconnected with the rest of the brain and more intuitive, enabling spatial, abstract, musical, and artistic thought and expression. The left side is more isolated, primarily connected through the corpus callosum to the right side. In isolation, the left side is able to process information in a linear, verbal, and rational form, undistracted by competing input from other parts of the brain.

As we mature, we effectively retrace our evolutionary history, operating reflexively through the reptilian brain, then emotionally through the limbic system, and later cognitively through the neocortex. Each layer of the brain has a will of its own, but through experience we learn to modify our behaviors and make neurological connections between the layers. We wire the three brains together as one, although each layer retains a degree of autonomy. We previously described the conscious/subconscious relationship as analogous to two separate brains inhabiting a single body. Now we discover that there are actually three brains. We navigate life with three partially integrated, partially autonomous brains, which greatly contributes to our multiple-personality-like behaviors.

For example, a child might say he will not steal or lie anymore, and in his conscious mind he believes that is true. Yet impulses take over from the older parts of brain as he walks down the candy isle at the grocery store, and without conscious consideration, the fingers reach out and pocket a few goodies. The ability to control these impulses is directly related to the degree that the three brains are wired together.

Similarly, ask a child how she feels about something, and she may not be able to tell you directly. The emotional, old mammalian part of the brain isn't adequately connected to the verbal parts of the brain for a child to consciously express her feelings. Unable to express the emotions consciously and directly, the child communicates subconsciously and indirectly through metaphor. For example, some psychologists use art therapy and play therapy to facilitate communication with kids in counseling. A child might not be able to verbally express her feelings, but she may be able to convey it in a drawing or act it out with dolls, without consciously being aware of it. A psychologist can initiate a two-way dialogue with the child about events in the game or about the drawing to understand the issues she is dealing with.

Likewise, when my daughter described how she appreciated the sturdy construction of our stone and log home in comparison to the shaky house of her birth parents, she was simply using a metaphor to express that she felt more secure now than before. With practice we can learn to express our feelings directly. The more we practice, the more we make neural connections between the emotional and the verbal parts of the brain, improving our ability to discern and describe what's happening inside. By exercising each layer of the brain and cross-wiring them together, we gradually mature through various stages of human development. These stages can be defined and categorized in scores of different ways, each based on the filters of the observer.

Filters for Human Development

In the language chapter we noted that labels can transform something formless, changing, and intangible into a noun with distinct characteristics and boundaries. In terms of human development, for example, we could label four obvious phases: infant, child, adolescent, and adult. Labels allow us to categorize these stages as if they are distinct and separate phases, even though they are not. The transition from one stage to another, such as from infant to child, doesn't happen overnight, but with labels we can contrast and compare each stage in absolute terms.

Psychologists have generated a variety of categorization schemes and labels to describe the stages of human development, each based on different criteria or filters. For example, Lawrence Kohlberg examined human growth through the lens of *morality* and noted six stages of moral development. James W. Fowler explored progressive levels of *faith*, and distinguished seven stages of faith development. Jane Loevinger examined human development from the perspective of *self-awareness* and described nine stages of ego development. Erik Erikson considered human growth from a *psychological* perspective and observed eight stages of psycho-social development from infancy to late adulthood. Jean Piaget identified four stages of *cognitive development*, including sensorimotor, preoperational, concrete operational, and formal operational.

The labels are primarily useful for research and educational purposes, and the boundaries remain as blurred as our progression from infant to child to adolescent and adult. There is no sudden dividing line between one stage and another, and so psychologists often subdivide the stages of human development into substages such as "lower, middle, and higher" for each stage.

Which model of human development is the correct one? Probably all of them are correct. By investigating issues of morality or cognitive development, certain patterns of psychological growth become visible. By labeling these patterns we can discuss and contrast these otherwise formless behaviors as if they were tangible things. We can compare the process of human development through many different filters and learn different truths from each perspective. For the purpose of this text, we are primarily interested in perceptions of reality, which can be thought of as worldviews.

German philosopher Jean Gebser (1905–1973) first catalogued human behavior based on different worldviews, which he described as *archaic, magical, mythical,* and *rational* in his book 1953 book *The Ever-Present Origin.*[2] Philosopher Ken Wilber noted similarities between Gebser's system and Piaget's four levels of cognitive development, and he started linking them together, along with the other categorization schemes. The result was a generalized pattern of worldviews that includes cognitive, moral, ego, faith, and psychological development all in one model. As with any categorization scheme, the boundaries are messy between one stage and the next. Rather than attempting to resolve contradictions with detailed substages, it is probably most useful for our purposes to retain a big-picture, generalized perspective of each of these worldviews.

In this text I have modified Gebser's system of worldviews with more intuitive labels: preconscious, magical, mythical, and sequential. I also apply the word "processing" to emphasize that each worldview is based on a specific pattern of thinking, resulting in unique perspectives on reality.

Preconscious Processing (0–2 years old)

It is amazing how much we take for granted as adults that we had to learn as infants. We know where our body ends and the rest of the world begins. We can recognize a chair, no matter what angle we see it from. We are born with the wiring to perceive sights and sounds, yet we lack instructions to know how to process that information. We come wired to move our limbs, but we lack the experience to know how to do it voluntarily. Yet, by firing neurons here and there, our limbs start to twitch and move this way and that, until the grey matter forms the neurocircuitry that enables us to reach out this way, or to crawl over there. Visually, the world may initially be a blur of meaningless light without depth, but by looking and touching we begin to discern three-dimensional space until we can see that some things are close up and others are far away. The meaningless noise of the world gradually becomes meaningful as our brains devote more circuitry towards familiar sounds and connects them with associated sights and actions. We begin to mimic the familiar sounds we hear, and ultimately teach ourselves language without organized instruction.

Infants are initially unable to distinguish between themselves and the rest of the world and thus have no ego or self-identity. They begin to coordinate their neurocircuitry, starting with completely reflexive skills such as sucking, following objects with their eyes, or grasping when something touches the palm of their hands. By about six weeks old they learn to grasp intentionally. Infants learn to reach for things, although the objects may be beyond their grasp.[3] However, they do not begin to differentiate between themselves and the rest of the world until about four months old. For example, a friend's daughter pulled her own hair when she was upset, which made her cry even more. By about five to nine months old a baby learns to physically distinguish herself from the rest of the world. Some researchers consider this the real birth of the physical self.[4]

Learning to see requires experience as well. Prior to acquiring depth perception, the world is perceived two-dimensionally. A chair looks like a different object when viewed from different angles. Infants learn to see three-dimensionally by first reaching out to faces around them, then by crawling around in exploration. They gradually learn that the world is three-dimensional and separate from themselves. By seeing and physically interacting with chairs and other objects, infants learn to recognize things from any angle.

Similarly, in two-dimensional perception, objects that are farther away seem smaller, a phenomenon that we learn to associate with greater distance. Colin Turnbull, author of *The Forest People*, brought his African Pygmy friend Kenge out of the jungle for the first time. Looking at some buffalo several miles away, Kenge asked, "What insects are those?" Kenge had normal depth perception in the jungle, but he had never been exposed to open vistas before, so he didn't realize that the "insects" were full-sized buffalo.[5]

In addition to wiring limbs and senses and learning to physically distinguish herself, the infant must also learn to emotionally differentiate herself from the rest of the world. The infant initially treats the world as an extension of herself, as if everyone and everything feels, sees, and desires the same things she does. The infant plays hide-and-seek in plain sight, assuming that you cannot see her if she cannot see you. By about fifteen to twenty-four months of age, the infant starts to wake up to the realization that she is an emotionally separate self from the rest of the world. This is the psychological birth of the child, and the beginning of the "terrible twos."[6]

Magical Processing (2–7 years old)

At approximately two years of age, a child begins to think symbolically, understanding that words or pictures can represent something that isn't physically present. While an infant might be able to close his eyes and recall an image of a dog, a child makes the connection that a picture of a dog or the word "dog" symbolically represents a dog. Between age four and seven years a child learns to generalize, to form the concept that a symbol such as the word "dog" can represent an entire class of objects—all dogs, rather than just a specific dog. In short, the child begins to acquire language and use it as a tool to perceive the world.

At this age, children engage in imitation, acquiring language and behavior through mimicry and accumulated experience. However, they lack an intuitive grasp of nature and science, so the world seems to work in magical ways. For example, when my son Edwin was four years old, he dreamed that the apple tree in the yard was covered in cookies. Upon waking, he ran out the door to see the cookies. That is reality to a four-year old. Food and toys magically appear; people appear, disappear, and reappear in their lives, and they simply have no concept of sequential cause and effect. They don't understand that cookies require ingredients and baking. Cookies just appear in their lives. Even if they recognize that they ate the last cookie, they don't understand why another batch cannot magically appear like the previous ones.

Robert Kegan provided an example of magical thinking in his book *The Evolving Self*: "*One day a mother of two was at the end of her rope with her sons' constant bickering. The current squabble was over the allocation of a dessert pastry. The mother had given two of the small squares to her ten-year-old and one to her four-year-old. She had explained to her aggrieved younger son that he had received only one because he was smaller, that when he was bigger he could have two. He was quite unappeased by this logic, as you can imagine, and he continued to bemoan his fate. The mother lost her patience, and in a fit of sarcasm she swept down on his plate with a knife, saying, "You want two pieces? Okay, I'll give you two pieces. Here!"—whereupon she neatly cut the younger boy's pastry in half. Immediately, all the tension went out of him; he thanked his mother sincerely, and contentedly set upon the dessert…. [The mother and older son] looked at each other; and in that moment they shared a mutually discovered insight into the reality of their son and brother, a reality quite different from their own.*"

The ability to accurately judge amounts was termed "conservation of matter" by Piaget. Young children lack the ability to accurately compare mass or volume, which can be demonstrated in the kitchen with a child up to seven years old. Take two identical pitchers with identical amounts of water and pour the contents into two separate containers, one that is short and fat, and another that is skinny and tall. Ask the child which one contains the most water. He will typically pick the one that is taller, as if it has more water, even though he just watched you pour an identical amount of water in both containers.[8]

Children's stories and movies tend to reflect magical thinking, which is something that remains part of all of us as we mature; hence the popularity of the *Harry Potter* stories and other magical adventures. As adults we may not spend a lot of time in a magical worldview, but it is still an important part of who we are. We continue to fantasize about wishes coming true or having magical powers. Frankly, I've always lived in a very magical world. One of my favorite movies is *Matilda*, based on the book by Roald Dahl, a story about a little girl with magical powers.

Childhood is also a timeless experience, bound up in the present moment. Children transition instantly from happy to sad, from laughing to crying, totally wrapped up in the moment as if the events of two minutes ago have no relevance to the present experience. Although capable of anxiety about the future, children exist largely in the immediate now, with little reflection on the past or speculation about the future.

Young children are entirely egocentric, aware of their own point of view but unable to perceive the world through the eyes of anyone else. They exist solidly in first person, not readily able to get outside of themselves to see the world through other people's eyes. They are aware of their wants and needs but they cannot readily acknowledge that other people have wants, needs, and feelings too. Children operate as if the entire universe revolves around them. They have a lot of expectations and demands. They want everyone to serve them. People are perceived in terms of their usefulness and what they can provide. At this stage of development, children are generally aware of their existence, but not in an introspective or self-conscious way.

Children do not experience guilt as we know it, since they are stuck in their own viewpoint. They have no concept of right or wrong or of guilt or remorse, until we tell them they are being good or bad and program it into them. Initially they learn that it is bad to hurt other people because they get in trouble for it. They do not understand the concept of hurting a person, either physically or emotionally, but they do understand consequences for bad behavior, which impact their own experience.

Nor are children capable of thinking through the consequences of their actions, whether it is lighting a fire in the basement or putting a cat in the dryer. In short, children at this stage of development remain highly impulsive. They tend to act without thinking through the consequences of their actions; they don't use their conscience to moderate their behavior. Children younger than about seven years of age who commit murder are typically exonerated in countries with due process, because they are not considered capable of understanding the consequences of their actions.

Most children mature through this first-person experience fairly quickly, but some teens and young adults remain stuck in first person. Lacking guidance, or traumatized by some childhood event, they don't perceive their actions through the eyes of other people. Those who remain first-person oriented and impulsive as teenagers and adults are typically very fun loving, living for the moment, heedless of future consequences. But without the ability to see the world through the eyes of other people, they can be boundlessly brash, saying or doing things that hurt people, and, like children, cycling from great joy to great anguish from moment to moment.

Mythical Processing (7–11 years old)

As children continue to mature, they begin to acquire an intuitive grasp of nature and science, recognizing that a short, fat glass can hold as much water as a tall, skinny one. They also understand reversibility, as observed by Piaget. For example, if 4 + 4 = 8, then it makes sense that 8 − 4 = 4. Children become very adept at serialization and classification, such as arranging objects in order according to size, shape, or any other given characteristic. Furthermore, they can understand that one set of objects can include another. In short, children of this age are very concrete thinkers.[9] However, children are not very flexible thinkers at this stage of development. They tend to process concepts in terms of simple opposites—short or tall, hot or cold—rather than as shades of grey.

I remember as a child, seeing bad things in the world and wanting to make a difference. I imagined that if I were president I could outlaw things like cigarettes and beer and somehow that would make the problems go away. Of course the world is a bit more complicated than that, as illustrated by the prohibition of alcohol in the United States between 1920 and 1933, which led to bootlegging, illegal imports, a violent black market, racketeering, and loss of tax revenues.[10] Children cannot perceive these complexities, so they see issues in black-and-white.

At this age children also lack critical reasoning skills or the ability to experiment through the process of elimination. For example, mixing paint to get the right color might be approached through random experimentation rather than systematically increasing the amount of color added.

As they mature, children learn to perceive the world through the eyes of other people. For example, if you put a teddy bear in a box in front of two younger children, then move it when one leaves the room, the other erroneously assumes that the child who left the room is aware of the new location. In contrast, an older child understands that the one outside the room cannot know the teddy bear has been moved. In effect, a child matures from a first-person experience, seeing the world only from his own perspective, to a second-person experience, seeing the world through the eyes of other people, even if not always accurately.[11]

As adults we actively cultivate this second-person perception by playing constructive mind games with our kids, saying things like, "How would you feel if Jimmy took *your* toy? Do you understand now how Jimmy might feel because you took *his* toy?" Over time we teach children to transpose their viewpoint to imagine the internal experiences of other people. Children further develop this skill by engaging in role-playing games, pretending to be other people—kings and queens, princesses and princes, cops and robbers. They act out the good and bad behaviors they see among people around them and on television, and admonish each other for breaking the rules. They shift into second person to act out these different roles, and in so doing they begin to get a sense of what it is like to see the world through other people's eyes.

Although it is difficult to accurately perceive the world through second person, it is also one of the keys to successful communication. The important part of communication isn't what is said, but what the audience hears, so the speaker has to understand the background experience of the audience. I used to find it paralyzing to talk to two or more people at once. I focused entirely on interpreting my words through their ears, based on what I understood of their background experiences. Of course, I imagine myself better at intuiting the thoughts of others than I really am.

A second-person perspective greatly encourages conformity, as behavior is molded by perceived expectations. As adults we admonish our children for bad or undignified behavior, telling them things like "What would people think if they saw you doing that?" We literally teach children to see themselves through the eyes of other people until they become completely self-conscious, as if everyone in the world is judging them. We make them self-conscious by the time they are teenagers, and then we wonder why they are suddenly embarrassed to be seen with their parents.

Role-playing is similar to learning scripts for a play. We learn to act properly in society, as if all of life were a stage. We learn basic scripts, such as how to act cool, how to put someone else down, how to perform in common situations. We learn to ask, "How are you?" to everyone we meet, and to respond by saying "Fine." The person asking isn't usually looking for a real answer. It is just a script we act out like automatons, performing without thinking about our behavior.

Mythical processing allows a child to see through the eyes of other people around them. Children role-play the behaviors of people they know and feel secure in conforming to the ways of their culture. The result is an ethnocentric viewpoint. Lacking exposure to other cultures and viewpoints, they understand only the code of conduct of their own culture and see it as the only way to do things. They interpret reality in black-and-white terms, believing the answers must be either this or that, based on their cultural background.

With role-playing, a black-and-white view of issues, and lacking a mature sense of cause and effect, the mythical worldview is typically associated with gods and strong opinions of right and wrong. While younger kids tend to perceive reality in very magical terms, kids of this age perceive reality in more mythical terms. For example, while a younger child might imagine he can make a picture of a candy bar magically turn into a real one, an older child might be motivated to pray for one instead, perhaps imagining that if he behaves well then he will be rewarded.

Sequential Processing (11 and older)

The next stage of human development is sequential processing. It is the ability to step outside of oneself into a third-person perspective, to engage in critical thinking, and to make objective comparisons between different sides of an issue.

For example, in a dispute you would be able to identify your side of the issue from a first-person perspective, then shift to second person to see the issue from the other person's perspective, and then shift to third person to view the situation as an outside observer where you can objectively compare both sides of the issue. This is an acquired skill, and not one that comes easily. You learn to see both sides of an issue—and sometimes admit when you are wrong. You learn to see issues in terms of many shades of grey, that sometimes there is no black-and-white answer, but rather that the truth is somewhere in the murky middle.[12]

At this phase of development, a maturing person begins to accept people who are different. Instead of seeing other beliefs or cultures as alien or threatening, he begins to understand that other viewpoints are as valid as his own. In the process of acknowledging the uniqueness and individuality of others, he also discovers his own individuality. He learns that his values and dreams are distinct from his culture and the expectations of others. By becoming increasingly aware of other people he becomes more aware of himself, maturing as an introspective, conscientious individual

Interestingly, however, only about one-third of Americans fully acquires sequential thinking. The majority essentially "solidifies" in a hybrid stage of development, with a partly mythical, partly sequential worldview. For example, an automotive engineer might perceive design problems in shades of grey, making trade-offs between fuel economy versus performance. Yet, he might retain black-and-white opinions about what is morally right and wrong.

Layers Like an Onion

Stages of human development can be thought of like the layers of an onion. The core of the onion represents subconscious, impulsive, animal like behavior, while each new layer added to the onion represents an increasing level of awareness, resulting in a new way of interpreting the world, a new worldview. Children initially operate entirely subconsciously, unaware of their own existence. In exploring the world they naturally discover their separation from it, and the self is mentally born. Children develop a magical map of reality, which is revised over time, through mythical and later sequential interpretations of their experience. Like an onion, we do not cast off previous layers, but encompass them in new layers of growth.

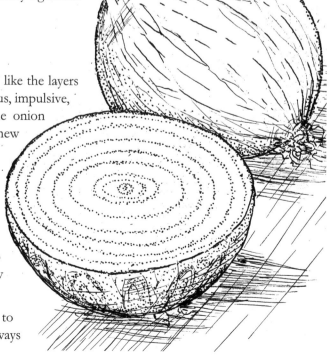

We are not aware of the transition from one stage to another as we develop, and we tend to assume that we always

experienced reality as we do today. However, one of the reasons many people struggle to remember childhood is because childhood is a different kind of reality, like living in another world. When we do recall the past, we subconsciously revise our memories to fit our current perceptions of the world. For example, in remembering an event from early childhood, we might recall what other people were thinking, even though we would not have experienced a second- or third-person perspective at that age.[13]

It was initially assumed that people matured from one stage to the next concurrently across all aspects of experience, but research indicates that people tend to advance more quickly in some domains than others. For example, a person may quickly grasp the principles of concrete thinking associated with the mythical stage, yet retain a strong first-person perspective from the magical stage. As noted by Ken Wilber in *A Brief History of Everything*, *"The self at any given point in its development will tend to give around 50 percent of its responses from one level, 25 percent from a level above that, and 25 percent from a level below it. No self is ever simply "at" a stage. And further, there are all sorts of regressions, spirals, temporary leaps forward, peak experiences, and so on."*[14] While there is a tendency to mature from one stage to the next, the transitions are not necessarily uniform, and not every person reaches the same end point before solidifying as an adult personality.

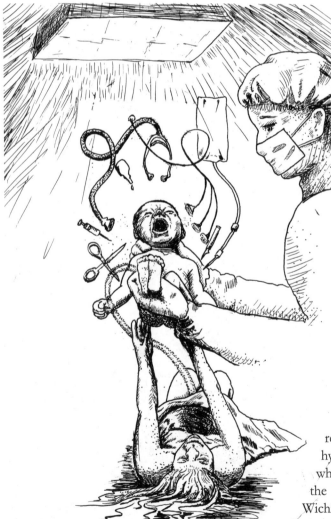

Mental Disorders

Traumatic events at any stage in a person's life can leave psychological scars, and typically the younger a person is at the time of the trauma, the deeper the resulting pathology. For example, an infant traumatized during the first months of life may never fully differentiate between himself and the physical world, leading to severe reality distortion and psychosis. He may confuse his own thoughts with those of other people.

Infants deal with issues of trust, which can impact their lifelong outlook on life. For example, if the mother disappears from sight, but reappears when needed, the infant tends to grow up perceiving society as largely trustworthy. However, if the maternal relationship is unstable, or if the child is abandoned at an early age, then the child may grow up to be mistrustful of the world and unable to form stable relationships of his own. Although he may act normally in other ways, he may remain plagued throughout life by poor relationship skills. These disorders are both psychological and neurological, making them especially difficult to deal with.

Disorders originating at the magical level may reveal themselves in neurotic symptoms such as obsessions, hysteria, compulsions, and depressions. For example, a girl who was beaten as a child developed a phobia about leaving the bathroom as an adult. She lived with her boyfriend in Wichita, Kansas and spent increasingly long sessions in the bathroom until she refused to come out at all. He thought it was a bit weird, but quickly adjusted to socializing in the bathroom and bringing her food and fresh clothing. She didn't come out of the bathroom for two years, until her skin grew around the toilet seat, and it had to be removed at the hospital.[15]

Mental disorders at the mythical level are frequently "script pathologies" dealing with an individual's role in society. Mythical processing is about learning roles or scripts and conforming to the expectations of society. A person can suffer from false scripts and depression, telling himself such things as, "I am a lousy person." These negative scripts may be reinforced by critical peers and adults who generalize one mistake by saying, "You can't do anything right." Small issues become distorted into big ones, and the individual may believe things like, "If Johnny doesn't like me, then no one will."[16]

Psychological trauma at any stage of development can stunt an individual's emotional growth, causing a small part of him to be "left behind" as he otherwise struggles to develop. As if tethered to an anchor, the individual struggles to move forward and mature properly. Danah Zohar described this emotional scarring in *The Quantum Self*: *"People who are in conflict—and this is most of us to some degree—have much less energy available to the main personality (their highest unity) than people who are more integrated. They have many poorly integrated subselves—pockets of childhood pain, pockets of personality that developed in different directions. Towards one extreme are those who need psychiatric help because they can't "get themselves together," who have so much of their mental energy siphoned off by subselves that they find it difficult to function as a self. At the other extreme are those charismatic people who sparkle with coherence."*[17] Thus, a thirty-year-old man may function normally most of the time, except for unexpected moments of infantile behavior, leftovers from some bad experience at the start of his journey. The grown man may be haunted by infantile behaviors for life, or at least until the original issue is addressed.

It is easy to imagine that an individual could consciously choose to cease inappropriate behavior, but the behavior isn't conscious to begin with. Emotional scars of childhood tend to be deeply embedded in the subconscious, and the subconscious controls most of our behavior. We like to think that we can consciously focus on better behaviors and choices, and that is partially true. However, in recalling the flashlight analogy of consciousness, we are only aware of a small part of our existence at any one time. When the flashlight of our consciousness is pointed one way, the subconscious mind is unsupervised to act impulsively in another.

In the next chapter we explore a startling phenomena: Similar to individuals, entire cultures seem to mature through magical, mythical, and sequential levels of development.

Six

Cultural Evolution

Technology and Worldviews

"Every society ever known rests on some set of largely tacit basic assumptions about who we are, what kind of universe we live in, and what is ultimately important to us. Some such set of assumptions can be found to underlie the institutions and mores, patterns of thought and systems of value, that characterize a society. They are not formulated or taught because they don't need to be—they are absorbed by each person born into the society as though by osmosis. They are accepted as given, obviously true—and throughout most of history, by most people, never questioned."

—*William Harmon, Global Mind Change*[1]

Like computers, humans come into existence with certain basic circuitry but must acquire programming and supportive files to be able to function. However, while computers typically have operating systems such as Macintosh or Microsoft to keep files organized, our operating systems consist of worldviews, such as magical, mythical, or sequential. Within each system, only certain programs or applications are compatible, so the programs that run within a magical operating system are different than the programs that run within a mythical operating system. We upgrade our operating systems as we mature through the stages of human development, transitioning from a preconscious existence to a magical, then mythical, then sequential experience of reality.

Interestingly, entire cultures seem to transition through similar stages of development. While no existing group of humans could be characterized as living a preconscious existence, there are plenty of cultures with distinctly magical, mythical, or sequential worldviews. Since individuals learn principally through mimicry, we tend to mimic current behaviors and thinking styles and mature to a similar stage of human development, leading to a common worldview across the culture.

A worldview is not a conscious choice, but a subconscious adaptation driven by the social-political organization of a culture. Social-political organization is directly linked to population size, and population size is largely dictated by the technologies utilized in production. While this relationship might seem complex, it is really quite simple. The bottom line is that cultural perceptions of reality are driven by technology in a sequence that works like this:

Technology > Population > Social-Political Institutions > Worldviews

61

Technology influences how cultures perceive the world, and as individuals we mimic those perceptions to build our own maps of reality. In this chapter we explore the connections to see how hunter-gatherer technology is linked to a magical worldview, while agrarian technology favors a mythical worldview, and industrial technology leads to a sequential worldview. In effect, we will step outside each version of reality to see what it looks like from an outside perspective.

Production Technology and Equality

Most hunter-gatherer societies had strict gender roles; men hunted and fished while women gathered roots, seeds, and berries. It must have been an effective pattern of behavior for survival, since ninety-seven percent of hunter-gatherer cultures were organized similarly. Aside from strict gender roles, these were largely egalitarian cultures in which everyone worked to survive and neither gender, nor typically any one individual, had a higher status or more political power than anyone else. Even spirits and gods were usually both male and female.

In horticultural societies women tended gardens with simple digging tools, and men continued to hunt. Strict gender roles remained; everyone worked to survive, and neither gender nor any individuals had significantly more political power than anyone else. However, since women produced most of the calories, these were often matriarchal, or at least "matrifocal" societies. In other words, in horticultural societies women generated most of the food, women generally led the households, and many of the spirits or gods were feminine.[2]

In contrast, agricultural societies were heavily patriarchal. Livestock were hitched up to plows and driven by men. Women experienced a significant rate of miscarriage running the plows, so men switched from hunting to farming. Men produced most of the calories, men became the heads of households, and consequently the gods became male gods. In a new twist, however, agricultural societies produced a surplus of calories. The surplus enabled population growth and specialization. For the first time, individuals could hold full-time jobs as soldiers, priests, or political figures rather than working to produce food. People no longer worked as equals in the quest for food, which led to hierarchical systems of power and a disparity in the rights of men and women. As Ken Wilber wrote in *A Brief History of Everything*, *"Because of the social relations that began to organize themselves around the basic forces of production—in this case the plow—men then began to dominate the public sphere of government, education, religions, politics. And women dominated the private sphere of family, hearth, home. This division is often referred to as male production and female reproduction."*[3]

Industrial societies are presently leveling inequalities that arose with agriculture. Women are as capable as men at working in most factories to earn a living. Men and women work side-by-side as equals in most factories and offices. In many families both parents work to earn a living, and in some cases only the mother goes to work to "bring home the bacon." Our society remains in transition towards equality today. The number of women in law and politics is continually growing, yet remains small compared to the number of men who hold political power. Massproduction generates a greater surplus and more specialization, along with the ability to communicate and transport goods over long distances. These factors enable larger populations, more consumption, and more interaction with other cultures.

These examples illustrate how production technology is connected to population size and the social-political structures of a society. Production technology heavily influences equality between genders and among individuals as well as the gender bias within religions. Production technology influences experiences and perceptions of reality across cultures, and individuals acquire that version of reality through mimicry and accumulated experience.

In this case, we grouped and classified cultures based on their production technologies, providing a unique perspective into our past and present history. However, as with stages of human development, there are multiple ways to classify human cultures. Each system of classification is based on particular patterns of behavior, resulting in slightly different delineations between groups, but each provides a unique insight into the nature of reality, both past and present.

Classifying Cultures

Early Western attempts at classifying cultures were highly flawed due to limited information about other cultures and the biases of philosophers, historians, and anthropologists. According to one popular model proposed in 1877, all societies must inevitably progress through seven stages: lower, middle, and upper savagery, lower, middle and upper barbarism, and finally civilization. Specific advances, such as the art of pottery, elevated a culture from one level to the next.

One of the first credible works on cultural evolution in popular literature was Peter Farb's *Man's Rise to Civilization*, based on the research of anthropologist Elman Service. Rather than linking cultural evolution to specific technologies or lifestyles, Farb outlined a connection between the size of a population and the complexity of its social, economic, and political institutions. He classified cultures according to patterns in their political structure as *bands, tribes, chiefdoms,* and *state governments*.[4] An additional level of distinction is the *divine kingdom,* used by some authors to describe cultures midway between chiefdoms and states. As with human development, there are no clear lines between individual stages, but all cultures fit somewhere along the continuum.

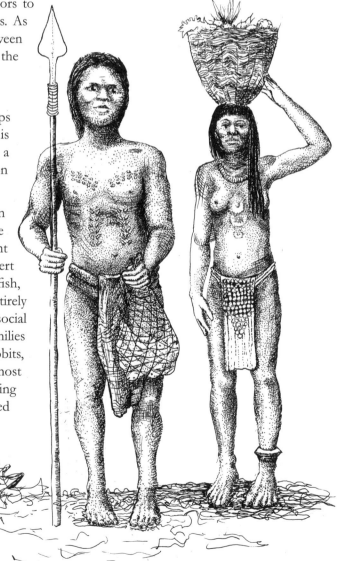

Bands: Cultures organized as bands were groups of families that cooperated with each other. The family is what Farb calls the *"irreducible minimum of human society,"* a socio-economic-political unit consisting of the association between a woman and a man and their children.[5]

The Piute Indians of the Great Basin Desert in Nevada and Utah were organized as bands. Lacking the technology to utilize the resources of their environment more effectively, individual families roamed the desert seeking pine nuts, roots, seeds, grasshoppers, rabbits, fish, or antelope that happened to be in season. It was an entirely egalitarian society, in which no person had a higher social status than any other. Through chance meetings, families occasionally met with other families when pine nuts, rabbits, or other resources were seasonally abundant. The most experienced hunter became the temporary leader, organizing all aspects of the hunt. Afterwards the families disbanded and went their own ways. Understanding the basic structure of Piute culture helps explain some of their behavior and interactions with Westerners.

For example, American explorers sought tribal chiefs to establish treaties, but the closest thing to a chief among the Piute was the "rabbit boss" who organized the hunt. There was no structure to bind the Piute people together as a single social-political unit. It was for this reason that the Piute were known as a largely peaceful people. They did not wage war on neighboring Indians, and they split up and ran away when attacked by others. They lacked the social-political structure to either mount an attack or to defend their territory.[6]

This isn't to say that people living in bands were free from aggression. Homicide rates can be shockingly high in band societies. A survey of one band of Copper Inuit revealed that each adult male had committed homicide at least once. Most homicides were related to quarrels over women.[7] An enlightening movie produced by the Inuit is *The Fast Runner* (2001). This fictional soap opera of Inuit life, lust, and murder, offers a glimpse of social life north of the Arctic Circle.

Bands may consist of temporary groupings of families, such as the Piute, or more permanent groupings consisting of up to a few hundred people, but they are all essentially egalitarian in structure, with no person having any significant political power or exemption from normal day-to-day work.

Tribes: Tribes are larger and more complex than bands, often consisting of multiple subgroups, such as the clans of the Zuni pueblos. Each clan has separate duties within the tribe. Like bands, tribes are composed primarily of related families living together. Specialization is minimal, without full-time soldiers, artisans, priests, or office holders. Everyone helps out with the effort to find food. A chief or council of leaders can recommend a course of action and make decisions, but they lack the power of state to enforce those decisions. In essence, a tribe is functionally a large gathering of independent individuals governed only by persuasion.

A society of free-willed individuals can be a recipe for internal conflicts, and homicide was common within many tribes. However, aggression was primarily directed outward towards neighboring tribes. Tribes often lived in a perpetual state of combat with their neighbors. From the Plains Indians to the northeastern Iroquois, as well as tribes in Africa, South America, and the South Pacific, war was a constant state of reality. Tribes rarely fought with the intention of conquering each other, and fighting had little to do with political disputes. Fighting released stress as warriors proved themselves in battle and earned prestige among their peers.

While bloodshed was common, the greatest glory typically went to warriors who merely touched or "counted coup" on an enemy and escaped unscathed. Pretty Shield, a medicine woman of the Crow Indians, described it this way, *"Striking an armed enemy with a bow, coup-stick, lance, or with the hand, or disarming him, without injury, counted the most honorable of coups. Killing and scalping an enemy did not entitle a warrior to count a coup."*[8]

In the book *The Falcon*, a narrative of the life of John Tanner, Tanner described his life among the Ojibway. Tanner was kidnapped at the age of nine years old by Shawnee warriors from his family's homestead in 1789. He was later traded to the Ojibway and raised by a woman who had lost her son. He remained a member of the Ojibway tribe his entire life and participated in several raids against the Sioux. The warriors traveled far to attack the Sioux, but in every "raid" the warriors were turned back by hunger, thirst, premonitions, internal strife, or simply because there was no cohesive structure to hold them together.

The Ojibway raids against the Souix became increasingly humorous throughout Tanner's narrative as raid after raid dissolved en route to the battlefield. In the mother of all raids, a mass of four hundred Ojibway warriors coincidentally met up with a thousand other Ojibway, Assiniboine, and Cree who were prepared to make war on the Sioux. As Tanner described it, *"On the first night after we came together, three men of the Ojibbeways were killed. On the next, two horses belonging to the Assinneboins, and on the third, three more [horses]. When such numbers of men assemble from different parts of the country, some must be brought into contact between whom old grudges and enmities exist, and it is not surprising that the unstable power and influence of the chiefs should be insufficient to prevent disturbances and bloodshed. On this occasion, men were assembled from a vast extent of the country, of dissimilar feelings and dialects, and of the whole fourteen hundred, not one who would acknowledge any authority superior to his own will. It is true that ordinarily they yield a certain deference, and a degree of obedience to the chief each may have undertaken to follow, but this obedience, in most instances, continues no longer than the will of the chief corresponds entirely with the inclination of those he leads."* Many Indians journeyed for months and some for more than a year to join the great battle. But the gathering dwindled to four hundred warriors by the time they were within two days striking distance of a Sioux village. When they finally reached the Sioux village, the war party consisted of a single chief and one or two warriors, who fled when they were discovered lurking around.[9]

Like a band, even if a tribe were able to organize and conquer a foreign territory, it still lacked the means to secure and administer it. The virtual absence of internal structure, along with the tendency to think in terms of battles, greatly aided the Europeans in conquering North America. Native Americans were fighting battles for honor and glory against European enemies who were fighting to conquer and rule over new territory.

Chiefdoms: The chiefdom is characterized by a surplus of food, greater specialization in labor, and a central figure to take in and redistribute wealth. While bands or tribes might migrate from one food source to another, a chiefdom has a larger, more permanent population spread across a diversity of environments. One group might specialize in fishing, while another specializes in farming or berry picking, and the resources from each are redistributed throughout the chiefdom. Chiefdoms formed along the northwest coast of North America and across the southeast from Virginia to Texas. Typically, a chief was pampered throughout life and provided with an elaborate house and other needs, all financed by the flow of goods within the culture. Chiefdoms were hierarchical, so much so that in northwest coast cultures an individual would know precisely whether his rank was 292 or 293 from the chief.[10]

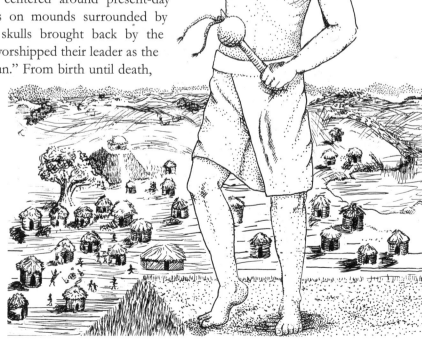

The largest chiefdoms in North America were the mound builders, such as the Natchez people centered around present-day Mississippi. The Natchez built temples on mounds surrounded by palisades, which were decorated with skulls brought back by the warriors. They worshipped the sun and worshipped their leader as the sun's brother, or simply as the "Great Sun." From birth until death, the Great Sun was treated as a living god and was the focal point of the entire culture. Every morning the Great Sun would greet the rising sun with howls, then raise up his hand and point the direction the sun must follow across the sky. The temple held the bones of the Great Sun's ancestors, as well as various idols such as ceramic models of men and women, snakeheads and tails, stuffed owls, crystals, and the jawbones of a large fish. The Great Sun went to the temple to worship and then announced what the idols foretold.

When a male heir was born to the Great Sun, the Natchez people brought their own children in the hope that they would be chosen as his lifelong aids and servants. The eventual death of the Great Sun was followed by a tremendous funeral rite, in which his wives, guards, and servants were also expected to die, and the rest of the population vied for the privilege of accompanying him into the afterlife. Volunteers swallowed a concoction of tobacco that rendered them unconscious, at which point they were lovingly strangled by relatives. The Great Sun's cabin was burned, and all the fires in the village were extinguished. He was temporarily buried at the temple. Later, the bones were exhumed and the remaining flesh was removed before placing them in baskets beside his ancestors.[11]

The Great Sun was powerful. He essentially owned all people and all property, and could do with them as he pleased. On a whim he could have any person executed on the spot, although there was no reason to use such power. More typically, a chief would have captive slaves executed on a whim, not in a display of power, but rather in a display of wealth. Among northwest coast cultures a chief might have his slaves executed to be used as logs for a visiting chief to roll his boat up onto shore. It was a show of extravagance to demonstrate that the chief had so much wealth that he could dispose of his people for frivolous purposes.

On the other hand, the power of a chief was secured not through any legal institutions, but through loyalty gained from the process of redistributing wealth. While there was a constant flow of goods and wealth towards the chief, the chief demonstrated his greatness by giving it away, bestowing it to all of his people. And although the chief might be able to send warriors to conquer new territory for the chiefdom, there wasn't any means to control that territory, except by redistributing wealth back to the people, so that they benefited by being conquered. If any group felt disadvantaged, they might splinter off to form their own chiefdom. While the chief had primary control of force within the chiefdom, it wasn't an exclusive power. Individual lineages within the chiefdom often feuded with each other and carried out their own justice, or launched their own raids into neighboring chiefdoms.

Divine Kingdoms: Large and complex chiefdoms, or proto-states, are sometimes referred to as *divine kingdoms*, as described by authors Robert Sharer and Loa Traxler in *The Ancient Maya*: *"The history of Maya political organization was dominated by the development of independent polities and centralized political power—the rise of the institution of divine kingship… Maya kings claimed a divine or sacred status, similar to that of Egyptian pharaohs, and were responsible for the prosperity, health, and security of their kingdoms and their subjects by maintaining a favorable relationship with the gods."*[12] Significant cities and grand architecture suggest a state level of organization, but divine kingdoms often consisted of only one or a few such cities. Most importantly, the ruler or king was perceived as a living god, much like the Great Sun of the Natchez, as was the case among the Maya, Aztecs, Inca, and Egyptians.

Divine kingdoms and large chiefdoms make up one of the most bizarre chapters of human history. Wherever our ancestors began building cities, they perceived their rulers as living gods, built great temples for them to communicate with the gods above, held mass sacrifices when their god-kings died, and seemed to be driven by unseen voices and idol-worshipping, as if the entire culture experienced mass schizophrenia. From our perspective it might seem like these divine kings or "living gods" were skillful con men, consciously making their subjects subservient to their will, but the evidence suggests otherwise. As noted by Ken Wilber in *Up from Eden*, *"These earliest kings, frequently submitting themselves to ritual regicide, served an integral function in the society at large, and tended to be subservient to that function. That subservience is glaringly epitomized in the sacrificial rites, where, no matter how barbaric they were, nonetheless the king voluntarily submitted himself…"*[13]

The Aztec civilization is a good example of a divine kingdom. Although the population was large enough to form a state government, the empire was functionally a divine kingdom ruled by Moctezuma, considered a living god by his people. The Aztecs told the Spanish that their history began when a statue from a ruined temple spoke to them and commanded them to cross a nearby lake in the heart of the valley, carrying the statue with them wherever they went.[14] To escape persecution by other tribes, the Aztecs colonized two marshy islands where they dug canals, piling mud into narrow gardens called *chinampas*. The gardens were typically fifteen to thirty feet wide, three hundred feet long, and completely surrounded by water. With the fertile soil, a constant supply of water, and the mild climate, the Aztec grew multiple crops per year. The surplus led to explosive population growth and power among the Aztec people. There were 200,000 to 300,000 people living in the capital city of Tenochtitlán (today's Mexico City) when Spain's Hernando Cortez arrived in 1519. It was about five times larger than London at the time.[15] Spaniards described Tenochtitlán as the most beautiful city they had ever seen. Moctezuma lived in luxury, with a magnificent palace filled with great numbers of dancers, a royal zoo, a display of people with physical deformities, and royal gardens with sweet-scented trees, ponds, and moving water flowing from tank to tank.

Moctezuma's warriors plundered outlying lands for wealth, but lacked the ability to administer the territory. They kept the trade routes open between distant cities and extracted goods and sacrificial captives from communities along the way, but they hadn't learned to build loyalty to the empire by giving anything back. Vanquished neighbors were unwilling participants in the Aztec empire, so they eagerly joined forces with Cortez's meager force to topple the empire.

Idol making was pervasive in divine kingdoms, and the idols typically had extra-large, hypnotic-looking eyes. Historical records indicate that these idols were often worshipped as if they were gods. In 1565 the Spanish administrator of one conquered Mayan city ordered an end to all such idolatry, and was shocked when upwards of a million idols were brought to him. One Mayan figurine was made of cedar, a holy wood to the Mayan people. They were carved by priests fasting in huts, then anointed with their blood and blessed with incense and prayers. The finished idols were lavishly dressed and cared for, and according to a sixteenth-century observer the Mayans believed the idols spoke to them. They sacrificed birds, dogs, their blood, and people's lives to the figures.[16] The Spaniards also reported that among the Inca of Peru, the devil spoke to the people out of the mouths of their statues.[17]

Clay figurines have been found in great profusion in most Mesopotamian cultures as well, often displayed in exactly the same way in each household, and sometimes buried with the deceased. Cuneiform literature frequently refers to the god statues as if people were guided by them.[18] Many of the larger cities were built around tall temples called

ziggurats, which scholars believed housed a god-statue. According to cuneiform texts, the god-statues liked eating, drinking, music, and dancing; they had beds to sleep in and occasionally enjoyed visits from other god-statues. They had to be washed and dressed, perfumed, and guided about on special occasions. The washing ceremony was likely done with a sprinkling of clean water, which may have led to later christening ceremonies. Tables placed before the god-statues later evolved into altars. In this case, however, food and drink were placed on the tables to feed the statues. According to some interpretations, the god statue was left to enjoy his meal alone. Later, a divine king entered the shrine from a side entrance and ate whatever was left behind by the god-statue.[19]

Some cuneiform tablets describe how statues were made in a divine craftsman's house, where craftsmen were directed by a craftsman-god. Before being installed in the shrines, the statues went through a ritual mouth-washing and mouth-opening ceremony. In later times, wooden statues with inlaid jewels were given a washing-of-the-mouth ceremony, apparently to renew their speech. The god-statues were carried by torchlight to a river, and with ceremonies and chants a statue's mouth was washed with special concoctions as it faced each of the four directions. After additional incantations, the statues were led back, helped along the path almost as if they were walking, followed by additional ceremonies at the temple gate and throne, where the mouth was washed again.[20]

Wherever divine kingdoms existed, there were always lavish funerals whenever a living god died. In the Mesopotamian city of Ur (in today's Iraq) five thousand years ago, a king was buried with all his servants, sometimes alive, in a crouched position around him. The vaulted tombs contained food and drink, clothing, jewelry, weapons, lyres, and sacrificed draft animals yoked to ornate chariots. Eighteen such tombs have been found at Ur, with others uncovered in the cities of Kish and Ashur.[21] In Anatolia (Turkey), royal graves were roofed with whole carcasses of roasted oxen to feed the dead.[22] The larger and more wealthy the culture, the more elaborate the tombs, rites, and burials for the dead kings, culminating with the extravagance of the Egyptian pyramids.

States: Most familiar to Western readers is the social-political organization of the state. State governments are associated with larger populations, more complexity, technological advancements, and more wealth. States arose with the transition from horticulture with hand implements to more intensive animal-driven agriculture. Men switched from hunting and fighting to farming. Technology made possible the necessary surplus to feed full-time armies, specialized labor, and religious/political hierarchies.

States are variously organized as monarchies, communism, or democracies, but each government owns the exclusive right to use force through its sanctioned police and military powers. Any faction within the state that tries to use force at its own discretion is considered a threat to the central state government. With full-time armies available to conquer and hold territory, state governments are typically expansionist, as demonstrated by the colonial powers of Europe. We explore different forms of state governments in greater depth in later chapters.

Similar to human development, the cultural transition from one level of social organization to the next typically is gradual, rather than abrupt. In *Man's Rise to Civilization*, Farb further delineated bands and tribes based on size and organization. Cultures organized as states can also be subdivided into intermediate levels. There are significant differences between agricultural states and industrial states, as we will see throughout this text.

Worldviews according to Social-Political Organization

We classified cultures according to social-political patterns as bands, tribes, chiefdoms, divine kingdoms, and state governments. In the section before that we classified cultures according to production type: hunter-gatherer, horticultural, agricultural, and industrial. These systems of classification do not correlate precisely with each other, although they share general themes, and each provides helpful insights into understanding our past and present.

In the table on the following page we can compare differences between various types of societies based on their social-political structure, while noticing that some characteristics overlap from one column to the next. None of the characteristics is absolute. For example, most societies organized at the tribal level depended partly on horticulture and lived in permanent villages, except nomadic tribes like the Plains Indians, or pastoral groups like the Massai of Kenya.

We could further classify cultures by worldviews, noting behavioral patterns among entire cultures that are similar to the previously described preconscious, magical, mythical, and sequential stages of human development. In other words, an entire culture might operate at a magical stage of human development, perceiving reality in magical terms, while other cultures might operate at the mythical or sequential stage. Each worldview represents a generalized interpretation about how the world works. In the bottom row of the table we see how these worldviews correlate with each form of social-political organization.

Classifying cultures according to their version of reality is logical in light of our quest to determine what reality is. At the beginning of our quest we determined that we needed to poke and prod at our illusions of reality to see our reality from the outside. If we can classify cultures by the type of reality associated with them, then we can effectively see those realities from the outside. We will step beyond those realities to arrive at a completely new perspective.

In brief, all people and primates prior to fifty thousand years ago lived a largely preconscious existence, without self-awareness as we know it. Hunter-gatherer bands and tribal societies typically operated with a magical perception of reality. Chiefdoms and divine kingdoms exhibit characteristics of both magical and mythical thinking, while agricultural states have a solidly mythical perception of reality. Emerging industrial states like ours encourage a sequential perception of reality. Through the remainder of this chapter we explore cultural realities based on magical, mythical, and sequential worldviews.

Classification of Cultures according to Social-Political Organization

	Primates	Band	Tribe	Chiefdom / Divine Kingdom	Agricultural State	Industrial State
Population	tens	dozens	hundreds	thousands	millions	tens of millions
Technology	foraging	hunting & gathering	horticulture, herding, hunting & gathering	horticulture, herding, hunting & gathering, craftsmen	livestock-driven agriculture, cottage industries	industrial agriculture, factories
Resource Distribution	sharing	reciprocal	reciprocal	redistributive, limited markets	markets, currency, taxes	markets, currency, taxes
Food Storage	none	minimal	minimal	moderate	large surpluses	excesses
Settlement	nomadic	nomadic	village	towns	cities	numerous cities
Decision-Making	social dominance	egalitarian	egalitarian, leadership by merit	centralized, hereditary	centralized monarchies or representative government	centralized, mostly representative government
Dispute Resolution	social dominance	social dominance or group discussion	social dominance or group discussion	centralized, arbitrary	religious laws, judges	secular laws, judges
Full-time Army	no	no	no	yes	yes	yes
Trade Networks	none	local	local	regional	international	global
Writing	none	none	symbolic	hieroglyphic	alphabetic, mathematic	alphabetic, algebraic
Voices †	universal	animistic spirits	animistic spirits	gods and god kings	external authorities, institutions	introspective, subjective individualism
Perspective	subconscious	first person	first person	first & second person	second person	third person
Worldview	preconscious	magical	magical	magical/mythical	mythical	sequential

† Voices are explained in chapters seven through ten.

Magical Worldview

The magical worldview is well illustrated by the previously described cargo cults that arose among indigenous groups after first contact with the outside world. The natives thought that they could mimic the white man's magic to make planes land or ships come in. They didn't understand sequential cause and effect—that raw resources had to be extracted, processed, manufactured into material goods, and delivered, all by human labor. In the hope of fixing the problem, the Australian government brought tribal members back to the mainland to see the processes where raw goods were manufactured into products. But the tours made no difference to the indigenous people because sequential processing doesn't exist in a magical world. Instead, they would wait and wait for their ship or plane to come until they became very hungry and uncomfortable. Then they would finally give up and go back to work to take care of themselves.[23]

One of the last surviving cargo cults celebrated its fiftieth anniversary in 2007 on the island of Vanuatu east of Australia. The villagers believe that their messiah, John Frum, was responsible for sending the U.S. military cargo ships during World War II. Every year they march in homemade army uniforms with the American flag. They hope to one day entice another delivery of cargo.[24]

Like individuals at a magical level of development, magical cultures tend to be highly first-person oriented, impulsive, and glued to the present moment, as suggested by this passage from filmmaker Lewis Cotlow's book *In Search of the Primitive*: *"The morning is dark and gray, which accounts in part for the excessive quarrelsomeness of the Pygmies, for they are as easily depressed as elated. A rainy or dull day puts them in bad humor, and the entire camp seems to get up on the wrong side of its logs. Since no Pygmy can conceive of repressing even the smallest and most insignificant emotion, he snaps at the first chance."*[25]

A first-person-oriented society is a largely carefree way of life with little self-consciousness or judging of others. Jamie Uys, director of the 1980 movie *The Gods Must be Crazy* described the !Kung people of Africa as uninhibited. *"All Bushmen are natural actors. I suppose it's because they don't have television, and they spend their evenings telling stories and acting them out. And they don't have any hang-ups or inhibitions at all,"* he said in a 1990 interview with The Associated Press.[26] Lewis Cotlow filmed primitive societies all over the world and reported similar natural acting talent, free from self-consciousness.[27]

In hunter-gatherer societies, people are often uninhibited about defecating in public or having sex in public, and although they might note homosexual behavior among members of their tribe as "curious," they don't judge whether it is right or wrong. For example, childhood playmates as well as adult men and women among the !Kung experimented with same-sex partners. Other !Kung regarded these relationships with *"curiosity and bemusement toward them rather than embarrassment or hostility."*[28] Similarly, men who dressed and acted like women among the Ojibway were simply recognized as women, without judgment.[29] Compared to the constant judging and ridiculing that people endure in our culture, the nonjudgmental, uninhibited ways of primitive societies seems highly civilized.

The downside to a first-person existence is the utter lack of restraint. For example, in moments of great anguish, such as following the death of a loved one, it was not uncommon in some hunter-gatherer cultures to demonstrate grief through acts of self-mutilation, such as chopping off a finger. It is easier to do such a thing if you exist in the moment and don't consider the consequences of your actions thirty seconds from now.

However, it would be foolish to label primitive peoples as ignorant or somehow less evolved than we are. The Asian Tsunami of 2004 caught 230,000 people unaware, but primitive tribes sensed the coming wave and escaped to higher ground. Tribal peoples on the Indian-administered islands of Andaman and Nicobar would normally have been out fishing at the time, but they, and apparently most of the animals, headed for higher ground long before the tsunami hit. The Jarawas, Great Andamanese, Onges, Sentinelese, and Shompens tribes are fiercely independent and do not like outsiders. When a government helicopter flew over the islands to check on the tribes after the tsunami, one Sentinelese man shot an arrow at it.[30] Aerial surveys indicated the tribes survived unscathed, which was later confirmed in a rare meeting with the Jarawas, who said that all members of their tribe survived the big wave.[31] Government officials and anthropologists speculated that ancient knowledge of the movement of wind, sea, and birds may have saved the tribal peoples. However, according to some of the tribal leaders, the earth communicates to them, and apparently, they could see the tsunami coming via "remote viewing periscopes." Closely related, tribes on nearby "civilized" islands lost thousands of people to the natural disaster.[32]

Indigenous peoples have encyclopedic knowledge about local flora and fauna, and modern pharmaceutical companies are actively seeking native herbal remedies as new sources of medicine. Indigenous people often look at Westerners as children that are intelligent in a technological sense, but unwise when it comes to understanding the real world.

Mythical Worldview

Mythical processing is directly linked to agriculture and the rise of state governments. Agriculture provided the surplus of food that enabled a specialized workforce with leaders, soldiers, and farmers of unequal status. In his book *Ishmael*, author Daniel Quinn correctly blamed agriculture for the subsequent exploitation of people and the environment. The egalitarian lifestyles of more primitive cultures gave way to hierarchical systems of power. Through achievement or lineage, individuals obtained greater wealth and status than their peers, creating social hierarchies. People held or advanced their status by dominating other people, livestock, and the land. In a pecking order that descended from kings to lords to peasants to women and children, dominance and abuse was endemic to the way of life.

Developmentally, mythical processing is characterized by role-playing, a strong belief in gods, and black-and-white viewpoints where there is only one right way to live. Mythical thinking is not just a phase of childhood, but the prevalent worldview around the globe today. Many adults have a black-and-white way of seeing the world, and we often hear it in the rhetoric of politicians. It is a highly ethnocentric, us-versus-them perspective characterized by a great sense of unity with one's own kind, while other groups are perceived as less human. It does not matter whether it is a sports team from another town, the followers of another religion, or communists on the other side of the world. Rigid mythical thinking often leads to extreme behavior, such as religious violence, riots at sporting events, and political wars.

There were no formal relations between the United States and Iran for a long period of time after the hostage crisis in 1979. A soccer game between the American and Iranian teams was one of the first steps towards rebuilding diplomatic ties. America lost this particular soccer game, which went essentially unnoticed in our country since it was just a soccer game. But to a starkly mythical culture with rigid viewpoints, the Iranians didn't just win the soccer game. From their viewpoint, they had beaten the Great Satan. People proceeded to demonstrate in the streets, overturning and torching cars, breaking storefront windows, and otherwise causing mayhem, while shouting that Allah is great and they had beaten the Great Satan. That is what a strongly mythical, black-and-white culture can look like.

Our own history is tarnished by similar black-and-white thinking. The conquest of the Americas was based on a mythical quest, in which our forebears labeled Native Americans as "savages" and tried to convert them from pagan magical ways into a mythical worldview. Colonists and conquistadors converted or killed the natives, and either outcome was equally acceptable. Through conquest, disease, and starvation, our forebears succeeded in wiping out at least ninety percent of the estimated thirty to one hundred million natives of North and South America.[33] Those who survived were forced to give up most of their traditional ways. They were punished for talking or dressing in the old ways, and their children were forcibly removed from their families and sent to boarding schools to learn the white man's religions. The tide didn't turn the other way until the 1970s when sequential processing started to dominate society and Native Americans began to gain respect and rights to be who they are. By then, however, they had already lost most of their cultural heritage.

Sequential Worldview

The next layer of cultural development is a sequential worldview. A complex society requires the ability to get outside of a problem and see it and oneself from a third-person perspective. From this perspective we can engage in critical thinking and make objective comparisons between different sides of an issue. In sequential processing there is a tendency to see issues in many shades of grey and to be more accepting of people that are different. Instead of seeing other beliefs or cultures as alien or bad, we are more accepting that there are other viewpoints equally valid as our own.

We are fortunate that, although the mass of American culture was immersed in a mythical and semimagical worldview when our country was established, the founders had enough foresight to create a system of government that was sequential in its structure. Our forebears came here largely to escape religious persecution and dictatorial monarchies in Europe. American colonies were often founded upon specific religious beliefs, but the

Revolutionary War helped forge a common American identity among the colonists. The founding fathers established a system of government that recognized all religions as equally valid.

Instead of having ethnic turf wars in America, people of many different faiths—Buddhists, Christians, Muslims and atheists—can all live on the same city block. We meet our neighbors and discover that they are decent people, not so radically different from ourselves. Familiarity makes it difficult to say that their beliefs are wrong or that they are somehow less human. We compare viewpoints side by side and find that the differences are not so great. We begin to acknowledge that every person has an equally valid take on the possible truth and an equally valid right to choose his or her beliefs. Thus, the transition from mythical to sequential processing is accompanied by a shift from an ethnocentric to an individualistic perspective.

The Olympic games were born out of a mythical worldview and were originally intended to give teams a chance to compete against each other for the honor of their countries. Athletes wanted to perform their personal best, but they were truly doing it for their country, as if their win would somehow glorify their entire nation. Over time, however, the Olympics have become increasingly individualistic. Athletes often migrate to the country where they can obtain the best training available to excel as an individual. We have retained ethnocentric customs, like playing the national anthem for each country that wins the gold, but a winning athlete might not be a citizen of that country.

As a culture, Americans remain on the cusp between mythical and sequential processing, not as black-and-white as in the Iranian soccer example, but not fully sequential either. American society is often polarized by issues that might be amicably resolved through critical reasoning and compromise, or by searching for completely new alternatives.

Like individuals, cultures do not suddenly jump from one worldview to another. A society in transition might interpret some events with a mythical worldview, and others with a magical or sequential worldview. The shift in the spirit of the Olympics is also evident in other aspects of our culture, such as television programming. Early television shows featured villains that acted mean and wore black clothes, and heroes that were faultless and wore white clothes, and of course the heroes always won. Over time, television shows evolved to reveal murky plots and many shades of grey. When our culture started to shift, television shows started to shift as well, picking up on emerging trends and role-playing them for a national audience. *Superman* and other superhero movies were remade for a new generation, revealing a darker, more human side to previously angelic characters. Although television often presents the worst side of humanity, it can become a driving force in changing our worldviews. Actors demonstrate lifestyles driven by different worldviews, which are passively absorbed into mainstream consciousness. Television deals with previously taboo topics such as death, homosexuality, abortion, and racism, providing the audience alternative perspectives on reality.

In summary, we have discovered that individuals and whole societies mature through magical, mythical, and sequential modes of processing information, each with its own worldview and predictable patterns of behavior. Coverage of these layers of consciousness was necessarily brief in this chapter. In Part II we explore these layers in greater depth to better understand where we have come from and where we are today. From the past to the present we will uncover the roots of our reality, mapping the preconscious, magical, mythical, and sequential levels of consciousness. The deeper we dive into these worldviews, the more they will seem like alternate realities, so different from our own that it would be like living in a different universe with its own laws of physics. With a solid foundation for these core layers of consciousness, we can explore new worldviews that are emerging in response to the increasingly complex nature of our society, language, and metaphors. We will explore the strengths and weaknesses of each worldview we encounter, and by poking and tugging at the fabric of reality, we will shatter the illusions and step through to new realities, in the hope of discovering the ultimate reality that encompasses all others.

Part II

Layers of Consciousness

—Seven—

Preconscious Processing
Aware of Everything but the Self

"Before my teacher came to me, I did not know that I am. I lived in a world that was no-world. I cannot hope to describe adequately that unconscious, yet conscious time of nothingness.... Since I had no power of thought, I did not compare one mental state to another."

"When I learned the meaning of "I" and "me" and found that I was something, I began to think. Then consciousness first existed for me. Thus it was not the sense of touch that brought me knowledge. It was the awakening of my soul that first rendered my senses their value, their cognizance of objects, names, qualities, and properties. Thought made me conscious of love, joy, and all the emotions."

—Helen Keller, *The World We Live In*[1]

W hen I accidentally step on my dog's foot, it is quite apparent from her yowls that she experiences pain. Her whimpering and twitching while she sleeps suggests that she dreams and has nightmares. But what is her experience of reality really like, and is she aware of her existence?

It is easy to anthropomorphize, to assume that my dog's experience is much like my own in some fundamental way. She likes to play and seems to have emotions and dreams, so it is natural to think that she is self-aware. Yet, the available evidence suggests that language and metaphor were required for our species to introspect and recognize our existence for the first time. Our ancestors apparently existed preconsciously up until the Cultural Revolution— aware of the world outside, but like sleepwalkers, unaware of anything on the inside.

> Snapshot: Preconscious Processing
>
> Technology: Foraging, grazing.
>
> Origin: Animals, early humans.
>
> Logic: Instinct, association.
>
> Perspective: No self-identity, nonjudgmental, hypnotic.
>
> Culture: Fused with nature, universal language.
>
> Social-Political Structure: Bands, groups.
>
> Notable People: Early humans, feral children, some autistics.
>
> Television/Movies: *The Wild Child, Mockingbird Don't Sing, Rain Man, Clan of the Cave Bear.*

Recall that a "subconscious" act is doing something without awareness, such as setting the keys down without consciously noticing it, while "preconscious" describes someone or something that has lived an exclusively subconscious existence, without self-awareness as we know it. In this chapter we formulate a plausible approximation of reality as it may have been experienced by our ancestors and by other creatures of nature. While it is impossible to know what the experience of non-experience is like from the inside, at least we can describe the behavior from the outside, based on observations of animals. We can also learn from autistic individuals such as Temple Grandin, who describes her own way of thinking as "halfway between animals and people,"[2] as well as from feral children who lack the ability or the opportunity to acquire full linguistic capabilities.

Aware, But Not Self-Aware

Konrad Lorenz (1903–1989) was considered the father of ethology, the study of animal behavior. The Austrian zoologist began raising and studying greylag geese in 1935. He discovered that adult geese pair for life. If one partner dies, the other returns to its own mother and never mates again. Lorenz incubated geese eggs until they hatched, and he noted that the goslings accepted him as if he were their mother. At maturity these wild geese flew away with other geese, but upon the death of their mates, they returned home to Lorenz. Lorenz also raised ducks, and the ducklings followed him as long as he bowed down and made clucking sounds as he walked.[3] Other species are similarly undiscriminating when it comes to identifying their own kind, which suggests a lack of self-awareness among most animals.

It is hard to imagine not being able to correctly identify one's own species, but most animals seem to lack the ability to compare themselves to other animals to determine which group they belong to. Rather, they seem to identify with whichever species they are raised with. In the words of Temple Grandin, author of *Animals in Translation, "You have to make sure animals are socialized to other animals, because most of what animals do in life they learn from other animals. Adults teach their young where to eat, what to eat, whom to socialize with, and whom to have sex with."* Orphaned male elephants have exhibited bizarre behavior after being raised without the benefit of an elder male elephant for guidance. Upon being released into the wilds, some orphaned elephants sought out rhinos instead of other elephants. Sometimes they tried to kill the rhinos. Sometimes they tried to mate with them.[4]

Many pet owners have noted that their pets "think they are human." This statement may be especially true for pets and livestock that have been hand-raised since birth. The caretaker becomes "imprinted" upon the animal to the extent that the animal grows up with the assumption that it is a person. This relationship can be hazardous in dealing with some species. For example, a hand-raised bull may challenge people instead of other bulls for social dominance.[5] Thus, when raising pets, livestock, or wildlife, it is important that the animals are properly socialized to their own species to learn what they are and how to act.

The degree of socialization required to learn normal behaviors varies widely by species. Most reptiles bury their eggs and walk away, leaving their offspring to fend for themselves. Mammals have more complex brains and tend to depend on some degree of socialization, especially herd animals and other highly social species. For example, horse herds are organized according to a dominance hierarchy. Introducing new horses incites temporary chaos as they push each other around to establish social rank. In wild herds stallions compete for leadership, and only the winner stays with the herd. The mares establish a "pecking order" of who is submissive to whom, until every mare knows her rank. However, the herd lives in relative peace once the horses have each determined their status. This hierarchical social organization makes it possible to domesticate horses, since the horses perceive people as dominant members of the herd. Unfortunately, problems arise when horses are raised in isolation from other horses. Stallions raised in isolation often have to be kept in isolation, because they never learn the social cues and don't mix well with other horses. Without the ability to recognize rank, such stallions have "raped" mares or relentlessly attacked other stallions.[6]

Humans are the most social mammals, and we acquire appropriate behaviors through mimicry rather than hardwired instincts. Children have not fared well without human interaction. For example, Frederick II (1194–1250) of Sicily hoped to discover what language children would speak if they were never exposed to any. He allowed foster mothers and nurses to take care of the physical needs of a group of orphan children, but forbade them to coddle or talk to them. Unfortunately, all of the infants died. Similarly, in 1915 a doctor at Johns Hopkins Hospital documented a 95 percent mortality rate among infants admitted to orphanages and foundling homes in Baltimore, even though they received adequate physical care. Studies since then have consistently revealed that an absence of social stimulus and maternal care leads to a high rate of physical and emotional retardation and mortality.[7] We may be born with the necessary wiring to become human, but lacking sufficient social stimulus, we cannot become anything at all. We only become human by mimicking other people.

Feral children—those raised in isolation from other people—exhibit behaviors that are hardly recognizable as human. At the age of twenty-three, Oxana, the girl raised by dogs, demonstrated her dog-like heritage for reporter Elizabeth Grice from the *U.K. Telegraph*. Grice wrote, *"She bounds along on all fours through long grass, panting towards water with her tongue hanging out. When she reaches the tap she paws at the ground with her forefeet, drinks noisily with her jaws wide and lets the water cascade over her head. Up to this point, you think the girl could be acting—but the moment she shakes her head and neck free of droplets, exactly like a dog when it emerges from a swim, you get a creepy sense that this is something beyond imitation. Then, she barks. The furious sound she makes is not like a human being pretending to be a dog. It is a proper, chilling, canine burst of aggression and it is coming from the mouth of a young woman, dressed in T-shirt and shorts."*[8]

In 1970 social workers discovered a thirteen-year-old girl in Los Angeles who had been locked away in a room for ten years, mostly tied to a potty chair. Researchers called her Genie to protect her identity. According to one of the researchers interviewed on PBS *Nova*, Genie had a strange bunny walk, sniffed and clawed, and constantly spat. She had been beaten for making noise and consequently learned to stay silent most of the time. She knew only a couple of words. A team of doctors, psychologists, and linguists worked with Genie to rehabilitate her. Studies of her brain waves indicated mental retardation, but it was never clearly determined whether she was born that way or became that way in isolation. Researchers discovered that she had a voracious appetite to learn new words and seemed to acquire a year's worth of learning in a year, as a normal child should. However, she never learned proper grammar, using only simple sentences, such as "Applesauce buy store," to indicate that they needed to buy more applesauce.[9] Genie's story was portrayed in the movie *Mockingbird Don't Sing*. Interestingly, Genie achieved the highest ever score on tests that measure a person's ability to see patterns and make sense out of chaos, and she aced an adult-level test that measured spatial abilities. She was able to recreate a complicated structure of colored sticks from memory. She recreated the layout and the colors exactly the same as the original design.[10]

There are also hundreds of stories about feral children raised in the wilds, and many of these stories may have some truth to them, but there are only a few cases that have unequivocal documentation. One was a twelve-year-old boy given the name Victor after he was captured in France in 1799. Victor was naked and mute, he acted like an animal, and his body was scarred from years of living in the wild. Victor was tutored for several years by a resourceful young medical student named Jean-Marc Itard. Itard taught him to understand basic speech, although Victor only learned to say two words. Victor's story was portrayed in the movie *The Wild Child*. Interestingly, Victor was completely comfortable while naked in cold weather. He would even leap about in the snow and throw it up in the air in joy, completely oblivious to the cold.[11] It is not clear whether he physically acclimated to the cold from years of living in the outdoors, or psychologically never learned to be cold in the first place.

Most interesting are the children who have apparently been raised by wild animals, including dogs, wolves, bears, monkeys, panthers, and gazelles. These cases are similar to the story of Mowgli in the *Jungle Book*, except that, unlike Mowgli, these children never learned to act human. At first it is hard to imagine what circumstances could lead a child to be raised by animals, but some peculiar incidents shed light on the possibilities. For example, in 2005 in Kenya, a dog found an abandoned two-week-old baby in a bag and carried it home, then sheltered the baby beside her own puppy until it was discovered by people.[12] In many cultures it has been common practice to nurse children on domestic stock and tamed wild animals, and in some cases the animals wandered off with wild herds, their human children in tow.[13]

In 1920, Reverend Joseph Amrito Lal Singh of India discovered two young girls living in a den with a wolf family. Reportedly, the she-wolf defended the children as if they were hers, and the children had to be forcibly removed. While there has been some speculation that the reverend invented the story to draw attention and fund-raising to his orphanage, Singh kept detailed journals and photos of the girls' behavior and his attempts to humanize them.

The older girl was approximately eight years old and the younger about eighteen months. He named them Kamala and Amala. It was initially assumed that the girls were sisters, but it is more probable that they were adopted by the she-wolf at different times.

In Reverend Singh's care, the girls behaved like wolves. They scratched and bit people who fed them, preferred raw meat, moved on all fours, and would not allow themselves to be dressed. They were mostly nocturnal and could see very well in the dark. At night they howled like wolves, apparently calling out to their family. They also had heightened senses of smell and hearing, and they seemed to be insensitive to heat and cold. The girls showed no visible human emotions other than fear, mostly of other people. Amala died a year later from a roundworm infestation. Kamala was eventually housetrained, learned to walk upright with assistance, and acquired a very limited vocabulary. She still reverted to moving on all four limbs when she wanted to get somewhere quickly. She died of typhoid at the age of seventeen.[14] These examples demonstrate that socialization is critical to normal development of social animals, especially people. Without proper role models, children seem unable to relate to the world in a human way. Even after intensive socialization and language therapy, the children seem unable to grasp their relationship to the world. Their neurological development is incomplete. They are aware, but not necessarily self-aware in the sense that the rest of us are.

Fused with the Universe

Through self-awareness we are able to differentiate ourselves from the universe, to recognize that we are separate from everything else. Prior to learning to think symbolically as children, we live fused with nature and unaware of our existence. For this brief period in our lives we see reality without questioning or defining it, without changing stars into constellations or clouds into bunnies. We simply exist in the moment, discovering the world around us without judging it.

As a naturalist, I have spent most of my life learning to define nature in order to better understand the world around me. Looking at a young spruce tree in the forest, I can determine its age by counting how many whorls of branches there are up the trunk. If the trunk is forked, then I know that the top of the tree was once injured, and two or more of the side branches took over the job of the original trunk. Upon seeing wildflowers, I can quickly group them into various categories based on evolutionary relationships that are readily visible to the trained eye. I can look at rocks and make a crude guess as to the geologic history of the area. Upon finding a discarded can or bottle, I see it as litter. I can even make some assumptions about the character of the individual who dropped it there.

My experience in nature is very different from that of a deer, which might see a can or a bottle as shiny. A rock is hard. Flowers either taste good or don't. Trees exist as they are in the present, without prior history or future possibilities. Creatures of nature experience reality as it is, without any analysis, subjective interpretations, or judgments about right or wrong. Yet, while fused with the universe, lacking self-awareness and the capacity for critical reasoning, it is astonishing how much a preconscious being can know just by instincts alone.

Instincts and Knowing

As I wrote in *Botany in a Day*, nearly 40 percent of modern pharmaceuticals contain ingredients that were first discovered in plants. Some of these constituents were discovered by randomly experimenting with plants in the laboratory. However, researchers save time and money by working with plants with a known history. Most ethnobotanists study the herbal lore of tribal cultures to discover new medicinal plants, but a few researchers have sought herbal wisdom by observing wild chimpanzees. Chimps demonstrate the ability to medicate themselves when ill by seeking out specific plants for their healing properties. When a chimp

significantly alters its behavior, stops eating and starts consuming different herbs, researchers send those plants to the lab for analysis.[15]

My son Donny demonstrated similar healing instincts as a baby. We left the door open one night, which allowed mosquitoes to flood into the house. His little face was covered with mosquito bites the next morning. When we gave him oatmeal for breakfast, he applied it to his face as a soothing facial. Similarly, my friend Bonnie had a container of horseradish sauce sitting out while she ate a sub sandwich. Her six-month-old daughter Vidahlia, who was sick with a cold, dipped her hand into the horseradish sauce and ate it straight. Spicy foods like that can be highly beneficial for fighting a cold. It is unknown why a six-month-old baby would recognize horseradish as medicine and tolerate the spiciness, or why chimpanzees would choose bitter wild plants to medicate themselves. Where does this innate wisdom come from when it cannot be traced directly back to either natural selection or cultural upbringing?

In one study, a number of natural, unflavored foods were placed before a group of infants. The infants demonstrated that they could select a nutritionally balanced diet for themselves from the selections at hand. If an infant initially binged on starchy foods, he would later seek out foods high in protein. If at first he ate foods lacking a particular vitamin, he would later eat what was needed to make up the deficit. Without any logical knowledge of diet or nutrition, the infants demonstrated an innate ability to make healthy choices.[16]

Unfortunately, we lose our instincts quickly as we grow up. Our parents teach us which foods are known to be good for us, and that if we can choke them down we will be rewarded with foods that are known to be bad for us. Even without this perverse sense of dietary rewards, we grow up, acquire language and culture, and lose our innate abilities. We acquire knowledge, but we lose knowing. For example, in wilderness survival situations, lost children typically seek protective cubbyholes to crawl into and stay warm, while mature, "rational" adults often wander around in the cold or rain until they die of exposure.

According to author Laurence Gonzales in his book *Deep Survival*, *"Despite the fact that small children lose body heat faster than adults, they often survive in the same conditions better than experienced hunters, better than physically fit hikers, better than former members of the military or skilled sailors... If it gets cold, they crawl into a hollow tree to get warm. If they're tired, they rest, so they don't get fatigued. If they're thirsty, they drink. They try to make themselves comfortable, and staying comfortable helps keep them alive. The secret may also lie in the fact that they do not yet have the sophisticated mental mapping ability that adults have, and so do not try to bend the map."* In other words, children survive best before they acquire enough language skills to build symbolic maps of reality. Gonzales reported that children between the ages of seven and twelve have the poorest survival rates. Kids in this age range have developed the ability to build mental maps, but still lack adult judgment.[17]

Universal Language

Previously, we noted a connection between metaphorical language and self-awareness. Our ancestors apparently existed in a preconscious state until the Cultural Revolution of 40,000 to 50,000 years ago. With language acquisition came the gradual loss of an apparently prelingual and universal interspecies mode of communication. Many Native American creation stories allude to this universal language, describing a time when people and animals spoke the same language and held council together.

In the book *Of Wolves and Men,* author Barry Lopez described apparent communication between predators and prey, observing that in the first moment of an encounter, wolves and their prey often stand absolutely still and stare at each other. Immediately afterwards, the encounter crystallizes into one of several possible outcomes: either the prey simply turns and walks away, or the wolves split, or the wolves charge and quickly kill the animal. Lopez called this encounter the "conversation of death," during which predator and prey come to a mutual understanding.[18]

In one anecdote, two buffalo bulls and two cows, one of them lame, were resting and ruminating. The three healthy buffalo ignored a group of wolves that came by to check them out, while the lame cow became highly agitated and stood up to face the wolves alone. The cow signaled herself out as prey, while her healthy companions were completely unperturbed by the wolves presence.[19] Many indigenous peoples similarly believe that animals will "gift" themselves to the people for sustenance. There is a moment of connection between the hunter and the hunted, and it seems as if the prey agrees to give up its life for the people.

Is it possible that our distant ancestors experienced some form of universal non-linguistic communication between people and animals? Did the rise of complex language and culture program this perception out of the brain? These questions are more speculative than hypothetical because we presently lack means to investigate the possibility, or even to theorize about it intelligently. However, some people do believe it is possible to communicate with other species.

There are people of all backgrounds in modern culture who claim to have achieved mutual understanding with animals. In his book *Talking with Nature*, Michael J. Roads described shooting wallabies on his farm to save pasture for the cows. Finally sickened by the experience, he stopped killing and asked the wallabies to leave the pasture for his cows. He offered the forage around the outside of the paddock instead. Much to his astonishment, the wallabies "agreed," and the pasture grew so much that he was able to increase the size of the herd. A few years after selling the farm, Roads spoke to the new owners and learned that the pasture was useless. The new owners shot six thousand wallabies in two years, yet the surviving animals still kept the pasture mowed down to nothing.[20]

In her book *Grandmother's Grandchild*, Alma Snell described a similar situation that occurred when she was sent from the Crow Reservation in Montana to a boarding school in South Dakota. She overheard one of her teachers talking about putting poison out for the ants in the tea room, so she warned the ants, *"You little ants, they're going to kill you. Tonight they're going to put something out to kill you. So you better move and get away from here."* The next morning the teacher noted that the ants were gone, but there were no bodies. However, one of Snell's friends told of encountering a column of ants while out walking. The ants were marching away from the tea room.[21]

Derrick Jensen met one man who worked on the Alaska pipeline, always carried a gun, and had killed many bears in self-defense. A native told him that he didn't need to shoot them. He could just apologize for being in their territory and walk away. He has never killed a bear since. Similarly, a woman described how her rancher parents gave stillborn calves to the coyotes with the agreement that the coyotes would leave the rest of the herd alone.[22]

Voices, Visions, and Channeling

Another form of "communication," most often experienced when self-awareness is switched off, are the voices, visions, and channeling that seem to originate in the subconscious mind. As Derrick Jensen wrote in his book *A Language Older than Words*, "*As is true for most children, when I was young I heard the world speak. Stars sang. Stones had preferences. Trees had bad days. Toads held lively discussions, crowed over a good day's catch. Like static on the radio, schooling and other forms of socialization began to interfere with my perception of the animate world, and for a number of years I almost believed that only humans spoke.*"[23] Similarly, children often have "imaginary playmates," which we adults dismiss as just that—imaginary. But children may perceive their playmates as very real. My friend Bonnie remembers having frequent conversations with two other children in her house, and she was surprised that nobody else could see them.

In his book *Born on a Blue Day*, autistic savant Daniel Tammet described how he spent his recesses at school in thoughtful conversation with an imaginary playmate. His "playmate" was an old, old woman, more than six feet tall and creased with wrinkles. She wore a long blue cloak and called herself Anne. Tammet never asked Anne where she came from, but they conversed about life and death, hobbies, fairy tales, and why Tammet was different from everyone else. She always listened patiently and reassured him. The relationship ended one day when, "*she asked me to look at her because what she had to say was important... She did not say anything for several minutes and then she spoke very, very softly and slowly and told me that she had to go and could not return. I became very upset and asked her why, and she told me that she was dying and was here to say good-bye. Then she disappeared for the last time. I cried and cried until I couldn't cry anymore, and I continued to grieve for her for many days afterwards.*"[24]

Prior to that, Tammet had an experience in which he began writing "*compulsively across long reams of computer paper, often writing for hours at a time, covering sheet after sheet of paper with tightly knit words…a whole page might be taken up in describing the various details of a single place or location, its colors, shapes and textures. There was no dialogue, no emotions. Instead I wrote of long, weaving tunnels far underneath vast, shimmering oceans, of cragged rock caves and towers climbing high into the sky. I didn't have to think about what I was writing; the words just seemed to flow out of my head. Even without conscious planning, the stories were always comprehensible. When I showed one to my teacher, she liked it enough to read parts of it out loud to the rest of the class. My compulsion to write soon disappeared as suddenly as it had first visited me.*"[25]

Was Tammet's automatic writing channeled from his subconscious, or from some other source? Was his playmate some kind of spirit, or a mere projection of his own mind? Tammet offers clues, noting that he and his playmate discussed things that were specifically of interest to him; they talked "*about my love of ladybirds, and my coin towers, about books, about numbers, about tall trees and the giants and princesses of my favorite fairy tales.*" However, there were some questions she would not answer, such as why Tammet was different from other kids. The old woman would seem to be a reflection of Tammet's own mind, and in retrospect, Tammet believes that his playmate's departure was his own painful decision to find his way in the world.[26]

In their book *Voices of Reason, Voices of Insanity*, authors Ivan Leudar and Philip Thomas observed that cultural perceptions of voices and voice hearers have changed over time. People once accepted that voices and visions came from angels, spirits, and gods. Now these phenomena are labeled hallucinations, and voice hearers are often institutionalized or medicated, although the tide is again turning the other way. Leudar and Thomas prefer to acknowledge that the phenomena are real to the people who experience them. Since we cannot know how these phenomena may be interpreted in the future, it may be a cultural assumption to label the experiences as mere "hallucinations."

The available information suggests that Daniel Tammet's automatic writing and his imaginary friend were the products of his own subconscious mind. It seems probable that similar phenomena, such as Bonnie's childhood playmates, were also subconscious projections. However, we should always be open to other possibilities. For example, Bonnie's two-year-old daughter often talks and laughs with unseen entities in the sky, and one time Bonnie caught a glimpse of colors out of the corner of her eye in the direction her daughter was looking. Thus, we must wonder if young children see things that become invisible as they become fully socialized into our culture. We must wonder if auditory-visual experiences, such as hearing voices or seeing imaginary playmates, are the mind's attempt to make sense of phenomena that are otherwise invisible to us.

Even if visual-auditory experiences are mere projections of the subconscious mind, it would be premature to dismiss their relevance. Great truths may emerge from revelations and prophecies. Furthermore, we cannot say with certainty how the source material gets *into* the subconscious in the first place. In other words, we cannot rule out the possibility that the subconscious mind might sometimes tap into information, inspirations, or future knowledge based on information that is not available to the physical senses.

Logic by Association

While there are benefits to living in an instinctive, preconscious reality as children do, the downside is that preconscious logic is dictated by coincidental associations. Preconscious beings lack a concrete sense of cause and effect to understand how the world works.

An association is the act of making a mental or emotional connection between one thing and another. A simple association connects names to objects, such that you recognize that an apple is a type of fruit rather than a piece of furniture. Pets learn to associate sounds like an electric can opener with food, and come running when they hear it. Negative associations are also common. A dog that has been abused by a man might distrust all men by association.

An animal that has a terrifying experience will associate that experience to something they see, hear, or smell at the time, which becomes a panic trigger whenever they encounter it again. For example, one horse that Temple Grandin worked with was terrified of black cowboy hats. It didn't mind baseball caps or other colors of cowboy hats, but it must have been abused by a person wearing a black cowboy hat. The horse was scared of a black cowboy hat even if the hat were sitting on the ground. Its panic level increased if anyone picked up the hat, and escalated the closer the hat was brought to the person's head. These kinds of associations are exceedingly common, even among people.

For example, I grew up in the country, hiking anywhere I wanted to, drinking out of streams along the way. I never used a water filter until one walkabout with friends across ranchlands downstream from towns where the water quality was suspect. We used a water filter, but I caught a germ that gave me a whopping case of diarrhea. Rationally speaking, it wasn't the water filter that made me sick. It was probably the bag of granola we dropped in a creek and ate anyway. However, I could not break the emotional association between the water filter and getting sick. Every time I looked at the filter I felt a mild panic, as if the filter was the cause of the diarrhea.

Most people are capable of revising or correcting associations over time, but severely autistic individuals are not. For instance, one young girl learned to associate clouds with "bad" and doors with "good." If asked how much she liked something, she would draw pictures of doors or clouds. Four open doors and no clouds meant really good, while four clouds and no doors meant really bad.[27]

Fear and Pain

Influenced by Galileo's mechanical view of the universe, philosopher René Descartes (1596–1650) perceived animals as mere biological machines. He believed that only humans had minds and therefore animals could feel no pain. Based on this belief, Descartes practiced vivisection, the dissection of live animals. This view of animals as mindless machines led to hundreds of years of barbaric science experiments on live animals, which have been moderated but not terminated in recent times.[28]

Ironically, Descartes was at least half right, since self-awareness is an emergent property resulting from language acquisition. Existing in a preconscious state, animals do not have minds as we think of them. However, it would be foolish to think they do not feel pain, as evidenced by my dog's howls when I accidentally step on her foot. It might be more accurate to say that animals experience a different sensation of pain than people. In her book *Animals in Translation*, Temple Grandin wrote that animals and many autistics tend to experience higher levels of fear than normal people, but are less sensitive to pain. While the pain might hurt just as much, they react to it less.

Fear and pain are inversely related to activity in the frontal lobes of the neocortex. The prefrontal lobes play a key role in language and perception, and they are deeply interconnected with older layers of the brain, moderating our reptilian and mammalian impulses. Many autistic people have reduced activity in the frontal lobes and tend to experience higher levels of fear but less sensitivity to pain. Other species have smaller frontal lobes and similarly experience more fear, but less pain.

Ordinarily, we depend on all parts of our brain, with higher brain functions moderating older, more impulsive survival instincts. For example, while strolling down a path, we might glimpse the curvy form of a snake hidden in the grass. The visual information is sent to the amygdala of the limbic system where it triggers a fear and flight response, flooding the body with adrenaline and quickening the heartbeat until we are ready to take evasive maneuvers. However, the same signal is simultaneously sent to the prefrontal lobes for additional processing. Processing may reveal that the "snake" was actually just a curved stick. The fear reaction is canceled an instant later, and we continue down the trail with only heightened senses.

Like fear, we would expect pain to be a primal sensation associated with the oldest parts of the brain, and pain is indeed associated with the amygdala. However, very intense pain is associated with the frontal lobes. People who have experienced crippling pains have been helped by severing the frontal lobes from the rest of the brain. Although they still felt the pain just as intensely, they were no longer bothered by it.

Temple Grandin pointed out that highly visual people never recover from post-traumatic stress disorder, while verbal thinkers often do. When people cross some threshold of linguistic development they seem to become less fearful, yet more sensitive to pain. The same could be said for perceptions of heat and cold. Feral children, apparently lacking self-awareness, often seem insensitive to hot and cold temperatures. They simply accept conditions as they are.[29]

Life on the Right Side of the Brain

If language enables us to become self-aware, then severely autistic people, unable to interact coherently with other people, would seem to be trapped in some kind of preconscious existence. However, some individuals with high-functioning autism have acquired enough linguistic skills to become self-aware and independent in society. Yet they still struggle with the deeper complexities of language, which provides some insight into what life may have been like for our ancestors before languages became so complex. It would be a bit like experiencing life from the intuitive, creative right side of the brain, without the filtering or reasoning of the linguistic left side.

Autistic savant Daniel Tammet often rocked himself rhythmically as a child, and he would frequently hum in the classroom, unaware he was doing it until the teacher or other students pointed it out. Self-awareness is an acquired skill. When touring London as a teenager, Tammet still lacked the linguistic ability to filter out extraneous sensory information. Overwhelmed by the sights, sounds, and smells of London, he wrote: *"There was too much information for me to mentally organize and it made my head hurt."*[30]

Daniel Tammet's savant abilities are due to a rare neurological mixing of the senses called synesthesia. He is able to do complex math problems in his head, experiencing it all in shapes, colors, and motions. For example, he can calculate 13 divided by 97 out to about a hundred decimal places in the form of a visual spiral that rotates downward in larger and larger loops. Multiplying two numbers, such as 53 and 131, is experienced as two different shapes, and the answer is experienced as the shape that fits between them, or 6,943. While Tammet's savant abilities are due to his unique neurological wiring, there is ample evidence to suggest that we are all capable of seemingly extraordinary accomplishments if only we could disengage the verbal filters that distort our experience of reality.

The Cost of Consciousness

In artwork, children simplify the world into symbolic stick figures of people, animals, trees, houses, cars and airplanes. It is so common for children to draw stick figures that we consider it completely "normal." It seems as if they draw to the best of their ability, then improve their artistic skills through practice and art lessons. However, from the chapter *Growing Up* we know that infants as young as seven months old see mental images, and by the age of two they begin to think symbolically. A young child learns that a stick figure of a dog can represent a dog, and by four to seven years old, the child learns that the stick figure can be generalized to apply to all dogs, even of vastly different breeds.

Many autistic individuals and feral children struggle with this kind of generalization, and don't acquire symbolic thinking as easily as other people. But they are not blinded by symbols either. Some autistic savants have produced intricately detailed drawings without training by simply drawing them as they remember them in photographic detail. Stephen Wiltshire, nicknamed "the human camera," was once given a helicopter ride over London. Three hours later he completed an accurate scale drawing of a four-square-mile section of the city featuring more than two hundred detailed structures.[31] Similarly, Genie, the girl left strapped to a potty chair, could precisely replicate complex patterns from memory. My son Edwin was remarkably adept at the memory card game at four years old, but lost that ability when he started learning to read. It could be said that people who are unobstructed by language are more capable of perceiving reality as it is, while the rest of us generalize reality into symbols and fail to notice our actual surroundings. We filter out extraneous information that might be distracting or overwhelming to the senses and see only what we want to see.

Temple Grandin learned to function in our world in spite of her autism. Extraneous stimuli, such as a computer screensaver, are impossible for her to ignore. She can be totally mesmerized by a screensaver, unable to focus on her work until she shuts it off. Grandin built a career designing humane stockyards to manage stock, especially cattle, without frightening the animals or needing to shock them with electric prods. She gets in the chutes and looks at the scene from their perspective, recognizing the kinds of stimuli that might scare them.

While "normal" people tend to see only what they want to see, Grandin, Tammet, and the livestock see *everything* and are unable to block anything out. Anything that is unfamiliar, such as a water bottle dropped in the middle of the path, can become a terrifying roadblock. The cows would cautiously explore the water bottle if given a chance, but being forced forward from behind magnifies their fears. Normal people filter out details like trash on the ground, becoming blind to the stimuli that frighten the animals, even when they look for them.

Temple Grandin is frequently hired by stockyards to figure out why the animals won't move forward through their chutes and pens. In addition to the trash on the ground, common problems include issues like a yellow coat hanging on a wall, people seen through the fences ahead, the shrill backup alarms on heavy equipment, a chain swinging in the wind, or bad lighting. Areas of high contrast can be particularly troubling for the animals, such as the transition from a well-lit room to a dark hallway, because it looks like a drop-off to the cows, similar to the dark shadow of a cattle guard. Grandin provides insightful solutions like turning on a light or moving a ladder out of the way. She has designed half of all livestock handling facilities in the country, all of them tuned to the psychology of the animals. She describes "normal" people as having inattentional blindness, since we don't see things that are right in front of us.[32]

Like an autistic savant, Temple Grandin produced a professional quality blueprint of a complex stockyard on her first try, after merely studying blueprints done by architects. She manipulates images of specific livestock chutes she has seen to design a vivid three-dimensional model of an improved stockyard in her mind. After creating a complex stockyard in her mind, she draws it from memory.

Interestingly, normal people can improve their artistic ability through exercises such as by turning pictures of people and landscapes upside down, making it difficult to resort to familiar symbols while drawing them. Furthermore, research has shown that people can instantly improve their perceptive and artistic abilities with transcranial magnetic stimulation to interfere with the frontal lobes.[33] The treatment apparently shuts down the symbolic mode of processing information, so that people can see reality without distorting it.

As parents we may be delighted to see our children reach developmental thresholds, such as learning to use a computer or learning how to read. However, there is a cost to such progress. There are indications that people may naturally have photographic memories before acquiring symbolic thinking. The fact that some adults do have photographic memories, including a few people without language impairments, suggests that all of us may be capable of it. Imagine how fantastic it would be to have the ability to recall page 47 in our minds, or to remember a scene in such detail that we could draw it realistically. More research is needed to document the extent of our photographic skills, and to determine if it is possible to permanently cement this skill, so that children won't lose the ability in transition to symbolic thinking. It may be beneficial to delay symbolic learning by a few years to facilitate children's photographic abilities.

Similarly, Temple Grandin believes that all people may be capable of extreme sensory perception. One of her students can hear a radio when it is switched off, as well as the hum of electric wires in the wall.[34] Other people have temporarily acquired heightened senses, such as one medical student who dreamed he was a dog while high on recreational drugs. He awoke with super-heightened senses, able to identify all twenty of his patients by smell, and capable smelling their emotions as well.[35]

In the next chapter we witness the transition from preconscious to magical processing and explore the psychological world of people living in bands and tribes. While significantly different from the preconscious existence of our ancestors, there are many holdovers and similarities as well.

—Eight—

Magical Processing

Life in Hunter-Gatherer and Tribal Societies

"Most Jivaros are not introspective or moody. They spend little time regretting the past or worrying about the future. Thye live in the present and find it good, most of the time, even though it is filled with dangers. The worst dangers are, in their minds, largely unseen. They fear the inguanchi, the demons or evil spirits, but not the jaguar, the white man or the Jivaro enemy. The Jivaro world abounds with spirits, some good, but most bad. As many things as there are in the world—trees, animals, plants, birds, rivers, fish, butterflies, ants, clouds, earth, and the shining things in the sky—that is how many spirits there are, and more."

—Lewis Cotlow, *In Search of the Primitive*[1]

Have you ever wondered why it is so difficult to remember childhood as an adult? Consider the obstacles: First there is a change in scale, since our perspective was different when we were short enough to look at the bottom of the kitchen table instead of the top of it. But we also processed information in an entirely different way. As children we lived in a magical world with no concept of cause and effect, where cookies would magically pop into existence, and when they were gone, it wasn't clear why more couldn't appear like the others. When we mature from a magical to a mythical to a sequential way of seeing the world, it becomes extremely difficult to remember anything clearly. The way we process and interpret events as adults is vastly different from the way we experienced them as a child; it is the equivalent of living in a different universe.

At the cultural level, magical processing is characteristic of hunter-gatherer and tribal societies where people are isolated in their exposure to the outside world. These societies are characterized by a strongly first-person existence with many hypnotic rituals and the ability to occasionally hear voices. Most of all,

> Snapshot: Magical Processing
>
> Technology: Hunting and gathering, subsistence farming.
>
> Origin: Stone Age technology and art, basic metaphorical language.
>
> Logic: Magical, symbolic, animistic.
>
> Perspective: First person, personal wants, personal glory, uninhibited, nonjudgmental.
>
> Culture: Isolated, bubbleverse, witchcraft, rituals and drama.
>
> Social-Political Structure: Egalitarian bands and tribes.
>
> Notable People: Surviving hunter-gatherers.
>
> Television/Movies: *Harry Potter, Matilda, The Chronicles of Narnia, The Serpent and the Rainbow, The Fast Runner.*

these cultures exhibit a heavily symbolic interpretation of reality and a magical view of how the world works. Tribal peoples might be puzzled by the behavior of other people, but they do not necessarily judge them for being different.

Magical Association

In the previous chapter, we saw that preconscious logic is dictated by association, like the horse that was terrified of black cowboy hats. Logic-by-association is the foundation upon which magical processing is based. In essence, if the horse transitioned from preconscious processing to magical processing, it would perceive the hat as something to placate to avoid bad luck, or as something that might be controlled to terrorize other horses. Horses apparently do not think that way, but hunter-gatherer bands and tribes do. This subtle perceptual shift is one of the few things that distinguished our hunter-gather ancestors as *human*, different from all other species on earth.

Sir James George Frazer (1854–1941) compiled notes about magical beliefs from primitive cultures around the world in his 1922 book, *The Golden Bough*. One can sense what daily life might have been like in a primitive culture from a single paragraph out of thousands of examples, somewhat condensed here, *"Esquimaux boys are forbidden to play cat's cradle, because if they did so, their fingers might in later life become entangled in the harpoon-line. Here the taboo is obviously an application of the law of similarity, which is the basis of homoeopathic magic: as the child's fingers are entangled by the string in playing cat's cradle, so they will be entangled by the harpoon-line when he is a man and hunts whales... So, too, among the Ainos of Saghalien a pregnant woman may not spin nor twist ropes for two months before her delivery, because they think that if she did so the child's guts might be entangled like the thread... a Blackfoot Indian who has set a trap for eagles, and is watching it, would not eat rosebuds on any account; for he argues that if he did so, and an eagle alighted near the trap, the rosebuds in his own stomach would make the bird itch, with the result instead of swallowing the bait the eagle would merely sit and scratch himself. Following this train of thought the eagle hunter also refrains from using an awl when he is looking after his snares; for surely if he were to scratch with an awl, the eagles would scratch him. The same disastrous consequence would follow if his wives and children at home used an awl while he is out after eagles, and accordingly they are forbidden to handle the tool in his absence for fear of putting him in bodily danger."*[2]

One can quickly sense how challenging it could be to live in a primitive culture, where every mundane action involves rituals to perform and taboos to respect to solicit good magic while avoiding the bad. As noted in the quote at the beginning of this chapter, people in magical cultures didn't necessarily fear physical threats, such as being killed by a rival tribe, so much as imagined threats like malevolent magic. The difference between waking and dreaming was often a blur.

In Jungian psychology, dreams are interpreted by recalling people and objects of the dream and reflecting upon what each of those elements might represent. Life in magical cultures was similar, except that people often did not distinguish waking from sleeping. The Australian aborigines, for example, described their way of life as the dreamtime, and they considered dreaming to be as real, or more real, than waking.

In a magical world everything has symbolic meaning. If a crow sitting on a branch means something in a dream, then it means the same thing if encountered while awake. The challenge of living in a magical world is that every possible association could be interpreted to mean *something*—every bird that flew overhead, every bunny, every clap of thunder or rainstorm, and every positive or negative experience. But what happens if you misinterpret the symbolism? What happens if a stray thought from your subconscious contaminates your dreams? Primitive cultures are often associated with a high degree of paranoia and ritual.

While staying with the Jivaro head hunters in the 1940s, filmmaker Lewis Cotlow fell ill with dysentery just before the warriors disappeared on a raid against a neighboring village.

After killing nineteen people in hand-to-hand combat, the victors sorted out the bodies. They did not take the heads of the women or children or any warriors that they recognized as relatives. That left nine people from which they carefully removed the heads just above the collarbone. They initiated the shrinking process at camps along the way home, first by removing the skins and discarding the skulls. The head skins were boiled down to about half size. Further shrinking with the aid of hot rocks and hot sand made it possible to reduce the heads down to fist size. Back at camp, the Jivaros fasted, feasted, and danced in ceremonies that could go on for months. Shrunken heads were stuck on lances in the ground and the Jivaro danced around them, thrusting lances at them to frighten and conquer the spirits. After months of these kinds of rituals, the heads had no further value and could be discarded.

Since Cotlow was too ill to get to Western medicine, his Jivaro companion Peruche insisted on going to a neighboring village to enlist his friend Nakata's shaman for help, since the shaman had cured a white man once before. But Peruche was bitten by a poisonous snake and died before he got there. In a magical culture there is no such thing as an "accident," so the shaman from Peruche's village imbibed an alcoholic drink and dreamed to learn who sent the deadly snake. Much to the shock of all in camp, the shaman named Peruche's friend Nakata, who was also a blood relative. Naturally, the only way to solve the issue was to organize a raid and kill Nakata, and Cotlow was unable to convince them otherwise.[3]

Interestingly, U.S. immigration officials arrested a woman from Haiti in 2006 after baggage screeners discovered a human head in her luggage at a Florida airport. The woman, Myrlene Severe, claimed that she practiced voodoo and brought the head along to ward off evil spirits. Voodoo is an Afro-Caribbean practice with roots that go back thousands of years.[4] The Haitian government recognizes voodoo as a religion, but the United States does not.

Magical thinking may seem distant from our modern world, but we are not so far removed from it in Western history. For example, in America as recently as the mid-1800s, it was well known that plants and trees came from seeds, but it was also popularly believed that plants and trees could spontaneously sprout where no seed had been, since some species would occasionally appear miles away from any others of their kind. American culture at the time was dominated by mythical processing, with some carryover from magical processing, and a growing trend towards the sequential.

Any transition from one level of processing information to another begins with a few individuals, then gradually spreads throughout a culture. Naturalist Henry David Thoreau was one of those individuals, systematically exploring the world around him with a thermometer, ruler, and note pad in the mid-1800s. He applied sequential processing to the issue of seed dispersal and documented how seeds could travel over long distances to "magically" sprout a new plant where none had been before. He never finished the book, but his manuscript was published in the 1990s under the title *Faith in a Seed*.

Magical thinking remains integral to our culture today, although in greatly watered-down form. Just about everybody has magical beliefs or illogical rituals they perform "for luck." One reason we cling to such beliefs is that they often come true. For example, black butterflies are a sign of bad luck in the Philippines. One Filipina woman living in Greece told of being surrounded by black butterflies while out jogging. Remembering her childhood folklore, she became frightened and ran home. The phone rang as she entered the house, and it was her mother calling to say that her father had died.[5] Anecdotes such as this are common, as are magical finds and serendipitous encounters.

Recently, my sister Jeanne was contemplating buying a house, but it needed a lot of repair work. In assessing her tools, she realized that she needed a small sledgehammer. The hammer she needed "magically" appeared while she was bicycling down the highway. The only time in her life she ever found a sledgehammer beside the road was right at the moment when she needed one. By the sequential logic of Western civilization, we would dismiss this incident as nothing more than coincidence. From a magical perspective, however, the sledgehammer could be perceived as a timely gift from the universe and a serendipitous sign to proceed with buying the property. Alternatively, the fact that Jeanne had to carry the eight-pound hammer for the next forty miles of her ride might be symbolic of the work she would endure to fix the place.

My own life is similarly full of serendipitous, magical moments. One must wonder if magical thinking actually works if a person or culture believes in it sufficiently. This is a subject we will return to in greater depth.

Timeless

Life in magical cultures is typically glued to the present moment. Hunter-gatherer bands and tribes focus on what is happening in the moment, rather than dwelling on the past, worrying about the future, or introspecting upon one's feelings. Warriors act out their bravery and accomplishments around the fire, and symbols are drawn on a hide to record major events, which are retold from generation to generation. But even when sharing this past history, people would *re-enact* events in the present tense, conveying a more dynamic story than merely saying, "They did this and then that."

Timelessness is a natural result of seeing the world from a first-person perspective; individuals are often highly impulsive and lack self-consciousness. They bounce along in the present moment, and like children may switch from laughing to crying and back to laughing again. Hunter-gatherer societies are often considered to be among the happiest peoples on earth, simply because they are not obsessed with introspection. They are less vulnerable to issues like self-pity or self-doubt, expressed in the D. H. Lawrence quote from the movie *G.I. Jane*: "*A small bird will drop frozen dead from a bough without ever having felt sorry for itself.*"[6] Although they may not know where tomorrow's food will come from, or even if they will find food tomorrow, hunter-gatherers exist largely unfettered by past regrets or future worries. In his biography, *The Falcon*, John Tanner imprinted the homestead routine of storing food for the winter before he was captured by Indians. Unlike his adoptive Ojibway tribe, he constantly tried to store food in preparation for hard times ahead.

Being alive in the present and not perceiving the future, hunter-gatherers may experience a sense of immortality, much like any young buck in our culture. As expressed by Ken Wilber in *Up from Eden*, "*Death is an abrupt, present, and magical occurrence, which might or might not happen now—it is not something that occurs in a distant future. Extended time does not yet pervasively enter the picture.*"[7] Yet, if death seems imminent, hunter-gatherers often embrace it without reservation, much as John Tanner described about his Ojibway brother after they fell through the ice on a frigid day: "*We were no sooner out of the water than our moccasins and clothes were frozen so stiff that we could not travel. I began also to think that we must die. But I was not like my Indian brother, willing to sit down and wait patiently for death to come.*" Tanner successfully built a fire and saved them both.[8] Indigenous peoples live in the now, they die in the now, and in a sense they remain immortal because they never imagine a future where they do not exist. They rarely dwell on the future at all.

At first glance, a lack of concern for the future might seem shortsighted and counterproductive to survival, but there are critical advantages to existing in a timeless state in a primitive lifestyle. For example, hunting with bows and arrows or other primitive weaponry requires being fully engaged in the moment. A hunter cannot hope to stalk up on his prey while distracted by thoughts of yesterdays or tomorrows. He will die of starvation or be killed by another tribe or predator. We seldom encounter dangerous predators today because most were killed off long ago, but there were an estimated fifty thousand grizzlies living between the Great Plains and the Pacific Coast in the early 1800s.[9] Among the tribes that shared grizzly habitat, natural selection favored those individuals who were totally engaged in the present moment.

Even better than a first-person perspective for awareness is no perspective at all, like our preconscious ancestors. Hunter-gatherers often used hypnotic rituals to return to a subconscious state of mind.

Chanting and Hypnosis

The human brain is wired to exist in hypnotic states with self-awareness switched off. Children spend a lot of time in hypnotic states, singing little rhymes over and over again, often with a subtle, glassy-eyed look. Most teenagers are wired to their music, almost like an addiction. They can hardly function without it. At this stage in life people are easily swayed by the power of suggestion. Even highly responsible teens are prone to significant lapses in judgment as they are swayed by suggestions from peers, songs, stupid stunts on television shows, or random impulses from the subconscious. These hypnotic states tend to subside as adult life forces people to depend more and more on the linguistic left brain. The songs that once ran endlessly through the mind gradually subside and disappear.

In tribal cultures, hypnotic rhythms and songs are woven into the fabric of everyday life, from grinding grain on a metate to planting crops, celebrating around the fire, or doing a war dance to prepare for battle. The passage of time seems to disappear in these hypnotic states, which is a great aid in accomplishing monotonously repetitive tasks, such as grinding grain between two rocks. A person in a hypnotic state can excel in action, as long as the body knows what to do.

Just as an athlete slips into the "body-mind" to excel without the distractions of conscious thought, hunters and warriors must also be able to act without thinking. An effective hunter must exist totally in the moment, operating on his accumulated experience without distracting thoughts. He cannot be thinking, "Geeze, I've got to get back to the village by four o'clock to file my taxes." If the hunter loses sync with the present moment, he will miss essential clues about game that is hiding nearby, or make some noise or movement to give himself away.

In warfare, hypnosis is essential for efficiently killing other people, especially in hand-to-hand combat. If you are going to bash people's heads in with sticks and rocks, or cut open someone's chest cavity to eat their living heart, it helps to exist in a completely hypnotic state so you can act without feeling empathy or fear. Any second thought or hesitation could lead to your demise, so you must function entirely on autopilot to be efficient. That is one reason why charging armies have often had a drummer boy or some other form of song or instrument to send troops forward.

In the book *In Search of the Primitive*, Lewis Cotlow described filming Masai warriors at a war dance. The only instrument they had was a drum, but they kept up *"a persistent beat that was hypnotic in effect."* The dancers became increasingly animated and emotionally charged as the dance progressed, reminding Cotlow of stories about warriors falling into epileptic-type seizures after getting worked up into such a frenzy. After the dance, he suggested filming them in a mock charge, so they set up a scene where ten warriors could charge up over a low hill at the camera. The only problem was that the charging warriors were so hypnotized by the re-enactment that Cotlow realized they were going to drive their spears right through him. Other Masai bystanders saw it too and threw themselves at the warriors in front, knocking them down. Cotlow wrote, *"The Masai who saved us were with difficulty holding down the two writhing, kicking warriors, both of whom were frothing at the mouth. One still jerked his arm violently as if throwing a spear."*[10]

Becoming a warrior typically involves extensive training and trials, and the more extreme the environment, the more extreme the initiation into manhood. The reason is simple—one cannot wimp out or have self-pity when trying to survive in a marginal environment. In his book *Facing the Lion*, Joseph Lemasolai Lekuton described growing up as part of two cultures in Kenya. He was trained as a Massai warrior at home, but the Kenyan government also required each family to send one child off to school. Lekuton's journey eventually led him to become a schoolteacher in America, although he travels back to Kenya to support his family and tribe every year.

Lekuton described taking his family's cows to pasture every day, often in searing, 100°F temperatures. He would stay out all day without food or water. When it was hot, he was hot. When it was raining, he was wet. If they had no food at home, he went hungry. Lekuton nearly died of dehydration during a drought, while grazing the cattle far from water for an extended period. He survived by licking the sweat off the noses of the cows.

Since his tribe was nomadic, it was often a challenge to find his family when school closed for vacation. Lekuton wrote, *"Sometimes I wouldn't know exactly where my family was. I had to search for them. So I'd set out with some other boys from my area. Sometimes the school car would take us to a point on the road as close as it could to where we were going. Then we'd walk. Usually, there would be plenty of people along the way, in villages and cattle camps. We could spend the night with any family. If we didn't encounter any people, we'd find a cave or sleep in a tree. The longest it took me to find my own family was about two weeks."* The boys had to evade poachers on one journey home when Lekuton was ten years old. They walked and ran forty miles in a single day to reach the safety of the village.

As a teenager, Lekuton underwent the initiation to become a man and a warrior. The initiates petitioned their elders for one to two years with songs and deeds to prove they were worthy, culminating in a ceremony where the boys were circumcised to become men. Initiates were given no painkillers, and drops of water and milk were placed on their eyelashes to prove they didn't blink during the seven-to-ten-minute operation. Their mothers stood by ready to beat them with clubs if they moved or showed any signs of cowardice. In high school, when the president of Kenya personally asked Lekuton to win a soccer game, Lekuton put himself into a warrior's trance and scored all three goals, bringing his team to a 3-to-2 victory.[11]

Voices from Nature

Hypnotic states are conducive for channeling thoughts and voices from the subconscious mind, so it was relatively common to hear animistic voices in primitive cultures, especially in moments of stress.

In 1931, Pretty Shield, medicine woman of the Crow Indians, told her life story to writer Frank B. Linderman. In one memorable incident as a child, she and a friend caught two baby antelope. They were tying the babies' legs together to carry them back to camp when the mother antelope returned. The crying babies made the mother crazy:

Bristled like a fighting wolf she ran at us, but stopped, stamping her hoofs, her eyes full of fear and fight. Suddenly, as though some medicine had told her what to do, she ran to the ledge of the rock, and began to beat it with her hoofs, as though beating a drum. And then she began to sing, keeping time on the rock with her hoofs. I understood her words.

"Who is going to have the smartest children?

The one that has straight ears.

Get up and run; run on."

The antelope sang this song four times, according to Pretty Shield. Pretty Shield was upset thinking about how she might feel if someone stole her children, so the girls set the baby antelope free, and Pretty Shield never forgot the song. She often sang it to her grandchildren to help them go to sleep. This was not an isolated incident, nor was Pretty Shield mentally ill. Besides the antelope, she described talking chickadees, ants, and bears, and told of a woman who kept a talking mouse in her pouch.[12] Similarly, in *Lame Deer, Seeker of Visions*, John Fire Lame Deer wrote, *"Butterflies talk to the women. A spirit will get into a beautiful butterfly, fly over to a young squaw, sit on her shoulder. The spirit will talk through that butterfly to the young squaw and tell her to become a medicine woman."*[13]

While it was common to hear such voices in primitive cultures, it is not entirely uncommon for people to hear similar voices today. At least five percent of the population has reported hearing voices. Many people hear voices for the first time during moments of stress, such as in grief over the loss of a loved one.[14] Naturalist Jon Young described how the birds would come to his grandmother's window in Poland and speak to her in Polish about her deceased loved ones and how they were doing.[15]

The Culture Is the Universe

The universe of a child is very small, typically consisting of bubbles of space around the home and Mom and Dad, connected by the car to other bubbles of space at the homes of friends and relatives, plus parks, stores, and gas stations. Yet within this "bubbleverse," all of the child's needs are hopefully met with food and shelter, love and growth. As the child grows the bubbleverse also grows, expanding with his or her awareness of the outside world. But imagine what it would be like to live in a bubble that stopped thirty miles from the place you were born. People lived that way for most of human history, including in recent times for isolated cultures.

New Guinea is home to about a thousand indigenous languages—some as different from each other as English from Chinese—among tribes living only a few miles apart. The diversity there is partly due to the inaccessible landscape. In 1910 a team of British ornithologists landed on New Guinea's coast and set out on an expedition for the snow-capped mountains only a hundred miles away (a five to ten day walk in my part of the world). Due to the impenetrable terrain, they gave up and turned back after covering only forty-five miles in thirteen months.

White explorers, missionaries, and settlers had been coming to New Guinea since the 1500s, but until the 1930s many highland tribes had not yet heard of whites, didn't know about the ocean (a hundred miles away), and assumed they were the only people in the world. Among other things, the frightened natives believed white people were returning ghosts, until they dug up and scrutinized their feces, or sent terrified young girls to have sex with the foreigners. Knowledge of their own neighbors was equally limited, such that one tribe believed that the people of a nearby tribe had their hands joined behind their backs and ate grass.

The geography of New Guinea greatly discouraged travel or exchange of knowledge, but an even greater obstacle common to all stone-age cultures was the social-political structure of tribal living. In the modern world we are accustomed to the constant input of information from the other cultures, and we have the freedom to travel widely, both within our own expansive borders and to other countries around the globe. But the nature of tribal living is such that each village or tribe is its own social and political unit, with shifting alliances among neighboring tribes. Relationships with adjacent groups would typically fluctuate from guarded social interaction and trade to outright warfare.[16] Even when circumstances were peaceable between two adjacent tribes, there was no means to meet or negotiate with the next tribe beyond them. In places like the United States or Africa, tribal territories were much larger, but the degree of isolation was similar.

Many indigenous tribal names, such as Inuit, Anishinabe, Nimíipu, or Khoi, translate simply as "the people," or "the real people," which is a reflection of their isolation. They did not perceive their neighbors as ethnic equals in the same way that we Americans think of Canadians or Mexicans. Rather, tribes often perceived of themselves as "the people" and applied less flattering epithets to their neighbors. These names were picked up by Western explorers as they asked each tribe what they called the next one. Thus, we came to know the Inuit as Eskimos, which means "fish eater" in Cree. We know the Tsitsitsa as Cheyenne, which came from a Dakota word meaning "those who speak strangely." The Mohawk tribe got its name from an Abenaki word meaning "enemies," while the Sioux got their name from an Anishinabe word meaning "snakes."[17]

The magical worldview was so vastly different from the mythical worldview of European explorers that cultural misunderstandings between them frequently bordered on the ludicrous. When explorer John Ross brought a young Inuit man named Poowutyuk onboard for training as an interpreter, neither comprehended the other's culture. In one incident, Poowutyuk went "foraging" on the ship and discovered the steward's cabin where the food was kept. He took a grouse and hare, which were intended for the captain, and while wearing wet furs seated himself in a bin of "warm snow" to eat the bounty. The warm snow turned out to be flour, making him ghostly white from head to toe by the time the outraged crew found the thief, as described by author Pierre Berton in *The Arctic Grail*, *"Poowutyuk was proud that he had been able to look after himself. The idea of theft was unknown to him… [Ross] ordered the Eskimo youth to suffer a dozen blows on the back with a stick. Poowutyuk was more puzzled than pained by this treatment. It didn't occur to him that he was being punished. But what was going on? Was it some sort of ritual or custom? A ceremony, perhaps? At last he had it figured out. Since it was too cold for him to disrobe, and since his garments were thick with flour, and since he couldn't reach his own back, the accommodating kabloonas were beating the flour out of him, as he had seen them beating rugs. He submitted quite cheerfully, while Ross, uncomprehending, drew up a code of punishment for any more immoral acts that might occur in the future, oblivious to the fact that no one had yet been able to teach the Eskimos what, in the white man's view, an immoral act was."[18]*

While the Inuit's inability to recognize punishment seems comical, the explorers lived in their own mythical fantasy, like actors in a play, wearing dress uniforms with polished buttons to dinner while stranded in the middle of nowhere. They transported trunks of frivolous items on expeditions to maintain an illusion of nobility. The Inuit lived successfully in the Arctic for thousands of years with the resources at hand, but well-equipped explorers lost scores of men to cold, starvation, or scurvy simply because they refused to copy what the Inuit did so successfully. They chose discomfort or death rather than adopting native lifestyles.[19]

Unexplained Phenomena

The notion of talking animals initially seems absurd from a Western point of view, and yet by mapping out the magical worldview we find that it was a common experience to hear voices, at least as projections from the subconscious mind. As outside observers, we applied logical, sequential thinking to generate palatable explanations for animistic voices and many other aspects of magical thinking. We created a map that enables us to perceive what life might have been like for our ancestors. Or did we?

We outlined reality as it was experienced in magical cultures, but we used our own worldview to generate that map. What if we only deluded ourselves into thinking we figured out the magical worldview, when we never stepped outside of our own viewpoint to get it? In the quest to define reality, we have to question our methodology. I am not suggesting that the reality we mapped out in this chapter is erroneous, but perhaps it is significantly incomplete.

Mark J. Plotkin, Ph.D., trained as an ethnobotanist at Harvard, Yale, and Tufts, then traveled to the Amazon rainforest in the 1970s and 1980s to learn about medicinal plants from indigenous tribes. While most of his experiences involved identifying and recording the uses of wild plants, there were other unexplainable events, as described in his 1993 book, *Tales of a Shaman's Apprentice*. In one terrifying dream, *"An enormous jaguar strode into my hut and stared deeply into my eyes, as if trying to divine my thoughts."* Plotkin believed the dream was some kind of visit from his teacher the Jaguar Shaman, which the shaman confirmed the following day.

Plotkin wrote, *"It became totally clear to me that different people, cultures, and places can have their own realities; that just as one can learn the spoken language of a foreign land, one can absorb its spirit— even if that spirit and its wisdom differ radically from those of one's own culture. In a society where people believe hallucinogenic experiences are caused by deities that inhabit sacred plants and that the reality we live every day is merely a dream, why shouldn't a medicine man who consults with the spirit world be able to turn himself into a mighty jungle beast? When I dreamed of the jaguar, I felt the Indians were communicating in a whole new language of exchange—beyond the plants that I had learned or the words that Koita had taught me, a language of other realities."[20]*

Like Plotkin, I was also interested in native lore. As a teenager I attended a sweat lodge ceremony in Montana. It was a spiritual and healing event for the Blackfoot and Salish Indians. This was a time of my life when I was trying to decide if there was magic in the world or if things only happened according to the sequential cause and effect of Western logic.

At the opening ceremony, the Native American elders described how they selected the site years before. Five eagles circled overhead in the sky, which they took as a good sign. That first night they saw a green glow over the horizon. While I was there, the elders engaged in what might be dismissed as pagan rituals, talking to the spirits, making offerings to the four directions, and performing healings. My experience in the sweatlodge was interesting, but not metaphysical. I enjoyed the experience and went to bed. The ceremonies went on for much of the night.

The next day the medicine men described how the hot rocks rolled themselves out of the sweatlodge, across flat ground, and went back to the fire pit. The spirits were apparently displeased with something about the encampment. Of course, I did not see any such thing with my own eyes, so what really happened? In our sequential worldview we say that it is impossible for rocks to move at their own will, so either there was a "logical" explanation for how the rocks moved, or it was an intentional fabrication, hallucination, or possibly a mass hallucination. Whatever our worldview is, there is a tendency to experience life within

that context, and to filter out anything that doesn't jive with our definition of reality. The evidence can be all around us, but it doesn't become part of our awareness. Is it possible to subconsciously arrange to be somewhere else when something happens that we don't believe in? I felt no closer to an answer to my questions about the nature of reality after the sweatlodge experience than before it.

What I have noticed over the years is that magical things do seem to happen, as long as we are open to the possibilities. For example, one time my wife Renee and I turned off at an intersection in the middle of nowhere. We came upon a railroad crossing when the lights flashed and the gates came down to block the highway. We sat there waiting for the train to come. We looked one way. We looked the other way. There was no train. While we were sitting there we took another look at our map and realized we had taken a wrong turn. We turned around to go back, and at that moment the gate raised up, as if it no longer needed to block our way, and still there was no sign of a train. In our normal way of thinking we would dismiss this event as a bizarre anomaly and not even ponder its meaning. I wonder, however, if it might be sensible to neither believe nor disbelieve anything, but simply to be open to possibilities.

For example, some indigenous remedies make sense to Western science, while others seem bizarre but tend to work within the context of the culture. Alma Snell, a Crow woman who taught me about native foods, described her own birth in her book *Grandmother's Grandchild*. She was a ten-pound baby, and the birth wasn't going well. The midwife called for an old Crow woman to assist with the birth. The old woman sent Alma's brother to the river with a tiny porcelain bowl and asked him to catch a fish in it. Alma wrote, *"He went down there, broke up the ice near the river's edge, and caught this little fish. Somehow, he got it into the bowl with the water in it. He came as fast as he could to the old lady. "Hurry!" she said. She agitated the water with her finger, teased the fish so that it swam around desperately. Then she took the fish out, gave it to my brother, simultaneously pouring the water into my mother's mouth. As soon as she drank that water, my mother had me. I was born. My father, who was in the next room, praying, heard my first cry. Then the old lady told my brother to take the little fish back to the river, "Release it. Watch it. Come back and tell me what it does." He came back and reported, "The fish wobbled on its side for a little bit and then swam swiftly away." The old lady said, "They'll be all right. The baby will live." I've always had a way with water. I love the water."*[21]

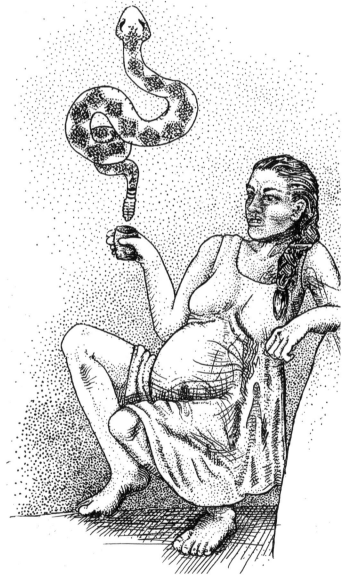

Lewis and Clark described the birth of Sacagawea's son Pomp at the Mandan villages before they headed west on the Missouri in search of a navigable water route to the Pacific. Sacagawea was having a difficult delivery, which might be assisted by ingesting rattlesnake rattles, according to the lore of the times. Lewis had a rattle with him, broke it up in some water and gave it to Sacagawea. The baby was born less than ten minutes later. From his mythical worldview, Lewis could not imagine why the rattle worked. Our sequential, scientific worldview is also unable to identify any properties that would facilitate delivery. Nevertheless, the rattle seemed to work within Sacagawea's magical worldview.[22]

Different cultures often have unique ailments that only their own doctors can diagnose and treat. Is it possible that a magical world works, but only for people fully immersed in it? Is it possible that voodoo works if the giver and the receiver both believe? I'm not going to say that it does, only that it might be sensible to avoid passing judgment too quickly. It may be helpful to set aside assumptions about cause and effect, to become skeptical of being skeptical, opening up to all possible versions of reality. In the next chapter we explore the mythical worldview, which is dramatically different, yet in some ways very similar to the magical worldview, depending on your point of perspective.

—Nine—

Mythical Processing

Agriculture, God, and Conquest

"The world of farming is the world of extended time, of making present preparations for a future harvest, of being able to gear the actions of the present toward significant future goals, aims, and rewards. The farmer works not only in and for the present, as does the hunter-gatherer, but also in and for tomorrow, which demands an expansion of his thoughts and deeds and awareness beyond the simple present, and a replacement of immediate impulsive discharges of the body with directed and channeled mental goals. In short, with the advent of farming, men and women entered an extended world of tense, time, and temporal duration, expanding their life and consciousness to include the future."

—Ken Wilber, Up from Eden[1]

Wouldn't it be grand if there were black-and-white answers to our problems? We could toughen laws and win against crime, drugs, and immorality. We could hunt down the terrorists and feel secure again. We could spell out the rules for our kids and they would behave like angels. Mythical thinking like this is characteristic of agrarian societies, it is the inevitable result of transitioning to permanent agricultural settlements with a larger population.

Agrarian civilizations are generally isolated and ethnocentric or nationalistic. Individuals engage in role-playing and learn a second-person, conformist perspective combined with a highly mythical, metaphorical interpretation of reality. They typically perceive issues in black-and-white, right-or-wrong terms. Socially and politically, agrarian societies are patriarchal and favor a "strict father figure" model of home life and government.

Agrarian societies are also hierarchical,

Snapshot: Mythical Processing

Technology: Agriculture with draft animals.

Origin: Early civilizations with harnessed livestock.

Logic: Principles, black-and-white choices.

Perspective: Second person, role playing, conform to expectations, listen to voices of authority.

Culture: Ethnic, nationalistic, us/them, religious, epic narratives, war and conquest.

Social-Political Structure: Hierarchical state governments, rigid classes.

Notable People: George W. Bush, Ronald Reagan, Pat Robertson, Joseph Stalin, Mahmoud Ahmadinejad.

Television/Movies: *Leave It to Beaver, Walker—Texas Ranger, Ben Hur, Die Hard, John Wayne westerns.*

101

with a few people acquiring a disproportionate share of the wealth and power. As a result of isolation and distrust of other cultures, combined with hierarchical ability to administer foreign territory, agrarian societies are driven by a thirst for conquest to shape the world according to their own ideals.

Rise of Agriculture

The transition from the magical to mythical worldview began with the digging stick and ended with the plow. Nomadic hunter-gatherers occasionally planted gardens and returned in the proper season to harvest them. Some tribes became semi-sedentary, growing gardens as their primary food source, supplemented by hunting and gathering until the soil and forest were depleted and the people moved on. When environmental conditions and technology favored intensive horticulture, human populations often exploded, enabling the rise of chiefdoms and divine kingdoms, as described in chapter six. Horticultural societies evolved into agrarian states if draft animals were tamed and harnessed by men to plow the fields.

The transition from hunting and gathering to farming changed the definition and experience of reality. Hunter-gatherers perceived magic by association, seeing or hearing potentially good or bad spirits in nearly every rock or tree or bird. They had to practice appropriate rituals and observe the right taboos to successfully find and kill game. Conversely, horticultural societies were dependent on the weather and the seasons for bountiful harvests. They looked up to the heavens and perceived gods who controlled the sun and rain and wind and cold. People prayed and offered sacrifices in hopes of appeasing the gods. They not only believed in these gods, but they heard them as well. The animistic voices heard by hunter-gatherer peoples gave way to the voices of gods, similar to those heard by Achilles or Moses. The people not only heard the gods, they became them, judging behaviors as moral or immoral.

As noted by Daniel Quinn in *Ishmael* and recorded in the book of *Genesis*, our ancestors lost their innocence to became aware like gods. They were banished from the carefree life in the Garden of Eden to make it on their own as farmers:

> *2.16: And the LORD God commanded the man, saying, of every tree of the garden thou mayest freely eat:*
> *2.17: But of the tree of the knowledge of good and evil, thou shalt not eat of it: for in the day that thou eatest thereof thou shalt surely die.*
> *3.4: And the serpent said unto the woman, Ye shall not surely die:*
> *3.5: For God doth know that in the day ye eat thereof, then your eyes shall be opened, and ye shall be as gods, knowing good and evil.*
> *3.6: And when the woman saw that the tree was good for food, and that it was pleasant to the eyes, and a tree to be desired to make one wise, she took of the fruit thereof, and did eat, and gave also unto her husband with her; and he did eat.*
> *3.7: And the eyes of them both were opened, and they knew that they were naked; and they sewed fig leaves together, and made themselves aprons.*
> *3.22: And the LORD God said, Behold, the man is become as one of us, to know good and evil: and now, lest he put forth his hand, and take also of the tree of life, and eat, and live for ever:*
> *3.23: Therefore the LORD God sent him forth from the Garden of Eden, to till the ground from whence he was taken.*[2]

The transition from magical to mythical thinking was completed with the switch from horticulture to agriculture as men took the reins of farming, diminishing the productive role of women. The rise of written languages in these patriarchal states slowly silenced the voices, until the gods were reduced to religious doctrines interpreted by men. Individuals who still heard the voices either founded religions, became canonized, or were persecuted and murdered. At last, the only voice remaining was the voice of authority of the hierarchical Church, and that voice guided men's actions much as unseen voices once commanded Achilles.

Like any other creature of nature, our hunter-gatherer ancestors only had to eat and live. They were not self-conscious of being naked, nor did they perceive themselves as separate from the world. It was only with the rise of agriculture that people learned to see themselves as separate from nature and judge what was right and wrong or good and evil. For the first time men set out to tame the wilds, to make nature bend to human will. With a newfound hierarchical lust for power, they set out to conquer the world and enslave other races, to subdue nature and women and children, and any other man who was less advantaged in life, as described by Daniel Quinn in *Ishmael*:

> *"If the king comes to a city that will not submit to his rule, what does he have to do?"*

> *"He has to conquer it."*

> *"Of course. In order to make himself the ruler of the world, man first had to conquer it."*

> *"You hear this fifty times a day. You can turn on the radio or the television and hear it every hour. Man is conquering the deserts, man is conquering the oceans, man is conquering the atom, man is conquering the elements, man is conquering outer space."*

> *Ishmael smiled. "You didn't believe me when I said that this story is ambient to your culture. Now you see what I mean. The mythology of your culture hums in your ears so constantly that no one pays the slightest bit of attention to it. Of course man is conquering space and the atom and the deserts and the oceans and the elements. According to your mythology, this is what he was born to do."*[3]

Voices of Authority

The animistic voices heard in hunter-gatherer bands and tribes became the voices of gods heard in horticultural chiefdoms and divine kingdoms. These early civilizations struggled to function cohesively as the gods seemed to voice conflicting commands to different individuals. The voices of the gods gradually faded with the transition to agriculture, patriarchal social structures, and writing. As fewer people heard the voices, they sought advice from those who still could, such as the Oracles of Delphi, until those voices were also lost. However, the human brain is wired to obey voices of command. The voices of the gods were immortalized in writing, to be interpreted and controlled by men. Religion codified many voices into a single voice administered through the Church hierarchy, commanding people how to live. In short, the many gods were replaced by a single external voice of authority.

An external voice of authority doesn't have to be religious at all to hypnotize a following. Adolph Hitler managed to warp the minds of his fellow countrymen into accomplices of grievous barbarity. In this waking nightmare, thousands of ordinary people committed the most horrendous of atrocities—starving, gassing, baking, and conducting experiments on their fellow citizens. As noted by Ken Wilber in *Up from Eden*, *"Just as a child creates visible gods out of his parents, even if they beat him, so men and women want masters, even if they enslave them."*[4]

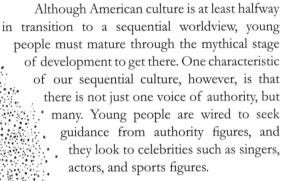

Although American culture is at least halfway in transition to a sequential worldview, young people must mature through the mythical stage of development to get there. One characteristic of our sequential culture, however, is that there is not just one voice of authority, but many. Young people are wired to seek guidance from authority figures, and they look to celebrities such as singers, actors, and sports figures.

Children are especially programmed to listen to voices of authority in the form of adults telling them what to do. Although children can be contrary at times, there is a powerful instinct to assume that adults know what is right and best, even when contradictory evidence is in plain sight. Becoming teenagers, kids often seem to disregard voices of authority, but it is more accurate to say they discover new role models, finding voices of authority in music and culture. As parents, we have to compete with the messages of their favorite music, sports, and television idols. This idol worshipping can become a form of hypnotism; people become so drawn to a rock star, actor, sports figure, cult leader, or mentor that they feel like their lives will somehow be better if they can be near this person. Young adults especially yearn for voices of authority as they search for answers to the complexities of life. They want something to believe in.

In 1997, coinciding with the passing of the Hale-Bopp Comet, thirty-eight cult members along with their leader all committed suicide with the aid of barbiturates, vodka, and plastic bags for asphyxiation, believing they would be transported aboard a spaceship hiding behind the comet. All were dressed in identical black shirts and sweat pants with new black-and-white Nike tennis shoes and purple armbands that read "Heaven's Gate away team." Each person had five dollars worth of quarters in their pockets, though nobody knows why.[5] Natural selection works against such cults, but they reappear on a regular basis. Other mass suicides included the 1978 People's Temple murder/suicide in Jonestown, Guyana (914 people), the 1994 to 1997 Solar Temple murder/suicides in Quebec and Switzerland (about 74 people), and the March 2000 Movement for the Restoration of the Ten Commandments of God in Uganda (780–1,000 people).[6]

There are hundreds of cults that do not make the news, and it is pretty easy for "normal" human beings to fall into such groups. Our brains are wired for it. Members are encouraged to socialize with each other inside a group, but not with outsiders. They hear only the commands of the cult leader. The cult may be physically isolated in a remote location, or socially isolated within a greater community. Many people are attracted to cults and religions because life is confusing. They desire guidelines to believe in and a voice of authority to tell them what to do. However, as Yatri observed in *Unknown Man*, *"Beliefs are cheap and they do seem great bargains at first. Ready-made answers are free. However, there is one small problem—there is no room for doubt. Doubt is the worm in the apple. It is always the fear of a true believer that somewhere, somewhen, someone will come along to disturb his cherished and borrowed ideas. Believers have to burn books, or heretics. At all costs they must repress that threat to their belief."[7]*

People of all ages seek external authority figures in difficult times. The need for guidance may be triggered by a personal tragedy, such as death or divorce, or a national one, such as 9/11. People who have been emotionally traumatized don't want complicated answers. They want a person or doctrine to give them simple solutions to get past the pain and back on their feet. Reporter Andrew Sullivan described his insecurity in *Time* magazine writing, *"I remember in my own faith journey that in those moments when I felt most lost in the world, I moved toward the absolutist part of my faith and gripped it with the white knuckles of fear. I brooked no dissent and patrolled my own soul for any hint of doubt. I required a faith not of sandstone but of granite."[8]*

This desire for guidance in difficult circumstances could be thought of as a retreat from the cusp of sentience. Self-awareness of inner turmoil is too painful, frightening, or depressing to face directly, and so we seek guidance from an authority figure. We copy and act out their answers to life's problems, rather than facing the issues directly. We relinquish to others our individuality and consciousness. We conform to external authorities rather than risk being alone as an individual.

Conforming to Expectations

Children approximately seven to ten years old are obsessed with rules and roles. In games they make up rules and they assign roles. They role-play cops and robbers, or princes and princesses, or mom and dad, and they act out stories and dialogue they have seen at home or on television. Through role-playing they learn to see the world from the perspective of other people in their culture. They want to define right and wrong, and they are confused when adults preach the importance of rules but then make exceptions, such as driving faster than the speed limit. Children transition through this intensive role-playing phase, but retain a powerful desire to conform to rules and roles.

My friend Sholei suggests that the need to conform is part of our evolutionary heritage, writing, *"The need to fit in is instinctual as well as a means to avoid loneliness and alleviate boredom. Deep down most pack or herd animals, humans included, understand that there is a certain safety in a group. Even now when there are few predators to worry about, an individual is far more likely to get bullied or attacked when alone, especially if that individual goes to public school."*

The tragedy of conformity is that kids mimic whatever they are exposed to and learn to identify with it whether they are interested in it or not. If kids are sufficiently exposed to diverse alternatives such as astronomy, dancing, theater, entomology, kayaking, or horsemanship, then they might choose a path that suits them. However, many kids lack the opportunity for such exposure, and if they do get excited about something, there may be no peer group at school to reinforce the interest. Instead, kids enroll in football, basketball, or whatever other sport is popular, because that is what everyone else is doing. The problem is exacerbated by artificially dividing kids into grades according to age. In tribal cultures children were part of the community. They had the opportunity to mimic people of all ages. In age-segregated classes, however, they have only each other. Kids mimic cues from the latest movies and act it out in front of each other, but that doesn't mean they actually care about it. They just don't have anything better to copy.

Another tragedy of conformity is that we adults chant the same mantra about the need to get good grades in school, to advance to college, to get a respectable and well-paying career. Well-intentioned parents can squash a child's dream to become an actor or an inventor in favor of something more secure, but less satisfying. Children are wired to follow this programming of shoulds and should-nots, and only regret it later. Many people have been astonished that I followed my own dreams. They described how they set aside their dreams to follow the career path of parents and teachers. Many became successful and productive members of society, but would give it up to start over and pursue their own dreams.

Logic by Principle

Mythical logic is driven by philosophical principles, rather than facts. Lacking a neutral, third-person perspective, and therefore the ability to engage in critical reasoning, the mythical mind perceives issues in terms of right or wrong in comparison to guiding beliefs. There are no in-between or shades-of-grey answers.

Strongly mythical cultures are usually governed by theocracies with little or no separation between church and state. Galileo, for instance, was not sentenced by impartial jurors on matters of fact, but by the Church on matters of principle. His astronomical data contradicted Church dogma. The Salem witch trials of 1692 and 1693 were also religious trials. The hysteria was probably the result of LSD-like hallucinations caused by ergot-infested grain, but Puritans interpreted the abnormal behavior as witchcraft. Nineteen women and men were convicted and hung by the Puritans. At least five other people died in prison while awaiting trial, and one elderly man was crushed to death under heavy stones for refusing to submit to trial.

Present-day Iran still lacks separation of church and state. Law and justice are conducted through religious institutions according to religious principles. Pakistan is in transition, with some factions trying to replace religious with secular courts. While we are fortunate to have secular courts and secular schools in America, there remains a strong influence of mythic ideas over objective facts.

Mainstream scientists complain that religious fundamentalists lack logic in their arguments for creationism. Fundamentalists start with the conclusion that the Bible represents the literal truth then seek evidence to support their beliefs. For example, creationists believe the earth to be 6,000 to 10,000 years old and that Noah's Great Flood occurred about 4,500 years ago. They say the flood caused catastrophic geologic events, such as formation of the Grand Canyon. Marine fossils on land, such as giant oysters found at 13,000 feet in the Andes, are perceived as evidence that the flood covered the entire earth. Contradicting evidence is ignored, such as the 4,700-year-old bristlecone pines and 13,000-year-old creosote bushes that escaped drowning under this imagined ocean. Creationists grab evidence at random, picking whichever argument sounds good at the moment, without any sequential thread of evidence. To a person with a mythical worldview, this kind of thinking is perfectly logical.

Similarly, some Islamic scientists use mythical logic to make reality fit the Koran. For instance, medical science has shown that the number of joints in the human varies from person to person, averaging about 307. However, since the Koran states that there are 360 joints in the body, Islamic scientists count things that some orthopedists wouldn't call a joint. By "finding" 360 joints in the human body, Islamic scientists distort reality to match the Koran, then cite each other as sources to validate their research. In an interview, Islamic scientist and chemistry professor Waheed Badawy of Cairo University stated that *"Islam has no problems with science... You can study what you want, you can say what you want."* Yet, when the interviewer suggested that the story of Adam and Eve might be just a story, Badaway responded that this claim would not be accepted unless there was proof: *"Nobody can just write what he thinks without proof. But we have real proof that the story of Adam as the first man is true."* When the interviewer asked, *"What proof?"* the professor looked at him with disbelief and clarified, *"It's written in the Koran."*[9]

As an adolescent I remember trying to make sense of the evolution-creationism debate, and I've seen my kids go through the same thing. Seemingly rational adults claim that the universe is billions of years old and that we evolved from apes. Other seemingly rational adults say evolution is an unproven theory, and that God created the world only a few thousand years ago. To children, lacking the tools to examine the natural world around them and unable to critically reason through the pros and cons of either argument, both arguments seem equally legitimate. Creationists will argue, and I agree, that students are taught to believe evolution on faith without any means of verifying it for themselves.

Given my background as a naturalist, evolution is not merely a theory or a belief, but something I can see in the world around me. I see flowers that have retained ancestral characteristics and those that have evolved new strategies. Sometimes I use clay to animate the stages of flower evolution in my botany classes. Without that kind of background and experience, a person has to swallow evolution on faith alone.

Creationists vocally challenge science in the schools, pushing the concept of intelligent design as an alternative to evolutionary theory. As "proof" against evolution, they might resort to metaphorical analogies such as *"evolution is as improbable as a monkey typing Shakespeare's Hamlet,"* or *"as likely as a pile of parts self-assembling to become a car."* Even if unsuccessful at introducing intelligent design into the schools, the challenge muddies the issue for a whole new generation of students. As a result, young people might believe whichever viewpoint seems to have the largest number of reasonable-sounding proponents. In other words, choosing one side or the other is not accomplished through critical reasoning, but through mimicry and role-playing.

It doesn't matter how logical your arguments and rebuttals are. It is futile to debate mythical thinkers. They reject sequential explanations and often interpret counter-arguments as evidence of persecution, entrenching their beliefs even more. However, the creation-evolution debate isn't necessarily an argument about the origins of life. It is a contest between mythical and sequential thinking.

As observed by Robert Kegan in his book *The Evolving Self,* *"Since what is most important for us to know in understanding another is not the other's experience but what the experience means to him or her, our first goal is to grasp the essence of how the other composes his or her private reality."*[10] A sequential thinker can imagine what it might be like to experience reality mythically or magically, because those layers of consciousness are nested within his own. On the other hand, a magical or mythical thinker cannot imagine a sequential worldview, because that perspective doesn't exist within his own worldview. Sequential processing is outside of his reality. By recognizing the layers of consciousness, it may be possible to shift public dialogue away from the origins of life to focus directly on the structure of mythical and sequential thinking.

The Ethnocentric Universe

Like tribal societies, agrarian states are typically isolated, much as North Korea is today. People frequently live their entire lives within a few days walk of the place they were born. Citizens might be aware that other cultures exist, but many would never see a neighboring community, let alone an adjacent country. Children mimic the cultural perspectives and values they are exposed to, and they may never be exposed to other viewpoints or religions. The result of this isolation is ethnocentric, nationalistic behavior and a mythical worldview. In the absence of contrasting viewpoints from other ethnic groups, the individual or culture is unable to shift to the next level of consciousness.

Imagine living in a small town, completely lacking media to describe the outside world. Unable to mimic and role-play other viewpoints, you would learn only one way to perceive the world. If you did finally encounter another culture, it would seem completely alien. Beliefs about right and wrong might be taken to great extremes, with the intensity of belief directly related to the degree of isolation.

Aside from the newspaper and radio, my mother's generation had very little connection to the world from their Montana farm during and after World War II. The nearest big town was thirty-five miles away, a trip made only twice a year. Not surprisingly, rural communities tend to be highly ethnocentric and conservative. People often preach a code of right and wrong based on religious beliefs handed down through generations. My mother and father grew up that way and subsequently made us kids dress up and go to church every Sunday. My mother later immersed herself in psychology, which greatly expanded her view of the universe. Although American culture is in transition from mythical to sequential thinking, rural communities typically shift more slowly. One local science teacher told me that 70 percent of her students come from families who believe God created the world just six thousand years ago.

Our local conservatism is nothing compared to that of more isolated cultures. After all, we live in peace with our neighbors, largely accepting who they are, whether we agree with them or not. In the Middle East, warring factions fought over differences between one version of Islam and another long before the meddling of Western powers. Colonialism brought European turf wars to the Middle East. France and Britain claimed land for their respective countries, pitting local forces against each other in skirmishes over the boundary lines. After World War I, the Middle East was carved up by French and British politicians in Paris, drawing national boundaries according to their own interests with little regard to ethic territories. After World War II, Western powers returned and carved out a new country for Israel.

In America, it is hard to understand why many Islamic people hate us so much. We espouse freedom from tyrannical governments and an opportunity to prosper in peace. But Islamic people have been the victims of imperialism for centuries, and now they are assaulted again by Western values. Imagine what it might be like for people who grew up exposed to only their own beliefs about Allah, Jesus, and morality. Today they are inundated with Western culture and media, which are as much of an assault on their lives as were past invasions by colonial armies. Islamic cultures had even more conservative dress codes and social rules than our European ancestors.

Our culture evolved gradually from Victorian times, when it was inappropriate for a woman to show her ankles, to today's world of baring as much skin as legally permissible. We can reasonably expect that Islamic cultures would be shocked by the deluge of imagery from the West. Their sense of morality is being challenged by Western culture. Worse, few Muslims have the means to connect directly with Americans to discover that we might have a lot in common after all. Much of what they learn about us comes from our movies, so it is no wonder that some Muslims believe we are all Satanic.

It is possible to be isolated even in the midst of a larger population. Many cults have risen in America and isolated their members from outside contact. Interestingly, while the Internet has increased connections across borders around the world, it is also leading to a higher degree of isolation. Multicultural communities previously led to the "melting pot" to blend and moderate ethnic extremes. Now it is possible to ignore one's next-door neighbors, while connected through the Internet to people around the world with similar viewpoints.

The Strict Father Figure

Previously we noted a link between the invention of the plow and the rise of patriarchal societies. Cultures became male-dominated as men became primary food producers. Hierarchical social structures emerged as farmers produced a surplus of calories to feed priests, politicians, and armies. In previous, egalitarian societies people achieved status by giving everything away, but in patriarchal societies people achieved status by gaining power over others in the social hierarchy, including at work and home. The father was the head of the household and the primary decision maker, hence the expression "father knows best." Children were made to conform and were beaten if they didn't. Women were often beaten into submission as well. The "strict father figure" became the foundation for European family values. In his essay, *"Metaphor, Morality, and Politics,"* George Lakoff described the strict father model this way:

> *Life is seen as fundamentally difficult and the world as fundamentally dangerous. Evil is conceptualized as a force in the world, and it is the father's job to support his family and protect it from evils—both external and internal. External evils include enemies, hardships, and temptations. Internal evils come in the form of uncontrolled desires and are as threatening as external ones. The father embodies the values needed to make one's way in the world and to support a family: he is morally strong, self-disciplined, frugal, temperate, and restrained. He sets an example by holding himself to high standards. He insists on his moral authority, commands obedience, and when he doesn't get it, metes out retribution as fairly and justly as he knows how. It is his job to protect and support his family, and he believes that safety comes out of strength.*

> *In addition to support and protection, the father's primary duty is to tell his children what is right and wrong, punish them when they do wrong, and to bring them up to be self-disciplined and self-reliant. Through self-denial, the children can build strength against internal evils. In this way, he teaches his children to be self-disciplined, industrious, polite, trustworthy, and respectful of authority.*

> *The strict father provides nurturance and expresses his devotion to his family by supporting and protecting them, but just as importantly by setting and enforcing strict moral bounds and by inculcating self-discipline and self-reliance through hard work and self-denial. This builds character. For the strict father, strictness is a form of nurturance and love—tough love.[11]*

As a child, I imprinted the strict father figure family model; it is a curse I have struggled with ever since. I don't remember much about my father except that he was gentle and loving and hated disciplining us kids. But that was his role in the family. My dad applied the belt to the butt because that was how a man's role was defined in our culture. Children learn through mimicry, and I can remember beating on the family dog for no particular reason. In later years, I attempted to discipline our dogs for killing chickens or chasing deer. It was the same act all over again: beat the dumb brute to make it understand. I have strived to learn more resourceful strategies since then, although my hardwired instincts remain.

The strict father model is appealing in its simplicity. There is instant gratification in being an authority figure with the ability to impose order right here, right now. Parents are bigger and more powerful than young children, making it easy to lay down the law and dish out consequences. We can intimidate them by my size and posture alone.

Most of the time Renee and I were patient parents, but the more challenging the situation, or the less resourceful we felt, the greater the temptation to take a command and control approach. For a short time, we even resorted to spanking. However, the problem with instant gratification is that it doesn't deal with the real issues; it just crushes the symptoms under the heavy hand of authority. More than that, it incites rebellion. Before long it was difficult to distinguish cause from effect. Did the behavior cause the spankings, or did the spankings cause the behavior? We quit spanking and regretted resorting to it in the first place. We strived to take an increasingly enlightened, more communicative approach to parenting. Unfortunately, children mimic everything, and we have seen the strict father role reflected in the way my kids intimidate or try to control each other. It is like looking in the mirror and seeing our least resourceful moments.

The Strict Father Figure in Government

Our perception of reality is built on metaphors, and the metaphors we act out at home carry over to the national level. According to George Lakoff, in the nation-as-family metaphor *"The nation is seen as a family, the government as a parent and the citizens as children."* Conservatives favor the strict father model of government to demand a high moral standard while protecting the nation from internal and external evils. To protect the nation from the evils of uncontrolled desires, they seek to define what is morally right or wrong, such as who is allowed to sleep with whom. To protect the nation from evils on the outside, they favor a strong military, and police action rather than diplomacy.[12]

Conservatives favor a tough-love approach, demanding self-disciplined, industrious citizenry. They believe every person should have an equal right to reach his full potential, but it is up to the individual to demonstrate the backbone to make it happen. A safety net such as the welfare system is believed to encourage slovenly behavior. Criminals who lack the moral fiber to be good citizens should be punished rather than reformed. It is not the government's job to help a criminal find a better path in life, only to punish them appropriately. Through the tough love of punishment, the criminal is expected to build character and make a fresh start as a productive, self-reliant citizen.

The relationship between government policy and family structure extends to schools as well. For example, Joseph Lekuton attended a school in Kenya run by American missionaries. Lekuton wrote, *"A part of every school day was set aside for punishing troublemakers, and I was often one of them... They used corporeal punishment—they beat us on the behind with a stick. It was painful, but it didn't stop me."*[13] The transition to sequential processing in America led to the end of corporal punishment in our schools, but many vestiges of mythical thinking remain.

Consider the link between team sports and foreign policy. The concept of sports and "teamwork" sounds holistic on the surface, but sports are not always holistic in practice. As noted by author Anthony Stevens in *The Roots of War and Terror*, *"Football, rugby, ice hockey and basketball are rituals of territorial conflict and war."*[14] Team sports are a form of controlled combat to motivate participants and spectators into a frenzy of ethnocentric us-against-them patriotism. This ethnocentric viewpoint is obvious when spectators holler chants like, "Go! Fight! Win!" or scream, *"We won!"* as if they were part of the action.

In small towns, community life revolves around school sports, and my own kids enjoy playing basketball and football. But many people take the games too seriously. Parents often rage against the coaches. Coaches sometimes yell at the kids until they are red in the face. I have watched coaches throw tantrums on the sidelines. Parents boo and hiss at the referees. Light-hearted games in elementary school become increasingly serious through junior high and high school, until the kids are as wound up about winning or losing as the adults. Through team sports, children learn to mimic the conservative, we're-right, your-wrong, let's-conquer-anyone-who-disagrees-with-us mythical thinking that ultimately leads to poor national policies. In short, we go to war as a nation because we go to war in high school, college, and professional competitions.

Granted, this perception of sports is a black-and-white statement in itself. Team sports are not all bad, and not all sports fans are mythical thinkers. My kids seem to shrug it off when other people get too wound up.

War and Conquest

Historically, the mythical worldview propagated a mentality of war and conquest, most notably through European colonialism. As our ancestors conquered tribal peoples around the world, they either converted or killed the heathen savages they subdued. In his book *The Discovery and Conquest of Peru*, Pedro de Cieza de León documented the subjugation of the Inca people by his fellow Spaniards in the 1500s. The conquistadors were not government soldiers as we might imagine, but mercenaries in search of treasure. Pedro de Cieza referred to them simply as "Christians." They marched across Peru, slaughtering Indians by the thousands, raiding their crops, burning villages, capturing women as servants and concubines, and stealing their gold and silver, all while preaching that the Indians should convert to Christianity and live in peace with the Spaniards.

As Captain Francisco Pizarro told one group of Indians, in the words of Pedro de Ceiza, *"They should forget their fallacious beliefs and useless sacrifices they made because it was only expedient to honor and serve God with sacrifices of good deeds and not with the shedding of blood of either men or animals. He declared that the Sun they worshipped was no more than an object created to illuminate and preserve the world, and that God Almighty had his seat in the most prominent place in the heavens, and that the Christians worshipped this God, whom they call Jesus Christ. Further if they did the same, He would grant them heaven's glory, and if they refused, He would cast them into hell forevermore."*[15]

In the conquest of North and South America, our ancestors killed at least 90 percent of the indigenous population through war, starvation, and diseases that were often introduced intentionally. We teach our children about the scale of Hitler's crimes against the Jews, but we don't really teach them about the crimes committed to settle our country. History is written by the victors.

We might assume our culture has progressed beyond mythical war and conquest, that American foreign policy is driven by reason rather than religion. Unfortunately, that isn't always the case. American foreign policy often resembles a religious crusade. According to CBS News *60 Minutes*, Evangelical Christians actively influence foreign policy in favor of triggering Armageddon.

Evangelical Christians believe Christ's second coming will be preceded by a series of violent events in Israel, culminating in the Battle of Armageddon. Evangelicals partnered with ultra-Zionist Jews who espouse a hard-line against the Palestinians and refuse to move out of the West Bank or Gaza, claiming that God granted every grain of sand of that land to the Jewish people. The association is unusual because Evangelicals also believe 1) two-thirds of the Jewish people will die in the war the Evangelicals are trying to create, 2) the Jewish people need to be converted to be saved, and 3) those who are not killed will finally have the good sense to embrace Christ and be "raptured" up to Heaven. Besides supporting warfare in the Middle East, Evangelicals don't see any reason to protect the environment, since 1) the end of the world is coming anyway, and 2) the world is supposed to be really messed up before the Messiah returns. Hard-line Jews embrace this twisted support because the Evangelical's political clout serves their own extremist agenda. In churches across America, Evangelical priests joyfully report upsurges in violence in Israel and cheer bloody battles. President George W. Bush was elected twice with the help of the Christian right and often favored the wishes of the Evangelicals in his policies towards Israel.[16] Our country is still emerging from the mythical age.

To get a sense of how American foreign policy might be experienced by others, try imagining what would happen if the Russians decided we were not doing enough to control gangs and drug trafficking in Los Angeles or Brooklyn. The Russians decide to fix the problem themselves, dropping bombs out of the sky on suspected gang hideouts, rolling down the streets with tanks and soldiers. The soldiers raid houses, speak a different language, and have a different culture. Would Americans run out into the street and welcome their Russian saviors, or would they be distrustful of them? Would young people see this invasive force and join the gangs that brought the Russians in the first place? That's basically what happens when our soldiers police other parts of the world.

It is important to note that mythical thinking doesn't require religion. For example, some antigovernment groups in the United States perceive the federal government as a threat to liberty. While they may have legitimate concerns about government as Big Brother, the black-and-white viewpoint leads to actions such as Timothy McVeigh's 1995 bombing of the federal building in Oklahoma City. In his mind he was attacking the government. But what is the government? McVeigh killed ordinary office workers, people like you and me, who applied for a job and had their kids along in daycare. By blowing up this building, McVeigh felt he was attacking the government, when he was actually attacking families, kids, and babies. The mythical mind is unable to make the distinction because they perceive issues in black-and-white.

Similarly, ecoterrorists may have legitimate concerns about the environment, but it is erroneous to think that terrorism helps the problem. Civilization is presently unsustainable. We are rampantly consuming resources, altering the climate, and pushing half of all life towards extinction. Ecoterrorists feel the need to get society's attention in order to make a difference in the world. They want to blow up buildings or burn down new houses to shake things up and

112

get people to pay attention to the environment. They might intuitively tap into a higher level of consciousness, recognizing our connection with the web of life, but at the response level they are operating in a mythical mindset. Ultimately, ecoterrorism consumes more resources to replace what was destroyed and casts a bad light on all environmentally conscientious people.

Mythical thinking is the single greatest threat to the future of humanity and the future of life on earth. If we are to survive into the next century without destroying each other, then we have to move our species beyond mythical thinking, and this is one statement that can be made in black-and-white terms.

Unexplained Phenomena

I was conversing with a fellow passenger on a train in Mexico about his work. He did exorcisms to help people who felt they were possessed by evil spirits or Satan. He would do a ritual to help them through their ordeal. He said, *"I don't necessarily believe in it myself, but to the people I work with, it is all very real and they get real relief from what I do."* If a person is immersed deep enough in their beliefs, and feel they are possessed by evil spirits, then yes, the spirits could manifest themselves in their life in horrible ways. By doing an exorcism and letting go of it, they can be free of the things have been haunting them.

In Uganda, Catholic pilgrims flock to a forty-foot-tall concrete cross on top of a hill in search of healing. Rumors have spread that people have been cured of minor ailments and bad habits after praying there and kissing the cross. One local woman complained of sleepless nights due to evil spirits in her house, but she has been able to keep them away and sleep peacefully since she started praying at the cross.[17]

Among the deeply faithful of any religious background, there are big and small miracles that cannot be explained in terms of physical cause and effect. For example, one older couple I met described how they bought land to build a home fifty years ago. Not knowing what else to do when they arrived in Helena, Montana, the husband said, *"God is going to help us."* He opened up the phone book to a random page, put his finger down and called the number he pointed to. The recipient of this unusual call coincidentally owned a lot in town and sold it to them on payments. Miracles do happen.

With a skeptical mind we can find a way to discount many "miracles," but cases remain that are difficult to explain. Do we discount such stories simply because they do not fit our particular map of reality, or do we leave it open to the possibility there maybe something lacking from our map of reality that makes it impossible for us to see how miracles could happen? It is possible that special things do manifest themselves to people who believe, just as in a magical worldview?

Regardless of the religion, people of faith see evidence of God's work in their lives, with miracles that serve as evidence that their beliefs are valid. However, while the evidence supports their worldview and their God, they may be unable to acknowledge that people with different concepts of God also experience God's touch in their lives. Objectively speaking, every God must be legitimate. If every religion works, at least some of the time, then there must be a more universal phenomenon at work. Whatever that phenomenon is, it may be impossible to perceive it as anything other than "God's will" to a person operating within a mythical worldview.

In the next chapter we begin to acknowledge that all religions have an equally valid take on the truth by shifting from an ethnocentric second-person perspective to the neutral third-person perspective of sequential processing.

Suggested Reading:

A Language Older than Words by Derrick Jensen. Hunter-gatherer cultures were largely egalitarian, while agricultural cultures are inherently patriarchal and hierarchical. Derrick Jensen effectively connects the dots between agriculture and conquest, showing how the rise of farming led to the subjugation and rape of women and children, indigenous peoples, and the environment. His book rants on the evils of civilization, which he delivers with appalling anecdotes mined from our history of conquest and genocide.

—Ten—

Sequential Processing

Science, Industry, and Material Wealth

"Culture makes a difference in the way evolution operates because it represents a second inheritance system, conveniently labeled memetic, additional to the genetic one, operating through the mechanism of social learning. There is increasing evidence that the importance of this mechanism for evolution in non-human species has been much underrated. The fact that cultural transmission operates through social learning does not make it less Darwinian than genetic transmission. Both are specific instances, with their own properties, of a more general category of information transfer processes that lead to the production of heritable variation and its modification through time."

—*Stephan Shennan, Genes, Memes, and Human History*[1]

Y ou probably have an intuitive sense of sequential processing, simply because you would not be reading this book if you were not already processing information that way. Sequential processing arose with science and enabled the industrial revolution, leading to the rise of powerful, wealthy nations.

It took only a few individuals processing sequentially to invent factories with interchangeable parts and assembly lines. When those factories were up and running, other people saw and mimicked the process. In a positive feedback loop, sequential processing led to linear, assembly-line developments that led to more sequential processing. In this chapter we turn the lens on ourselves to investigate what it means to have a sequential worldview.

Sequential processing is associated with increased intermingling among cultures and a

> Snapshot: Sequential Processing
>
> Technology: Industrial assembly line.
>
> Origin: Newton's mechanical universe, natural history, manufacturing.
>
> Logic: Sequential cause and effect., critical thinking, many shades-of-grey, economies of scale.
>
> Perspective: Third person, skeptical, individualistic.
>
> Culture: Multicultural, inclusive of others.
>
> Social-Political Structure: Hierarchical state governments, equal opportunity.
>
> Notable People: Isaac Newton, Henry David Thoreau, Charles Darwin, Henry Ford, Bill Clinton.
>
> Television/Movies: *M.A.S.H., Simpson's, The Godfather, Pursuit of Happyness, The Fugitive, Titanic, James Bond.*

third-person perspective. Individuals acknowledge the uniqueness and rights of other people and cultures. Issues are perceived as shades of grey, rather than in purely black-and-white terms.

115

Socially and politically, industrial/sequential societies remain hierarchical, but the drive to conquer and exploit is a holdover from the agrarian, mythically driven societies from which they evolved. Mature industrial cultures have no need for conquest, nor the desire to administer foreign territory, although the ideal of equal opportunity for all people may lead to military action.

Religion: Cradle of Science

Sequential processing in Western culture emerged in the separation between religion and science. While science and religion give us two dramatically different stories of reality, it didn't start out that way. Science did not intend to disprove either the Bible or the teachings of the Church, but rather to document and understand the amazing diversity of God's creation. However, as the sciences blossomed into astronomy, geology, biology, and later paleontology, early scientists observed peculiar discrepancies that didn't fit the biblical story of creation.

As with many early scientists, the astronomy of Nicolaus Copernicus (1473–1543) was funded by the Church. After reading the work of earlier astronomers and making his own observations and calculations, Copernicus formulated the hypothesis that the earth orbited around the sun. His work, *De revolutionibus orbium coelestium* (*On the Revolutions of the Celestial Spheres*) was published just before he died, and it is still considered one of the most important scientific hypotheses of all times, marking the beginnings of modern astronomy. The Church funded astronomy partly due to the need for a more accurate calendar system. Theologians were interested in Copernicus' work and were only somewhat perturbed that it contradicted an account in the Old Testament (Joshua 10:13) that the sun went around the earth. When the book was published it contained an unauthorized preface by a Lutheran cleric, possibly trying to soften the Church's reaction. He stated that Copernicus wrote the work as a mere mathematical hypothesis—not as an account that contained truth or even probability.[2]

The conflict between religion and science didn't come to blows until Galileo Galilee (1564–1642) observed the phases of Venus as predicted by Copernicus. Galileo saw that the universe operated by predictable mathematical laws and models, like a machine. This mechanistic viewpoint was expanded upon by Sir Isaac Newton (1643–1727) in his 1687 book, *The Mathematical Principles of Natural Philosophy*. Newton argued that the universe operated in a rational and predictable way that could be mathematically explained. The impact of this scientific revolution was, according to Richard Hooker in *World Civilizations*, "*in reality, a series of changes in the structure of European thought itself: systematic doubt, empirical and sensory verification, the abstraction of human knowledge into*

116

separate sciences, and the view that the world functions like a machine. These changes greatly changed the human experience of every other aspect of life, from individual life to the life of the group. This modification in world view can also be charted in painting, sculpture and architecture; you can see that people of the seventeenth and eighteenth centuries are looking at the world very differently."[3]

In biology, scientists started cataloging and organizing everything in God's creation. For example, by looking at two different types of roses one can find enough differences to clearly determine that each is a different species of plant, yet at the same time both are roses. This simple duality led to the modern system of classification, originated by Carolus Linnaeus (1707–1778), in which each species is given a first and last name, or more properly, a last and first name, such as *Rosa alba* (rose, white) and *Rosa mulitflora* (rose, multiflowered). *Rosa* is the group or genus for all species of roses. The Linnaean system of classification enabled early scientists to begin cataloging the massive biodiversity of life on earth. However, it didn't take long before the process revealed evidence contrary to the biblical story of creation.

At first it would seem obvious that two different species of plants or two different birds are classified with their own names, but after centuries of trying to classify every living thing on the planet, scientists haven't been able to agree on a perfect definition of what constitutes a species. The problem is that there are degrees of variation among all plants and animals, and scientists have to determine when a variant constitutes diversity within a species or warrants classification as an entirely separate species.

For example, the Baltimore oriole (*Icterus galbula*) of the East Coast is significantly different from the Bullock's oriole (*Icterus bullockii*) of the Midwest. But how do you classify birds in the middle that share characteristics of both species, and cannot be properly grouped with one type more than the other, or split off into their own group? Drawing a line between them is similar to determining the difference between two neighboring cities. In Texas, for instance, Dallas and Fort Worth are close together. If you were downtown in one or the other, then you would clearly know which city you were in. But how do you define a line between one and the other when you are in the shared suburbs? The two orioles were classified separately, then grouped together as the Northern oriole, and are now again recognized as separate species that tend to hybridize. However, the currently favored definition of a species is based on reproductive isolation, meaning that organisms naturally breed with their own kind. Therefore, it seems that the orioles should again be classified as variants within a single species.

When scientists tried to catalog God's creation, they struggled to define the line between one species and another. Through natural variation as well as domestic breeding programs, early scientists could see that species were in flux, changing from one thing into another. Their initial reaction wasn't to refute the Bible, but rather to generate possible theories to make the world they observed fit the creation story described in the Bible.

Speculation about evolution arose as naturalists tried to make sense of their observations. The naturalist Georges-Louis Leclerc, Comte de Buffon (1707–1788) of France speculated about evolution in his thirty-six-volume series, *Histoire naturelle*. He could see that variation occurred within a species, and he wondered if similar species, such as horses and donkeys, might have originated from a common ancestor. He then rejected the idea in the text, possibly to avoid controversy. Leclerc also suggested that the earth might have formed from a ball of white-hot matter that cooled over 70,000 years. In private he wondered if the earth might be much older, but to minimize conflicts with the Church, he and other early naturalists tried to reconcile these ideas with the biblical version of creation, suggesting that the six "days" were not days in a literal sense. He divided his 70,000-year history of the earth into six epochs that corresponded with the six days of creation.[4]

Jean-Babtiste de Lamarck (1744–1829) took evolution to the next step, outlining the first theory of evolution in his 1809 book *Philosophie zoologique*. Lamarck proposed that simple forms of life constantly arose from non-living matter and gradually evolved to become more complex. He believed that the mechanism driving evolution was one of acquired characteristics. For instance, by reaching up to eat leaves off the trees, ancestral giraffes stretched their necks a little bit, a characteristic that was passed along to the offspring until all giraffes had long necks. It is the equivalent of suggesting that we could pass a suntan along to our children.[5]

While biologists tried to make sense of their observations in the living world, geologists were trying to make sense of what they saw in the layers of rock all around them. The research of Abraham Werner (1749–1817) of Germany and William Smith (1769–1839) of England helped establish that rocks were formed in distinct layers sequentially through time. Smith further recognized that fossils were linked to specific strata, effectively turning the layers of rock into a sequential record of past life.[6]

The science of paleontology arose concurrently as fossil discoveries led to more questions about the history of life. Like many people, Thomas Jefferson found it inconceivable that any species could have been created only to die out. Jefferson found the remains of an extinct giant sloth, which he believed to be a rare lion that had merely gone undiscovered. But by 1811, with Mary Anning's (1799–1847) discovery of an ichthyosaurus in England, it was undeniable that some forms of life had died out in the past, contradicting accepted biblical dogma. To account for this discrepancy, it was concluded that the fossils were the remains of species that lived during earlier creations, which had subsequently been wiped out. It was thought that all living species were formed in the most recent creation, as documented in the Bible.[7]

In England, Dr. Gideon Mantell (1790–1852) found some fossilized teeth, which he correctly deduced belonged to a lizard-like reptile like an iguana. He named it Iguanadon, meaning "iguana tooth," and estimated it to be about forty feet long. Richard Owen (1804–1892) coined the term *dinosaur* in 1841. Evolution was openly discussed among scientists by then, usually linked to the idea of progress. Scientists believed that evolution worked in one direction, towards improvement or perfection. However, Owen showed that dinosaurs were physiologically more advanced than modern reptiles, evidence which undermined the idea of evolutionary progress. Owen fiercely opposed evolutionary thought, although he eventually arrived at a hybrid belief that evolution existed in a limited form according to a divine plan.[8]

In 1844 Robert Chambers (1802–1871) published *Vestiges of the Natural History of Creation*, proposing that the earth and evolution were not created directly by God, but rather that they were driven by laws that followed God's will. Like others of his time, he believed that evolution was progressive, but he also proposed that man arose from animals. Chambers' work was severely criticized by scientists and clergymen alike. The criticism served as a warning to Charles Darwin about the potential repercussions of his own work.[9]

Charles Darwin (1809–1882) was raised with a literal interpretation of the Bible and considered becoming a clergyman. But he also had an interest in the natural sciences, travel, and the outdoors. In 1831 he began his historic five-year trip aboard the *HMS Beagle,* not with an official position, but simply at the invitation of the captain to provide educated companionship to relieve the tedium of months spent bobbing around on the ocean. As a passenger, Darwin had freedom to explore his interests wherever they landed. According to prevailing views of the time, all plants and animals were created to fit the environment they lived in. But in South America Darwin observed that the habitat as well as the anatomy of the flightless greater rhea was similar to that of the African ostrich, and he questioned why there were two species, when only one would seem to suffice.[10]

On the Galapagos Islands he encountered thirteen slightly different species of finches, each specialized to different foods on different islands. Darwin wondered why the Creator would have gone to the trouble of making thirteen separate species solely for a scattering of rocky outcrops in the middle of the Pacific Ocean. Darwin later speculated about the finches, writing, *"Seeing this graduation in diversity of structure in one small, intimately related group of birds, one might really fancy that from an original paucity of birds in this archipelago, one species had been taken and modified for different ends."*

Pigeon breeding and racing was a British obsession at the time, and Darwin took an interest in it because it allowed him to witness change in living organisms. He studied the methods of the pigeon breeders in detail and concluded that the great diversity of pigeons had all been bred from a common ancestor through artificial selection for specific traits. But that didn't answer the question of how species could evolve through *natural* selection, without breeders to do the selecting.

The answer didn't come to him until 1838, when he read Thomas Malthus' *Essay on the Principle of Population*, which described the geometric growth of the human population and predicted that at some point the population would exceed the food supply. Malthus suggested that the ensuing competition for limited resources would ultimately lead to a struggle for existence. In a flash of insight, Darwin realized that under these circumstances in nature, the organisms most well adapted to the situation would have the best chance of surviving to pass their characteristics along to their offspring.[11]

Darwin did not publish his ideas right away, fearing the negative reaction that his work might receive. Instead, he spent years refining the concepts, gathering data, and discussing it with his associates to gauge their reactions. It wasn't until 1858, upon learning that Alfred Russel Wallace had independently arrived at the same conclusion and was about to publish his own work, that Darwin finally decided to go public.[12] Darwin published *The Origin of Species* in 1859, a moment that changed the world. Science and religion have been persistent adversaries ever since.

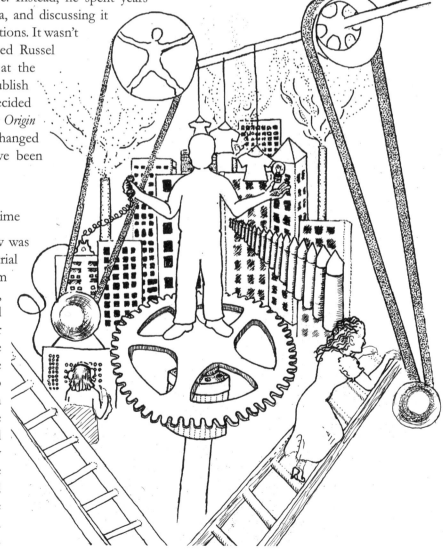

The Industrialization of Space and Time

The emerging scientific view was paralleled by the emerging industrial world, which led to ideas that seem utterly commonsense in retrospect, such as interchangeable parts and assembly line production. For example, like everything else in the 1700s, guns were manufactured one at a time by gunsmiths, and no two guns were identical. Every broken gun had to have custom parts made to fix it. Interchangeability originated in France near the end of the century and quickly spread to America, where Eli Whitney is commonly credited with the invention. In about 1798 he built ten guns with identical parts and assembled them from piles of parts in front of Congress. Congress was immensely impressed, and subsequently issued standards for United States equipment.[13]

Eli Whitney's idea of interchangeable parts became the foundation for another simple idea: assembly line production. Whitney initiated division of labor, with different people in the same factory specializing in different parts. Henry Ford perfected the assembly line for construction of the Model T in 1913, forming the factory model for modern industry. The assembly line slashed production costs, making automobiles affordable for ordinary people. More importantly, industrialization, combined with growing literacy in science and evolutionary theory, helped mainstream consciousness shift towards sequential processing.

To appreciate the depth of this perceptual shift, consider that, prior to trains, human travel was fused with the natural world. People traveled overland by foot, horseback, or buggy, intimately connected with the passing of every house and farm, keenly aware of the fatigue and smells of the livestock and every bump in the road. It was an intensely first-person, present-moment-oriented experience. The railroads changed human perception, as noted by Wolfgang Schivelbusch in his book *The Railway Journey: The Industrialization of Time and Space in the 19th Century*. Early passengers were shocked to break free from nature to speed along at twenty or thirty miles per hour. Englishmen described it as the *"annihilation of space and time,"* as their country seemed to shrink. All destinations seemed two-thirds closer together than before.

We might imagine that passengers would have reveled at the thrill of speed, racing through the scenic countryside. However, the foreground sped by at such a pace that passengers were forced to look at the bigger, panoramic view of the landscape. The first-person experience of bouncing along in a buggy was replaced with a detached, third-person perspective looking out the windows. Passengers found it tedious. Traveling was no longer about the journey, but the destination. Travelers moved faster than ever before and impatiently awaited the end of the ride. They took up reading to pass the time.

Society gradually adjusted to the new reality, until the detached, panoramic perspective became normal. The changes brought on by technology filtered throughout culture. Small, traditional stores gave way to department stores with wide, railroad-like aisles and panoramic views of products on the shelves.[14] Industrialization changed the perception of reality, such that most people become impatient with a slow, first-person oriented travel experience. We prefer the sweeping big picture to the mundane details of every street and farm.

Subjective Consciousness

Industrialization and science led to a detached, third-person perspective and the linear, cause-and-effect thinking that characterizes sequential processing. One result of this new way of thinking was the rise of subjective consciousness.

In preconscious times our ancestors lived fused with nature, unaware of their existence. They operated entirely on subconscious impulse without reflection. The rise of hunter-gatherer technology and simple metaphors enabled a first-person sense of self-awareness with an external, rather than introspective focus. People operated largely on impulse and occasionally experienced those impulses as animistic voices of command. With the rise of horticulture, those voices were heard as gods. The voices of the gods faded out with the rise of complex agricultural societies and the spread of written language. Agriculture led to second-person, role-oriented societies, where people listened to and conformed to external voices of authority. The scientific and industrial revolution facilitated an increasingly detached, third-person perspective and the rise of critical thinking. Rather than merely conforming to voices of authority, individuals learned to consider both sides of issues and arrive at their own conclusions. People truly began thinking for themselves for the first time.

In his book *Discourse on Method* philosopher René Descartes (1596–1650) proposed great skepticism. In a thought experiment similar to the virtual reality question posed in the first chapter, Descartes imagined that reality was a lie created by the devil. How could a person prove anything was real? Even scientific knowledge was suspect. He literally stopped believing in everything but found it impossible to live that way. In desperation for a certain truth to work from, Descartes realized that his thinking proved he existed, leading him to proclaim, *Cogito, ergo sum,* *"I think, therefore I am."* Descartes rejected all traditional beliefs and knowledge, perceiving individual subjective experience as the foundation of truth.[15]

We encounter a surprise when we try to pinpoint the dawn of consciousness. A limited sense of self-awareness arose with the Cultural Revolution 40,000 to 50,000 years ago. The ability to see oneself through the eyes of other people didn't become widespread until the rise of agriculture just 3,000 years ago, as proposed by Julian Jaynes. However, subjective third-person consciousness remained uncommon until the rise of science and industry only a few hundred years ago. Indeed, as we discovered through previous chapters, our behaviors suggest that we still operate like automatons.

A cultural shift from one way of perceiving reality to another doesn't happen overnight. The transition starts among a handful of people then gradually disseminates to the masses. Henry David Thoreau, best known for his book *Walden* and his essay *"Civil Disobedience,"* was processing sequentially long before it became mainstream. Thoreau was an amateur scientist, always measuring and recording natural phenomena, such as the depth of local ponds and the weather. As discussed previously, he conducted research dispelling popular myths that plants and trees could spontaneously spring up without seeds. The result of his sequential processing was a fully modern and individualistic view of the world.

While other people unconsciously mimicked the same behaviors from generation to generation, Thoreau mentally separated himself from his culture and consciously questioned its meaning and purpose. He noted that people seemed to go through life much like automatons, working endlessly to mimic a cultural standard without ever asking why. Instead of being awed by the wonders of ancient Egypt, for instance, he wrote, *"As for the pyramids, there is nothing to wonder at in them so much as the fact that so many men could be found degraded enough to spend their lives constructing a tomb for some ambitious booby, whom it would have been wiser and manlier to have drowned in the Nile, and then given his body to the dogs."*[16]

Thoreau conducted an experiment at Walden Pond to see how little work he could do to sustain himself. While a typical house in his time cost $800 and required many years of work to pay for, Thoreau built his cabin for $28. He demonstrated that by living simply he could work about six weeks per year and have most of his time free to pursue personal interests. By temporarily removing himself from civilization, he effectively shifted to a third-person perspective of his culture. He was an outside observer of society, not blinded by cultural biases. He believed in a person's right to be an individual without conforming to society's expectations.

Not surprisingly, Thoreau's writing did not sell well in his time, but his work later inspired Gandhi, Martin Luther King, and John F. Kennedy. His writing career didn't flourish until American culture caught up with him in the 1960s, one hundred years after his death. Young people questioned and rebelled against the status quo en masse for the first time. Instead of conforming to expectations to get a good education and a respectable job, young people pursued music and art, tried new haircuts, and protested against war. Subjective consciousness rose to prominence in the 1960s and continues to filter into human society. We might imagine that our ancestors perceived reality much as we do today, but it is evident that we are still emerging into sentience.

Cause and Effect and Critical Thinking

Sequential processing alters one's perception of cause and effect. For example, a collapsed building in a magical worldview might be interpreted as the result of voodoo or some kind of "bad luck." From a mythical worldview, the structure might have been pancaked due to a failure to honor one's God, or as retribution for sins. However, from a sequential worldview, we would seek a physical cause, a flaw in the structure that led to the building's collapse. We might sort through the rubble for clues to the collapse or compare this structure with others that have collapsed.

Sequential cause and effect is the quest to isolate specific variables. If, for example, we discover that clay hardens in the fire to become pottery then we might do a series of controlled tests with various types of clay, different amounts of temper, and a range of firing temperatures. We systematically control the variables, changing just one factor in each test, rather than merely trying things at random.

Critical thinking is also a form of sequential processing. It is the ability to objectively compare two different versions of an argument to recognize the merits and the flaws of each side. This type of processing does not come naturally to the human brain, and our ancestors were able to live their entire lives without it. But our culture is very different. The more complex our society becomes, the more we depend on sequential processing for problem solving.

Sequential processing is an essential skill taught in public schools—a skill which is being introduced at younger grades now than in the past. When my grandmother was a child, schools emphasized rote memorization of poems, dates, facts, and math tables. There was far less memorization when I was a child, and I see my own kids doing word problems in younger grades. It is easy to program basic math into the brain, like $2 + 2 = 4$, until you can recall the information without thinking about it. But you cannot navigate a word problem with your subconscious mind. You have to consciously process the information and write the math down in sequential order before you do the calculations. If Betsy has 10 apples and eats 1 and gives 3 to John and John eats 1 and gives 1 to Veronica to eat, then how many apples are there left? You have to read the problem and determine the proper order to do the math.

Unfortunately, a 2006 study by the American Institutes for Research revealed that the majority of college students struggle with critical reasoning, reporting that, *"More than 75 percent of students at 2-year colleges and more than 50 percent of students at 4-year colleges… lack the skills to perform complex literacy tasks, such as comparing credit card offers with different interest rates or summarizing the arguments of newspaper editorials."*[17]

One problem may be that people have less real-world experience to critically reason from. For example, a person who has grown up exclusively with lights, an electric stove, and a thermostat, does not relate to energy in the same way that an experienced camper does after collecting firewood to stay warm and cook food. Being directly connected to the energy supply, the outdoorsman develops a physical concept about quantity and sources of energy. The camper is better empowered to critically reason through conflicting energy policies.

Similarly, many people don't realize that flowers have any function other than beauty. They don't understand that flowers are the sexual organs of a plant, that pollination is akin to impregnation, or that a seed is like the embryo of a new plant. Lacking gardening experience, many people have reverted to a nearly magical relationship with food, as noted by author and gardener Barbara Kingsolver. They don't understand where it comes from, or why farmland and soil health is so important. Kingsolver was telling an urban friend that the peas, potatoes, and spinach were up in her garden. Her friend was puzzled, wondering which part of the potato was "up." She was unaware that potatoes grew leaves and stems, leading Kingsolver to speculate that the *"disconnection from natural processes may be at the heart of our country's shift away from believing in evolution. In the past, principles of natural selection and change over time made sense to kids who'd watched it all unfold. Whether or not they knew the terminology, farm families understood the processes well enough to imitate them: culling, selecting, and improving their herds and crops."[18]* Our nation may be in danger of reverting to a mythical worldview if we cannot keep our young people connected with the natural world.

The Nurturing Parent Model

In contrast to the strict father model of parenting associated with mythical processing, sequential processing favors a liberal, nurturing approach to raising a family. Nurturing parents believe children should have a childhood rather than be pressured to act like adults. They want children to develop imaginations and play. In the words of George Lakoff,

> *The primal experience behind this model is one of being cared for and cared about, having one's desires for loving interactions met, living as happily as possible, and deriving meaning from one's community and from caring for and about others.*

> *Through empathizing and interacting positively with their children, parents develop close bonds with children and teach them empathy and responsibility towards others and toward society. Nurturant parents view the family as a community in which children have commitments and responsibilities that grow out of empathy for others. The obedience of children comes out of love and respect for parents, not out of fear of punishment.[19]*

In *Last Child in the Woods*, author Richard Louv noted this distinction between himself and a friend, writing, *"Nick and I have fished together for years, but we are very different men. I have described him as a doubting nineteenth-century father; I am a doubting twenty-first century dad... Nick believes that violence is inevitable, that suffering is redemptive, and that a father must teach his children about the harshness of life by exposing them to that harshness. I believe that, as a parent, it's my job to protect my sons from the brutality of the world for as long as I can."[20]*

Nurturing parents tend to be highly protective of their children. They concern themselves with threats of all kinds, from the obvious dangers of crime and drugs to additional concerns such as diseases, pollution, pesticides, flammable clothes, dangerous toys, cars without seatbelts, and so forth. Nurturing parents can be overprotective, shielding their children against every possible natural and human hazard, to the point of sheltering them from such things as playing unsupervised in the woods.

On the other hand, nurturing parents tend to be indulgent and permissive, allowing children to explore their individuality instead of making them fit a mold. For example, nurturing parents often ask their children what they want to eat, rather than setting the agenda and making them eat whatever is on the plate. In this way, the individuality associated with sequential thinking is role-modeled throughout childhood. Obviously, indulgence can get out of hand; one family I heard about would drive to three different fast food restaurants to please every member of the family. Individuality must be tempered with empathy and compromise.

Government as a Nurturing Parent

In the nation-as-family metaphor, sequential thinkers perceive the role of government as a nurturing parent, with the responsibility to take care of its citizens like children. As a nurturing parent, it is the government's responsibility to provide for the basic needs of the people, including health care, education, and, if need be, food and shelter. In support of individuality, they believe government should embrace multiculturalism and equal rights for all people, regardless of race, gender, or sexual preference. If women and minorities are not being treated as equals, then it is the government's job to provide them the opportunity for self-fulfillment.

Just as nurturing parents are protective of their children, they believe government should be protective of the people, regulating pollution, disease, unsafe products, job hazards, and unscrupulous businessmen. Nurturing parents are also more environmentally aware, advocating government protection of natural resources for future generations. And unlike the tough-love conservatives of the strict father model, nurturing parents believe it is the duty of well-to-do citizens to contribute more in taxes to help those who are more in need.[21]

In terms of education, the sequential worldview protects the rights of children against the physical discipline associated with education in mythical cultures. However, the sequential perspective remains hierarchical in that the teacher possesses knowledge and the student is the recipient of that knowledge. Educational theory is oriented towards finding ways to effectively spoon-feed knowledge to students whether they desire to receive that knowledge or not. Competency tests are required to rate how effectively the knowledge has been transmitted. In the coming chapters we will see this hierarchical approach fade out in favor of allowing children to help envision their own education.

The Multicultural Culture

The more we incorporate sequential processing into our lives, the more likely we are to have an individualistic outlook. If we interact with neighbors of diverse ethnic backgrounds, then we probably won't judge them the way we might if they lived half a world away. We discover that these are real people, and they may become our friends. Our opinions about their beliefs become less rigid, and we see that everyone is entitled to their own viewpoints, even when we disagree. Ultimately, we acknowledge that their claim on the truth is just as legitimate as our own.

In his book *Sidewalks on the Moon*, Iranian architect Nader Khaliki wrote that he was schooled as a conservative Muslim and trained to be a mullah or preacher. However, he also read literature from all over the world, acquiring a more expansive viewpoint. He learned to question everything and seek answers beyond his own faith, of which he wrote, *"I used to go to Orthodox Catholic churches in Tehran in my high school years, since I had a deep belief that God must be everywhere… To me it was simple logic to believe that the God who sent the holy Quran is the same God who sent the holy Bible and the holy Torah."*[22] Although Khalili's book follows his quest to improve housing for the poor, it is also a journal of consciousness. The reader can follow his shift from mythical to sequential thinking, continuing on to additional layers of consciousness described later in this book.

With sequential processing we are less likely to perceive issues in strictly black-and-white terms, such as jobs versus the environment. Rather than being either for or against logging our national forests, for example, we may consider the issue in many shades of grey, that there is truth to both sides, and that perhaps the best answer may be found somewhere in the middle. Through sequential processing it is possible for nations to achieve reasonable compromises without resorting to war to decide who is right or wrong.

Some people might argue differently—that industrialization has facilitated further imperial and corporate conquest to better exploit people and natural resources around the world. However, it should be noted that this *need* for conquest is a holdover from mythical processing, not necessarily endemic to sequential processing. Our culture remains deeply immersed in mythical perspectives, which is the primary drive behind all forms of conquest.

Interestingly, some of the most effective efforts to foster peace in the Middle East have been driven by individuals and non-governmental organizations. For example, before Ariel Sharon came to power in Israel, there were projects that helped Israelis and Palestinians move beyond their ethnic boundaries. Some non-governmental organizations initiated business ventures with the requirement that half the employees were Israeli and half were Palestinian. People worked side by side, where they could make friends with their counterparts and see that they were people like themselves with legitimate hopes and dreams of their own. A similar program for kids taught martial arts to Israeli and Palestinian children together, helping to forge friendships between them. These efforts to unite people were ultimately sabotaged by the maneuverings of governments and political organizations that wanted to preserve a mythical world. As President Eisenhower once said, *"I think that people want peace so much that one of these days government had better get out of their way and let them have it."*

Beyond the Mythical

At times it seems that our society is stuck in a mythical worldview. Our culture has been incrementally shifting towards sequential processing for a long time, but mythical thinking remains a powerful force. We have the cumulative knowledge and experience to move forward, but mythical thinking continues to drive our culture. Perhaps it is because mythical thinking provides a great story to believe in and establishes a code of ethics to live by. It doesn't matter if there is overwhelming evidence documenting evolution; people need a vision to hold onto, something to guide them through life. In contrast, a purely sequential worldview lacks any attractive grand vision. There is no specific code of right and wrong, other than the rule of law. There is no apparent purpose for being, other than by accident. There is no apparent afterlife, just a brief flash in the pan of meaningless existence, and then "poof," it's all over.

Not surprisingly, many sequential thinkers remain religious, but without the fervor of fundamentalists. They might acknowledge evolution, yet still believe in a higher power, a God that exists as an amorphous energy in the universe, and believe that the Bible is open to interpretation. Or they may go to church simply because it is familiar and comfortable, or expected as part of their role in society. One concern, however, is that sequential thinkers tend to legitimize all faiths, a trait not reciprocated by mythical thinkers. Mythical thinkers typically claim that theirs is the only truth and everyone else is wrong, while sequential thinkers have a more individualistic worldview, where everyone has an equal right to believe what they want. Sequential thinkers indirectly endorse a mythical worldview, while watering down the strengths of their own views. This unintentional endorsement can skew election results towards the religious right.

Compounding the election issue, mythical thinkers are often driven by a common vision and a black-and-white set of values. Sequential thinkers, however, are diverse and individualistic, lacking a clear set of values to unite them. Compared to a flock of truly faithful mythical thinkers, getting sequential thinkers to the polls is more like herding cats, so mythical thinkers are disproportionately favored in elections. While these are significant obstacles, the challenge of moving beyond mythical thinking isn't as daunting as it seems.

In writing this book, it is my hope that readers will be able to initiate a dialogue about the different modes of processing reality. Becoming aware of our thought processes is an essential step towards becoming a sentient species. With awareness of the way we operate, we can solidify more resourceful worldviews within our society and shift power away from mythical extremes. When we achieve that in America, it will change the way we interact with and influence the world.

I am not suggesting we abandon religions or close down our churches. On the contrary, churches provide an essential community of support to help people through transitional moments in life such as marriage or death. Churches provide a sense of community and stability. Instead, I simply propose that religions should reflect the reality of the world we live in, as they did in the past.

To his credit, Pope John Paul II apologized in 1992 for the condemnation and house arrest of Galileo in the 1600s, which he suffered for his claim that the earth moved around the sun. The Pope also apologized for burning numerous scientists at the stake, and went so far as to acknowledge evolution in 1996, stating that *"new knowledge has led to the recognition of the theory of evolution as more than a hypothesis. It is indeed remarkable that this theory has been progressively accepted by researchers, following a series of discoveries in various fields of knowledge. The convergence, neither sought nor fabricated, of the results of work that was conducted independently is in itself a significant argument in favor of this theory."[23]*

The Church could also learn from some of its open-minded pastors, such as the late Father John Kirsch, who was an elk biologist before entering the priesthood. His lifetime of experience with nature combined with his theological views to form a mystical experience of the world around him. Although his philosophies were unorthodox by Vatican standards, Kirsch obtained permission from his bishop to establish the Living Water Contemplative Center to guide people on spiritual explorations in nature. No center was physically built for it, but Father John became the center himself, intermittently leading individuals on contemplative nature walks. In his seventies and eighties he was leading people to the top of ten-thousand-foot peaks in southwest Montana.[24] I joined Father John on some of his excursions. When he later conducted our wedding, he wore hiking boots under his robe, a symbol of individuality by this open-minded man.

As one who was raised Catholic, I wish to see the Vatican fully embrace science as an ally in discovering the mysteries of the cosmos. I also wish the Pope would encourage world peace by reaching out to all faiths in reciprocal recognition. Whether or not the Pope could convince Muslims, Hindus, or Buddhists to stand with him in a universal call for peace, the invitation wouldn't go unnoticed. The fact that the Vatican has not yet made a substantial effort towards reconciliation with other faiths greatly implies that the Church lacks commitment to peace.

Sequential Shortcomings

While religions need to embrace science to better understand the nature of the universe, science also needs to look beyond its own dogma to explore the possibility that there may be more to our existence than can be found in a Petri dish or an atom smasher. Like the nineteen-year-old who has it all figured out and doesn't need any more advice, science has tried to leave home without looking back.

There is a tendency among sequential thinkers, as with any worldview, to assume that theirs is the only legitimate view. Especially among scientists who are trained to think through problems sequentially using the scientific method, there is a tendency to dismiss phenomena that do not fit the universe as it has been defined. Science is supposed to be objective, which would suggest that it is equally open to all possibilities, but the reality is that alternative viewpoints are often either dismissed or scorned, even when those alternatives are put forth by fellow scientists who have a new explanation for something that was presumed to be known already. In his book *The Structure of Scientific Revolutions*, Thomas Kuhn writes, *"No part of the aim of normal science is to call forth new phenomena; indeed those that will not fit the box are often not seen at all. Nor do scientists normally aim to invent new theories, and they are often intolerant of those invented by others. Instead, normal scientific research is directed to the articulation of those phenomena and theories that the [existing] paradigm already supplies."[25]* On the other hand, perhaps the greatest benefit of sequential processing is that we can see how much we *don't know* and cannot easily explain about the universe, which ultimately forces us to try new ways of thinking.

Sequential processing is great for linear processes, such as designing better products, but one of its shortcomings is that environmental and social problems are often too complex for linear solutions. For example, modern agriculture is inherently sequential. Rich ecosystems are plowed under and replaced with rows of monoculture crops. Fertilizer is used to grow the crops and pesticides are sprayed to kill the bugs and weeds. Sequential farming results in bountiful harvests to send to market, but at the cost of poisoning the environment and eroding away the topsoil. We are sending our farmlands on a linear trip downriver to the ocean. Besides being unsustainable, since we are steadily losing soil, the dirt and pesticides create a dead zone in the estuaries where the rivers enter the ocean. Sequential processing is unable to deal with problems of this complexity.

Science brought itself to the boundaries of its own limitations, finding it impossible to control every variable when dealing with extremely complex systems, such as the functioning of ecosystems, making a climate model, or understanding connections between the health of the human mind and body.

In terms of consciousness and worldviews, the progression we have followed (preconscious > magical > mythical > sequential) serves as a logical, sequential means of explaining human behavior throughout human history up to present times. But because it is a sequence, it ultimately requires that we ask what comes next in the sequence. Is there anything beyond sequential processing, or have we already found the ultimate definition of reality? In the next two chapters we go beyond the sequential to explore two emerging levels of consciousness: systems and holistic processing.

Suggested Reading

    Or Perish in the Attempt by David J. Peck. From 1804 to 1806 the Lewis and Clark expedition traveled by boat, horseback, and foot from Saint Louis up the Missouri River to the Pacific Ocean and back. David Peck critiqued the mythical/magical medicine of the expedition from a modern medical perspective. The book is written from a distinctly sequential worldview, in which Peck dismisses the expedition's techniques as doing more harm than good, while praising the benefits of modern medicine. However, it should be acknowledged that the expedition survived injuries and ailments that may have thwarted a modern crew with modern medicine. Also, Peck fails to acknowledge that his medical practice will also seem equally primitive from a future perspective.

—Eleven—

Systems Processing

Informational Networks and Personal Destiny

"In the early 1950s, the Dayak people in Borneo had malaria. The World Health Organization had a solution: spray DDT. They did; mosquitoes died; malaria declined; so far, so good. But there were side effects. House roofs started falling down on people's heads, because the DDT also killed tiny parasitic wasps that had previously controlled thatch-eating caterpillars. The colonial government gave people sheet-metal roofs, but the noise of the tropical rain on the tin roofs kept people awake. Meanwhile, the DDT-poisoned bugs were eaten by geckos, which were eaten by cats. The DDT built up in the food chain and killed the cats. Without the cats, the rats flourished and multiplied. Soon the World Health Organization was threatened with potential outbreaks of typhus and plague, and had to call in RAF Singapore to conduct Operation Cat Drop—parachuting a great many live cats into Borneo."

—Amory Lovins, Rocky Mountain Institute[1]

Systems thinking arose from the field of systems dynamics, founded in 1956 at the Massachusetts Institute of Technology (MIT) to provide a better means of understanding the interactions of complex systems based on feedback loops. It is an integrated approach that results in a dramatically different interpretation of reality from sequential processing.

In a sequential world, an architect designs a house and passes it along to a heating contractor to calculate the size of the required heating and cooling system. In systems thinking, however, all aspects of house design are considered together, such that money invested in efficient design might allow a less costly heating system or none at all. In this approach, one might construct a map of the system to determine leverage points where change could have the greatest impact. Systems processing makes it possible to think laterally about issues in order to come up with solutions from completely new angles.

Snapshot: Systems Processing

Technology: Computers, information, networking.

Origin: Described at MIT in 1956.

Logic: Interconnected webs, integrated design.

Perspective: Self is an object, purpose and morality are self-determined.

Culture: Transnational networking, cyberspace, virtual reality.

Social-Political Structure: Collaborative government, United Nations.

Notable People: Amory Lovins, Bill Gates, Steve Jobs, Al Gore, Buckminster Fuller.

Television/Movies: *Seinfeld, CSI, Crash, Magnolia, Castaway, The Island, Pulp Fiction.*

Systems thinking is characteristic of the Information Age, the cause and the effect of creating interconnected communications networks. Informational societies are associated with a high level of intermingling among cultures and the global sharing of ideas. Citizens of informational societies begin to see themselves as malleable entities capable of choosing their own behaviors rather than reacting automatically to outside events. Issues and solutions are perceived in complex, interconnected ways, rather than in black-and-white or even shades of grey. Cause and effect is not perceived as linear, but involves multiple feedback loops and unintended consequences.

Web Logic

Systems processing was alien to the general public when personal computers first became popular in the 1980s. Entrepreneurs developed and marketed their products sequentially, and employees sought to work their way up corporate ladders one rung at a time. Software was designed for specific tasks and marketed toward a narrowly targeted audience, such as image processing for the publishing industry. That changed when Bill Gates developed Microsoft Windows and forged alliances to integrate Windows with other applications and pre-install it on new computers. Before long, Microsoft Windows was virtually required for anyone to operate a computer, and Bill Gates soon became the richest man in the world.

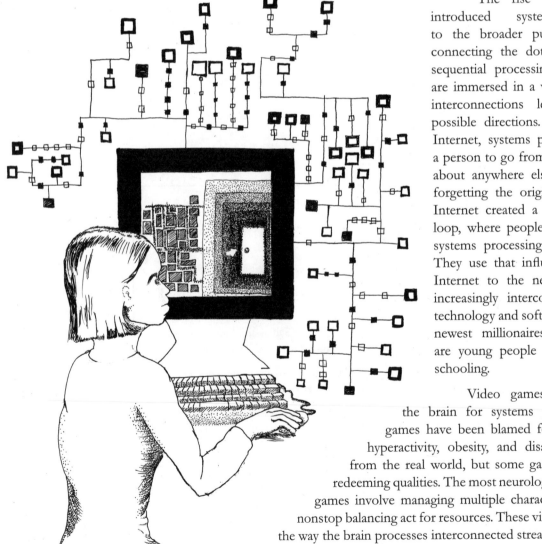

The rise of the Internet introduced systems processing to the broader public. Instead of connecting the dots in a line with sequential processing, young people are immersed in a world of web-like interconnections leading in many possible directions. Like surfing the Internet, systems processing enables a person to go from one point to just about anywhere else, at the risk of forgetting the original mission. The Internet created a positive feedback loop, where people mimic and learn systems processing on the Internet. They use that influence to take the Internet to the next level, creating increasingly interconnected web-like technology and software. Many of our newest millionaires and billionaires are young people with little formal schooling.

Video games also help wire the brain for systems processing. Video games have been blamed for contributing to hyperactivity, obesity, and disassociating people from the real world, but some games do have their redeeming qualities. The most neurologically constructive games involve managing multiple characters or cities in a nonstop balancing act for resources. These virtual worlds mirror the way the brain processes interconnected streams of information in the physical world.

In daily life we run mental simulations of possible actions in our minds before we act. Video games externalize the process, giving players the opportunity to try different scenarios to solve problems. The rules may be different, but video gamers use the same neurocircuitry for processing real situations. Studies of video gamers in comparison to nongamers have shown that gamers are consistently more social, more confident, and more comfortable solving problems creatively, and their attention spans are just as long.[2] While too much video gaming cannot be healthy for anyone, it is reassuring to know that time spent at the game console may not be a complete waste. Playing video games may become a virtual necessity for future generations to simulate the complex types of problems they will encounter as adults, provided that their virtual experiences are balanced by physical experiences in the real world.

Integrated Design

Businesses are often faced with seemingly insurmountable problems when they decide to pursue sustainable paths. A common approach is to sequentially design products or build a factory first and then wonder what could be done to make the products and processing more environmentally friendly, leaving sustainability as an afterthought. This approach is akin baking a cake without leavening, then trying to add baking powder after the fact—it is problematic and costly!

Businesses attempting to evolve efficient products from inherently inefficient predecessors run into similar problems. For instance, basic design concepts for modern cars can be traced back to the Model T. All advances since then have been incremental improvements band-aided over each other. According to Rocky Mountain Institute, *"Cars are extremely complicated, so automotive engineers and designers specialize. Their job is to make a given component or subsystem the best it can be. This is how the modern automobile has evolved, through an incremental process of small improvements to individual components, without much change to the overall concept. The trouble is, optimizing isolated parts often "pessimizes" the whole: integration and synergy are lost; complexity, oversizing, and inefficiency abound. What's lacking is a sense of the big picture, the whole system."[3]*

We have the necessary technology to build quality passenger cars that get 150 miles to the gallon. It is not that difficult to do, and auto manufacturers have built working prototypes using sleek designs, ultralight carbon fiber construction, and hybrid engines—all while testifying to Congress against raising mileage standards, since such cars cannot be built. The problem is that it is impractical to evolve 150-mpg cars from a system that is currently producing 25-mpg cars. Every part of the car, and every part of the car factory, needs to be redesigned and built from scratch. In other words, the transition to high-efficiency cars must be *"revolutionary, rather than evolutionary,"* as Amory Lovins often points out. Unfortunately, instead of starting from scratch, automakers pursue an incremental approach to the problem, by modifying existing cars with hybrid engines. The result is cars that get 50 to 70 mpg, which is better than 25 mpg, but a far cry from 150 mpg. The first companies to bring ultra-efficient cars to market may not be traditional automakers, but new start-ups that are unhindered by preconceived notions about automotive design. For instance, several start-up companies are developing high-efficiency cars propelled by compressed air.

Architects and home builders also talk about going green but apply a sequential approach, attempting to evolve efficient houses from inherently inefficient traditions. Paradoxically, our ancestors intuitively achieved systems-like results in the architecture of pueblos, cliff dwellings, and other indigenous structures. Houses were built of local materials, oriented to take advantage of solar heating, and typically designed to facilitate natural cooling. They did not apply systems thinking as we know it, but subconsciously applied intuitive principles that seemed to work. These behaviors were mimicked from generation to generation and improved upon with accumulated experience.

Modern architecture is also driven by mimicry with little conscious thought, but builders lost the link to the landscape and energy efficiency. Instead, houses are strewn about the landscape at random. Many houses in Montana are built on the north-facing slope of hills in spite of our six-month-long winters. The sun sits low on the horizon, and may not be visible at all when needed for solar input and psychological well-being. Houses are built in prime wildlife habitat, in subdivisions with names like "Elk Meadows," describing what was bulldozed for the development. Houses are built with highly processed materials shipped over long distances. I am appalled to see the complete lack of attention to local materials, energy efficiency, solar design, or commonsense land planning.

Most houses are built with little regard for solar orientation, costing their owners tens of thousands of dollars in heating bills that could be avoided just by rearranging the blueprint. The same is true for air conditioning systems, which are installed to mechanically make up for the lack of planning. Although absurd, such construction is considered completely normal. Builders work like automatons, constructing house after house without conscious thought. The same could be said for customers who compare prices on different brands of tuna at the grocery store, but think nothing of buying a house that will cost hundreds or thousands of dollars every year for unnecessary heating and cooling. People have learned to expect large utility bills—an assumption that is passed down through generations hand-in-hand with poor building practices.

In a world with dwindling resources and a destabilizing climate, we need to wean ourselves off fossil fuels completely and immediately. Imagine what the world would be like if every house were so efficient that it didn't need a heating or cooling system at all, and so efficient that it could cost-effectively generate its own electricity from a few solar panels on the roof. If houses had been built efficiently in the past, then our energy woes and global warming would be minor problems today. Fortunately, some builders are constructing more efficient homes, but unfortunately these houses are usually more expensive and still require heating systems.

As noted earlier, architects design houses, then forward the plans to engineers to calculate the size of the furnace or boiler required to heat the space. To design for greater efficiency, architects approach the issue sequentially, relying on familiar construction techniques. For example, four-inch walls become six-inch walls, requiring more wood and insulation. However, the law of diminishing returns dictates that each additional layer of insulation costs just as much as the previous layer, yet conserves less energy. A six-inch wall is better than a four-inch wall, but not efficient enough to entirely eliminate the need for a furnace, while an eight-inch wall is prohibitively expensive. Rather than making thicker walls, builders install a furnace to make up the difference. The finished house costs more than standard construction, yet still depends on fossil fuels.

Systems processing frees us from sequentially trying to evolve a better product or solution from an existing one. Instead, we start with a clean slate and consider all possible designs and all possible building materials to design a house that costs less than conventional construction and needs no furnace at all. The house is designed as a whole system, rather than as a collection of unrelated parts. Renee and I applied this kind of whole-system thinking towards designing our home. Without prior experience, we successfully built a 2,300-square-foot passive solar stone and log home with minimal energy needs, all for about the cost of a new car. Our electric bill was so low that we were later able to add solar panels to generate all our electricity.

Unfortunately, while neither the plumbing nor the orange trees are in danger of freezing if we lock up the house and leave for the winter, we are still dependent on firewood to warm the place up when we come home. Furthermore, since we didn't plan the solar water heater into the house, we built it separately in the yard, which was more expensive and less efficient. The photovoltaic panels we use to generate electricity are also beside the house rather than integrated into its architecture. It is for these reasons that I am working to take integrated building design to the next level.

The house we are currently building is intended to be 100 percent passive solar, without the need for firewood or fossil fuels for supplementary heating. In a nutshell it works like this: The walls and roof are superinsulated with scrap insulation free from a local factory, with no studs or rafters cutting through the insulation. All the doorways have airlocks, such that one must enter a porch or greenhouse before coming into the house. Most of the windows face south for free passive solar energy. Solar water heaters are built into the face of the greenhouse so that hot water thermosiphons to a tank upstairs without need for a pump. While primarily intended to heat water for faucets and showers, excess solar hot water can be pumped through tubing in the basement floor. The warm mass of the basement floor is intended to keep the house warm through cold, cloudy days. In addition, a large section of the roof is oriented southward and sloped at the ideal angle to eventually add solar electric panels. That way the panels will look like they belong on the house, rather than being tacked on afterwards.

We continue to see new ways to increase energy efficiency as we build the house. I documented past projects and our latest ideas for "what we would do next time" in my book *Living Homes: Integrated Design and Construction.* Each time we build a house, I update the book with what works and what doesn't. It seems astonishing that a handful of like-minded individuals should have to conduct this basic research in the first place. The need for self-sufficient houses is obvious. The reason houses continue to be built poorly is only because systems processing is still new, and the old ways of building are deeply entrenched in our culture.

Productivity

There is a direct relationship between higher levels of consciousness and increased productivity and efficiency. For example, consider the history of food production through the levels of consciousness. In primitive cultures, food production can be very magical. Walk through the woods and an edible plant or an animal seems to magically appear. In agricultural societies, people plant crops, tend livestock, and pray to mythical gods for good rains and a bountiful harvest.

In an industrial society, farming is a sequential process that involves controlling variables to achieve high yields: plowing, planting, fertilizing, irrigating, and spraying pesticides—doing everything possible to control the outcome. Agribusiness is expensive and usually generates waste, such as cornhusks or cornstalks, but the farmer hopes to deliver a product at a price sufficient to recover expenses and make a profit. In terms of livestock, a feedlot owner might buy hay and grain for the cows but end up with great piles of manure waste. This waste has to be disposed of properly to avoid leaching nitrates into the groundwater.

Systems processing leads to more interconnected operations. The farmer might dedicate some acreage to corn and some to cattle pasture. The cows are fattened on the corn, and the manure is returned to the fields to grow more corn. The farmer saves money on fertilizer, waste disposal, and feed. Making web-like connections increases the efficiency and decreases waste.

Systems processing enables an interconnected approach to any task. Instead of having single purpose goals, such as, "I'm driving to the store to rent a video," we have multipurpose, integrated goals, such as, "and along the way, I'm going to take the cardboard and bottles to the recycling center, get a gallon of milk, and make a bank deposit." Although such thinking is obvious and necessary for many parents, it is shocking how many adults do not operate that way. It is common to hear of people driving five miles for a gallon of milk or sixty miles to buy a shirt.

A trip to town can be made more efficient by avoiding it entirely. It is easy to fixate on a single goal and organize a trip to town just to get a new cutting blade for the lawnmower. However, it may be a better allocation of time and resources to do another project now and procrastinate buying the blade until it is necessary to drive to town for something else. One can also constructively procrastinate projects until the required materials arrive on their own. For example, rather than rushing out to buy new 2 x 4s for a building project, secondhand scraps will often turn up for free with enough patience.

For the first seven years of our marriage, Renee and I typically drove sixty miles to town twice each week to run errands. Even a short list seemed to consume an entire day. I didn't realize we were spending one hundred days per year driving to town and back until we adopted our children. I had to choose between writing, being a parent, or running errands. By asking what was truly necessary, I reduced my trips to town to one day every six weeks, giving me ninety additional days per year for more rewarding activities. Renee continued going to town about once a week to visit family; she often picked up the supplies I needed.

Governments are notorious for a lack of systems processing. Each issue, such as an unsightly hole in the ground, is considered a problem by itself, so government programs are likely to dig another unsightly hole in order to get the necessary fill material to eliminate the first one. Governments typically attack a problem by itself without considering impacts of the "solution," such as using DDT to kill mosquitoes.

Systems thinkers, however, talk of "win-win" situations, or even "win-win-win-win" situations, in which one action results in many different benefits, or two separate problems are used to solve each other. For instance, I once built a Mandan-style earthlodge on our property for the primitive skills classes we offer. It was a circular shelter twenty-three feet in diameter, built of poles covered with straw and dirt. The earthlodge had an opening in the peak over a central fire pit. It was a great shelter for several years until rot set into the poles, making it unsafe to use. Bulldozing the lodge would have created an impossible mess of mixed poles and dirt, so I put off doing anything until a better solution came along. Finally, my brother reshingled the local church and needed to dispose of the old wooden shingles. He considered burning the shingles in his driveway (you can do things like that in a small town), but the shingles would have blown all over town before he had suitable weather for a burn. Fortunately, his problem solved my problem. We piled the shingles in the earthlodge, creating a mound two feet deep around the inside. The shingles served as the kindling needed to consume the wooden poles. I waited for a snowy winter day to light the match.

The burn was spectacular, with a twenty-foot-high torch coming out the smoke hole, followed by the collapse of the dome. The dirt smoldered for a month, but all I had to do afterwards was to rake the site smooth. Instead of two separate and potentially costly disposal problems, our problems solved each other for zero cost and essentially zero labor. In hindsight, we could have harnessed the heat for a constructive purpose, such as firing pottery. That's the power and benefit of systems thinking. It enables one to achieve personal and business goals more effectively than perceiving each problem as a separate issue.

From a sequential perspective, rising population and increasing demand for electricity seems to require more power plants and more energy. But from a systems perspective, energy conservation also increases supply, thereby avoiding the need to build new power plants. A standard 100-watt incandescent lightbulb can be replaced with an equally bright 30-watt compact fluorescent bulb. Switching bulbs saves 70 watts of electricity that can be used elsewhere, effectively increasing the supply. Newer LED lightbulbs save even more energy. Amory Lovins of Rocky Mountain Institute in Colorado coined the term "negawatts," referring to energy supplied through conservation. In the 1980s Lovins determined that we could utilize energy efficient technologies to cut our carbon emissions in half for less cost than we were spending on power. Dollars saved through conservation are equal to profit, as Benjamin Franklin understood when he said, *"A penny saved is a penny earned."* Amory Lovins was one of my primary mentors when I was a young adult. I devoured his writing and role-modeled systems thinking until I learned to operate that way myself.

A favorite mental exercise is to look at opportunities to reduce waste wherever I go. For example, the local dump accumulates enough wood waste in the form of tree branches and boards to generate nearly as much electricity as the town of six hundred people consumes. But all that energy goes up in smoke as the pile is torched a few times each year. This wasted resource is an obvious potential business opportunity. I notice similar unused or underutilized resources just about everywhere I go—old trailer houses that could be recycled, useful building waste at construction sites, and free piles of wood chips, manure, lumber, and rocks. The point is that engaging in mental exercises enhances your neural network for systems processing, even if you reject ninety-nine percent of your ideas.

When we take our kids out for fast food, I find myself thoroughly dissatisfied with the quality of the food, and shocked by the amount of waste. I rethink the fast-food system, imagining ways to provide better quality fare without the waste. There is clearly a market for such a business. Over the years I have thought of about fifty "green" businesses and products that I would like to bring to market. However, recognizing that I cannot do everything myself, we launched our Green University® program with the mission to mentor other people in launching their own green businesses.

Systems-level creativity is exploding across our culture in response to rising fuel costs and concern over global warming. It is astonishing to witness the rapid pace of innovation as entrepreneurs design more efficient cars, lightbulbs, and appliances, and develop new and less costly ways to harness electricity from sunshine, wind, and ocean waves. These and more emerging technologies will enable our species to rapidly reduce and potentially eliminate our carbon emissions to abate global warming. With systems processing we can easily create a sustainable civilization. Unfortunately, the road to sustainability may be shockingly inefficient.

The ideal way to build a sustainable civilization is to make everything inherently efficient, such that buildings conserve water and electricity and require no heating or cooling. With intelligent architecture, it is easy to add a few solar panels to achieve self-sufficiency. However, the greater likelihood is that we will massproduce our way to sustainability by bulldozing rural landscapes for solar and wind developments and blanketing every roof with masses of solar panels.

135

The irony is that there is a difference between creating a sustainable civilization versus achieving a sustainable environment. Systems processing could enable us to create a sustainable civilization on the moon in the total absence of life. That is the risk of systems processing, that we might create a sustainable civilization while destroying half of all life on earth. As we will discover in the following chapter, true sustainability requires a more holistic approach to decision making.

The Self as an Object

Systems processing changes the way we perceive the world, and it also changes the way we perceive ourselves. We begin to see the self as a system, like an object that can be manipulated. This perception is the beginning of true sentience. Instead of behaviors being automatic reactions to outside events, we develop the ability to choose our own programming. We become fully cognizant of our behaviors for the first time.

It is easy to go through life as a perpetual victim, allowing one's internal state to be dictated by actions of other people. Many people go through life reacting to everyone and everything without having much control over their own behaviors. At the magical level, people tend to exist in first person, largely oblivious to the perspective of others. In mythical processing people improve their ability to shift to second person, to see themselves through the eyes of other people within their ethnic group. At the sequential level they develop the ability to step outside of themselves into third person to objectively assess multiple sides of an issue. This third-person perspective facilitates the transition to systems processing, where individuals begin to perceive themselves as a programmable object.

Often, we act as if other people control our thoughts and feelings, such as when we complain, *"You make me so angry."* But when we learn to see the self as a system, we realize that anger is one of many possible choices, and nobody can make us feel that way. Only we are responsible for how we choose to act in any situation. Many survivors of Hitler's concentration camps came to this realization. Regardless of how badly they were treated, how much the Nazi's tried to humiliate and dehumanize them, or how little control Jewish prisoners had over the fate of their physical bodies, there was nothing the Nazi's could do to control the prisoners' outlook on life. Their thoughts and feelings were entirely of their own choosing regardless of how bleak circumstances were on the outside.

In *The Teachings of Don Juan: A Yaqui Way of Knowledge* and other books by Carlos Castaneda, Don Juan sent Castaneda on psychedelic experiences to break him free of his mental habits, to demonstrate that instead of being a puppet to circumstances, Castaneda could determine his own actions, which Don Juan referred to as his "controlled folly." Suppose we are being yelled at. We might react and yell back without thinking through our actions. But with controlled folly, we can access a menu of choices and determine which choice might be the most desirable for the situation. One choice is to yell back. Another choice would be to shift from a confrontational face-off to a collaborative position, such that we are both looking in the same direction as we discuss the problem. We could also run away, or pick some other choice. If we decide that the best choice is to get angry, then anger is our controlled folly. In other words, instead of being angry, we would act angry. That is a different ballgame than reacting without thinking and letting other people control our behaviors.

Learning to consciously choose one's own programming is a great challenge. With a computer we can input new programming, and it will immediately do whatever it is programmed to do. To rewrite our own programming, we literally have to grow new neural pathways, while letting go of the old ones. For example, if other people make us angry, then our goal is to find more resourceful ways to respond. We need to consciously switch from automatic to manual programming in tense situations. That is easier said than done. However, with practice, we can learn to see the self as a system that can be reprogrammed at will.

In his book *The Power of Now,* author Eckart Tolle suggests practicing with the little things, such as *"the car alarm, the dog barking, the children screaming, the traffic jam. Instead of having a wall of resistance inside you that gets constantly and painfully hit by things that 'should not be happening,' let everything pass through you. Somebody says something to you that is rude or designed to hurt. Instead of going into unconscious reaction and negativity, such as an attack, defense, or withdrawal, you let it pass right through you. Offer no resistance. It is as if there is nobody there to get hurt anymore. That is forgiveness. In this way, you become invulnerable. You can still tell that person that his or her behavior is unacceptable, if that is what you choose to do. But that person no longer has the power to control your inner state."[4]*

One of the most influential factors in learning to see myself as a reprogrammable system was that my mother never let me say, "I can't." Whenever I said I couldn't do something, she would put it back on me and say, "You can't, or you won't?" Or she would say, "What stops you?" Seemingly insurmountable tasks were broken down into many individual steps of "I can." She made me evaluate every use of the phrase until I could plainly see that saying "I can't" was a personal choice, or at least a response to a large project that hadn't yet been broken down into bite-sized chunks. On the one hand, it helped me to detach from my personal ego, to see myself as an object that could be reprogrammed at will. On the other hand, I could be accused of having a boundless ego, because to me, anything is possible. I cannot even say "I can't" to a task as large as changing the world. It is simply a project that can be broken down into many specific tasks that are each physically possible to accomplish.

Overall, Americans utilize a combination of sequential and mythical processing for most situations, but sometimes access magical and systems processing for other issues. An individual who has grown up with the Internet and mimicked systems processing may be very talented at systems-related work, yet childhood traumas may keep him psychologically locked in first or second person, unable to objectively evaluate or modify his own behaviors.

It is important to note that successful reprogramming only comes with the genuine desire for change. We all have our shortcomings and limitations, and just because we learn to rewrite some of our programming doesn't inherently mean that we will become flawless human beings. With each obnoxious or harmful behavior, we have to decide if we really want to let go and change that programming.

Systems Culture

Imagine the challenges teenagers face as they mature. In a mythical society there is pressure to conform to one's ethnic culture. If everyone wears school uniforms or follows the same basic fashion, each unique individual must go through the mold to fit society's expectations. A teenager in American culture grows up mimicking both the conformity of mythical processing and the individuality that is characteristic of sequential processing. The first challenge is that there isn't just one model to conform to, but many diverse cliques at school: jocks, geeks, nerds, preppies, goths, punks, and others. A teen may drift towards a particular clique, mimicking that look and behavior among peers, while possibly toning it down around parents. There is enormous pressure to conform to a peer group, as well as enormous pressure to distinguish herself as an individual. To put it another way, the teen has to distinguish herself as an individual in a way that conforms to her peer group!

Most teen mimicry is relatively harmless, aside from the emotional pressures. Teens try to walk the walk and talk the talk to meet the current definition of cool. However, since there is no fixed model of cool, teens merely mimic each other mimicking each other, like a reflected image bouncing around in a house of mirrors without an original source. Teens must mimic carefully to conform to their peer groups, without it being obvious that they are mimicking at all, and then they must find an "edge" to be slightly more cool in an individualistic way.

It is challenging to demonstrate individuality while conforming to one's peer group; yet consider the added challenge of trying to define oneself on the greater world stage with seven billion other unique individuals. In the effort to demonstrate individuality, young people can go over the edge, trying to pierce body parts that nobody else has pierced, tattooing the body from head to toe, seeking the most outrageous hair style and color, or doing all of the above at the same time. These youths demonstrate the absurdity of both conformity and individuality. None of it is real. Teens or adults who arrive at this realization are left falling into a great abyss of chaos and emptiness: If none of it is real, then there is no foundation upon which to form a coherent worldview. The apparent lack of a worldview is a worldview in itself.

This emerging perspective is systems culture, similar to existentialism. In this version of reality, the universe has no intrinsic meaning or purpose. The individual is self-programmable and must take responsibility for her own actions and shape her own destiny. She is left floating in a world where preconceived notions of right and wrong as well as notions of purpose and meaning are perceived as cultural fabrications, and none of it is real. Lacking a cultural context for a reference point, the individual must decide for herself what morality is. Like the Creator forming the universe from nothing, the individual must build a foundation beneath her feet from nothing but her own reflection.

Not many people survive the plunge into this abyss of emptiness long enough to establish firm footing. Instead, they drift without a compass, debating all possible versions of morality, never settling on any one version, or they may retreat to a previous worldview with more solid footing.

As more people shift to a systems worldview, it changes our entire culture in positive or negative ways, depending on your perspective. Consider views on sexuality, for example. Sexual desire is driven by primal instincts, as evidenced by the body's remarkable ability to hypnotize the faculties of otherwise rational adults into impulsive behavior, such as extramarital affairs or one-night flings without protection or contraception. However, viewpoints about sexuality fall into predictable patterns associated with the levels of consciousness outlined in this book.

Sex in magical cultures is often associated with magic and power. For instance, on their way up the Missouri River in search of a navigable water route to the Pacific, the forty men of the Lewis and Clark expedition wintered with the Mandan Indians in present-day North Dakota. The native warriors wanted the white man's "power" and sent their wives to sleep with the explorers, believing that the women could serve as a conduit for the magic. The women had sex with the explorers, then had sex with their warrior husbands to transfer the magical power. Many of the Indians were particularly enchanted with Clark's slave York, and one warrior stood guard outside the lodge while York had sex with his wife, to prevent anyone from disturbing them.

In mythical cultures sexuality is typically viewed in black-and-white terms, where sex is permitted only in marriage. Unmarried and extramarital sex is considered sinful. Until recent times, women were stigmatized for adulterous behavior, and children born of such relationships were labeled bastards. Although innocent of wrongdoing themselves, they bore the lifelong stigma of their mother's shame. As barbaric and backwards as that sounds today, such thinking persisted into the middle of the twentieth century.

Sexual liberation in the 1960s was the result of sequential processing, as people began to view sex as part of our evolutionary heritage. Sex was no longer constrained by religious ideas of right and wrong. People enjoy sex recreationally, and many couples choose to live together before committing to marriage. If this lifestyle lacks morality from a mythical perspective, then systems values must seem like evidence of a disintegrating civilization.

From a systems perspective, all human customs are artificially created, and morality is consensual. Right and wrong are subject to individual interpretation. Anything is okay, as long as one's actions are not injurious to other people. Men and women may have "intimate friendships," in which they are good friends and occasionally lovers, without being locked into the traditional roles of a relationship. However, given that individuals are theoretically capable of choosing their feelings, sex is sometimes purely recreational, lacking any relationship at all. On college campuses there is a trend towards consensual one-night stands. Previously, a person who slept around a lot was considered bad, especially a woman. But now, on some campuses, those who *don't* sleep around may be treated as freaks. Unfortunately, achieving detachment is easier said than done, and the recreational experience can leave many people feeling used, compromised, or emotionally scarred, along with the potential for lifelong suffering from a sexually transmitted disease. The holistic worldview, which is the subject of the next chapter, brings goals and values into the decision-making process. Unmarried sex is not considered good or bad, just potentially complicated. Sex isn't wrong, but even with proper protection and the best intentions, it can unnecessarily complicate a person's life.

From a systems perspective, the tradition of marriage is perceived as artificial, which might make one wonder how a couple could have a stable relationship long enough to raise emotionally balanced children. A well-known example is the relationship of Kurt Russell and Goldie Hawn, who have been unwed partners since 1982. Russell described that legally tying the knot might make him feel tied down and bound, to which he might react by wanting freedom. By choosing to remain free, Russell finds that he is perfectly content where he is.

As celebrities, Hawn and Russell have inspired other couples to become devoted partners rather than conventionally bound by marriage. Studies by Marion Willetts, associate professor of sociology at Illinois State University, indicate that these "life partners" are just as committed to their relationships as married people. Some couples choose to remain unmarried as a political statement, noting that marriage discriminates against gay and lesbian couples. Other couples object to marriage based on its origins in patriarchal or mythical culture, and some object to the mixing of church and state in marriage. Interestingly, middle-aged and senior singles, who we might presume to have conservative values, are primarily seeking companions rather than spouses. A survey of 3,500 single Americans aged 40 to 69 by The American Association of Retired Persons (AARP) found that just 8 percent dated in the hope of finding someone to marry, while 49 percent said they were searching for a companion to be with and to talk with.[5]

Consensus-Based Parenting

In comparison to the strict father model of parenting in mythical cultures, or the nurturing model favored in sequential cultures, systems processing favors parenting by consensus. The strict father model is strongly hierarchical, the nurturing model less so, while the consensus approach to parenting recognizes children almost as equals.

According to humanist psychologist Carl Rogers (1902–1987), *"These parents have a new way of dealing with the child, from infancy through late adolescence. His earliest tears and wails, his beginning smiles and his mouthing of sounds are efforts to communicate, and an earnest and respectful attention is given to those primitive communications. The effort is also made to allow the child the right to choose, in any situation in which he seems capable of bearing the consequences of his choice. This is an expanding process, in which increasing autonomy is given to the child and adolescent, autonomy bounded only by the feelings of those who are close to the youngster. If this sounds like a completely child-centered family, it is not. The parent has feelings and attitudes too, and tries to communicate these to the child in a way this smaller person can understand."*[6]

In consensus-based parenting, the entire family is involved in decision making and every viewpoint is considered. A conscious effort is made to reach decisions that work for the entire family. Consensus-based parenting is effective for teaching communication skills, since each person takes the time to hear what the others have to say. The challenge to parenting by consensus is that it is easier said than done. Simple decisions, such as where to eat, or what to do as a family, can evolve into extended conversations to generate mutually satisfying answers. The larger the family, the greater the challenge to achieve consensus. It is much easier to impose decisions, telling the kids, *"Load up, we're going to the beach today."*

In terms of morals and discipline, the consensus-based systems approach requires parents to trust that their children are basically good and desire to make positive choices. Poor choices are cause for discussion rather than discipline. The trust between parents and children is dramatically different than the strict father model, in which kids feel compelled to hide things from their parents to avoid getting busted. In other words, learning to trust one's children is the easy part. The challenge is for parents to demonstrate to their children that they can be trusted. If the child trusts his parents enough to be open and honest with them about anything, then a family is able to function as a team of equals. In other words, the burden is on the parents to prove themselves trustworthy.

Renee and I have applied a consensus approach to parenting with varying levels of success. In the beginning, we held many "family meetings" to talk about issues and goals, though it was challenging to facilitate the meetings rather than to dictate them. Usually the meetings would drag on too long, until the kids were squirrelly. We abandoned the meetings after three and half years, but we always try to be reasonable and achieve consensus in less formal formats.

The greatest obstacle is proving ourselves trustworthy, so that our children feel safe talking to us. It is easy to revert to discipline and assign consequences for poor behavior. I do not intend to imply that there should never be consequences for bad behavior, but only that those consequences need to be discussed and agreed upon by the child. Through effective communication, the child needs to see his behavior through the eyes of other people to understand his error. Only then can he agree that a consequence, such as no computer time for a week, is a reasonable and acceptable way to acknowledge that it was a poor choice. The same standard of conduct and discipline must apply equally to the parents.

The biggest challenge we have faced as parents is that, since our daughters were older when we adopted them, we were forced to face our shortcomings on an accelerated schedule. We had to learn to listen deeply to our children, to acknowledge when they were right and we were wrong, and at times apologize for our own poor choices. We are not infallible as parents, and that is the biggest obstacle to building trust for children to feel like they can safely talk about anything.

Consensus-Based Education and Government

In discussing the nation-as-family metaphor we noted that the parental model favored at home becomes the model favored in government. Strict father households lead to black-and-white, tough-love policies in government. Nurturing households lead to supportive programs for people that need a hand up. By extension, consensus parenting leads to consensus-based education and government. For example, according to Carl Rogers in his book *Freedom to Learn*:

> *The traditional teacher—the good traditional teacher—asks her or himself questions of this sort: "What do I think would be good for a student to learn at this particular age and level of competence? How can I plan a proper curriculum for this student? How can I inculcate motivation to learn this curriculum? How can I instruct in such a way that he or she will gain the knowledge that should be gained? How can I best set an examination to see whether this knowledge has actually been taken in?*
>
> *On the other hand, the facilitator of learning asks questions such as these, not of self, but of the students: "What do you want to learn? What things puzzle you? What are you curious about? What issues concern you? What problems do you wish you could solve?" When he or she has the answers to these questions, further questions follow. "Now how can I help him or her find the resources—the people, the experiences, the learning facilities, the books, the knowledge in myself—which will help them learn in ways that will provide answers to the things that concern them, the things they are eager to learn?" And, then later, "How can I help them evaluate their own progress and set future learning goals based on this self-evaluation?"*[7]

Of his own experiences as a facilitator, Rogers wrote, *"To my surprise, I found that my classrooms became more exciting places of learning as I ceased to be a teacher. It wasn't easy. It happened rather gradually, but as I began to trust students, I found they did incredible things in the course, in blossoming out as growing human beings. Most of all they gave me courage to be myself more freely, and this led to profound interaction. They told me their feelings, they raised questions I had never thought about. I began to sparkle with emerging ideas that were new and exciting to me, but also, I found, to them."*[8] In the consensus-based approach to education, students are usually asked to grade themselves. In this system, when there is a disagreement between teacher and student over a grade, it is usually because the teacher thinks the student deserves a better grade.

In terms of government policy, consensus building is common for achieving citizen input on many public programs. I have attended numerous forums sponsored by government agencies or non-profit organizations on topics such as land-use planning, weed management, and programs to promote sustainable living. Typically, each forum involves breaking into small groups to brainstorm possible solutions. These ideas are reported back to the larger group, then voted on to decide which ideas to pursue in greater depth. Consensus building seems like a fair and democratic system to involve everyone while quickly identifying the most promising ideas for additional development, and compared to traditional models for solving problems, it is a monumental step forward. However, two key problems remain.

First, other than popularity, there are no guidelines to distinguish between good and bad ideas, so voting can kill the best ideas. Second, the sessions typically lack clear goals or may be based on negative goals. For example, consider generating ideas to control weeds, deal with teenage drug abuse, or fight terrorism. These goals are all stated in negative terms. The negative goal of weed control favors taking actions against them, such as using herbicides, rather than doing anything to build soil health and encourage competition from desirable species. Similarly, we may seek to crack down on troubled teens without doing anything to give them positive alternatives. We drop bombs on terrorists, making people fear and hate Americans even more, rather than investing in schools and economic programs to improve quality of life in impoverished countries. These problems can be better addressed with comprehensive goals stated in positive terms, combined with guidelines to objectively evaluate proposed solutions.

In other words, consensus building reveals the great weakness of systems processing; it is a random process without clear goals or values. Consensus building insulates decision making from the irrationality of individuals, but doesn't insulate decision making from the irrationality of the collective consciousness. As demonstrated in the aftermath of 9/11, an entire nation can be swayed in favor of poor choices. In reaction to trauma, America's collective consciousness reverted back to mythical processing, and the consensus was to go to war.

To achieve more holistic choices we need to establish positive goals and a system of testing and implementation guidelines to ensure success. Adding goals and guidelines to systems processing brings us to a new level of consciousness, called holistic processing. As you may sense by now, our species will survive only if we can embrace this holistic way of processing information. Our survival requires that we adopt a holistic model of parenting at home and extend it through the nation-as-family metaphor to a new way of making collaborative decisions.

Suggested Reading

Guns, Germs and Steel by Jared Diamond. Diamond applies a systems perspective to the question of why Europeans and the Chinese were able to advance more quickly in their technological and industrial revolutions than the rest of the world. This fascinating read includes an analysis of the development of different cultures with respect to indigenous domesticable animals, the orientation of landmasses, and other socio-geopolitical factors.

Collapse by Jared Diamond. Jared Diamond takes a sequential and systems viewpoint and tries to answer the question of why some past civilizations collapsed and why some survived. He then draws parallels to our current society, and what we might do to better ensure survival. Issues addressed by Diamond include political events, environmental stewardship, climate, and natural amenities. Case studies include Easter Island, Japan, Greenland, Montana, and more.

The Tipping Point by Malcom Gladwell. Gladwell provides an enlightened systems-level perspective to make positive change in the world and to achieve it with limited resources. For example, a logical, sequential approach to fighting serious crime is to focus resources on prosecuting and rehabilitating the worst offenders, or at best on programs to prevent crimes. However, Gladwell demonstrates that sometimes little things, like fixing broken windows or persistently painting over graffiti, can do more to lower crime rates than putting additional officers on the streets.

—Twelve—

Holistic Processing

Mutualism and Sustainable Prosperity

"No one, it has been said, will ever look at the Moon in the same way again. More significantly can one say that no one will ever look at the earth in the same way. Man had to free himself from earth to perceive both its diminutive place in a solar system and its inestimable value as a life-fostering planet. As earthmen, we may have taken another step into adulthood. We can see our planet earth with detachment, with tenderness, with some shame and pity, but at last also with love."

—*Anne Morrow Lindbergh, Earth Shine*[1]

It is hard to imagine, but prior to the Apollo space program in the 1960s, no human had ever seen the image of the earth against the backdrop of space. Children today are inundated with such imagery and don't think much about it. But the first images from this new perspective had a profound effect on the American psyche. From space there are no visible boundaries or cultural divides, just a beautiful blue marble alone in an infinitely large universe.

From space it is readily apparent that all life is interconnected, that the fate of humanity is directly linked to the fate of planet earth. Many people consider the Apollo program as the beginning of the environmental movement and the inspiration for Earth Day, a day that is recognized and celebrated around the world. The Apollo program gave birth to a new perspective: the holistic worldview.

> Snapshot: Holistic Processing
>
> Technology: Earth-monitoring sensors and satellites, permaculture.
>
> Origin: Apollo space program, ecosystem management.
>
> Logic: Integrated goals and testing, assume wrong until proven otherwise.
>
> Perspective: Strands in web of life.
>
> Culture: Global village.
>
> Social-Political Structure: Goal-oriented, transnational, moral duty reflected in policies.
>
> Notable People: Allan Savory, Bill Mollison.
>
> Television/Movies: *Forrest Gump, The Amateurs, It's a Wonderful Life.*

Holistic processing is similar to systems processing in that reality is perceived as a web of networked connections, but holism is more integrated. We learn to mentally step beyond ourselves, to see our lives as individual strands within the web of life. We become aware that everything we do in life causes a ripple of impacts, big or small, good or bad, to

travel throughout the web and ultimately back to us. For example, consuming gasoline can fund terrorism and contribute to global warming, melting the Arctic ice pack too early for polar bears to hunt seals. Our actions are reflected back to us in the form of an increasingly dangerous and impoverished world with a destabilizing climate and disappearing wildlife. Holistic processing isn't merely a guilt trip, but rather a values-driven perception of the world and a means to make a positive difference.

Holistic thinking is characterized by a high level of mutualism, in which people seek quality of life, prosperity, and a clean environment for each other as much as for themselves. Issues are perceived in terms of well-defined holistic goals, rather than as piecemeal problems. Socially and politically, boundaries between nations become more symbolic than rigid as cultures meld into a global community, working together for the betterment of all. A holistic approach is desperately needed to achieve global sustainability in the twenty-first century.

Quest for Sustainability

I became concerned about social and environmental issues at an early age. I wanted to do something to make a difference. With a youthful, mythical perspective, I imagined that if I were president I would pass laws banning smoking and everything else bad in the world, and that would solve our problems. The news media encouraged this black-and-white perspective, showing environmental issues pitted against industry, and economic progress against workers. In order for one side to win, the other had to lose.

Through my interest in wilderness survival skills and primitive living, it was logical to perceive civilization as the problem. The answer to our woes was to return to the Stone Age and live in harmony with nature like the Indians. Unfortunately, Stone Age living is only sustainable if we eliminate 95 percent of the existing population first, so that nature can recover from the impacts of the remaining few. Besides, how could I convince everyone to give up their creature comforts and toys to live in huts in the woods? It was a non-goal from every angle, so I looked elsewhere for answers. Interestingly, I have met hundreds of people over the years who still believe the only viable answer to our problems is to return to primitive living.

Next, I thought the solution to sustainability was to live like nineteenth-century homesteaders, raising livestock and gardens, doing our own home canning, butchering, and firewood harvesting. I grew up around my grandmother's wood cookstove, and it is a very satisfying way to cook, but it is terribly inefficient. It would not be sustainable if everybody else depended on firewood too. Besides, neither I nor most other people I know really want to do all their own food growing, harvesting, processing, and canning. This "solution" was also a dead end.

I soon realized that it wasn't enough to search for "the right way to live." To be truly sustainable, a way of living also had to be desirable. I had to search for technologies and ideas that meshed with people's expectations for quality of life, rather than trying to force something on them. For example, driving a high-efficiency car is much more acceptable than returning to the horse and buggy. I also had to search for ideas that were financially sound, so that it would make economic sense to live more sustainably. Not everyone can afford to buy enough photovoltaic panels to generate their own electricity. As a litmus test, I started looking for ideas that were socially acceptable, economically viable, and environmentally sound. Finding answers was easy once the question was clearly defined.

One of the first technologies that passed my litmus test was the use of plants for filtering polluted water. Artificial swamps with water-loving hyacinth, cattails, reed grasses, and irises were used to clean polluted waters. Microbes on the plant roots do most of the actual cleaning by breaking down and metabolizing organic and inorganic compounds in the water. These water treatment systems purify water better than conventional chemical treatment systems, and at a lower cost. In some cases the swamps serve as wildlife habitat and city parks. It didn't take long until I started seeing viable answers all over the place. I began to realize that we have the answers we need to achieve a higher quality of life, in a way that is completely sustainable, and at a cost savings compared to the way we live now. But if the answers are right in front of us, then why do so few people know about them?

In my quest I discovered Allan Savory's book *Holistic Resource Management*, later retitled: *Holistic Management: A New Framework for Decision Making*. Savory described a process for setting and achieving holistic goals. It starts with defining one's desired quality of life in general terms, such as "We seek to be healthy and happy, to travel a lot, and to be part of a healthful community." Next comes a production goal defining in general terms what kind of work we want to do to earn a living to support our desired quality of life goal. Third is a description goal, which is a general description about how our production and quality of life goals can be indefinitely sustained. After loosely defining a three-part goal, we brainstorm possible solutions, then run them through a series of testing guidelines to ensure our ideas will achieve the desired results. *Holistic Management* didn't just pass my litmus test, it was my litmus test.

From a mythical perspective, goals are typically conflicted. We have to choose between one thing and another; we can have good jobs or a healthy environment, but not both. From a sequential perspective we learn to see issues in terms of many shades of grey; there are compromises, so we give up a little bit of one thing to have more of another. But in a holistic worldview, we seek to have our cake and eat it too. Balancing quality of life, work, and sustainability isn't about compromise; it is a matter of brainstorming enough ideas to arrive at a proposal that satisfies each component of the three-part holistic goal. Easier said than done, but it is a very satisfying way to live.

In my quest to discover solutions to our environmental problems, I quickly discovered that we have all the knowledge and most of the technology to cost-effectively build a sustainable civilization. It is possible to build affordable houses that don't require heating or cooling equipment and generate more electricity than they consume. It is economical to retrofit most existing structures to be nearly as efficient. It is possible to meet water demands of our surging population with simple technologies that capture runoff, utilize water efficiently, and recycle wastewaster or downcycle it to other uses. It is possible to profitably grow and distribute a healthy food supply without massive petrochemical inputs. Even the ability to build radically efficient cars is within our reach. Our biggest environmental problems are relatively easy to solve, yet we keep doing things the hard way.

I acquired an interest in economics to better understand how people make choices, which eventually led to my book *Direct Pointing to Real Wealth* (soon to be revised and released as *Green Prosperity: A Manual for Changing the World*). In a nutshell, it is economically advantageous to go green. We can save money and profit more through sustainable approaches to our homes and businesses. It is more cost effective to go green than to continue on our current path. In writing *Direct Pointing*, I believed people would make the best choices they had available. It appeared that people made poor choices only because so few people were aware that better alternatives existed.

I eventually realized that the problem was deeper. The solutions were in front of us all along, but invisible due to the way we perceive reality. In attempting to write a guidebook for sound decision-making, I was effectively outlining the neurocircuitry for holistic processing. The reason people do not make holistic decisions is because holistic thinking is not yet part of the neural network mimicked from one generation to the next. In my quest to make a difference in the world, the next logical step was to write *Roadmap to Reality* to emphasize that holistic thinking is more than an idea in a book; it is an entirely new experience of reality. *Roadmap to Reality* outlines the big picture, while *Green Prosperity* serves as a how-to manual to apply holistic processing towards achieving one's dreams.

A New Way of Seeing the World

In comparing viewpoints between conservatives and liberals, it is generally assumed that differences relate to opinions about the issues. However, through this text we can see that the opinions are connected to the way people process information. Conservatives tend to perceive issues in black-and-white as associated with mythical processing, while liberals tend to perceive issues in complex shades of grey, as associated with sequential processing. Conservatives and liberals basically swim in different universes. Interestingly, a study of on-line book-buying patterns reveals just how isolated these groups are from each other.

Valdis Krebs, a social-network analyst (i.e., systems thinker), was curious about patterns in consumer purchases of political books in election years, which led to a project analyzing book sales at Amazon.com and BarnesandNoble.com. Using a software program to gather information, he started with the list of best-selling books from the *New York Times*, then used the "customers who bought this book also bought" feature on the websites to hop from book to book to see what patterns emerged. The result was a diagram showing that conservatives and liberals almost exclusively purchased books that reinforced their own viewpoints. Neither read material from the opposite viewpoint.[2][3] It could be said that, "You are what you read." Interestingly, subsequent analysis of book sales revealed a third cluster of books. The third cluster includes titles such as *The Tipping Point*, *Collapse*, and *Guns, Germs, and Steel*, all written from a systems-level perspective.[4]

As a teenager and young adult, I read books written by systems and holistic thinkers such as Amory Lovins and Allan Savory. I connected with their ideas on an intuitive level, but it took a long time to exercise and develop the neural pathways to apply systems and holistic thinking to my life. Regurgitating these viewpoints to other people proved especially difficult, due to their web-like nature. Interconnected thoughts had to be understood and translated into sequential series of words. However, I still struggled with sequential processing, so my initial experience with holistic literature was mythical. I recognized in black-and-white terms that we needed to live harmoniously with the earth.

I intuitively connected with holistic concepts, but it was like being submerged in a swimming pool of ideas. It was difficult to surface with them in my conscious mind. I could feel them, but struggled to translate them into a string of words. However, as a result of reading books by holistic thinkers and spending time digesting, utilizing, and trying to express the information, I learned to become a holistic thinker, so that my own books are written from a holistic viewpoint.

For example, *Botany in a Day* is organized holistically, providing tools to recognize the patterns of identification and uses among related plants. It is much easier to learn these broad patterns than to attempt to identify and memorize the uses of individual plants. I've been told that it is a revolutionary book, that there is nothing else like it in the world. I've never taken a botany class myself, yet the book is used as a text in many universities. It is not an issue of intelligence, just one of organization. *Botany in a Day* is organized holistically, which enables people to get the big picture first, followed by increasing levels of detail. *Roadmap to Reality* is also organized holistically, outlining patterns of consciousness in the same way that *Botany in a Day* outlines patterns of plant identification. Each layer of consciousness is a worldview of its own, which is nested within the next worldview. By reading holistic writing you begin to think holistically yourself.

Changing the World

I frequently meet people who desire to live a more sustainable lifestyle. Many people are especially interested in starting a green business to make a living while making the world a better place. They like the idea, but holistic processing does not come naturally to them, and it certainly did not come naturally to me. It is my primary mode of processing now, and I can see numerous opportunities to start profitable green businesses, ideas that are essentially invisible to other people. Since my wife and I have four children and more businesses than we can handle, we established Green University as a place to mentor people in holistic thinking and help them shortcut the learning curve to launch their own green businesses.

Holistic processing has the potential to solve basically any social, environmental, political, or economic issue that exists in the world today. Holistic processing is not an answer in itself, but rather a goal-oriented way to generate integrated solutions to social, economic, and environmental problems. It is not a matter of choosing between one extreme or another, or of compromising with some shade of grey. Rather, it is the mentality that we can have our cake and eat it too. The three-part goal discussed in Allan Savory's book *Holistic Management* is the beginning of the process, and we simply generate as many possible combinations as necessary to find a solution that satisfies the entire goal. But how do we move our species towards a holistic worldview when most of the world's population remains deeply entrenched in a mythical worldview? In America people are still struggling to shift from mythical to sequential processing.

Fortunately, not everybody has to think holistically to create a holistic world, because relatively few people make the decisions that drive business and government. As mentioned earlier, it would be relatively easy to start a sustainable fastfood restaurant. The restaurant could provide organically grown foods from a network of local farmers, served in compostable packaging, within a super-efficient building with natural appeal. In addition to organic appeal, the lobby could exhibit a display of articles from independent sources revealing all the cardboard and garbage fed to other cows to produce beef. As Jo Robinson wrote in *Pasture Perfect*, commercial beef is raised on feedstock that includes: *"1) recycled human food, such as stale candy, pizza, potato chips, brewery wastes, and hamburger buns; 2) parts of our fruits and vegetables that we don't eat, such as orange rinds, beet pulp, and carrot tops; and 3) stuff you don't want to know about including chicken manure, chicken feathers, newsprint, cardboard, and "aerobically digested" municipal garbage."*[5] By providing a better business model and competing with mainstream businesses, it is possible to force change across an entire industry.

Similarly, American auto companies were out-competed for the second time by more efficient overseas companies with better products. Losing sales and forced to cut jobs, General Motors and Ford must provide more efficient cars if they want to stay in business. If they take a revolutionary step forward to produce 150-mpg cars or desirable plug-in hybrids, they could recapture lost market share and once again lead the world in innovation and production.

What we need to change the world is a handful of people of great consciousness who want to pursue green business projects that will ultimately force wasteful old businesses to go green to stay competitive.

The Climate Bomb

Global warming and other man-made natural disasters is forcing our species to shift towards holistic processing. Global warming was ignored for decades when we could have most easily turned it around. It started out like a back page story that read something like, *"And by the way, there is a nuclear bomb ticking underneath the city."* Few people were interested in global warming at first, but now it makes the headlines. The story doesn't go away. It pops up again and again, getting louder with each passing year. The question is: Will our species internalize the message in time to do anything constructive about it?

The general public is largely aware that fossil fuel use puts carbon dioxide in the air. To a lesser degree it is understood that the world's tropical forests function like planetary lungs, taking in carbon dioxide and breathing out oxygen. Cutting and burning tropical forests destroys the oxygen recycling capability and releases organic carbon into the atmosphere. Unfortunately, neither the public nor most scientists are aware that a major factor in global warming may be right beneath our feet. By considering issues of soil carbon sequestration, we can better understand the holistic level of consciousness.

In short, the substance that gives rich topsoil its dark color is carbon. Without the aid of humanity, nature itself built topsoil from little more than air and water. Plants breathe in carbon dioxide from the atmosphere, convert the carbon into vegetative matter, and exhale oxygen back into the atmosphere. Over time, dead vegetation is decomposed to become rich brown or black soil. Worldwide, soils contain an estimated 1,500 gigatons of carbon, compared to 750 gigatons held in the atmosphere and 650 gigatons held in plant matter like the tropical forests. A gigaton is a billion tons.[6] About 110 gigatons of carbon are removed from the atmosphere by plants every year, while another 2.5 gigatons diffuse into the oceans.

Carbon naturally cycles back to the atmosphere through the respiration of living organisms (50 gigatons), oxidation of the soils (61–62 gigatons). Human contributions include deforestation (2 gigatons) and fossil fuel emissions (5 gigatons). The net result is that atmospheric carbon levels are increasing at the rate of about 6 gigatons per year. By this accounting, fossil fuels and deforestation contribute enough carbon to account for the changing climate. However, the role of soil carbon and desertification may be seriously underappreciated.

Forests contain significant quantities of organic carbon, but trees often grow very slowly. An acre of grass can absorb more carbon per year than an acre of forest, and much of that organic carbon can be composted into soil under favorable conditions. More than half of the earth's land surface consists of grasslands, but these grasslands are turning to deserts at an alarming rate. Desertification contributes to global warming by reducing the acreage available to remove carbon from the atmosphere. Compounding the problem is that desertification releases gigatons of carbon stored in once-fertile soils.

Desertification is caused by numerous factors, including natural climate variation, excessive use of fire, poor livestock management, and farming. Australian Aborigines used fire extensively 50,000 years ago to hunt big game animals, hunting many species to extinction, while contributing to desertification of the continent.[7] Ten thousand years ago, much of the Middle East supported forests and grasslands, which turned to desert due to deforestation, agriculture, and poor grazing practices. Likewise, the rich soils of the Sahara once grew the grain that supported the Roman Empire. But now the soil is gone, oxidized back into the atmosphere or blown out to sea, leaving barren sand and rock covering an area nearly as large as the United States.

In China, human-caused desertification was first documented in the fourth century B.C. and has spread ever since. Desertification accelerated over the last hundred years due to a combination of deforestation, grazing, and over-cultivation. Twenty-seven percent of China is now covered by useless sand, which threatens to bury the capital of Beijing under advancing dunes.[8]

Newsweek magazine reported that 40 percent of American crop and rangelands have turned to desert due to poor management.[9] But there are many degrees of desertification, and we have seen only the beginning. With deserts spreading at alarming rates across North America, Asia, and Africa, we are losing carbon to the atmosphere and losing the ability to extract it again. Merely plowing soil increases the surface area exposed to oxidation, converting soil carbon into carbon dioxide. Our fertile soils were built from atmospheric carbon by nature, while human agriculture and poor grazing practices have caused epidemic soil loss. The loss of soil carbon may be the reason global warming is occurring much faster than originally predicted.

The Cycle of Life

From a mythical viewpoint, it is often said that God made the world for the benefit of people, so it is okay if livestock graze the grass down to its roots. Sequential thinkers, on the other hand, see a linear relationship in which favorable environmental conditions grow the grass that supports grazing animals. If the range is in poor shape and starting to show signs of desertification, then it is logical to assume that removing the stock will allow the range to recover. However, that too is flawed thinking in arid environments. The grass may grow taller as if the land is healing, but the bare ground between the grass continues to spread. From a holistic viewpoint, it is all connected: the soil grows the grass that feeds the animals, *while the animals plant the grass to build the soil.*

Western rangelands were historically grazed and maintained by massive herds of buffalo. The important part was not the buffalo, but the sequence of grazing. Before the arrival of Europeans, predators forced the buffalo to stay clustered in tight herds for safety. Some herds were so massive that observers described them as miles wide and hours or days long in passing. They crushed everything in their path, trampling the grasses and sage, every bit of organic matter, into the soil. Their hooves and urine killed the moss while plant seeds were pounded into the soil. Old or dead vegetation was trampled into the ground where microbes could break it down. The organic debris helped retain moisture for plant growth.

149

Gradually the debris rotted and returned nutrients to the soil. The migrating bison allowed the prairie to recover without further interference, enabling lush and unrestrained growth. Over time, the bison helped build the fertile prairie soils.

Fencing and stocking the land created a new sequence of grazing, which logically has a different effect on the land. Without predators, cattle spread out and graze over wide areas; they no longer trample standing dead grasses from previous years. The dead grass blocks incoming sunlight, killing new growth below. Old vegetation stands for years, slowly decomposing through oxidation and weathering. Valuable nutrients in the old growth are unavailable to living plants. In fenced pastures livestock eat tender new growth before the vegetation can recover. Burning the range accelerates desertification by stealing the organic matter that protects the soil and new seedlings from drying out.

Loss of organic matter also results in poor soil structure. Raindrops strike the exposed soil, pulverizing and separating loose, aggregated clumps. The fine particles of silt, sand, and clay solidify as a hard surface crust. Seeds and water cannot penetrate the capped surface, so bare patches develop between the plants. Weeds, brush, and grasshoppers thrive in the open patches. New moisture is lost as runoff and contributes to flooding. Water bypasses the water table and old springs dry up. In northern climates, freezing and thawing can cause the top inch of soil to become so porous and fluffy that seeds dry out before they germinate.

In South Africa, Dutch settlers established communities around free-flowing springs they called "fontiens." They named their towns after the springs and the abundant wildlife: Elandsfontein, Springfontein, Buffelfontein. Settlers described herds of springbok (like antelope) so vast that they trampled everything in their path as they migrated through, including teams of oxen that could not be unhitched in time. Now the grasslands, the springs, and the wildlife are gone, and the remaining range supports very few livestock. The climate did not change according to weather records, but the land still turned to desert.[10]

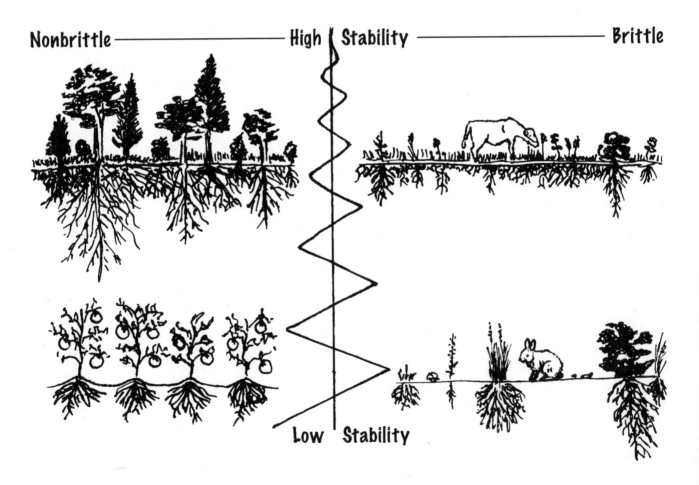

150

Seedling germination in seasonal rainfall environments is always a challenge, even under the best of circumstances. Seeds must be thoroughly mixed with soil and covered with organic matter and manure fertilizer to retain moisture and protect them from the sun. Otherwise, the delicate seedlings dry out and die before they become established. The more extreme or brittle the climate, the more difficult it is for new seedlings to germinate. The Salt Lake City area was once described as having grass "belly high to a horse," yet that is not the landscape today. The landscape is grey because the grass is gone.

Halting desertification and turning these barren wastelands back into fertile, productive landscapes is relatively easy, but it requires playing by the rules of the ecosystem. In other words, it requires holistic thinking. If we listen and learn the ways of the ecosystem, then we can restore the health of the land and still get the productivity we desire. Don and Cleo Shaules, who live near Billings, Montana, embraced holistic thinking to run a sustainable ranch. They mimicked the historical sequence of grazing with the aid of carefully planned fences, putting more animals in smaller spaces for shorter periods of time. Additional impact is achieved by herding the animals, or by putting feed or supplements in areas where impact is especially desired. The cows trampled organic carbon into the soil and inoculated it with bacteria from the manure. With animal impact the Shaules successfully trampled cactus and sagebrush into the dirt, while "rototilling" the soil to favor new seedlings. The rich, brown soil humus increased from 1/4 inch up to 1 1/2 inches in just ten years! They literally built soil from air, and more than doubled their livestock numbers along the way.[11] That is the power of holistic processing.

Similarly, Colin Seis, a farmer in Australia, doubled the organic carbon in his soil in little more than a decade by sowing cereal crops into his perennial pastures. In other words, he grows harvestable crops on the same land he manages for intensive grazing, which translates to increased productivity and higher profits. Thousands of other Australians are now adopting his methods.[12]

To successfully reverse desertification, climate change, and other global disasters, we have to think and act holistically. We have to recognize that everything we do impacts everything else and ultimately affects us. Perhaps the best way to learn holistic processing is to immerse oneself in the literature of holistic thinkers. In addition to *Holistic Management* and *Green Prosperity*, there are numerous other books that offer tips for living more holistically.

Holistic Parenting

The consensus-based parenting associated with systems thinking is a monumental leap forward from previous parenting models. Fortunately, the transition from consensus to holistic parenting is an easy one. Other consensus-based processes typically lack holistic goals and values, but those goals are implied in consensus parenting. The difference between consensus versus holistic parenting is primarily a matter of expressing those values and goals.

As a young adoptive parent, I was confident that I could be a holistic parent to my children. Although I had no roadmap for guidance, I sensed the need for a holistic approach to parenting. I envisioned a household where we would define common goals and individual goals and strive to achieve them together. I imagined that we would develop a family bond deeper than that found among mythical or sequential households. While we have been blessed with four wonderful children, it would be a stretch to call our lifestyle or parenting "holistic." In our family meetings years ago, however, we successfully outlined a basic quality of life goal with our children, as follows:

"We want to treat people the way we want to be treated ourselves. We want to treat each other with respect and kindness. Sometimes we want hugs and kisses. We need to listen to each other when we say 'stop.' We need to gently remind each other about not yelling. We want to treat animals with respect. When we catch

live mice we will take them a long ways from the house and let them go, instead of killing them. We will have our family meetings on Mondays, and we will close our meetings by holding hands and saying how we feel." We also listed personal goals and discussed specific behaviors we wanted to change. My daughter Cassie, for example, said she didn't like being tickled. It was very empowering to be able to say that in a family meeting. We listened.

Looking back at the minutes of our family meetings and the quality of communication we were developing, I am not sure why we ever quit. Perhaps our lives became too busy, or it took too much effort to communicate holistically on a scheduled basis.

The biggest conundrum I faced as a parent is the conflict between my desire to raise our family holistically and my not-so-small mission to make the world a better place. I believed it was possible to do one or the other, but have struggled to figure out how to do both at the same time. For example, I had the great privilege to spend most of my childhood outdoors. In California we had a big yard and gardens. I was intimately familiar with the plants and artifacts of vacant lots around the neighborhood. Bicycling pathways from Los Altos to Stanford University was like following a nature trail through a seemingly rural countryside. My parents limited our access to the television. We returned to my grandmother's house in Montana every summer and spent months playing in creeks and fields, or going on picnics in the mountains. Thankfully, Grandma Josie did not own a television set.

As a wilderness survival instructor, it seems likely that my children would have similar opportunities, but through my writing career I role-model spending thousands of hours in front of a computer. Naturally, my children mimic that behavior and want to play endlessly on the computer. My boys mimic me and write their own books, and I am very proud of that. However, we get habituated to the computers through our blustery, frigid Montana winters, until nobody seems to remember how to do anything else. The kids want to play on the computers even on the most beautiful days. After months of living that way, my son Edwin says he doesn't like to go outside or do anything but play the computer. I carry him kicking and screaming out the door to go on a picnic, knowing that he will have fun when we get there. Travel vacations are more satisfying; we seem focused on each other and more engaged in the outdoors. Every time we camp in a national park, Edwin tells me he wants to move there.

When I wake up in the morning, there are things that I know I must do to make an impact on our current world situation. Otherwise, our species will not survive, and there is little point in having a family. Yet, it is also obvious that it is pointless to try "saving the world" without also "saving my family." This is the crisis and conundrum I face daily as a parent, sometimes focusing on my family, sometimes focusing on my vision. I don't know if we will ever achieve a truly holistic lifestyle and family unity, but in the spirit of holistic processing we keep striving towards that goal.

Holistic Government

Based on the nation-as-family metaphor, we can predict that if enough families adopt a holistic parenting model, it will inevitably change government policies. Conversely, it is possible that holistic leadership in government could lead to an increase in holistic parenting. At present, however, government is anything but holistic. Congress rarely defines goals in positive terms or guidelines to determine whether or not legislation achieves the intended results.

For example, Congress approved $110 billion in emergency aid and reconstruction funds after hurricane Katrina in 2005,[13] but without any grand vision on how to spend it. At least $1 billion was lost to fraudulent claims in the first year. In addition, the Federal Emergency Management Agency (FEMA) purchased 26,000 manufactured and modular homes to help rebuild New Orleans, as well as 114,000 camper trailers for temporary housing. However, the manufactured homes were banned for use in flood plains by FEMA's own rules. Ten thousand of these homes were left sinking in the mud near Hope, Arkansas. Meanwhile, the "temporary" camper trailers out-gassed formaldehyde making them a health hazard to long-term residents.[14] Our government will only be able to make sound decisions when Congress, the president, and federal agencies start defining goals in terms of quality of life, production, and sustainability, along with a set of guidelines to test whether or not each proposed action will help achieve those goals.

It is important to remember that when we shift from one layer of consciousness to another, we don't necessarily stop using the previous layers. We incorporate all levels of consciousness into who we are and how we process our world. For example, political debates originated out of mythical processing. Political candidates attempt to make it clear in black-and-white terms why you should vote for them and not the opponent. As a result, mythical thinkers are often favored in politics because they naturally see the world in simplistic terms. This is especially the case during hard times, when we are faced with terrorism, wars, or a sluggish economy. People want simple, black-and-white answers, even if such thinking contributed to the problems in the first place. A sequential thinker might have reasonable proposals, but his or her answers could come across as too much information, or too grey and fuzzy in a debate.

It is even more challenging for a holistic candidate to express his or her viewpoint. To be an effective leader, a holistic politician must translate holistic concepts into a sequential format to demonstrate a solid plan, and then simplify that plan down to a handful of black-and-white statements that people can easily connect with. For example, a candidate could emphasize a plan to halt global warming at a profit, growing the economy in the process. The political system runs on simple messages like that.

Holistic Living

Living holistically involves more than just thinking. It involves being in touch with our emotions, playfulness, creativity, sexuality, and spirituality. Many intelligent and well-educated individuals make unwise choices because they have not matured as emotionally balanced adults. In a worldview where everything is intertwined, living holistically primarily means being connected to each other and ourselves. By being emotionally in touch with ourselves and balanced in our relationships, we can build a truly sustainable way of life. In short, our thoughts, feelings, and behaviors need to converge in working harmony to fully realize our dreams.

Sequential healthcare, for example, typically focuses on symptoms and subsequently prescribes a pill, diet, or operation for various ailments, while ignoring the bigger picture. Holistic healthcare, on the other hand, begins with a vision of healthy living, such as "being physically fit and feeling good." Once the goal has been defined, then all possible therapies can be evaluated to achieve that goal, including conventional treatments as well as herbs, meditation, psychotherapy, faith, wilderness camping, a new job, or more quality time with family. My friend's father is a radiologist who treats cancer patients. He uses pharmaceutical medicine and advanced scientific equipment for treatment, but he also writes prescriptions that include weight loss, healthy eating, stress reduction, and practicing yoga.

Limitations to Holistic Processing

As we have seen through this chapter, it is possible to achieve true sustainability if enough people incorporate holistic thinking into their lives and work. We can build a sustainable civilization without destroying the environment in the process. We can begin to reverse desertification, making rich black topsoil from atmospheric carbon. However, even holistic processing has its limitations. The biggest problem with holism is the human factor. People are fallible, and most people have their hands full trying to keep their lives together and raise a family. Even well-intentioned, holistically managed ranches have fallen victim to divorces and subdivisions.

Another limitation is that technology is evolving so fast that we may need to rapidly shift to higher levels of consciousness to deal with the increasing complexity. But what exactly is this concept of higher consciousness? To some people it may sound like New Age spiritual babble. And yet, through this text we have examined several tangible, practical levels of consciousness already. Transitioning from one worldview to the next is effectively "transcending" to a higher level of consciousness, which we have all done at least once or twice in our lives. Higher consciousness is simply about learning a new way to perceive reality. In Part III we explore the concepts of transcendence and higher consciousness as we continue our quest to define a universal, all-encompassing reality to which all other realities belong.

Suggested Reading

Three Cups of Tea by Greg Mortensen and David Oliver Relin. *Three Cups of Tea* is a fascinating story about Greg Mortensen's efforts to build schools in Pakistan and Afghanistan. Mortensen provides a holistic perspective on the war on terror, showing how U.S. military efforts often make the situation worse. Mortensen's low-cost schools educate both girls and boys, and compete with the religious-funded *madrassas*, where young boys are brainwashed to become fundamentalist extremists.

Holistic Management by Allan Savory. *Holistic Management* is a guidebook for holistic thinking to assist businesses, organizations, and governments in setting and achieving holistic goals. The user defines a three-part goal in positive terms for quality of life, a generalized statement of production, and a generalized description for long-term sustainability. Next, the holistic practitioner generates ideas to achieve the defined goal, and culls poor ideas through a series of testing and implementation guidelines. The book is primarily focused on land-management issues, but is broad enough to be used by anyone, even for running a donut shop.

Part II

The Road to Sentience

—Thirteen—

Transcendence

Transitioning from one Worldview to Another

"Ego is the unobserved mind that runs your life when you are not present as the witnessing consciousness, the watcher. The ego perceives itself as a separate fragment in a hostile universe, with no real inner connection to any other being, surrounded by other egos which it either sees as a potential threat or which it will attempt to use for its own ends. The basic ego patterns are designed to combat its own deep-seated fear and sense of lack. They are resistance, control, power, greed, defense, attack. Some of the ego's strategies are extremely clever, yet they never truly solve any of its problems, simply because the ego itself is the problem."

—Eckhart Tolle, *The Power of Now*[1]

To one who is unfamiliar with the different modes of processing information outlined in this book, any talk about transcending to higher levels of consciousness might sound like New Age babble. But as we have seen, transcending from one level of consciousness to another is a natural part of growing up. The definition of transcend is simply *"to rise above or go beyond the ordinary limits of."*[2]

As we mature we naturally transcend from the magical to the mythical and usually to the sequential, sometimes to even higher levels of consciousness, whether we are aware of it or not. In this chapter we focus directly on this concept of transcendence, to examine what happens when we transition from one level of processing information to the next. Then we consider some of the possible triggers that stimulate a shift in consciousness. Surprisingly, we find that environmental destruction and/or feelings of guilt can trigger higher levels of consciousness. We discover that there is such a thing as higher consciousness, and that we are all walking the same path. We find, as Yatri wrote in *Unknown Man*, that, *"Man exists in a twilight zone between a beast and a Buddha, for he is in a constant process, knowing that he is, but not who he is."*[3]

Fusion > Separation > Integration

There are three phases in the transition from one level of consciousness to another, as recognized by psychologists and outlined in Ken Wilber's *A Brief History Of Everything*: 1) fusion and unawareness, 2) differentiation and separation, and 3) integration.[4] For example, a preconscious infant is so psychologically fused with his mother that he doesn't recognize he and she are separate entities. But through time, and the baby's inability to make his mother meet his wants and needs at will, he becomes aware they are separate. Discovering this separation can be a traumatic process for an infant, and the source of a lot of crying and fussing, but over time the baby integrates this realization into his own reality, becoming his own person.

A child at the magical level is fused into a first person perspective, with little or no awareness that other people have their own feelings. It can be unsettling to realize that other people have their own emotional experience, but once a child becomes aware of it, then they can move to the next phase, role playing doctors, firemen, or mommies, to find out what it is like to be in somebody else's shoes. When they integrate a sense of other people's emotions into their perspective they transcend from a magical to a mythical worldview.

The transition from the mythical to the sequential is similar. At first we are so fused with our cultural perspective that we assume it is the only way to perceive reality. When we encounter people who think differently, we assume their ways are wrong. But if we interact with them long enough then we become aware that other cultural viewpoints are not necessarily wrong, just different. When we learn to objectively compare two viewpoints from a neutral perspective, then we transcend from mythical processing to sequential processing.

In sequential processing we remain fused with linear cause and effect to the extent that we may perceive ourselves as victims of circumstances. Events happen and we react to them. Other people can make us sad or mad. They are responsible for the way we feel. When we learn to differentiate between their actions and our emotional experience, we begin to integrate a new experience into our life. We learn to choose our own actions and feelings, independent of what other people say and do. In doing so, we transcend to systems processing.

However, at the systems level, we may not yet be aware of the connection between our actions and everything else. We may be so fused with the routine of putting gas in the car, or steaks on the grill, that we never think about what it means to the rest of the world. It might seem outrageous when suggested that our actions could contribute to terrorist bombings. But as we become aware of the interconnections in life, we begin to see that buying gas often channels money towards people who see our culture as a threat to their own. By using that gas we contribute towards global warming and melting Arctic ice earlier in the spring, making it harder for polar bears to hunt seals. We experience a disharmonious, dissatisfying, disgruntled initial realization that our actions can harm the world and ultimately harm the lives of people we know and care about.

As a result, we gradually move towards holistic integration and modify our behavior, starting with simple efforts such as minimizing unnecessary car trips, carpooling, and buying more fuel-efficient vehicles. We might switch to a car that gets the best mileage possible, or switch to something that runs on alternative fuels, hopefully from sustainable resources. We transition from a state of fusion, unaware of the impacts of our actions, to differentiation, intimately aware of our connection to the web of life, to a point of integration where we begin to incorporate a web-oriented perspective as we define who we are and how we live our lives.

Every time we transcend from one way of seeing the world to another, we go through this three-step process. We start from a point of fusion or unawareness, transition to a state of differentiation and awareness, and then arrive at a state of integration with a new perspective. Along the way we transcend old notions about the nature of reality and discover whole new perceptions. We correct for some of the distortions and arrive at a worldview that is increasingly reflective of the true nature of reality. We become increasingly detached from our own ego, which will ultimately enable us to transcend the ego altogether.

Transcending from one level of consciousness to another is also known as a "paradigm shift," which can happen at an individual or cultural level. Thomas Kuhn, a science historian, coined the term paradigm shift to describe the transition from one scientific theory or explanation to another. The term has been expanded to include changes in consciousness.[5]

People resist paradigm shifts more than they resist any other kind of change, but paradigm shifts gradually become inevitable. It starts with a few individuals perceiving something in a new way. They might point out the anomalies and failures of the old perspective and demonstrate better approaches. A few open-minded individuals soon embrace the new viewpoint, while most cling to familiar ways, even in the face of overwhelming evidence. The new paradigm gradually gains momentum, until it becomes the dominant mode of perceiving reality.

A paradigm shift is rarely a pleasurable experience. In order to transcend from one perception of reality to another, we must first realize that our original beliefs were misconstrued. This conflict was one of the greatest personal struggles Charles Darwin had to deal with. His theory of evolution contradicted everything he learned from the Bible. He didn't set out with the intention to shatter his reality, or anyone else's, but he could not deny the evidence he found.

Environmental Destruction and Consciousness

Imagine that we have returned to the Stone Age, and our tribe is migrating to a new island where no humans have ever been before. We find an island rich with life and lacking other predators. The native species have no defenses, no fear, and not even the ability to run away. We walk up to a flightless bird and club it to death for dinner. Life is so easy that we hardly have to work at all. It would make sense to steward the resources, to make sure that we have a sustainable supply of flightless birds so that we can live easily, without having to struggle for food. The reality, however, is that whenever our ancestors migrated to new lands they acted more like nonsentient predators than conscious stewards.

Like the skunk that killed fifty chickens in my neighbor's hen house some years ago, our ancestors were fused with nature and uncapable of foreseeing resource depletion. They hunted whatever game they could easily kill. If they couldn't find one species, they simply hunted something else. Prior to the arrival of the Maori people in New Zealand around A.D. 1000, there were about two-dozen species of flightless birds called moa, along with scores of large ducks, geese, swans, eagles and other bird species that lived there for millions of years, free from predators of any kind. The Maori ate the meat, used the skins for clothing, made fishhooks and jewelry from the bones, and blew the eggs out to make water containers. In more than one hundred known archaeological sites, many of them several acres in size, the Maori processed their game and discarded the remains in massive quantities, leaving behind the skeletons of an estimated 100,000 to 500,000 birds per site. The moa and dozens of other unique species were extinct less than five centuries after the Maori people arrived.

Similarly, Madagascar was first colonized by Africans and Indonesians around A.D. 500. They wiped out more than a dozen species of flightless elephant birds, including some that weighed up to a thousand pounds and laid eggs that were more than two gallons in size. They exterminated fourteen species of large lemurs—some the size of a gorilla, as well as giant tortoises, aardvarks, and pygmy hippos. In both New Zealand and Madagascar the climate was known to be stable during the time of the extinctions.[6]

Similar extinctions occurred in the wake of human migrations all over the world. While climate change and numerous other factors may have contributed to the demise of some species, human presence was the final, decisive factor. In North America, for example, scores of species survived twenty-two previous ice ages before dropping dead at the end of the twenty-third, shortly after the arrival of the first Americans. Among the exterminated were North America's horses, giant armadillos, mammoths, and saber-tooth cats.[7] On every new island and continent, our ancestors arrival coincided with the extinctions of seventy to eighty percent of the megafauna—the big game worth hunting. One consequence of this loss of biodiversity is that it made life harder for our ancestors, which leads to the question: could we achieve higher levels of consciousness without harming the environment?

Whenever a species loses its resource base, it must do one of three things: 1) move to new territory, 2) adapt in a new way, or 3) die. The archaeological record is filled with the remains of past civilizations that perished or dispersed. Disrupting ecosystems and wiping out food resources forced our ancestors to work harder. They had to develop more complex weapons and better social coordination to be successful hunters. The tribes that adapted were able to survive and pass on their genes and knowledge. They worked together to drive herds of animals over cliffs, or they successfully killed from a distance using newly innovated spear throwers or bows and arrows. Harming the environment made life more difficult for our ancestors, which ultimately forced them to use their brains in new and more complex ways.

As hunter-gatherers it was possible to consume resources in one area with little consequence because the tribe could move on and let the land recover. In permanent settlements, however, the problems could not be left behind. Our ancestors had to learn to steward their resources to ensure that they had sustainable sources of wood and food. Jared Diamond's book *Collapse* details the fall of many past civilizations that failed to manage their resources sustainably, as well as the adjustments other civilizations had to make to avoid a similar fate. In learning to steward their resources, successful civilizations had to adopt more complex ways of dealing with and perceiving their world. The origins of human consciousness are tied to this increasing complexity. Our ancestors were guided by mimicry and accumulated experience. They did not worry or speculate about the consequences of their actions. But, as human society became increasingly complex, new problems arose that preprogrammed reactions could not solve. People had to adapt and use their brains in new ways to resolve the issues.

Many animals, including deer, defecate wherever they are, even walking through good forage or clean water. They give no conscious thought to protecting the resources, but the impact is spread out enough that it is not a problem anyway. The same was true for our hunter-gatherer ancestors. They could defecate anywhere in the woods or near camp, and it wasn't an issue. After hunting out the local animals, harvesting the edible plants, and stinking up the area around camp, the band or tribe could move on to new territory. However, transitioning to larger, permanent settlements required new solutions, such as centralized latrines. According to tribal historian Joseph Medicine Crow, many Crow Indians became seriously ill or died when they were first confined to the Crow Reservation, because as a nomadic people they had no concept of maintaining sanitary surroundings.[8]

Increasingly complex societies required increasingly complex solutions to deal with basic sanitation. The distributed defecation common in magical cultures was replaced by outhouses in mythical cultures, which were replaced by the complex piping systems common in sequential cultures. In trying to grapple with sanitation problems, larger cities used cesspools to store human waste until it could be transported away by "honey wagons." Early sewage systems consisted of ditches built into city streets, channeling raw sewage to the nearest river or lake. Cesspools and sewage ditches persisted in New York City until the early 1900s. Although the ditches helped remove human waste, they were a major source of disease, ultimately leading to the massive piping systems and wastewater treatment systems we have today.

Unfortunately, wastewater treatment remains a sequential process, sending half-clean water and copious nutrients on a one-way trip downstream. Wastewater and other pollutants have created huge dead zones in estuaries where rivers pour into the ocean. However, bigger environmental problems force people to innovate new solutions. Future sewage plants will close the loop on waste, perhaps by capturing methane gas for fuel and recycling wastewater and nutrients through hydroponic farms to grow more food.

In terms of garbage, hunter-gatherer societies hand-made everything from locally available materials. Old shelters, baskets, and clothing rotted back into the environment they came from. The only permanent trash consisted of broken stone tools, which quickly disappeared into the soil. There was no such thing as litter, so garbage was dropped anywhere. Filmaker Lewis Cotlow noted this lack of stewardship in his travels, writing, *"we came to one small Pygmy clearing, with ten or eleven beehive huts in it. I saw no resident Pygmies, and the ashes looked quite dead. It was an abandoned camp, as the general messiness and smells indicated, aside from the absence of humans. Pygmies are not very tidy, except for their persons, and when a camp becomes too dirty, or when the game is hunted out, they just move on to another location. They have so few personal or household goods that moving is no great chore, and housebuilding takes less than an hour."[9]*

Western cultures gradually evolved a concept of garbage as products were developed. It was not a big problem at first, but the more cans, bottles, stoves, couches, clothes, toys, and hazardous waste that were generated, the more garbage there was to dispose of. People often dumped garbage in pits in the backyard. But as people crowded close together, it became necessary to develop systems to cart it away to centralized landfills or incinerators. While none of today's solutions are remotely perfect, at least we have a concept of garbage management. Other cultures have catapulted into the industrial age without evolving a cultural heritage to deal with trash. That is one reason why litter is common in developing countries and among indigenous populations where people are new to industrial abundance.

It is easy to romanticize natives, to imagine that they should be environmentally conscientious and wouldn't think of littering. But many indigenous people tend to drop garbage without a second thought. In many Inuit towns, for example, broken down snowmobiles and trucks are left beside the road where they quit. I first noticed the phenomenon while participating in a sweat lodge ceremony on a reservation in Montana. The elders did a ritual prayer to the four directions and brought an offering of food out in the woods. Later, while hiking in the woods, I was surprised to see plastic plates all over the ground, the remains of past offerings. But the offerings were not fully accepted, since the four directions had no way to assimilate the trash. It was shocking to see native people litter when they otherwise seemed so close to nature.

Likewise, I was surprised to see Tarahumara Indians discard soda bottles on the ground in Mexico. However, our species did fail the sentience test. The idea that it is wrong to throw a can or bottle on the ground is a human judgment that evolved over time. We cannot blame other cultures for littering when the concept simply is not part of their culture.

Fortunately, many indigenous cultures around the world are beginning to forge new identities as the original stewards of the land. They are proactively taking steps to protect their homelands from outside exploitation. For example, the Northern Cheyenne in Montana have opposed coal mining, despite of a 46 percent unemployment rate on the reservation. According to Duane Champagne in his book, *Social Change and Cultural Continuity Among Native Nations,* "*an estimated 80 percent of the Northern Cheyenne opposed commercial coal development… [although] 66.8 percent of the Northern Cheyenne thought that commercial coal development would improve reservation economic conditions. They expected more numerous and better paying jobs, more local businesses, improved financial conditions for the tribe as a whole, and a better standard of living. Thus the Northern Cheyenne clearly had an appreciation for the economic and material benefits that would derive from coal development. The negative aspects of coal development were indicated by the Northern Cheyenne as damage to the environment, threat to the Cheyenne way of life by allowing too many outsiders onto the reservation, an expectation that most of the jobs would go to non-Cheyennes, fear of increased alcoholism and drugs, and threat of total destruction of Cheyenne culture.*"[10]

Picking up trash is part of the collective heritage we teach our kids and pass on from generation to generation. Unfortunately, our concept of trash is still a sequential one, where used goods are hauled away as trash, never to be seen again. We need to transition to a systems or holistic approach to dealing with garbage, where everything is pre-designed to be recycled or to degrade naturally. Imagine a world where plastic drink bottles are thrown in the compost bin to decompose into soil. That future is coming, the result of transitioning from sequential to systems processing.

In returning to the issue of species loss, it may seem like nothing has improved since the wave of extinctions that began with human migrations. The problem is worse than ever before. Human impact will leave a notable mark on the fossil record, similar to the mass extinction events of 65, 210, 250, 364, and 444 million years ago, when planetary-wide disasters killed off half or more of all life on earth. Millions of years from now paleontologists will discover a line in the rock strata where countless species suddenly ceased to exist. In the same layer they will discover the residue of billions of human artifacts.

Fortunately, one thing has changed, and that is our awareness of the problem. Our ancestors had no way of recording the loss of a species. They may not have noticed when the

162

last of a species disappeared, especially when the numbers dwindled gradually over centuries. Despite a precipitous decline, the population would seem stable within any one person's lifetime. Flightless birds, for example, might be superabundant for one generation, but a rare treat hundreds of years later. The hunters that killed off the last bird couldn't know it was the last one, and probably perceived the find as a moment of great luck or magic anyway. However, with written records and long distance communication, we are becoming aware of our actions, recognizing for the first time that we cannot just hunt wildlife, we also have to manage populations and habitat for sustainability.

This awakening can be traced back to one moment more than any other: June 3, 1844. Feather collectors started hunting the great auk, a flightless seabird, in 1785 for stuffing pillows and mattresses. The industry systematically wiped out every auk on every island from Scotland to Iceland, until the day two fisherman, Jon Brandsson and Siguror Islefsson, killed the world's last breeding pair—and smashed their single egg—at Eldey Rock.[11] Like an embarrassingly stupid criminal act, the event was recorded and added to our collective consciousness. The tragedy doesn't fade away, even though it happened more than one hundred fifty years ago.

The demise of the great auk marked the beginning of a shift towards wildlife management. Human cultures started evaluating what it would take to maintain sustainable population levels. The result is that deer and dozens of other species that were once scarce from unlimited hunting are now abundant. Wildlife managers consciously adjust hunting policies and manage habitat to maintain desired population levels.

Despite glimmers of awareness, we will likely exterminate half of all life on earth this century.[12] We are more aware of our impact than ever before, and scientists are struggling to catch up. We are monitoring species all over the world and mapping native habitat. We know the problems are there. We know we have to change our relationship to the environment. If we expand this awareness to enough people, we will start dealing with these issues more holistically.

In terms of environmental policies, mythical thinkers typically believe we have to choose between protecting the environment versus having a robust economy. Sequential thinkers seek compromise, in hopes of finding the middle ground. Economic growth can be balanced with environmental progress by limiting development and perhaps by spending more to clean up pollution or to restore abused landscapes. But this is still a compromise. Systems thinkers begin to see the situation differently, seeking to radically reduce environmental impacts by reinventing industrial practices to minimize waste or to channel it towards constructive ends.

In a typical coal-fired power plant, for example, sixty percent of the energy in coal is lost as waste heat out the smoke stack. In Kalundborg, Denmark, however, much of that energy is captured in steam and piped to nearby business and 3,500 homes as a source of heat. Sulfur dioxide in the exhaust is scrubbed out with calcium carbonate, resulting in waste calcium sulfate or gypsum, which is used by a neighboring company to make gypsumboard. The remaining desulfurized fly ash from the power plant is used in a cement plant. Hot water discharged from the power plant is used by a commercial fish farm. Diverting these wastes towards additional uses conserves resources, reduces environmental impacts, and saves money.[13]

Holistic thinkers take environmental stewardship to a whole new level by generating goals for a satisfying quality of life and a high level of prosperity, combined with a description goal of how to sustainably and indefinitely achieve those goals. More time might be consumed in the creative processes of generating and testing ideas to meet those goals, but the outcome is an approach to living and working that results in improved environmental health and greater prosperity. This "green prosperity" is not that difficult to achieve.

In a holistic approach to achieving our own livelihood, Renee and I built and paid for our solar home on a shoestring budget. Owning our home made us rich, rather than impoverished in debt. Applying our own labor and building with inexpensive and locally found materials enabled us to live without a mortgage or a big utility bill. Our limited power bill made it easy to switch over to solar, so that our house generates approximately as much electricity as it uses. Many people assume they need to launch a successful career to afford a house, but they end up buying a mortgage and endless bills. In our case, it wasn't a career that enabled the house, but the house that enabled the career. Without a mortgage or utility bills, I could afford not to work a regular job. It took ten years of writing to launch my career as an author and publisher. Our path wasn't necessarily the answer for other people, but it made holistic sense for our situation. It is unlikely that I would have succeeded as a writer if I had to work to pay bills.

In terms of global warming, American contributes more greenhouse gasses to the atmosphere per capita than any other country. And yet, through simple energy efficiency measures we could greatly reduce our carbon outputs and make ourselves richer in the process. Moreover, by seizing the opportunity to lead in sustainable technologies, we could eliminate most of the rest of our carbon emissions and export the technology to the rest of the world. But the reality is that, as long as we are guided by mythical and sequential thinking, we will continue increasing our carbon emissions, destabilizing global climate, and compromising our nation's security through dependence on foreign energy. While other nations are promoting sustainable technologies and developing products for the twenty-first century, the U.S. is losing the opportunity to lead, and we are indicting ourselves as the country most liable for the impacts of global warming.

Our children and grandchildren will consider us as shortsighted and irresponsible. Not only did we saddle them with trillions of dollars in national debt for indulgences in our time, and not only did we burden them with the highest ever proportion of elderly people in need of healthcare, but we also left them with the responsibility to pay for the impacts of a destabilized climate. As crop failures lead to hundreds of millions of environmental refugees in need of food and safe harbor, our children will have to handle the resulting political instabilities. They will face the responsibility of housing and feeding those in need. It won't be a mere moral responsibility, but a necessity to maintain global political stability in the face of unprecedented human migrations and turmoil. These problems could be solved right now at a profit if approached from a systems or holistic perspective. But to a culture that is still processing the world in mythical and sequential terms, the solutions remain invisible, and thus effectively non-existent.

Guilt and Consciousness

Ironically, transcending to higher levels of consciousness entails achieving higher levels of guilt. Call it the downside of higher consciousness. Feeling guilty about our actions indicates awareness of a problem, which can lead to change. Change is based on the three phases of transcendence. First we are fused with a worldview and unaware of the problem, then we separate or differentiate from the issue, becoming aware of and feeling guilty about our actions. Next we modify our behavior to compensate and integrate the awareness and behavior into our consciousness. Ultimately, we learn to live with greater consciousness, which is good for everyone.

Chimpanzees appear to live a preconscious existence, operating entirely through mimicry and accumulated experience. There have been instances of deception, where individual chimpanzees hid bananas while waiting for other chimps to leave the area, so they could feast by themselves. Humans might define this deception as a negative or bad behavior, but without self-awareness, there is no such thing as good or bad behavior. There are only behaviors that work versus those that do not, and chimpanzees do not experience guilt about their actions.

In our culture, small children exist entirely in first person and have no concept of second person, or how their actions might affect other people. If a child harms another person it is recognized that they were not aware of the consequences of their actions. They are unable to shift out of first person to experience what it is like to see the world through someone else's eyes. Young children are not capable of experiencing guilt until we teach it to them through repeated admonishments, such as telling them that hitting is bad and hurts people. Children initially learn it is bad to hit other people because they get in trouble for it. Over time they learn that it is bad to hurt people because those people have feelings too. Through role-playing associated with mythical processing, children learn to see themselves through the eyes of other people and learn to feel guilty if they offend them. The guilt is passed on from generation to generation. We teach our children that being mean, stealing, or lying is wrong and they should feel bad about themselves if they do it. Not all guilt is good or properly placed, but appropriate guilt can lead to greater consciousness.

The ability to feel guilty over environmental issues is indicative of higher levels of consciousness. Most people flip on light switches, shop, and pump gas without feeling a glimmer of guilt about the impact of their actions on the rest of the world. Sequential thinkers connect the dots to see the big picture, but it was systems thinkers and holistic thinkers that outlined the big picture in the first place. As pointed out by biologist and conservationist George Schaller, *"People must understand that everything they do is an ecological act. How much does it cost to bring grapes here from Chile? Not just the grapes, but the fuel spent in carbon emission? If you have a cup of coffee, that means some rain forest in Columbia is being cut down to make coffee plantations. Do you have a cell phone? OK, inside it there's a mineral called coltan, mined mostly in the eastern Congo by a lot of the Rwandans who fled after the genocide, and they're living in the forest, and they're killing gorillas and elephants for meat because they don't have much else to eat."*[4] We are creating an increasingly complex world where our actions impact everything else. With rising awareness of interconnected cause and effect, there is a wave of guilt percolating through our society about the way we consume resources. Mostly it makes people feel badly about themselves and the prospects for the future, but the guilt has the potential to trigger new and better ways of solving problems. Environmental guilt can lead to a whole new level of consciousness.

Unfortunately, guilt at any level can become a stumbling block that a person cannot circumnavigate. For example, an individual may live in perpetual guilt, feeling that he should conform to the expectations of family, friends, and society, while he would rather pursue his personal hopes and dreams. Guilt may lead to depression, illness, or suicide in some cases. Other individuals may bow to the pressure to conform, reluctantly pursuing a well-paid and

respectable professional career at the cost of being perpetually unhappy.

Many Americans feel guilty about consuming most of the world's energy and resources, but don't see a practical means to do anything about it. It would be easier if they could see a neighbor down the street who has "gone green" already. As long as the house and landscape are tastefully done, then word will spread down the street, *"Did you know that the Jones' don't have a power bill? And their yard is full of the most spectacular butterflies and birds. It is like an oasis over there! Have you tasted their delicious home-grown apples?"* It is easier to see a path forward from guilt to integration when role models have previously blazed the way.

From a parenting perspective, the link between consciousness and guilt raises some interesting problems. On the one hand we want to raise children who are very conscientious in the way they live. We want our children to think about things and make wise choices, but the problem is that too much guilt can become counter-productive. Try feeling guilty about environmental pollution or child labor every time you flip on a light switch, every time you ride in a car, and every time you buy a product.

Concerning child labor, as noted by Megha Bahree in Forbes magazine, *"Every time you buy an imported handmade carpet, an embroidered pair of jeans, a beaded purse, a decorated box or a soccer ball there's a good chance you're acquiring something fashioned by a child. Such goods are available in places like GapKids, Macy's, ABC Carpet & Home, Ikea, Lowe's and Home Depot. These retailers say they are aware of child-labor problems, have strict policies against selling products made by underage kids and abide by the laws of the countries from which they import. But there are many links in a supply chain, and even a well-intentioned importer can't police them all."*[15] According to UNICEF statistics, *"An estimated 218 million children aged 5-17 are engaged in child labour, excluding child domestic labour. Some 126 million of these children are believed to be engaged in hazardous situations or conditions, such as working in mines, working with chemicals and pesticides in agriculture or working with dangerous machinery."*[16]

It is wrong for impoverished children to be forced to make the products we buy, but it isn't right to saddle our own kids with guilt. We want to raise conscientious children, but we don't want them to carry the burden of guilt for problems that were created by adults. The sad reality is that just about everything we spend money on has a negative consequence to it, because the world is not yet holistic and we are exploiting people and the environment with most products presently on the market.

My philosophy as a parent is that I want my children to be aware of the impacts of their actions, but not excessively burdened with guilt. I do not want to drive the guilt in too deep. On the other hand, I hope they develop their awareness and make positive choices as adults. We try to model a positive lifestyle and business practices so that our kids might think about how they can have a positive effect on the world as they become adults.

A Global Shift in Consciousness

Many consciousness writers espouse the belief that the world is on the verge of a global shift in consciousness, that people are going to suddenly start thinking and acting more holistically towards each other. I am skeptical based on the fact that we remain a primitive, volatile species, and it is hard to imagine a rapid transition from killing each other to achieving world peace and unity. Nevertheless, we have observed previous shifts in consciousness from preconscious to magical to mythical and sequential processing. It is evident from the rise of the Internet and global communications, people are transitioning towards systems and holistic worldviews. As you may have gathered, shifts in consciousness seem to accelerate as we move through time.

Our ancestors existed in a preconscious state for hundreds of thousands of years then acquired a magical worldview for tens of thousands of years. The mythical perspective is a few thousand years old, while sequential processing originated only centuries ago. Already there is a transformation underway towards systems and holistic worldviews. Unlike the transition from the magical to the mythical, change today is happening too fast to give the mass of humanity a chance to catch up.

The accelerated shifts in consciousness parallel evolutionary trends in biology and technology. For example, life on Earth consisted of nothing more than single-celled, asexually reproducing organisms for 2.5 billion years. Sexual reproduction enabled the exchange of genetic material, which can be thought of as sharing information. Multi-cellular organisms arose 900 million years later, leading to the Precambrian explosion that filled the seas with increasingly complex life forms. Complex life forms colonized land only 500 million years ago, quickly diversifying into countless plants and animals. Interactions between unrelated organisms, such as plants and fungus, have allowed novel genes to flow back and forth, accelerating the changes. And while evolution favors reproduction over intelligence, there is a small percentage of species that have survived by investing in brain mass. For good or bad, one of these species has learned to manipulate genetics to further accelerate evolution.

Technological innovation similarly moved at a glacial pace in the preconscious millennia before the Cultural Revolution. With the rise of the hunter-gatherer lifestyle, our ancestors suddenly created tools, weapons, clothing, jewelry, cooking utensils, shelter, games, and boats, all from nothing more than the available plants, animals, and minerals. The rise of agriculture and increased trade led to more information exchange and the eventual rise of the industrial revolution and sequential processing. Industry enabled the rise of the informational, systems-based world. The resulting information exchange is leading to the recognition that we need a more holistic approach to solve our problems.

Technological innovation is occurring faster than ever, and we can realistically expect change in the next fifty years as profound as those of the last five hundred. Where technology leads the way, shifts in consciousness must follow, or we risk descending into chaos. Perhaps with awareness of the various levels of consciousness, it will be easier to transition through them.

Detaching from the Ego

At the beginning of this quest to define reality, I suggested that we, 1) distinguish cultural reality from universal reality, 2) assume that everything is true—at least within the proper context, 3) proceed with unbounded open-mindedness tempered by equally unbounded skepticism, and 4) look for consistency to test the probability or improbability of any particular version of reality.

Without these guidelines we might have discarded an idea like transcendence as

New Age babble. But by being open-minded and seeking the truth behind every reality, we have discovered that "transcending to a higher level of consciousness" is a literal expression for normal processes of human development. We all transcend to higher levels of consciousness as we mature, and we all have the opportunity to continue growing and expanding our worldviews.

Transcendence often sounds like spiritual fantasy because the idea isn't grounded in our day-to-day reality. It is for that reason I avoided the use of the word transcendence through Parts I and II of this text. But transcendence makes complete sense when we look back from our present perspective. We sequentially traced transcendence through time, seeing it unfold in the history of our species as well as within our individual lives. With our expanded vocabulary we can review the layers of consciousness from a new perspective, in terms of detaching from and transcending the ego.

At the magical level we are so fused with our individual perspective that we are oblivious to the views of other people. However, through the process of role-playing we detach from a first-person perspective to see ourselves from a second-person perspective filtered through the eyes of our own culture.

As we continue maturing we begin to acquire a third-person perspective and transcend to sequential processing. It enables us to occasionally detach from our ego to observe our actions from a neutral viewpoint. In an argument, for example, we might engage in a spirited debate, then transition to second person to truly listen to our opponent's side of the story, and finally shift into third person to objectively compare the two sides. If the evidence weighs against our case, then we may have the grace to admit we were wrong.

Transcending to systems processing brings a whole new level of detachment, where we are sufficiently free from the ego to see the self as an object that can be programmed at will. Instead of moving through life in a series of knee-jerk reactions controlled by external events, we realize that we are free to choose our own actions. No one else is responsible for how we feel or respond to any situation.

In holistic processing we detach from the ego even more. We not only move beyond our first-person perspective, we begin to observe the self from outside the web of life. We imagine an interconnected web and see ourselves as one small part of the web. This perspective reveals a high level of connection with the natural world, and yet, also highlights a lingering separation. We are part of the web, but a distinct and separate part. We perceive ourselves as individual units linked together by our actions in the web of life. There is a tendency to look in the mirror and say, "This is me. This is who I am."

In the quest to define reality we must dissolve the concept of self and transcend the ego altogether. The reason is simple; we cannot claim to be objective when our perceptions are filtered through our ego. In other words, a holistic worldview is a valid experience of reality that encompasses all previous worldviews, but the true nature of reality remains skewed through attachment to our self-identity. In the next chapter we transcend to a new level of detachment by dissolving the concept of self, breaking down the boundaries that separate us from the natural world.

—Fourteen—

Mystical Processing

Dissolving the Concept of Self

"Look at the millions of life forms on this planet alone. In the sea, on land, in the air—and then each life form is replicated millions of times. To what end? Is someone or something playing a game, a game with form? … The individual life forms are obviously not very important in this game. In the sea, most life forms don't survive for more than a few minutes after being born. The human form turns to dust pretty quickly too, and when it is gone it is as if it had never been. Is that tragic or cruel? Only if you create a separate identity for each form, if you forget that its consciousness is God-essence expressing itself in form."

—Eckhart Tolle, The Power of Now[1]

Mysticism has long been associated with deep meditation and enlightened sages, but the rise of mystical processing in mainstream culture can be traced back partly to the work of a biologist hired by NASA to search for life on Mars. James Lovelock initially assumed he would need to invent sophisticated equipment and send it to the red planet, but then realized we could test for life from here via a spectrographic analysis of the Martian atmosphere.

Our own atmosphere is composed of a highly improbable mix of reactive molecules that could not exist without living organisms to continuallfy modify the environment. Lovelock investigated the biosphere and observed that our planet has retained optimal conditions for life in the face of circumstances that could have either frozen or boiled the oceans. Just as our bodies are self-regulating to maintain a stable internal temperature regardless of the weather, the earth somehow acts like a living organism to regulate conditions in a way that is favorable for life. The diverse life forms of the world cooperate as if they were organs of a larger being. Lovelock called this the Gaia theory, after the Greek goddess of earth, creating a new metaphor, a new way of perceiving reality. The Gaia metaphor is a step beyond the web-of-life metaphor of holistic processing; it suggests that we exist like cells within a larger organism.

> Snapshot: Mystical Processing
>
> Technology: Microbiology, genetics.
>
> Origin: Eastern religions, exobiology
>
> Logic: Pluralistic.
>
> Perspective: Planetary identity, no ego.
>
> Culture: Gaia, global ark.
>
> Social-Political Structure: Personal responsibility, green anarchist.
>
> Notable People: Albert Einstein, James Lovelock.
>
> Television/Movies: *Seven Years in Tibet, The Astronaut Farmer, Cocoon, Osmosis Jones.*

Meanwhile, there is an emerging view that the human body is similar to Gaia in design, more like a colony or ecosystem of organisms working together than a solitary individual composed of many parts. Such thinking tends to dissolve any remaining concept of self, leading to a new identity that is "we" rather than "I". No longer bound by an identity tied to a specific body, the self is free to identify as anyone or anything, ultimately taking on the identity of the planet itself in a mystical perspective of reality. In this chapter we endeavor to transcend the ego by dissolving the sense of self that separates us from everything else to experience a reality in which we are again "one with nature," but totally aware of the connection.

The Gaia theory

Our species has been tinkering with nature for centuries, developing the sciences of agriculture and forestry, experimenting with fertilizers and pesticides. We are so used to managing and manipulating the ecosystem that it is difficult for many people to believe that no one controls the ecosystem, and nature can function without our help. One European tourist in Yellowstone National Park asked my sister, who worked there as a guide, *"Where do you put all the animals at night?"* In the tourist's native country, the farm animals were led back to the barns every night. It was unthinkable to imagine that these wild animals could survive on their own, without someone to bring them in at the end of each day!

Our planetary biosphere is inconceivably complex, yet created itself from nothing, materializing and prospering on a chunk of wet rock hurtling through the cold vacuum of space. The fact that life started at all on this planet is certainly a miracle, yet it is equally miraculous that life has continued to survive over the last 3.8 billion years. The sun has increased it's heat output by 25 percent in the natural course of it's own life-span, yet the temperature on earth has remained comparatively constant. Without the presence of life on earth, the oceans should have either frozen or boiled by now, or the water molecules should have broken apart and the lightweight hydrogen atoms escaped into space, taking with them any possibility of water. Even without freezing or boiling, the oceans should have become too salty to support life by now, given the amount of salts that wash off the continents each year. How could mere algae and bacteria, trees, grass, fungus, insects, birds and mammals, manage to keep the biosphere intact and hospitable in such a hostile universe?

The principle of the Gaia theory is simple. Life has modified and been modified by the biosphere, a process called co-evolution. Organisms that survive and thrive on the planet are those that help maintain the biosphere in a way that is favorable for life. An easy way to understand this concept is through an analogy that Lovelock calls "Daisy World." A hypothetical planet is colonized by black and white daisies. The black daisies absorb light as heat and warm the planet, while the white daisies reflect light and keep the planet cool. Too many black daisies cause the planet to overheat, making the world uncomfortable for them, but better for the white daisies. Too many white daisies cause the world to become too cold, thus favoring the black daisies that can absorb heat.

The real biosphere is much more complex, with billions of independent life forms functioning as a spontaneous check-and-balance system to maintain a comfortable environment for life as a whole. Algae and other plants, for instance, removed carbon dioxide from the atmosphere and buried the carbon in the form of calcium carbonate (limestone) on the ocean floors as well as in fossil fuels such as coal, oil, and gas. This carbon sequestration has reduced the greenhouse effect and kept the planet cool, even while the sun has become warmer. Likewise, moisture over the ocean forms around sulfur particles out-gassed by marine algae, thus bringing much-needed sulfur to land organisms while also controlling the amount of cloud cover over the planet.

Bacterial colonies along the seashores coat salt crystals with a sort of varnish that inhibits the salt from dissolving back into the water, helping to remove salt from the oceans. The combined weight of salt and limestone deposits on the continental shelves may be a factor in triggering plate tectonics—the movement of the continents across the globe. No detectable entity manages the globe, but each of the independent life forms on earth seems to contribute to the stability of the whole.[2]

In addition to preserving favorable conditions on earth while facing long-term threats, the Gaia effect successfully stabilized the biosphere after numerous large-scale catastrophes, such as the asteroid impact that apparently wiped out the dinosaurs sixty-five million years ago. Evidence suggests that a chunk of space rock, approximately six miles in diameter, slammed into Mexico's Yucatan Peninsula, sending a 500-foot tall tsunami towards North America.[3] [4]

Atmospheric oxygen levels were exceptionally high at the end of the Cretaceous, due to abundant plant life. In the oxygen-rich environment, global wildfires may have torched a quarter of the world's biomass, while dust and soot in the air shut down photosynthesis. The fires consumed the oxygen and loaded the atmosphere with carbon dioxide, creating a greenhouse effect. Most of the species that died out, both on land and in water, depended directly on plant or animal food chains, while those that survived were dependent on detritus. Survivors included insects and worms that consumed decaying organic matter and the small mammals and reptiles that hunted them. It took ten million years, a blink in geologic terms, for the Gaia effect to remove the carbon dioxide from the atmosphere and stabilize the biosphere.[5] [6] [7]

Ordinarily we assume that Earth was conveniently favorable for life, and living organisms merely adapted to the conditions at hand. Yet, as we have seen, life modified the biosphere, filled the atmosphere with oxygen, and built rich soils from atmospheric carbon. Life became a geologic force. We climb mountains of limestone that were built from the remains of microorganisms in ancient seas. We use coal deposits hundreds of feet thick, formed from the remains of ancient plants. Even iron and uranium deposits were formed from bacterial action eons ago. Living organisms built an Eden on this wet rock in space without the helping hand of man.

The Gaia theory was initially criticized by many within scientific circles because it sounded more like religion than science. In actuality it is a science and a worldview. As a scientist, Lovelock relied on traditional investigative methods to reveal the hard evidence of the Gaia effect, gradually building widespread acceptance in the scientific community.

Microbiology, Genetics, and Mysticism

One irony of consciousness is that technological progress physically separates us from nature, yet increases our ability to perceive our connection to nature. Mystics of past ages intuited an intimate connection with nature, and science is presently confirming that connection. Just as the Apollo space program gave birth to global consciousness and more holistic thinking, microbiology and genetics are dissolving perceptual barriers, enabling us to see that we share common ancestors and a common genetic code with all other species of plants and animals. We are learning to recognize kinship with all life, with all of Gaia.

Richard Louv inadvertently described this shift in consciousness in *Last Child in the Woods*, writing, *"Think what it means for children to grow up now, and how different their experience of nature and definition of life is, or soon will be, from the experiences of us adults. In our childhood, it was clear enough when a man was a man and a mouse was a mouse. Implicit in some of the newest technologies [such as growing a human ear on a mouse's back] is the assumption that there's little difference between living and nonliving matter at the atomic and molecular level... Not since the predominance of hunting and gathering have children been taught to see so many similarities between humans and other animals, though now those similarities are viewed in a very different, more intellectualized way."*[8]

171

The modern mystic arose from these advances in microbiology, genetics, and Gaia science, blooming into a counterculture of "Gaia worshippers," often characterized by dreadlocks, incense, and talk of honoring our Earth Mother. However, this is not a hippie revival. These individuals no longer perceive themselves as individuals in the conventional sense. They have dissolved their self-identity to degree that allows them to identify with everything else. Most have an intuitive sense of the mystical worldview, but otherwise operate at previous levels of consciousness. Yet, to the extent that they have embraced the mystical, they have begun to transcend the ego. Instead of defining themselves according to the face in the mirror, they identify with every plant and animal and rock and tree and person.

These and other budding mystics experience a new road cut into the side of a mountain as if it were cut into their own flesh. They perceive a dead coyote shot and left to rot as if it were one of their own kind. They feel guilt over every product in every store that was manufactured at the expense of desecrated environments and enslaved people. Mystics feel it all because they have dissolved their ego and expanded their identity to perceive reality from a planetary, pluralistic, all-species perspective. They are the voices of the voiceless, speaking out for the indigenous people and species that have no voice of their own.

The Self as a Community

While the Gaia effect enables us to see the earth as a collection of independent species unconsciously working together to maintain a stable biosphere, an emerging view sees the human body in a similar perspective. We exist more like ecosystems of interdependent units rather than as mere individuals. We can systematically dissolve our self-identities to better perceive reality from a pluralistic perspective.

It is natural to perceive the skin as a boundary that defines us as different from the rest of the world. However, our skin barely qualifies as a boundary, since it isn't a solid boundary, but a porous one, where water and toxins can be sweated out of the body, and medicines and poisons can easily soak into the body. For example, excessive sun exposure damages the mucopolysaccharide hydrogel between our skin cells. *Aloe vera* plants contain similar mucopolysaccharides in the leaves. The slimy substance is slathered over a sunburn to reduce the severity of the burn or turn it into a tan. We usually assume we must ingest herbs so the body can modify and utilize them for repair, but in this case, we substitute plant parts for damaged human parts. It is interesting to feel the *Aloe vera* soak in and become part of the skin.

So our skin is a boundary, but a porous one. Now, let's take it a step farther and think about our lungs. We normally assume that the boundary separating us from the world is on the outside, yet we inhale outside air deep inside of our bodies to breathe. Membranes in our lungs allow oxygen from this outside air to pass through to our bloodstream on the inside. So we could say that the boundary separating us from the world isn't on the outside, but actually wraps through to the inside, following the intricate contours within our lungs. The lungs as well as the digestive tract are lined with epithelial cells similar to our skin.

In the next step we can imagine eating a carrot. When is the carrot separate from our being and when does it become part of our identity? Is it part of our identity when we have chewed it thoroughly? Is it part of our identity when it is being digested in the stomach or traveling through the intestines? Where do we draw the line to say that a meal has crossed the boundary to become part of who we are, rather than an outsider, a carrot, that is passing through? Where do we draw the line that separates us from everything else? It is challenging to find a definitive point where we end and the rest of the world begins. This exercise is intended to cast some doubt on the concept of self-identity. Where do we end and where does the world begin? Can we distinguish ourselves as separate from the rest of the world?

Five hundred different species of microflora (bacteria) inhabit our intestinal tracks and help digest our food. We are greatly out-numbered in our own bodies by these microorganisms. Estimates vary widely, but the typical adult consists of about one hundred trillion cells, of which only ten percent are human. The other ninety percent are bacteria. Bacteria are smaller than human cells, yet out-number cells in our bodies, with the majority of them living symbiotically in the large intestine. Helpful intestinal microbes produce vitamin B12 and vitamin K and assist with digestion by breaking down carbohydrates.[9] A study of rats in a completely sterile environment showed that they could digest food without the aid of bacteria, but needed to consume thirty percent more calories.

Bacteria begin colonizing our intestines after birth. Early arrivals condition the immune system to favor their survival, while limiting the survival of competing species. Studies of the microflora of infants and young children have shown that those who develop allergies tend to house more harmful species and fewer beneficial species. Since helpful bacteria stimulate the immune system and train it to respond properly to antigens, it is theorized that a lack of beneficial bacteria in early life could lead to an inadequately trained immune system, which tends to overreact to antigens. Good bacteria also serve as a protective barrier against harmful bacteria by filling up the available habitat niches.[10] Bacteria are part of who we are, and we would not function properly without them, but are they part of our identity? Perhaps they should be.

Beneficial bacteria also live in our mouths. For example, leafy greens are rich in nitrates. Nitrates in our diet are converted to nitrites and secreted in our saliva, then converted to nitric oxide by bacteria on the back of the tongue. Nitric oxide helps kill *E. coli* and other harmful bacteria in the stomach, and may kill acid-producing bacteria in the mouth that contribute to tooth decay.[11] By using mouthwash we kill off the bacteria that are there to help us. There are even microorganisms that live inside our bloodstream, our organs, and sometimes our brains. Some are beneficial and others may be harmful.

The more we think about the human body and how much we share it with other living organisms, the more we seem like walking ecosystems rather than individuals. For example, after antibiotics have wiped out the microflora in the gut, we can restore balance by eating yogurt with active cultures. The beneficial bacteria happily reside in the digestive tract and assist with digestion. In the past we had a very sequential view of bacteria, seeing them as separate from ourselves and totally dispensable. But now we are learning how interdependent we really are.

Scientists are discovering that some medical problems, such as ulcers and certain forms of cancer, can be caused by bacterial outbreaks. Yet, we also know that taking too many antibiotics can kill beneficial bacteria, which could potentially lead to an outbreak of the bad ones. Scientists are finding that exposure to a few pathogens can be beneficial to keep the immune system busy, since an otherwise idle immune system can attack just about anything else, leading to allergies to dogs and cats, pollen, and food.

Thus, good health is a matter of establishing a balanced personal ecosystem with a diversity of beneficial microorganisms to ward off potentially dangerous pathogens. Excessive use of antibiotics and antibacterials not only weakens our own bodies, it ultimately breeds more resistant, more dangerous bacteria that could cause greater harm in the future. A sequential view of human health has put us at great risk, due to the overuse of antibiotics and other drugs. Viewing the human body more like an ecosystem promises to lead to better health for all.

Our human cells can also be thought of like an ecosystem or colony. Specialized cells produce enzymes to digest food, transport materials in the body, search out and destroy pathogens, and repair wounds. It is as if the human body is a densely packed city with billions of individuals working in unison, and we are largely oblivious to it. We see an individual in the mirror, yet we exercise little control or awareness about what goes on inside. We identify our mind space as our own, and we control the major motor functions of the physical unit we associate with, but for all practical purposes, this colony of cells is its own community. Our conscious existence is merely along for the ride. The "individual" we see in the mirror is a fabrication. We exist as a vast collective of life forms, most of which are not human, unconsciously working together as cohesive unit.

In terms of identity, we have to make a choice. Do we define ourselves as the sum total of this walking, talking, portable ecosystem which functions autonomously without our awareness, or do we identify with the mind space associated with it? Let's consider it from another angle.

Almost all life forms on earth are either single-celled organisms like bacteria or multi-celled organisms like ourselves. Only a handful of species, such as cellular slime molds, are able to exist both ways. Cellular slime molds exist first as single-celled organisms that feed on bacteria in decomposing organic matter on the forest floor. After consuming the available nutrients, they emit a chemical signal to attract nearby slime molds, and the individual cells slowly migrate towards each other through the detritus. Up to 100,000 cells merge to form a tower. In the absence of light, the tower becomes prostrate like a slug and migrates as a single organism, much like a slug. When light is found, the cells differentiate into a base, stalk, and a top with encapsulated spores. The spores are released to start the cycle as single cells again.[12] Imagine if we existed as single cells in the lawn but suddenly decided to congregate in one spot to build a human body in the middle of the yard. That is essentially what these slime molds do, but on a smaller scale. Thinking about this example, we have to ask: what is the difference between ourselves and slime mold? Not much. Like slime mold, we exist as a colony of cells working together to make something bigger.

What if the sole reason for our existence was simply to allow the cells in our big toe to see the mountains? No cell by itself can see the mountains or ponder its own existence, but by working cooperatively, a colony of cells is able to achieve new perceptions of reality. Cells probably lack such intentions, but it is a useful mental exercise to break free from static thinking. Interestingly, single-celled organisms can sometimes control the behavior of multi-cellular life forms. We like to think that we are in control of our behaviors, but as we have seen throughout this book, we react to the world on autopilot, using scripts that have been mimicked and passed down from generation to generation. But what if we were even less sentient than that? What if our behaviors are controlled by microorganisms? There are many known pathogens that can alter the behavior of their host to better suit their needs.

For example, the lifecycle of a common fluke, *Euhaplorchis californiensis*, includes stages in a snail, a fish, and a bird. Studies in a California salt marsh revealed that forty percent of the snails were infected by flukes. However, the fluke is not an idle passenger. The parasite neuters the snail, making it unable to reproduce, so the fluke becomes the sole beneficiaries of the snail's resources. The nearly mature fluke swims free of the snail to search for a killifish. It latches onto its gills and enters the bloodstream, eventually following a nerve to the brain. The fluke forms a thin layer over the brain and waits until the fish is eaten by a shorebird. However, to increase the odds of being eaten, the parasite manipulates the fish to swim close to the surface of the water in a shimmying motion that exposes its shiny underbelly to the light. Shorebirds are thirty times more likely to catch one of these infected fish, which appears to be a good deal for the birds. The parasites, meanwhile, break out of the fish head and live in the bird's gut where they steal food and produce eggs. The fluke eggs are distributed back over the marsh through the bird droppings to be consumed by snails grazing on algae.

Similar studies have shown that the lancelet fluke (*Dicrocoelium dendriticum*), which cycles between ants and herbivores, can make its ant host climb a blade of grass and cling to it until eaten by a passing cow or deer. Similarly, hairworms can sabotage a grasshopper's nervous system, causing it to drown itself in water, where the hairworms swim free. One of the world's smallest tapeworms (*Echinococcus granulosus*) can cause a massive cyst in the lungs of an herbivore host, such as a moose, weakening it until it is susceptible to predators like wolves, which is where the parasite needs to be to complete its lifecycle.[13] So, if parasites can manipulate the behavior of fish, ants, grasshoppers, and the relationship between wolves and their prey, we have to wonder what might manipulating our behavior? What if our wants and needs are driven by parasites?

Even if we successfully dissolve our self-identity and learn to see ourselves as colonies more than as individuals, we may still associate our individuality with our DNA. DNA is like a fingerprint that makes each of us unique and different from anyone else in the world. It is the basic building block that defines us, the set of instructions that we are designed from. But keep in mind that our DNA has its own life, and like a fish that has been commandeered by a fluke, we are the equivalent of temporary hosts for our DNA to migrate from one living being to the next.

Our DNA is part of an unbroken chain of life that can be traced back 3.8 billion years to the beginning of life on earth. The concept that is hard to fathom is that it is truly an unbroken chain. In all of 3.8 billion years our DNA has never died. It has been miscopied extensively to create many unique life forms, but it is still an unbroken chain of living code that has been splitting in half and making copies of itself over and over again for nearly four billion years. Many copies were flawed and failed to continue replicating, and many species were killed out before they could pass their DNA on to a new generation, but our DNA has successfully stayed alive for 3.8 billion years.

From a purely sequential, Darwinian perspective, the origin of life in all its diversity was completely accidental. DNA replicates itself over and over again and gradually accumulates various errors, many of which turn out to be fatal flaws, but some miscopied versions turn out to be successful mistakes that lead to new life forms. The vast majority of new organisms are simple life forms that can efficiently replicate without wasting precious energy on grey matter, but occasionally organisms evolve a degree of intelligence that proves to be beneficial for survival.

While our DNA has been alive for 3.8 billion years, obviously neither you nor I have. To further dissolve the concept of self, we could anthropomorphize our DNA to suggest that it has the desire to perpetuate itself, and we exist solely as temporary hosts, vessels to transport it from one life form, our parents, to the next, our children. We could imagine our DNA as a virus, and having children is the way that it is transmitted from one host to another. Once we have passed the virus on to our children, then we have limited remaining utility, other than to protect them until they can infect the next generation. Looking at it from this perspective, does our DNA really define our identity, or are we just being used by our DNA to get from one host to another, to perpetuate its own seemingly eternal existence?

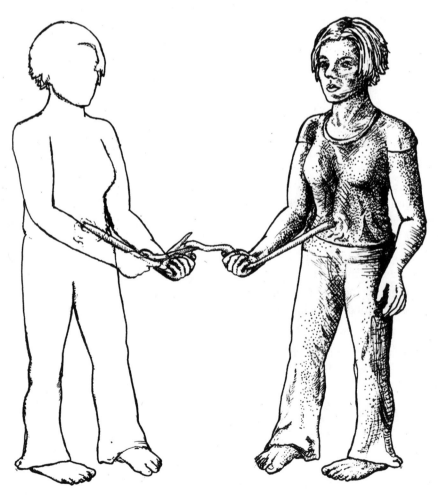

The point of this mental exercise is to completely dissolve our concept of self-identity. When we look in the mirror we may no longer see the self as an individual, but as a collective, and not the product of our DNA, but a temporary host for it. Through these mental exercises we can begin to detach from our physical identity, transcend our concept of self, and dissolve the notion that our identity is our body. When we dissolve our physical identity we are left with only our mental space. We can imagine, that like a slime mold in reverse, we can dissolve the physical body into its constituent organisms. Our cells are parting ways and disappearing back into the lawn. All we are left with is the mind.

Letting go like this is a challenging, because we identify so strongly with our bodies that the idea of dissolving the self triggers an instinct for self-preservation. But keep in mind that this is merely a mental exercise, a momentary shift to get a new perspective on the nature of reality. If you can mentally detach from your physical identity and dissolve the concept of self, then you are prepared to explore reality in unique and exciting ways. Aware of the possibilities, you may experience reality from this new perspective at sudden and unexpected moments. When you have dissolved your sense of self in this manner, then you are free to identify with something else, with anything else you see. You can look at a deer and become the deer. Look at a tree and become the tree. Float free from your physical limitations and become any rock, flower, or mountain.

The first time I consciously felt this level of connection to the natural world was in July of 2000 on a canoe trip with our kids. We were floating the upper Missouri River in north central Montana, and I was looking at a frog in a pond at our campsite. I had the mild sensation that I wasn't looking at a different being, but rather that I was looking at myself, and the frog in the pond was me. While difficult to describe in words, it is a profound way to experience the world.

In my years of learning and practicing primitive wilderness survival skills, I desired to achieve that feeling of being "one with nature," but usually ended up feeling as though I didn't belong, especially after my shelters leaked rain or I couldn't find food. And yet, here I was tent camping with the family and cooking on a propane stove, when suddenly *I knew* I was one with nature. It wasn't a mere belief, but a feeling of deep connection. It is a feeling I have experienced many times since, that I share my identity with all of nature. I am the trees, the mountains, the river, the highway, even the keyboard that I type on, and all the people I meet in my life.

John Kirsch, the Catholic priest who wore his hiking boots when he performed our wedding ceremony, often described himself as a mystic. Kirsch was an elk biologist before joining the priesthood. In his years of field research in the mountains of Montana, he developed an intimate connection with the natural world, which gradually fused with his religious practice. At first he felt out of place bringing this deep connection to nature into the church, but he quickly found an enthusiastic following when he started sharing his spiritual experiences publicly. Of his relationship to the elk, he once wrote, *"...every entity is related to every other entity and is part of the total unity. Therefore, how can I mark off where I end and the elk begins, or the elk ends and I begin?"*[4] He connected with the world at a mystical level, seeing, feeling, and breathing the reality that he and the elk shared the same identity.

177

It is challenging to dissolve one's sense of identity by merely reading a chapter, but you can imagine a mystical perspective. How would it feel to fly like a robin? How might it feel to be a rabbit in a plot being bull-dozed for a subdivision? What would it be like to experience the evening news as if you were watching yourself? As described by Roshi Philip Kapleau in *The Three Pillars of Zen*, *"…all of nature, mountains and rivers, are seen as oneself. In this deeper realization of oneness you will feel the preconsciousness of each object in the universe, rejecting nothing, since things as well as people will be seen as essential aspects of yourself."*[5]

Similarly, as noted by Ken Wilber in *A Brief History of Everything*, *"You are not a part of nature, nature is a part of you. And for just that reason, you treat nature as you would treat your lungs or your kidneys. A spontaneous environmental ethics surges forth from your heart, and you will never again look at a river, a leaf, a deer, a robin, in the same way."*[6] It may not be easy to dissolve your personal identity to experience this worldview, but if successful, you will experience life in a mystical way, and it will totally change your perception of reality. For one thing, if you dissolve your self-identity, you may also dissolve all remaining sense of culture.

The End of Culture

In the quest for the real reality we have explored many worldviews, each with its own definition of what reality is. While each worldview offers a unique perception of reality, it should be noted that our perceptions change, not reality itself. We assume we can look at reality and see it for what it is, but each worldview is skewed by attachment to our self-identity. It is only by letting go of the ego that we begin to detach from one worldview and shift to the next. We learn to see ourselves from the outside, and we learn to observe our own behaviors. In so doing, we detach not only from our self-identity, but also from our cultural identity. Culturally introduced rules and roles seem black-and-white from a mythical worldview, becoming murky shades of grey from a sequential viewpoint. Rules an roles are rejected as artificial fabrications from a systems perspective. At the holistic level we begin to set goals and create our own rules and roles of mutual respect. At the mystical level, all of human culture is recognized as inherently artificial.

I never fit into the social scene as a teenager and young adult, so the scene always seemed artificial. If I had to go to a social function, I pictured everyone around me as animated skeletons. I could better grasp what was and wasn't real by seeing people as walking, talking skeletons. From this perspective it was obvious that the make-up, the clothes, and the conversations were all artificial fabrications. People were attracted to bright lights and loud sounds, and pretended to have a good time at a party, yet none of it was real. To borrow from Shakespeare it was, *"A tale told by an idiot, full of sound and fury, signifying nothing."* I'm not sure if I started seeing social functions this way because I was a social misfit, or if I became a social misfit because of my perceptions. Either way, I did not fit in. My alienation wasn't limited to social functions either.

In the black-and-white perspective of my youth, I wanted to know what was real and what wasn't real. I observed that, like a child drawn to a clown in a bright costume or the tooting of a party horn, the spotlight of our cultural attention swung around to whomever could make the most noise and commotion of self-importance at the moment. That which was revered as real and important in our culture shifted back and forth like the wind. People talked and gossiped about people and events that were relevant only because everyone was talking about them. Tomorrow they would talk about something different.

Culturally, I enjoyed a good movie, play, or song as much as the next person, but I learned to see culture itself as full of self-importance but lacking substance. While our entire culture revolved around things that were temporary, I was drawn to the natural world where change was measured in millennia.

Human drama is merely drama, but the natural world beckoned to me as the real world. I spent much of my youth learning plant identification and wilderness survival skills, including stalking wild animals to watch them eat and play. I liked to stalk deer to see how close I could get without being detected. Sometimes I let them know I was there and non-threatening. I grazed as if I were another deer to gain their trust so they wouldn't run away. Instead of ignoring nature as if it were mere wallpaper in the background of illustrious human endeavors, I appreciated the birds in a parking lot as having lives as important or unimportant as our own. Their drama was as meaningful as our own.

The downside to being intimately connected to nature is seeing it destroyed by civilization. I felt stricken every time I saw senseless development. I couldn't understand why people were blind to the destruction. The moment of insight came when I volunteered to drive my teenage daughters to a dance at the county fair. Upon arrival I was overcome with raw instinct that the dance was the root cause of all environmental destruction. I am blessed and cursed with this ability to connect even the most mundane events to a global perspective, and I realized that the greatest threat to the planet might be that most people were completely absorbed in personal dramas and human culture, totally oblivious to the natural world.

We could exterminate half of all life on earth and few people would notice the difference, which is exactly what we are doing. Consider that billions of passenger pigeons once blanketed the skies before being hunted to extinction, yet the skies seem perfectly normal without them. The world outside the window will continue to look perfectly normal until every last species is gone.

It was a beautiful night outside at the dance, and I couldn't shake the sense that my kids were drawn to the lights and music like insects to a bug zapper. There was nothing inherently wrong with this particular dance, but I found myself in tears trying to cope with it. My kids never knew when Dad would lose it for no apparent reason.

Green Anarchism

The common definition of anarchy is chaos. Without the guiding hand of government to lay down the law and maintain order, we imagine unfettered theft and violence, mass panic and the fall of civilization. Indeed, I have met anarchists who were angry at society.

179

They perceived civilization as enslaving people and nature. They blamed civilization for programming people, taking away their humanity, and turning them into consumers without a conscience. In their view, children are schooled to limit their thinking and freedom. They are taught to jump through hoops to get anywhere. They learn to become cogs in the mindless machinery of civilization.

Green anarchists join demonstrations to protest global trade, which they see as an instrument of corporate greed to exploit people and natural resources. They want to burn down houses and blow up dams to do their part to help the environment. Clearly, this is a mythical, good versus bad, black-and-white perception of reality. Yet, behind the anger there is an undercurrent of emerging mysticism and deep conscience. With my background in wilderness survival skills I have sometimes been a magnet for green anarchists who want to escape civilization and live in harmony with nature. Through extensive conversations I learned to see through the anger and hatred to understand the future they envisioned. Between outbursts of railing against the evils of society, these individuals described a remarkable and positive vision.

They intuited a mystical connection with the world, but processed it through the wiring of youthful, mythical minds. Filtering out everything they stand against reveals what they stand for. Green anarchists propose a world of unbounded freedom and self-actualization tempered by an ethic of personal responsibility and mutual respect for all people and all life. The passion of this green anarchist movement is underestimated in our country, and there is potential for a large-scale ecoterrorism attack. Green anarchists are usually not bad people, just desperate individuals who have intuited a deeper meaning in the world and don't know what to do with it. The civilized world is presently incapable of hearing them, and these mostly young

people don't know how to channel their message in a positive direction.

The situation is analogous to a rabbit trying to stop a bulldozer. The bulldozer operator is oblivious to the rabbit. If the driver sees the rabbit at all, it will be a fleeting glimpse as it runs for safety or disappears under the blade. Green anarchists perceive the world from the perspective of the rabbit. They feel deeply and identify with every life lost to the machine of civilization. A bulldozer is not just a symbol of development and progress, but of murder. Green anarchists are as panicked as the rabbit and hope to speak for the voiceless denizens of the world.

Ironically, green anarchists are just as voiceless. Nobody would hear them if they stood on the street corner and screamed all day. Their message cannot be heard from a mythical, sequential, or systems perspective. The difference is that, unlike rabbits, anarchists are capable of committing arson or wielding dynamite, uranium, or anthrax. They imagine, wrongly so, that people will get the message if they can draw enough attention to it, or life will be better if there are fewer people on the planet. Fortunately, the anarchists I have met were so heartfelt and apologetic about taking the life of a squirrel or chicken that they could never bring themselves to physically harm another human being.

In talking with green anarchists, I was surprised at how passionately they felt trapped by the machinery of civilization. I realized that I grew up completely unfettered by that perception. The world of my youth was largely free of the pressures and expectations of society, and virtually devoid of government regulation. It was a place of boundless freedom where it was okay to walk across other people's property, and it was a world of mutual respect for others. I felt free to pursue my interests and live my dreams. I was unaware that other people experienced a different reality.

There were puzzling clues, but it was a mystery to me. I recall one friend's mother commenting on my idealism, saying that I would find out what the world was really like when I became an adult. I was shocked when my high school computer teacher lectured our class about the need to work hard to get good grades to get into college to study hard to eventually get a good-paying job to endure until retirement. At least that was my perspective of the lecture. What a dismal picture he painted of the future! I didn't realize until I was in my thirties that everyone else in the class probably accepted that future as fate long before the lecture.

Never realizing that our dreams were impractical, Renee and I bought land and built our house without a reliable source of income or any significant building experience. Without taking any botany classes, I wrote *Botany in a Day* to simplify plant identification. Without prior business experience I started my own publishing company and other businesses. The freedom to self-actualize, to follow one's dreams without jumping through hoops or becoming enslaved by civilization, is the essence of what green anarchy is really all about. A large part of why I grew up feeling so free had to do with when and where I grew up.

Montana is often perceived as a conservative, anti-government, guns-God-and-glory state, which it is. However, Montana is also a very pro-environment state, as evidenced by the preamble to the constitution, *"We the people of Montana grateful to God for the quiet beauty of our state, the grandeur of our mountains, the vastness of our rolling plains, and desiring to improve the quality of life, equality of opportunity and to secure the blessings of liberty for this and future generations do ordain and establish this constitution."* Furthermore, the declaration of inalienable rights begins with *"the right to a clean and healthful environment."* Historically, Montana has been neither truly conservative nor liberal, but more accurately green anarchist, in the positive sense of the word. Montanans' mystical relationship to the land is reflected in the preamble. Evidence of green anarchist thinking is revealed by such legislation as the "reasonable and prudent" speed limit on our highways. It was legal to drive as fast as conditions safely allowed, until the law was deemed unconstitutional in 1998.

Montana was largely settled by disgruntled southerners who wanted to escape government oppression after the Civil War. They came to Montana where there were few people and no laws, and they kept it that way. Although there was a quiet beauty and grandeur to this untamed state, it was a tough place to live. The winters were long, cold, and windy. The summers were hot, dry, and too short to grow many crops. Montana was often low on the income scale, and people persisted only because they valued the connection to the land more than they valued material wealth. Farmers were pleased to see wildlife eating their profits and content to find trespassers fishing, hiking, and hunting on their land. Police were so scarce that one could drive all day without seeing a patrol car. Montana was so free of regulation that we needed only a septic permit by mail and a cursory electrical inspection when we built our home. It was a place where, until recently, people didn't bother to lock their doors, ever.

I walked into a public restroom recently and felt the passing of a way of life. Here was an unsupervised building with light fixtures and mirrors that could be easily shattered, doors that could be mangled, porcelain fixtures that invited vandalism. The white walls were free of graffiti and entirely immaculate. How sad I thought, that such facilities will likely disappear in another ten or twenty years, to be replaced by vandal-resistant facilities. How ironic that Montana was most civil when it was least civilized.

I am dismayed to travel around our country to see gated communities, houses with bars on the windows, highways lined in litter, and no trespassing signs everywhere. It is only in recent times that the machine of civilization has discovered Montana. Newcomers arrived oblivious to our traditional way of life. They bought land and posted signs to keep everyone else out. They bulldozed the tops of hills to put houses where they could get the best view, ruining the view for everyone else. I wondered if I was naive as a young man, hiking across farms and ranches as if they were public property, but I have talked to other people who grew up the same way. One rancher told me how pleased he was to find people fishing on his property. After he retired and sold the ranch he was shocked to see the "no trespassing" signs go up. He was no longer allowed to be on the place he had lived his entire life!

Although conservative in ideology, traditional Montanans are mystics and green anarchists at heart. To me, Montana was an environment of boundless freedom and mutual respect that fostered a perspective of unlimited possibilities. The freedom we took for granted is the vision espoused by green anarchists today. They seek freedom for themselves, freedom and respect for all people, and freedom for all species.

Home, School, and Government

There is an old tribal proverb that states, *"It takes a village to raise a child."* As may be evident by now, higher levels of consciousness return back to nature and our hunter-gatherer roots. The values and ideals espoused by Gaia followers and anarchists resemble hunter-gatherer lifestyles. Many tribes functioned like big families; everyone shared food and shelter and responsibility for the children. Any adult could fill the role of mother or father as appropriate. It was an inherently anarchist lifestyle. Children learned by being in a rich community of younger and older people without structured classes. They were not segregated into groups according to age as they are in our culture. And, weather permitting, people lived nearly or completely naked, as some tropical tribes still do today.

Images of tribal people living in the nude seem completely natural to most of us. We don't think twice about it. But imagine a modern American family living that way, with mom, dad, and teenage boys and girls all naked together doing family activities like cooking, reading books, watching television, or playing catch in the backyard. It is a jarring image even to many "liberal" sensibilities, yet no more unnatural than tribal life. To a person growing up in a nude household, nudity is natural and sensual or tactile rather than sexual. Many modern families do practice such nudism and sometimes take vacations to nudist resorts, where kids can hang out with other kids in the nude. It is a sensual lifestyle because one's entire skin is constantly exposed to the flowing air, the textures of the furniture, warm and cool surfaces, or the bare skin of other people.

I once brought my summer interns on a joint wilderness survival trek with another instructor and her interns. We were told to expect some nudity, which didn't bother us. I've always enjoyed hiking up to a mountain lake for a quick skinny dip. It is part of our Montana heritage. Just about every grandmother or grandfather can fondly recall skinny-dipping in their youth. We were surprised, however, to learn that the other group lived nude together all summer. On the first day of the trip my co-instructor threw a watermelon in the lake, which these guys and girls were fighting over naked, and it was completely natural. My group sat on the shore and watched, because we knew it would be too arousing to swim out there and wrestle with naked men and women. However, with each passing day we became increasingly comfortable in the nude. Nude was beginning to feel natural towards the end of the week.

Our ancestors lived nude for at least ninety-five percent of human history. Clothing was invented with the Cultural Revolution primarily for survival in colder climates. People did not need to hide themselves in modesty or insulate themselves during warm weather. Clothing only became "necessary" at the dawn of agriculture, when people became self-conscious and separate from nature. Clothing outwardly expressed an internal perception of reality. As we connect again with our true nature, we may find less need for clothing.

In terms of education, the mystical/anarchist equivalent of hunter-gatherer schooling, or lack of it, is "unschooling." Unschooling is usually practiced as a form of home-schooling, but it is also the philosophy of some private schools. The guiding belief is that children naturally desire to learn and formal instruction can squelch that desire, turning learning into a chore. Thus, unschooling allows kids do virtually whatever they want. Parents or teachers are there to facilitate learning only when the child desires it. If a child wants to do nothing but play video games for a year, then he can do that. Eventually, he will get bored with it and want to do something more interesting. The point is that real learning doesn't take place until the student desires to know something. At Sudbury Valley School in Framingham, Massachusetts, for example, a group of students asked a teacher to teach them math skills. The teacher only consented when it was evident that the students were serious about learning. With the aid of the teacher, the students eagerly devoured the math and homework, mastering six year's worth of addition, subtraction, multiplication, division, long division, fractions, decimals, percentages and square roots in twenty hours of class instruction over twenty weeks.[17] It should be noted that, as with traditional schools, unschooling does not achieve miraculous results with every student. Some students still fall through the cracks.

The most important skills learned at schools like Sudbury are not necessarily reading, writing, nor arithmetic, but self-management and social organization. For instance, one teenage girl expressed anger at having wasted two years of her life without learning anything, to which the teacher replied, *"If you learned how bad it is to waste time, why then you could not have learned a better lesson so early in life, a lesson that will be of value for the rest of your days."*[18]

At Sudbury students learn to take ownership of their lives and education, as reported in the magazine *Psychology Today*, *"At weekly town hall-like school meetings, every student, like every staff member, has one vote, and students govern the school completely, debating and deciding on staff hires, budgets and all rules. That 5-year-olds have as much say as 17-year-olds may explain why all sit raptly through a two-hour meeting. Day-to-day, an elected eight-person judicial council representing every age group enforces the rules voted in school meetings. A student might be charged with bringing illegal substances on campus or disturbing someone else's right to quiet; students and staffers alike can file a complaint; they come to see it as a way of protecting their special community."*

Psychology Today reported that Sudbury *"students go on to lead deeply satisfying lives. Most are unusually resilient. Almost all feel that they are in control of their destiny. In disproportionately high numbers—42 percent—Sudbury graduates become entrepreneurs. The alumni study shows that a "spectacularly high number" pursue careers in the arts—music, art, dance, writing, acting. Math, business and education are popular routes, too."*[19]

In the nation-as-family metaphor, as one may sense from these examples, the mystical state would be a self-governing, clothing-optional society with minimal institutional structure or laws. It would also be a society that recognizes that all species have a fundamental right to existence.

Worldviews and Wolves

We know that worldviews greatly affect our perception of reality, but the depth of our filtering can be challenging to grasp. Even gazing at a wild animal, we filter the experience based on our cultural heritage. Author Barry Lopez noted perceptual shifts in his book *Of Wolves and Men*, writing that *"...in the wolf we have not so much an animal that we have always known as one that we have consistently imagined."*[20] He noted that we don't merely observe wild animals; we create them in our minds.[21]

In primitive hunting cultures people typically revered and emulated wolves. Wolves are highly social, playful, and care for each other, by bringing food back from the hunt. Hunters copied wolf strategies, such as chasing prey animals onto frozen lakes so they lose their footing on the ice. Hunters admired wolves because they could feed themselves even when humans struggled to survive. Consequently, hunters often wore wolf skins and wolf masks in their rituals and magic.

The transition to agriculture and livestock led to a radically different perception of wolves. Wolves were a constant threat to livestock, so they were demonized and eradicated. Wolves could also be seen on battlefields in the *"eerie twilight of dawn and dusk"* eating the human dead. In folklore the wolf became *"the Devil, red tongued, sulfur breathed, and yellow eyed; he was the werewolf, human cannibal; he was the lust, greed, and violence that men saw in themselves."*[22]

In this mythical era, wild and domestic animals were sometimes put on trial for murder, based on the Judaic law of retribution, an eye for an eye. In Germany in 1685 a wolf was put on trial because it was preying on livestock and it was believed to have killed some women and children. People thought the animal was the reincarnation of a local, hated magistrate, so they hunted and killed the wolf, then dressed it in a suit of flesh-colored cloth and fitted it with a mask, wig, and beard to look like the magistrate. Then they had a trial, convicted the dead wolf, and did a ritual hanging in the town square.[23] Our concept of werewolves comes from this period in European history, when it was believed that some people could become wolves at night. If a person fended off a wolf with a sharp stick one night, then discovered a neighbor with a scratch the next day, it was evidence enough that the person was a werewolf. Thousands of people were burned at the stake based on less substantial evidence.[24]

In colonizing America, Puritans saw wilderness as an insult to the Lord and a challenge to men to prove their religious conviction by taming it. Wolves symbolized wilderness as well as man's former bestial nature. Men hunted bears, mountain lions and bobcats, but not with the fanaticism that was unleashed against wolves. Other predators were typically hunted to the extent that they threatened livestock, but wolves were hunted to eradicate them all.

Poisons became widely available for the first time with the settling of the West. Settlers shot buffalo and other wild animals and poisoned the carcasses to kill wolves and coyotes, inadvertently killing every other creature that fed on the meat, including ferrets, skunks, badgers, foxes, dogs, raccoons, weasels, eagles, ravens, hawks, ground squirrels, wolverines, and bears. The dying animals often slobbered poison on the grass where it dried in the sun, eventually killing horses, antelope, and buffalo.[25] Even children succumbed to the poison frenzy.[26] Lopez noted that people didn't merely kill wolves, they tortured them. Some people set wolves on fire, or cut their Achilles tendons and turned dogs loose on them. People burned their own forests just to remove any cover where wolves could hide.[27]

The religious fervor died out with the gradual transition to a sequential worldview. However, as a result of the mechanistic perspective of Newton and Descartes, people perceived wild animals as mere biological machines. Wolves were hunted for sport as trophy animals, or merely for the joy of blasting them apart with big guns. But the primary justification for continued killing was that wolves competed with hunters for big game animals. Based on linear thinking, killing the wolves left more deer, elk, caribou, and moose for hunters.

Lopez noted that modern biologists study wolves as if they genuinely hope to understand them, yet they still process the data through their own filters. Biologists accept only statistical, repeatable data in hopes of creating a consistent model of wolf behavior, as if wolves were mere biological machines. In actuality, wolves and wolf packs exhibit tremendous individuality, which is unrepresented in the scientific perspective.

Our culture is transitioning towards a more holistic view of wolves, that they are part of the web of life, essential for controlling herd size and culling weak or diseased animals. Wolves have been reintroduced into some of our last remaining wild places, such as Yellowstone National Park, to restore balance to the ecosystem. It is recognized that wolves do sometimes prey on livestock, and programs are in place to selectively hunt problem wolves and to compensate ranchers for their losses.

The mystical worldview brings an entirely new perspective on wolves, that they have as much right to exist as we do. Visionaries are dreaming and strategizing the rewilding of the North American continent to bring back open prairies, buffalo herds, and the wolves that herded them.

Automated Technology and Rewilding the Continent

Green anarchists rail against the evils of technology, but the irony is that technology is both the inspiration and solution to their mystical vision. These are not disadvantaged youths reacting with jealousy against the rich, but usually people who grew up with material abundance and found it empty. They are more prone to question the meaning of life than people who live a hand-to-mouth existence. As Japanese farmer Masanobu Fukuoka noted in his book *The Natural Way of Farming*, "*agonizing over life and death, and wandering through ideological thickets in search of truth were the pastimes of idle city youth.*"[28] For lack of any obvious answers to the meaning of life, some people turn to drugs, others shrug and become good consumers without a conscience, while some become conscientious protesters.

In their search for purpose and meaning, green anarchists voluntarily choose a lifestyle of extreme simplicity. Many anarchists feel extreme guilt and avoid buying anything if they can help it. They don't want their money to cause harm to other people or organisms. They often shop for basic needs and food out of dumpsters and wear the same ratty clothes until the patches and duct tape fail to hold them together.

Paradoxically, the green anarchist quest for meaning hints at what will happen to mainstream society when mass production makes everything essentially free. In many ways, we have nearly reached that point already. The cost of most material goods has steadily dropped for the past ten thousand years. Consider the cost of clothing.

Being experienced in primitive wilderness survival, I have scraped and tanned deer hides and sewn clothes as did our hunter-gatherer ancestors. It is a load of work to make one set of clothes. A simple agricultural society is slightly more efficient with a handful of tanners or weavers that specialize in the craft and trade clothing for other goods and services they need. In an industrial society textiles are made far more efficiently with the aid of better machinery and assembly lines. In an informational society the process becomes increasingly automated as computers do the work. Clothing is also more customized, as individual parameters can be programmed in without retooling the factory. In essence, we started with a system that made shirts one at a time, evolved to a system that could make ten at a time, to making a hundred, to making a thousand. The promise of profit drives endless competition to streamline production.

Making more shirts for the same amount of labor lowers costs and results in greater profits. Therefore, we can afford to lower prices below the competition's to steal market share. The problem is that when we lower the cost of production, then our competition must follow suit to stay in business. They streamline operations to compete, leading to a price war with each side dropping prices until the profit is nearly gone. Thus, if we were able to feed our family and pay the mortgage while making a hundred shirts per day in the industrial economy, we might have to make a thousand shirts per day just to stay in the same place in an informational economy. Fortunately, the same phenomenon hits every other industry as well, so that prices are lowered on all mass-produced goods. Today, the cost of a new shirt is a pittance, due primarily to automation, but tragically also due to cheap sweatshop labor. I've been astonished to see my kids buy new clothes for about the same cost as used clothes from a thrift store. Clothing is practically free already, which is why most people have more of it than they can handle.

The cost of most other products continues to fall in a similar way, and some things are already free. For example, there were only a handful of wilderness survival guides on the market when I was a teenager. Today, there are hundreds of books in print, and more importantly, thousands of free articles, guides, and videos on the Internet. Meanwhile, computers are rapidly increasing in capability while costs are holding steady or falling. Even the cost of food has fallen steadily for ten thousand years. It takes progressively less work to grow bushels of wheat or heads of lettuce, leading to steadily lower prices over the long-term, when adjusted for inflation. Farms of the future will likely be automated, indoor facilities.

The first vertical farm is being constructed in Las Vegas, Nevada. A thirty-story tall building will grow a hundred different fruit and vegetable crops, providing enough food for 72,000 people. Indoor farms reduce transportation costs to market, and have the potential to become closed-loop systems, where city sewage becomes nutrients to grow the crops.[29] A similar idea has been proposed to build vertical farms in New York City. Each building would fill an entire city block and feed 50,000 people. It would take 150 such buildings to feed all of New York.[30]

In another development, researchers are working to bring artificial tissue cultivation to market, meaning that it will be possible to grow meat while eliminating the need for wasteful bones, guts, hide or hair. It may soon be possible to grow a steak in something like a bread machine using only a few starter cells and some growth medium.[31] [32]

Factory-grown food might sound like a green anarchist's worst nightmare, and reactively offensive to mainstream sensibilities. However, tissue cultivation will facilitate the rewilding of the continent. In short, most of the world's land and oceans are exploited to produce food and goods for people. Even scenic "wild lands" are mostly utilized and degraded to raise beef or timber. Due to mass production, farmers still get paid the same amount for their goods as they did decades ago, while operating costs have risen. The result is that farms and ranches are steadily consolidated into ever-larger operations. At some point it will no longer be economical to compete with factory-grown food. That is the moment when farmlands could revert to wilderness. The Great Plains have been experiencing depopulation for decades due to the challenge of making a living at ranching. These lands will be the first to be reverted to wild lands, with the promise of restoring the massive herds of buffalo that once roamed the plains. Where humanity has failed to manage the land and carbon cycle sustainably, nature will have the opportunity to heal itself.

Human culture is in for a revolutionary shift as we continue to speed towards the point when everyone's material needs are satisfied by automated systems. When people no longer have to work for material gain, they will be left searching for deeper meaning in life. Free from enslavement to the machine of civilization, individuals will seek meaning in their lives through such things as introspection, the arts, curiosity, or working for the betterment of humanity. In the next chapter we will explore emerging technology that will complete the transition to an economy where everything is free.

Beyond the Mystical

When you dissolve your concept of self so that you no longer have a personal identity, but now identify with all of Gaia, then you are also ready for the surreal experience of detaching from your preconceived notions about matter and time, which we begin to do in the next chapter. The journey ahead will challenge your most cherished notions about the nature of reality. As was first expressed by physicist Arthur Eddington, *"Not only is the universe stranger than we imagine, it is stranger than we can imagine."*[33] But there is no harm in trying. The only way to discover the true nature of reality is to embrace it, no matter how bizarre it seems.

In our day-to-day lives of working a job, paying bills, and getting kids off to school, it can be challenging to imagine the relevance of such an endeavor. It seems as if the cosmos have no direct relevance to our lives in the here and now. But counter-intuitively, the universe is not "out there" separate from our existence. By exploring the universe, we are effectively looking in the mirror and exploring ourselves. In this journey we transcend our notions about matter and time to find a completely new worldview, a new experience of reality, within the mundane routines of our daily lives.

If your brain is not wired for processing paradoxes, then it may be helpful to read or watch science fiction. Sci-fi often plays out paradoxical stories based on themes from quantum physics, parallel universes, and time travel. Immersing oneself in science fiction is helpful for developing the neural network required to process the ideas presented through the rest of this book. Science fiction helps loosen preconceived notions about the nature of matter, space, and time to make it possible to perceive the world in new and exciting ways. If the coming chapters seem challenging, then consider immersing yourself in sci-fi and reading them again.

Suggested Reading:

Guerrilla Gardening: A Manualfesto by David Tracey. Guerrilla gardening is about growing flowers, vegetables, shrubs and trees in "public" places with or without permission. The mystical/anarchist worldview is evident in the author's Gaia perspective and his philosophy that we can make our world a better place even when we don't own the land. Rather than asking permission, Tracey advocates seeking forgiveness afterward, if necessary at all.

Ishmael by Daniel Quinn. Ishmael is an easy-to-read fictional dialogue detailing the connection between the rise of agriculture/mythical thinking and the drive to conquer people and nature. The book gives the impression that civilization has failed and the only answer is to return to hunter-gatherer/magical thinking, but even Quinn describes that idea as "inane," suggesting we need a "new paradigm" instead. He doesn't try to define the paradigm, yet from his pluralistic, all-species viewpoint, it is clear he is writing from a mystical/green anarchist worldview.

—Fifteen—

Observer Processing

Collapsing Reality into Existence

"Thoughts become things… once a thought is thought, it's as if it's instantaneously endowed with a power and a force all its own, and it's as if it's given a single, solitary mission: to reappear in your life within time and space. If you think thoughts of material things, your thoughts will strive to become those material things, if you think thoughts of events or circumstances, your thoughts will strive to move the players and conditions around in your life, so as to yield those events or circumstances. And if you think thoughts of love, or hate, or of other emotions, again, your thoughts will shift around the conditions of your life so that you can experience those thought-of emotions all over again."

—*Mike Dooley, "Thoughts Become Things."'*

At the beginning of this journey we mentally stood on the front doorstep and observed the world around us. We determined that our basic senses cannot be trusted to give us an accurate perception of reality, although with the aid of tools such as infrared imaging, we could correct for some of the distortions. Then, over a breakfast of mealworms, we determined that our cultural biases further distort our perception of reality, that most of our beliefs and actions are nothing more than unconsciously mimicked behaviors. Since then we have worked to identify and detach from our cultural biases to embrace a more expansive view of reality.

We discovered that there are many layers of consciousness, and that each level completely

> Snapshot: Observer Processing
>
> Technology: Nanotechnolgy.
>
> Origin: Quantum physics
>
> Logic: Paradox.
>
> Perspective: Self as Creator.
>
> Culture: Global Web Consciousness
>
> Social-Political Structure: Unknown.
>
> Notable People: Niels Bohr, Werner Heisenberg, Stephen Hawking.
>
> Television/Movies: *What the Bleep, Groundhog Day, Matrix, Stranger Than Fiction.*

changes one's perception of reality. We examined past and present human behavior in relation to the layers of consciousness, and investigated the benefits and shortcomings of each. Being aware of the layers of consciousness enables us to see the forces driving the world today, whether reading the newspaper or talking to a person on the street. We can observe language and behavior clues to determine if they are operating out of a mythical, sequential, or other worldview.

189

Recognizing levels of consciousness, rather than being totally immersed in them, is in itself a whole new level of detachment and objectivity. However, while this roadmap to reality seems more accurate, or at least less distorted, than our starting perspective, there are still many biases and distortions to correct. To experience a truly universal perception of reality, we have to empty our cup and detach from old notions about how the universe works to embrace the bizarre nature of matter and energy. After all, we are part of a universe with black holes that can crush entire solar systems into nothingness. We are part of a universe where subatomic particles shoot through our bodies and the entire planet, without hitting anything. We are physically made of stardust recycled from earlier stars. To have a worldview with the least possible distortions, we must incorporate the bizarre nature of the cosmos into our daily lives—into our meals, into our jobs, into our recreation. When we study the universe we are not merely studying something else; we are ultimately studying ourselves.

Tools of Creation

Each worldview discussed in this book is linked to a particular type of technology. The magical worldview is linked to hunting and gathering. The mythical worldview is linked to the rise of agriculture. The sequential worldview is linked to industry. The emerging systems view

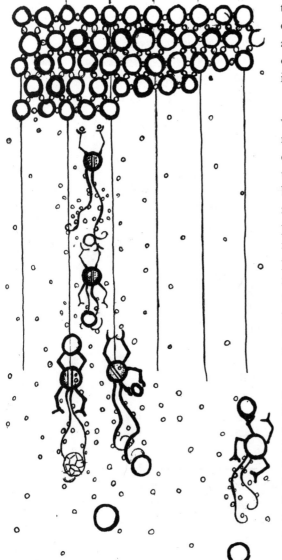

is linked to the Internet and the sharing of information. Holistic thinking is linked to sustainable technologies and the ability to live on this planet without destroying it. The mystical worldview is associated with microbiology and genetics, enabling us to perceive our connection to everything else. The rise of observer processing is linked to nanotechnology.

Nanotechnology changes all previous notions about the way we build or repair material objects. It is the ability to manipulate matter at the molecular level. The effort started with simple demonstration projects, such as arranging individual atoms to spell the acronym "IBM". Since then, the field of nanotechnology has been jumping molecular-sized hurdles, reported occasionally in the media. News articles typically feature some microscopic machinery part, such as a gear or switch built from just a few atoms. It doesn't mean much to our daily lives at the moment, but eventually these parts and pieces will come together in the form of one very small robot or nanobot called a "general assembler." Although small in the extreme—small enough that you could permanently lose one if you dropped it in an empty teacup, it will take only one such robot to change everything. The general assembler is the holy grail of nanotechnology.

A general assembler is a tool that can pick up individual atoms and assemble them according to whatever instructions it is provided with. It only takes one general assembler to change everything, because that one can be used to build more of its own kind, essentially self-replicating until instructed to stop and build something else. General assemblers could be instructed to build anything that doesn't violate the laws of physics. For example, we could use general assemblers to construct rockets out of diamond, the strongest known material, leading to thinner, lighter, and stronger spaceships than anything we have today.

Building with nanotechnology is similar to the way living organisms build themselves. In a pond, for example, a single-celled organism floats in the nutrient stream and follows the instructions of its DNA to grab specific materials needed for construction. Molecule-by-molecule, the cell builds itself from the raw materials of nature. In multi-cellular organisms such as ourselves, the nutrient stream is contained on the inside, but the process is the same. Starting in the womb of the mother, a single fertilized egg cell contains instructions to build an entire human being, and it does so bit-by-bit from the available nutrients. Similarly, a nanobot with the instructions to build a spaceship could be planted in an oversized test tube, like an artificial womb, which would be flooded with the raw ingredients needed to assemble the ship. Fabricating the fuselage out of diamond wouldn't require diamonds, but common carbon, which the nanobot would assemble into diamond. While undeniably complex, building a rocket out of diamond is easier than the natural process of building a multi-cellular life form.

Human beings, for example, are not designed from scratch like a rocket. We evolved out of the haphazard process of modifying available parts to make something new. The tiny bones in our ears that facilitate hearing were once part of the jawbones of our reptilian ancestors. Some of the bones gradually fused together to make the mammalian jaw, while others migrated backward to form ear bones. The instructions in our DNA are the equivalent of building a tricycle and then remodeling it into a car, an airplane, and finally a spaceship. Evolution repeats itself inside the womb, making primitive parts, then rearranging and modifying them to make the final product.

For instance, research has found a genetic link between the pumping action of the peduncle in a simple marine organism called a hydra and the pumping action of our own heart. Heart tissue originates at the tip of the human embryo, corresponding with its position on the hydra, before it migrates to the center of the body.[2] The human body re-enacts the evolutionary process as it builds itself from the mother's nutrient stream, developing and later losing evolutionary holdovers such as gill slits and a tail. More recent evolutionary holdovers are not yet gone, so we still carry the atrophied appendix and troublesome wisdom teeth, sort of like having an 8-track tape player built into a spaceship.

New technologies can be designed from scratch, without repeating the messy process of evolution. Starting with a single nanobot, a product would assemble itself from the raw materials in the test tube. The implications of nanotechnology are almost too much to fathom. For one thing, it will lead to a world where material goods and energy are essentially free, requiring new ways of thinking about careers, money, and wealth.

Even without nanotechnology, we have the necessary technologies to construct self-replicating solar panel makers. It would cost at least $10 billion to build the first set of these solar-powered robots that could scoop up barren desert soil and refine it to manufacture copies of themselves. However, once the first set was completed, then it would be a self-replicating system that would replicate until directed to stop. In the desert or on the moon, a self-replicating system would grow exponentially until there were potentially thousands of square miles of solar panels generating electricity for free. We only need one self-replicating unit to start the process. The rest are effectively free, which ultimately drops the cost of production to zero. [3]It is hard to imagine how the economy as we know it could persist in an era when material goods are free.

Nanotechnology promises more benefits and more potential perils than any previous technology. It is hard to imagine the impact of this technology on a species that is still struggling to transition from mythical to sequential worldviews. We are barely in motion towards the systems level, and we desperately need to achieve holistic consciousness to be sustainable. The seeds of a mystical worldview have barely been planted, and yet innovation is careening towards observer-level technology. The social implications are so outrageous that I have merely skimmed the less-shocking technological consequences.

For a taste of the full implications, imagine the ability to repair cells at the molecular level, creating the possibility of living "forever," or at least until killed in an accident. The concept may trigger knee-jerk reactions of great optimism or great pessimism, depending on the filters used to process it. Besides redefining the physical world, nanotechnology will shatter cherished belief systems and values even more than Charles Darwin's *Theory of Evolution*, and no amount of denial will make it go away.

Nanotechnology might sound like science fiction, but every step required to build the first general assembler was mapped out back in 1986 in Eric Drexler's book *The Engines of Creation*. Drexler forecast nanotechnology to emerge by the middle of this century, but it appears that he was wrong. The technology is evolving faster than anticipated.[4]

While nanotechnology is primarily oriented towards manipulating physical matter, there are parallel advances in cybernetics linking the human brain to technology with equally far-reaching implications. Researchers link sophisticated prosthetic devices to the human nervous system, and individuals can learn to control these artificial limbs by thought. We are rapidly approaching the point when people will be able to install a hard drive for assisted memory, making it easier to recall names, dates, facts, and figures. Further, it may be possible to surgically implant the necessary technology to browse the internet by thought alone.

In her book, *Consciousness: An Introduction*, Susan Blackmore suggests that interfacing with such technology might be as intuitive as our natural systems. Consider the question, "What is the capital of France?" We don't know where the answer comes from. "Paris" just pops into mind. Blackmore writes, *"With implanted electrodes detecting your intentions you only have to think clearly enough about what you want to search for, and it pops into your mind just as the word "Paris" did. It's all there. The whole of the web is part of you, and it is part of every other fully wired person as well."* Blackmore notes that this kind of technology could redefine consciousness in unknown ways, possibly leading to some kind of global web consciousness.[5] The nature of such a culture and government, or lack of it, is equally hard to predict.

While these technological advances remain in their infancy, the metaphorical aspect of observer processing is already diffusing into the collective consciousness from quantum physics.

Smoke and Mirrors

Stand on the front porch again in your imagination and look around, correcting for the distortions. Imagine you can see the world in ultraviolet like a bee, or infrared like a snake. Imagine experiencing the neighborhood with the nose and ears of a dog, what it might be like to fly through the air like a robin, or to wriggle through the earth like a worm. Try detaching from preconceptions about right and wrong, religion and politics, likes and dislikes, and imagine what it might be like to experience your world through the eyes of a !Kung bushman from Africa, or a Saudi woman who must hide behind a veil. If you are able to detach from cultural notions of the way things "should be," then you may begin to catch a glimmer of reality as it is, right? Actually no, not even close.

Everything we experience is real and not real, solid but not solid. From the viewpoint of physics, everything that exists in our world is mostly empty space held together by energy fields. Magnify one atom to the size of a football field, and it would consist of a cloud of electrons surrounding a nucleus the size of a grain of sand. The rest of it is empty space.[6] There is so much empty space inside solid matter, inside every rock, tree, bird, and skyscraper and inside our own bodies, that subatomic particles from space go careening through us without hitting anything. Subatomic particles travel through the roof, through our heads, through the floor, and usually through the entire planet without hitting anything at all. We are made of smoke and mirrors more than substance. The only reason we cannot walk through walls is because the negatively charged electrons in our bodies repel the similarly charged electrons in a wall.

But that is only the beginning of the weirdness. If we are going to discover an accurate perception of reality then that perception must include the basic facts about our existence. We need a worldview where we see and experience the world as illusion and energy more than substance, as possibilities more than certainties. We need to detach and dissolve our concepts of matter and physics to embrace the true nature of the universe.

We are familiar with Newtonian physics, where commonsense laws govern the way things work. When we throw a baseball, for example, we can predict where the ball will go. However, to embrace the true nature of reality we must go beyond Newtonian physics to explore quantum physics where matter behaves in peculiar and unexpected ways. We must explore this realm until we experience it not as something else, but as a study of our existence.

Wave-Particle Duality

A wave can pass through multiple points at once, much like an ocean wave flowing through the supporting pilings of pier, while a particle, like a baseball, can pass through at only one point. Subatomic particles such as photons and electrons exhibit both behaviors. Project a beam of light through two parallel slits in a barrier and it will produce an interference pattern of light and dark stripes on a screen. Like water waves on the surface of a pond, two crests combine to make a bright stripe, while a crest and a trough cancel each other, creating a dark stripe. Thus, nineteenth century scientists believed light was a wave.

With the rise of quantum theory, however, physicists realized that light was not just a wave, put rather a wave-like particle called a photon. The discovery suggested a new experiment, that it should be possible to send light through the slits one photon at a time onto photographic film. Logically, there should be no interference pattern, since there would be nothing for the photon to interfere with. Scientists tested this assumption in 1909 and were astonished to see an interference pattern develop as photons accumulated on the photographic plate. The interference pattern could only develop if a photon passed through both slits at the same time and interfered with itself like a wave.

Physicists conducted many tests to determine the speed and locations of these wave-particles. When they tested the speed they discovered a wave, but when they tested the location they discovered a particle. It is not presently possible to determine speed and location of a subatomic particle at the same time.[7] In the words of Willis Harmon, *"the wave and particle descriptions represent complementary aspects of a reality that cannot be fully conceptualized in either metaphor alone. We are free to measure either the wavelength or the position of a photon as precisely as we choose. But the two quantities do not appear in the same conceptual model, and an attempt to think in terms of both at the same time leads to a paradoxical situation. For the principle of uncertainty states that the more precise our knowledge of the wavelength, the greater is our ignorance regarding the position, and vice versa."*[8]

A wave has an infinite number of points, while a particle exists at only one point. The wave, no matter how large or small, can always be divided in half, and then in half again and again and again. Like plotting points on a line, you can always divide the space in between any two points and put another point in the middle. For a wave to become a particle it must collapse, out of an infinite number of possibilities, into one particular point. Scientists found this distressing because they like to run controlled tests, where they have completely removed themselves from affecting the outcome. Yet in this case the scientist apparently causes the wave to collapse while he or she is trying to determine a location. The popular analogy of this situation is a cat in a box, where a random event has a fifty-fifty chance of releasing a deadly gas that kills the cat. In the old view of physics, something did or did not happen, and we open the box to see the result. But from the viewpoint of quantum physics, nothing happens until we remove the lid. The possibilities remain in flux, and it is only when the observer removes the lid that the wave collapses into one reality or another. It is called the "observer effect." Scientists would like to be impartial observers, but it is they who collapse the wave of possibilities into a single point.

Quantum physics has revealed a conundrum in our quest to determine what reality is. Like physicists, we endeavored to remove ourselves from the experiment. We endeavored to detach from our preconceived notions of reality to discover what reality really is. Now we discover that reality is paradoxical. We cannot remove ourselves from the experiment because we are part of the equation. We affect reality in the process of attempting to define it.

Is this observer effect merely a queer fact of science, an interesting tidbit of trivia, or does it have any tangible relationship to our daily experience? Is reality something we adapt to like passengers or victims? Or is reality malleable, something we help create? We begin by considering the observer effect from a purely metaphorical standpoint.

Waves of Possibilities

The metaphor of the observer effect is that our lives exist in waves of possibilities and we collapse these possibilities into specific events through our actions. We collapse our reality into existence. The concept should seem obvious enough: Make lousy choices and we collapse a miserable reality into existence. Make smart choices and we collapse a more favorable reality into existence. The movie *'What the Bleep'* dealt with this issue extensively. Surprisingly few people see the world that way.

From the perspective of a mythical or sequential worldview, reality is what it is, and we must cope with whatever life deals us. In other words, we are victims of reality, rather than creators of it. Over the years I've been shocked at how many people exist that way, experiencing life as a crapshoot to be endured, rather than as a miracle to be celebrated. They get wasted on the weekends in an effort to obliterate their experience of reality and temporarily feel good, only to wake up with a hangover. Somehow this is supposed to improve their situation before they return to the treadmill on Monday. What a dismal way to experience life!

Rather than being victims of the universe, let's try a new worldview and imagine ourselves as creators of reality. We exist within an unlimited wave of possibilities, and as observers, we collapse those possibilities into specific realities. Let's consider some examples, starting out shallow and increasing in depth as we go along. This first example is not about creating reality at all, but about how we choose to experience it.

In this instance, a friend called to say that her truck slid off the icy road into a ditch. She felt like she was being tested by God, and this was only one in a series of endless trials she had to endure. An hour earlier I spilled half a can of paint on the floor, and I realized that I cleaned it up without reacting to it. I could have sworn, or I could have believed God was testing me, but I didn't do either. I cleaned up the mess without reacting, and it made me realize how much our interpretation can color our experience of reality. Getting the truck out of the ditch was no more difficult than cleaning up the paint spill, but the reality each of us experienced was dramatically different. I only wish I could respond to other crises as resourcefully.

We each define reality in our own way, and our beliefs and actions affect the type of reality we bring into existence. The bottom line is that a person who believes they will be successful probably will be. They will aim higher and pick themselves back up if they fail the first time. Likewise, a person who believes they will go nowhere in life usually doesn't, and if nothing is going to work out, then why bother trying anyway? The reality we perceive is the reality we create. As Gandhi said, *"Be the change that you want to see in the world."*

The bottom line is that it is impossible to seek a definition of reality as an objective observer. We can step into the world to see what happens, but there is no way to set aside our history of experience. Our pre-conceived ideas about the world alter our perceptions and our actions in every situation we encounter. As observers we affect the outcome of our experience. Whatever we focus on becomes our reality.

Granted, there are some limitations to creating our own realities. If we were to create all aspects of reality, then we might decide to have three arms and exist on a tropical beach where the world is at peace and nobody has to work. Apparently, we do not create our reality to that extent.

Individual vs. Collective Reality

No two people experience an event in exactly the same way. Imagine going for a walk with a group of people from various professions. An artist observes colors, lighting, and forms. An entomologist notices insects. A geologist pays attention to landforms and rocks. A botanist notices the plants and trees. A tracker reads the soil and notices which animals have come and gone through the area and what they were doing there. A meteorologist is keenly aware of the weather, while an ornithologist recognizes all the birds and bird songs, and a mycologist notices fungi we didn't know existed. You may have no such background at all, so you walk along oblivious to almost everything. Each person experiences a different version of the walk, as if we exist in separate universes, even while together.

Similarly, four people in a car share the reality of moving down the road together, while each person perceives a unique experience of reality. One passenger-observer watches the scenery go by, while another listens to music, the third sleeps, and the fourth is experiencing stress and hypertension. Each person creates her own reality while also agreeing on the collective reality of traveling together.

The same is true on a broader scale. Our individual realities exist alongside those of other people within our collective version of reality. We create our individual realities within the parameters of our culture, but we also contribute to the collective vision of reality. Individual opinions contribute to collective choices, such as our nation's decision to go to war. In return, the collective decision to go to war impacts our individual realities, as friends and family members risk their lives in the armed forces and tax dollars are diverted away from domestic schools and infrastructure.

It is reality by democracy. Our individual actions contribute to the collective definition of the way things are. In America we have defined reality in a particular way with a broad set of values, beliefs, laws, circumstances, and opportunities that make up the American experience and perception of reality, which is different from the version of reality experienced in Japan, Kenya, or Brazil. The reality we collectively collapse into existence affects our individual realities, and our individual realities impact our shared reality.

It is surprising how much the collective definition can color our perspective of reality. I recall one television show where the narrator described brain surgery in rural African tribal cultures. The farmers did not like the village medical clinic, so they often practiced their own medicine, including brain surgery. They used unsterilized knives and no anesthetics. It sounds barbaric to us, and we can feel pain just by watching it. We also expect the patients to die of shock or gangrene, but they don't. They have different expectations, and they have a 95 percent surgery success rate. After watching people sitting there being operated on, the narrator suggested that perhaps pain itself was a "cultural phenomenon."

Similarly, many diseases may be creations of our culture. As one doctor wrote, *"a patient does not go to a physician with a disease. A negotiation takes place in which the vague, formless discontent of the patient is shaped into a disease almost as a sculptor shapes clay."*[9] Guided by the doctor's questions, the patient describes his symptoms, inevitably focusing on some issues more than others, until the doctor arrives at a diagnosis previously defined by the collective culture. Diseases like fibromialgia and bipolar disorder are not well defined and likely consist of numerous symptom combinations of internal 'dis-ease'. The patient comes in with the possibility of an illness, and negotiates with the doctor until the possibilities collapse into a particular reality.

In reality by democracy, our individual realities overlap with the collective realities of our family, community, country, and the world. The way we choose to define our individual realities impacts the collective reality, while the collective definition of reality impacts individual realities. Recognizing our influence in the world is a sobering discovery. It requires us to completely reconsider our daily actions and our perception of reality. Individually we typically find whatever we seek. If we focus on being sad then we are sad. If we focus on happiness then we find happiness.

In our interpersonal relationships we must consider the effects of our influence. In marriage we must realize that our focus determines the outcome. If we focus on having a loving marriage then we can create that. If we focus on something else, then we will have that instead. In any conflict we must realize that we are a contributor. We can always see the other person's problems, but we so rarely acknowledge our own. My mother, a psychologist, always encouraged me to ask, *"What am I doing to facilitate this person's behavior? What behavior am I doing that encourages them to act the way they are?"* We must consider how our thoughts might impact other people's lives. If we believe our kids will be failures, then they may prove us right. If we tell them the world is unfair, then that may be the world they discover. On the other hand, if we believe they will be successful and tell them the world is basically good, then they may find life positively rewarding. We exist as observers and creators of reality. If we want to live in a world of peace and abundance then we must see that in the world today, and we must create it in the world tomorrow.

In Limbo

Wave-particle duality suggests that possibilities remain in a state of limbo until an observer collapses them into one reality or another. It is a bit like the 2000 election between George W. Bush and Al Gore, where the nation existed in a state of flux for weeks while it wasn't clear who would be the next President. Both possibilities hung in limbo, a kind of formless wave of uncertainty, until an observer, the Supreme Court, collapsed one reality into existence and not the other.

Sometimes it is beneficial to leave questions in limbo. We previously discussed voodoo, miraculous healings, and other phenomena that do not mesh with a sequential worldview. We speculated that seemingly impossible phenomena might be possible within a worldview with different expectations of reality. Now we can learn from the metaphor of the observer effect. We can allow our questions to float in limbo awhile longer without trying to pin down any particular answer. We may discover novel aspects of reality if we remain open to the possibilities. For example, the exorcist I met in Mexico didn't necessarily believe in God and the devil himself, but by accepting other people's versions of reality, he was able to help them find peace. Likewise, he would not have shared his experiences with me if I judged him too quickly.

Similarly, I met an interesting character after a public presentation on wilderness survival. There was nothing magical or mystical about my speech, but afterwards one individual came up and described an unusual encounter he had in the woods. One time he came upon a six-foot tall rabbit and followed it, in something that sounded reminiscent of *Alice in Wonderland*. We might ordinarily dismiss the person as a loony crackpot in need of therapy. But we would be collapsing reality into existence based on a preconceived definition. I made an effort to accept his story without collapsing it into any particular opinion. I said to myself, *"This is a highly unusual story, but it goes to show that his definition of reality is a lot more interesting than mine."* His reality was legitimate to him, and it showed me how limited I am in my perceptions of the world. I have never encountered a six-foot tall rabbit in the woods, but with my interest in wilderness survival, it would certainly make a nice meal!

Mind Over Matter

We considered the observer effect in a metaphorical sense, revealing that our perceptions and choices shape our individual and collective realities. However, a literal view of the observer effect suggests mind over matter, that our thoughts can affect physical reality. But is that going too far? Do our thoughts manipulate the physical world?

The laws of quantum physics describe the behavior of atoms and subatomic particles, but these laws do not apply to big objects. According to science, a hunter-gatherer with a magic charm cannot collapse a rabbit into existence from the surrounding matter. Nor is there anything in quantum physics to suggest that a rain dance could produce rain, or that an image of Christ could bleed, and yet, there is no shortage of people who claim to have witnessed such inexplicable phenomena. Are human minds capable of altering physical reality in some way, or are these people con artists or victims of mass delusions?

Sequential cause and effect can explain many seemingly magical or mythical manifestations. Other phenomena may be revealed as elaborate hoaxes or fabricated stories. However, it would be foolish to extrapolate the results of some investigations to conclude that all reports of mind over matter and other metaphysical events are hoaxes or misinterpretations. The answer to the question of mind over matter is partly a matter of semantics.

Consider that the Big Bang brought about a universe of only hydrogen and helium. These basic elements were fused together in the belly of ancient stars to form the heavier elements then exploded across space in supernova explosions. Our sun and planets eventually formed from the debris. We emerged from the primordial ooze of this debris to become walking, talking, thinking globs of pond muck. That is mind over matter. Try looking at pond muck and connecting with it at an identity level. It is you and you are it. We are matter that has mind.

Now reach out and pick something up. Here you are using your mind to instruct your body to pick up matter. That is mind over matter in a very literal sense, although maybe not what you anticipated as "mind over matter." But it is mind over matter, and there is immense potential in this kind of mind power. I have personally envisioned houses of stone and manifested them into existence, albeit slowly and one piece at a time. Yet, for mere pond muck, such as myself, to build something as elaborate as a house is definitely a testament to the potential of mind over matter. With bulldozers, trucks, and backhoes directed by our minds, we humans move more matter every year than all of the planet's winds, waves, rivers, glaciers, and geologic mountain-building forces combined.[10]

We can also move matter without touching it. Rather than building a house ourselves, we could dream it up and manifest it into existence through the labor of other people. With

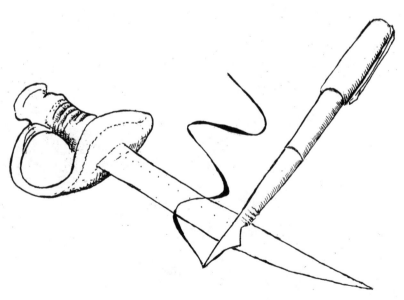

our mind we have other people move the matter. Optionally, we could inspire people to action with words alone, much like the old saying, *"The pen is mightier than the sword."* A few words in the right place at the right time can influence great numbers of people to change their behaviors, affecting how matter is manipulated on a daily basis. I have personally caused large piles of rock to become stone houses in several states and countries by merely producing a book and video about stone masonry. That also qualifies as mind over matter, and it raises an issue regarding the serenity prayer: *"God grant me the Serenity to Accept the things I cannot change, the Courage to change the things I can and the Wisdom to know the Difference."* How do we determine the difference?

We can easily help out with a community service project, such as landscaping or fundraising for a park. If we do that, then we always can take another step to help the world in a bigger way. There is no clear line to say when a person is unable to create additional change. Individual minds, such as Washington, Jefferson, Edison, Ghandi, and Martin Luther King, clearly changed the world in ways that mattered. Running for President might be hard to imagine, but it is just one more step beyond something else, and real human beings have done it.

The question of what I can and cannot do to make the world a better place has haunted me since childhood. I might like to live in a cabin and hike and camp all the time, but that wouldn't change the reality that woods and wildlife are steadily disappearing in the name of "progress." I ask myself, *"What if the difference between saving life on earth and losing it came down to the actions of one person, and that person didn't act?"* I feel a personal responsibility to make a difference, and see no clear line to determine when I have done enough. I am working to reinvent housing, to make houses that need no outside energy sources. I advocate sensible development to preserve what we have left of the natural world. I work with school children and ideas to reform education. I have fifty green business ideas and products I wish to bring to market. I work on nonprofit projects, such as preserving local watersheds that are of great importance to me. And I have this book, which I wouldn't write if I believed it wasn't possible to make a difference.

Readers of my other books have written to say they were inspired to change their lives in positive ways, but the question still remains, where is the line between what we can change and what we have to accept? In terms of mind over matter, it seems that the limits are way out there. If we want to make a difference we can. I've always had the feeling that we are very close, extremely close to a positive shift in the world, which might require only a handful of words at the right place at the right time to make it happen. I imagine it like inserting a few lines of computer programming to change how the computer behaves. Hopefully, my actions and the actions of other mindful souls will make that difference. I am hopeful that if I am mindful enough, it will eventually matter.

In the train of thought we are following, we have determined that, 1) our minds have emerged from matter, which constitutes mind over matter, 2) we can physically manipulate matter, which constitutes mind over matter, 3) we can hire somebody to do something for us, which qualifies as mind over matter without touching it, and 4) we can inspire other people in a way that changes their choices about how they deal with matter, which is also mind over matter.

So it is possible for the mind to manipulate matter; it is a normal part of our daily existence. But it probably wasn't the discussion of mind over matter you expected. I dodged the question through semantics to emphasize how miraculous it is that mere pond muck has achieved mind over matter. If pond muck can do all that, then what else is possible? Can we influence the world with our thoughts? Is it possible to heal oneself or other people with positive thought and energy?

Spontaneous Healings

In 1974 John Matzke noticed a lump in his armpit and was diagnosed with malignant melanoma, a highly fatal form of skin cancer. That tumor and several others were removed by surgeons, but within ten years the cancer had spread to his lungs. He was told he had eighteen months to live, and his doctor recommended immediate surgery to improve his odds. Instead, Matzke took time to strengthen his body. He went on long hikes in the mountains, ate healthy foods, and meditated. He visualized strong immune cells destroying the cancer. A month later he checked in for a new exam and x-ray. To his doctor's astonishment, the tumor was completely gone.[11]

Similarly, in 1985 Alice Epstein was diagnosed with cancer in her left kidney and told she should have it removed right away. A month later the cancer spread to both lungs and she was told she had two or three months to live. Epstein turned to psychosynthesis, a *"combination of psychotherapy and spiritual therapy."* In therapy she learned to express herself, rather than suppressing her needs to please others, and she overcame depression. Epstein never received any medical treatment or surgery, but the tumors began shrinking within six weeks and were gone within a year.[12]

Matzke's and Epstein's spontaneous remissions are considered authentic, while many other claims have been proven to be the result of mistaken diagnosis or scams to promote books and videos. Spontaneous remissions are estimated to occur in about 1 out of every 60,000 to 100,000 cancer cases. Were these miracles the result of mind over matter? Or did they recover due to some other factor, such as pathogenic stimulation of the immune system? Matzke survived another eighteen years before the cancer returned as a brain tumor that took his life. Epstein was still completely healthy twenty-two years later at the age of eighty.[13]

Studies have revealed conflicting, mostly dubious results on the medicine of positive thinking. A 1989 study of women with terminal breast cancer showed a significant survival advantage for women enrolled in supportive therapy, but follow-up studies failed to reproduce the results. All the patients enrolled in these studies have since died. Similarly, doctors at Duke University conducted a multi-center study using prayer to help patients in cardiac surgery for stint placements. But their study revealed no reduction in six-month mortality.[14] One possible factor is that positive thinking may be insufficient to heal physical ailments if we fail to deal with deeper issues that may have contributed to the illness in the first place.

Sometimes a person who faces death will let go of the past, to "die" in a mental-emotional-spiritual sense. By accepting and embracing one's own mortality, the ego dies and the individual suddenly has nothing to fear. She is reborn as a new person with a new outlook on life. That would seem to be the case with Epstein, who claimed to have had a "cancer prone personality" prior to her affliction, such as suppressing her needs to please others. In the face of death she let go of unhealthy psychological habits and became a new person.

Manipulating Matter

Suppose that every time we drive we fantasize about junking our car so we can replace it with a flashy new model. Can such thoughts affect our car over an extended period? Is it possible that our thoughts could cause metal fatigue on the molecular level that would ultimately lead to a breakdown at the macro level? Do our thoughts manipulate matter, or is this just another face for magical thinking? I don't know, but I am constantly daydreaming about someday buying a 150-mpg car. I cheerily imagine delivering our existing cars to the junkyard for demolition, never to guzzle gas again. Although I am good with basic maintenance, such as checking the oil level, we seem to have improbably bad luck with cars. It seems like our cars are always in the shop for repairs. It may be premature to declare that our thoughts manipulate matter on a molecular level, but we shouldn't dismiss it either.

Our cultural heritage includes countless claims of telekinesis or mind over matter, as well as telepathy. For every report of paranormal ability there seems to be an equal and opposite report refuting such abilities as sleight-of-hand magic tricks by con artists. Paranormal researchers have attempted to document telekinesis and other unusual abilities in controlled laboratory settings with mixed results. Some studies have produced positive results, only to be shot down by other scientists for poor methodology. Studies with proper controls have produced positive results for some researchers, but inconclusive or negative results for other researchers who attempt to duplicate the experiments. It is unclear whether paranormal researchers are biased in their research or if control itself is an illusion in paranormal experiments. We must wonder if a "double-blind" experiment is impossible in paranormal research. It may be the nature of reality that scientists tend to get the results they expect. The worldview they operate from influences the outcome of the experiment no matter how much they attempt to remove themselves from it.

Whether or not it is possible to prove paranormal phenomena in the laboratory, such things are part of normal life for millions of people. For example, my daughter Felicia is a student of natural horsemanship. She described one of her lessons this way, *"Our horses were tied around the perimeter of the indoor arena, and we were asked to sit in a half circle facing away from the horses. Bill, our instructor, played a recording of ambient sounds and waves, and asked us to completely relax—to empty our minds, and let the energy drain out of our bodies like water. After a few minutes he turned the tape off and asked what we observed. The horses were calm. They stopped fighting and pawing and stood quietly; some were beginning to fall asleep. Then Bill asked us to focus our collective energy into the timbers and walls of the building itself, to imagine them glowing with our energy. The horses were immediately agitated, pulling back until they broke their ties and ran loose in the arena.*

After calming and retying the horses, Bill worked with a young woman who was scared of her horse. He explained that horses are keenly aware of their bubble of personal space. They pay attention to their space within a herd, allowing them to run and turn as smoothly as a flock of birds. People also have a personal bubble, and we can focus our energy on controlling the size of the bubble. Bill instructed the woman to close her eyes and build up her internal energy. The horse was twenty yards away, but he told her to stand and focus her energy to push on the horse's left hindquarter. Momentarily, the horse shifted his weight and stepped away. He removed himself from the pressure of her expanded personal bubble." Science is unable to explain this energy work with horses or many other phenomena that mainstream people deal with every day. Consciously or subconsciously, our thoughts seem to affect the world around us.

Interestingly, while I was editing this chapter, Renee lamented to me that she would like to have a second chance with our pet iguana. We bought the iguana for Edwin's birthday a few months ago, but it escaped the terrarium in our bookstore. Given that iguanas require a heat lamp, humidity, and leafy greens to survive, we assumed that it died within a couple days. We didn't think it was mature enough to survive the desiccating heat of the furnace or the cool nighttime temperatures of the store. After a couple days we gave up all hope of finding the iguana alive. It was three weeks later that Renee voiced her wish for a second chance. An hour later there were two small children in our store exclaiming, "It's wheel! It's wheel!" I didn't know what they were talking about since we don't have wheels in the store, but they found the iguana, and it was real and alive. The universe works in mysterious ways.

Matters of Scale

If I daydream about the planet blowing apart, meditate and pray for such a thing, it is not likely to happen, which is fortunate for us. If we could pick up cars with our thoughts and send them hurtling at other people, then we would never have lasted this long. On the other hand, I previously described a Native American ceremony where rocks purportedly rolled themselves out of a sweat lodge and back to the outside fire pit, which the Indians took as a sign that they were offending the spirits. The idea seems preposterous to those of us living in a world of sequential cause and effect. But we have to wonder if such things are possible within a worldview where people are unfettered by skepticism. It is unlikely that anyone directed their thoughts towards making the rocks get up and roll back to the fire, but what if the collective consciousness, the collective system of beliefs, were intense enough to make magical things happen once in awhile?

Rocks that move on their own do not violate the magical perception of reality. Such things are expected, as suggested by this passage from *Lame Deer, Seeker of Visions*: *"In the old days one man had a stone which he sent out to look for buffalo. He always spread a red-painted buffalo skin for the stone to return to. One moment the hide would be empty and then, suddenly, the stone would be there in the center of it. Sometimes the stone brought back a pebble or a sprig of some medicine plant. The owner then questioned the stone and would make known to the people what it had told him. One Sioux tribe had a scouting stone which they would send out to see what their enemies were up to. This stone also had a returning place, a square earth altar made of fine red powder. The ancient yuwipi men unloosed rocks to search for lost objects. The farther such a stone had to travel, the longer it needed to return. Some medicine rocks don't like to be alone. They have helpers, smaller pebbles."[15]* Granted, these seeking stones could have been nothing more than sleight-of-hand tricks. But it is also possible that, like the divine kings who volunteered themselves for sacrifice because they believed themselves to be living gods, the shamans may have fully believed that stones could move.

Similarly, many deeply religious people have seen or experienced miracles in their lives. Their experiences proved to them that their faith, their God, really exists, even while people of opposing faiths report similar experiences. We may find that magic and miracles do occur if we shift to a worldview where such things are possible, yet it is apparently impossible to bring such thinking back to a sequential worldview and still believe it. Do our thoughts and beliefs affect physical reality? I prefer to avoid pinning the answer down either way. Rather than collapse the question into one opinion or another, let's allow it to float as a possibility. Let's be open-minded and skeptical at the same time and see what happens.

Playing Cards

Our family frequently played card games when I was growing up, and over time I began to observe that there seemed to be more happening in a card game than chance and strategy. I especially played a lot of pinochle and casino with my grandmother.

Grandma and I played cards for entertainment, but we were pretty competitive. I initially tried to make logical plays in a card game called "casino," but over time I experimented with a more intuitive approach. I searched for a light or dark or neutral feeling with each card to decide which one to play, even if the choice didn't seem logical. Naturally, I was often uncertain if I was intuiting anything at all, or just imagining it. I was frustrated when I lost a card game, not because I cared about winning or losing, but because I was distraught that my intuition could let me down. I focused even more intensely on my intuition in the next game.

Gradually I learned to track my plays through the games and observed something interesting: I could intuitively play every card correctly and still lose. I realized I could not win through intuition if I did not have the right cards.

It seemed like there was this element of power that would float back and forth across the table. One of us would hold it for a while and then the other, and our winning streaks would reflect who held the power. I realized that I had to be dealt the right cards to begin with, which ultimately led me into explorations of *intent* and *will*.

In Carlos Castaneda's stories with Don Juan, he described learning to focus will or intent towards specific goals that would seem to violate the laws of physics.[16] In our card games I observed that the winner, regardless of what we played or who played, was the person who seemed to have the strongest will and intent at that moment. That person was dealt better cards, as if a shuffled deck wasn't randomly mixed; it was stacked according to the competing will and intent of the players. Grandma was an especially fierce competitor. I could feel her will and intent.

My point of discovery came during a three-handed game of casino with Grandma and Renee. Renee was winning. She had all the right cards. I was losing badly until I realized I needed Renee's cards. As the cards were dealt for the next hand, I assumed Renee's physical posture. I subtly matched her outward body posture and internally imagined that I was her, sitting in her chair and experiencing what she experienced. As I picked up my cards I had the sensation I had her cards, and when I looked at them, I had the cards I wanted. I had stolen the power, and I led the games from there on out. I realized that intuition was only a small part of winning a game. Power was everything.

Over time, I observed that card games seemed to reflect each person's inner states. I noticed that people with strong personal power and will at the time of the game were closely matched. Also it seemed that the "power" had a way of getting stuck. One person would have it and keep it for a while, and then the next, and thus the winning streaks. It took extra will and intent to dislodge it from them. During our card games I tried to sense what each person was experiencing, how strong they were inside, and what their power level was.

When Grandma dislocated her wrist she temporarily lost much of her independence. With her loss of personal power, she lost much of her card power. If inner strength enabled her to hold power in a card game, then conversely, I wondered if gaining power could be a source of inner strength. I found, however, that it was difficult to gift the power. As long as my internal power was higher than hers I was still dealt the right cards to win. As her arm healed, so too did her card-playing ability

It was during a game with my great aunt that I fully understood the power of will in a card game. It was the first opportunity I had had to challenge her in almost a decade. I had won most or all of the games with her back then, and that really frustrated her. However, I forgot that, and I just wanted a good, stimulating challenge. I came on strong, saying that I was going "take her to the cleaners." I said that with my words, with my tone, and with my body posture. I wanted competition, but there was no resistance. I won the game before I sat down. Our inner power was at such different levels that I took virtually every point, even when I tried to channel strength back her way. I was dealt incredible hands, and I could do nothing to equalize the game. I intuitively monitor each person's relative power during card games, and hers was flat. There was nothing, and I felt terrible because I was creaming her and couldn't stop it.

My grandmother and I never talked about intent or will power, but I sensed that she intuitively understood it and used it when we played cards. We seemed to converse or battle on a subconscious level in our card games. I sometimes felt that she subconsciously tutored me in skills she never consciously knew she had. To borrow from *Star Wars*, I would say, *"The force was strong within her."*

Grandma was not as coherent in her later years, but we still played pinochle games with the extended family. Her playing wasn't logical, and she would let the opposing team take absurdly low bids, much to their initial glee. But glee turned to disappointment as they lost hand after hand against statistically improbable odds. Conversely, when Grandma wanted a bid, she would take it at any cost and somehow succeed in pulling it off. It did not matter who her partner was; her team won regardless of how illogically she played.

One of my best moments in pinochle happened when I was invited to play a game when I didn't have the time for it. I said, "Well, okay, but I'm going to have to win the game in the first hand." I had a strong hand, took the bid, and assembled a 1500 double family, the only one in my life, winning the game in minutes. Then I left.

My interest in power and intent in card games came to a screeching halt when we adopted our children. It was impossible to lose a card game, much to the consternation of my daughters. I switched off that programming, and haven't re-activated it yet.

Obviously, one cannot blindly accept personal anecdotes as proof of mind over matter, but it is sensible to be open to the possibilities. Given the sheer volume of seemingly inexplicable anecdotes in circulation, we could say there is a preponderance of underwhelming evidence to suggest that metaphysical things do happen, at least some of the time. I say, let it float; don't try to collapse the question into one opinion or the other.

Transcending Matter

At the beginning of this quest, we discovered that our ancestors were fused with the natural world, unaware of their own existence. In many ways, we remain nonsentient, reacting to events according to behaviors that were copied from generation to generation. However, there are glimmers of sentience as we learn to detach from our egos, to see ourselves through the eyes of other people, and then from an impartial, third-person perspective. We learned to see ourselves as objects, that we can choose our internal experience rather than have it dictated by outside events. And we learned to step even farther outside ourselves, to see our place in the web of life. Then we practiced dissolving our personal identities.

In this chapter we moved to another level, exploring the observer effect and the concept that we are not victims of reality, but creators of it. In the quest to define reality we discovered that reality isn't objective. How we perceive the world affects our experience of it. If we expect good things in life then we may be pleasantly surprised at our blessings. If we expect bad things in life, then we may be tested. In a sense, we are beginning to transcend matter itself, to realize that our thoughts and feelings might manipulate the physical world around us. But where do we go from here?

If we detached from the natural world to recognize our existence, if we detached from our personal egos to perceive ourselves as objects we can manipulate, if we dissolved our personal identities so we are no longer stuck within our physical selves, and we detached from our notion of a fixed reality to see reality as something we create, then I propose the next logical step would be to detach from time itself, which is the subject of the next chapter.

—Sixteen—

Nonlinear Processing

Transcending the Notion of Time

"Wherever one starts, there is always the question: 'What was before that?' This question comes from our sense of objective causality—that everything must be preceded by its cause. Must everything have a cause? If 'no,' then one leaps immediately to invoking mystical beginnings. If 'yes,' then the beginning is a logical impossibility. There can, by definition, be no beginning if everything must have a cause. By the logic of causality, beginnings are illogical. The logic of causality requires (because we do exist) the initial existence from which we are derived to erupt spontaneously from nothing. Clearly, the notion of objective causality must violate its own logic to get started."

—*Thomas Campbell, My Big TOE*[1]

In the previous chapter we explored the paradox of the observer-effect, wherein the objective view of reality is that reality isn't objective; it is shaped by our observations of it. The next step defining reality is to incorporate the weirdness of time. In this chapter we take paradox to a new level to experience a worldview that is entirely based on contradicting dualities. The goal is to detach from the notion of linear time to achieve a worldview that is essentially timeless, where time does and does not exist. Instead of merely perceiving our experience as a series of sequential cause and effect events moving forward through time, we may begin to experience a sense of nonlinear cause and effect, where events in the future have the potential to impact the past. The trick to achieving such a mental state is to shake loose our attachment to time.

> Snapshot: Nonlinear Processing
>
> Technology: Science fiction time travel.
>
> Origin: Relativity, quantum physics.
>
> Logic: Time paradox.
>
> Perspective: Past and future in flux.
>
> Culture: Unknown.
>
> Social-Political Structure: Unknown.
>
> Notable People: Ray Bradbury. Fred Allan Wolf, David Bohm.
>
> Television/Movies: *Star Trek, The Butterfly Effect, Frequency, Back to the Future, The Philadelphia Experiment, Twelve Monkeys, Déjà vu.*

Detaching from Time

Consider the passage of time among animals. Anthropomorphize a bit, and imagine experiencing time as a fly, where your entire life existence begins and ends in a matter of hours or days. What would that be like?

Imagine being a desert toad, buried in the sand in a state of suspended animation, waiting an entire year, or years, for rain to bring puddles to the desert. You awaken from your hibernation to experience the desert the only way you will ever know it, wet and full of puddles. You go about your life, eating and reproducing for the week or two while puddles exist, then return to suspended animation to wait for the next big rain. Even if you were aware of the passage of time while awake, you would have no way of counting down the days while in suspended animation. How would that affect your perception of reality?

Imagine being a male emperor penguin in Antarctica, incubating an egg until it hatches. Hold still with the egg balanced on your feet for sixty-five days in -40°F weather without eating, while the wind is blowing up to 120 miles per hour. What would that be like? How long until you would get hungry, or cold, or tired of standing around, bored and ready to do something else? Fortunately, emperor penguins don't seem to recognize the passage of time the way we do, or they would very likely be extinct.

Among people, many cultures live intimately connected with the cycles of the natural world see time as circular, not linear. They move at a more relaxed pace, and appointments at a specific time are meaningless. Even in western cultures, time had little meaning until relatively recent history. Time is always a factor in the sense that there is a time to wake and a time to sleep, a time to eat, a time to build shelter, and a time to plant or harvest crops, etc. Yet, our ancestors experienced a sort of static world, where people commonly lived their entire lives within a short distance of their birthplace, and little seemed to change within a lifetime. In the early 1800s, it took weeks or months to transmit a message across the country to or from Washington DC, even though the country ended at the Mississippi river. Life moved at a different pace, as revealed by handcrafted details in carpentry and metalworking. The experience of time as we know it didn't exist until the invention of the telegram and the railroads. Interestingly, according to historian Stephen Ambrose, in the early days of the railroads it was believed that people could not survive moving at sixty miles per hour.[2] But railroads and telegrams sped up the rate at which people and information could travel, changing the experience of time.

Prior to railroads, all clocks were set according to local solar time. Noon was the moment the sun was at its highest point in the sky, which made noon a different time in every town. That wasn't an issue in a culture that wasn't run by the clock, but the rise of railroads necessitated standardized timekeeping so that trains could run on a consistent schedule. The railroads initiated time zones and ran by the clock so that they could post a reliable schedule in each town. Today life moves at a faster pace, and most of us watch the clock to keep hopping from one appointment to another on time. We live in a culture that is hyper-aware of the passage of time.

The conventional wisdom is that time passes at a constant rate and only in one direction. But reality, and Einstein's theory of relativity, tells us otherwise. Tests have verified that increased velocity makes time pass more slowly. In 1971 four cesium atomic clocks were put on jets to go around the world, first eastward, and then westward, to physically measure this time distortion. Planes move faster going east due to the spin of the earth and its atmosphere, so the eastbound clocks slowed down by 332 nanoseconds (billionths of a second) relative to the westbound clocks. As phrased by Michio Kaku in Discover magazine, *"time is more like a river that meanders across the universe, speeding up and slowing down as it snakes across stars and galaxies."*[3]

By comparison, a clock onboard a spaceship traveling at 87 percent of the speed of light would tick only half as fast as a clock on earth. You would experience time normally onboard the spaceship, but upon returning to earth you would find that you aged only half as much as your friends and family. Time slows down the faster you travel, and would come to a complete stop at the speed of light.[4]

Similarly, time slows down due to the effects of gravity. A small object like our planet causes a barely perceptible time dilation compared to objects in orbit around it. The Global Positioning System (GPS) corrects for this time dilation to preserve accuracy.[5] A massive gravitational object, such as a black hole, causes time to slow down to a crawl. If your ship fell into a black hole, the event would happen quickly to you, but to an outside observer, the tragedy might unfold over thousands of years. By any objective measure, time is not constant, and our normal perception of it is highly skewed.

The motion of our planet may also effect the passage of time in a small way. As our planet rotates through its daily cycle, we rotate with it, flying eastward at 1,000 miles per hour, without noticing that we are going anywhere. The whole ball hurtles through space at 67,000 miles per hour around the sun, while the sun moves at 500,000 miles an hour in rotation around the galaxy. The entire galaxy itself is careening towards the neighboring Andromeda Galaxy at 288,000 miles per hour. How does the tick-tock of time compare to planets in other solar systems and galaxies that are moving faster or slower than we are?

To complicate matters, time did not exist prior to the Big Bang. Time is part of the space-time continuum and does not exist without space. Contrary to commonsense, empty space is something rather than nothing, and space-time continues to stretch as galaxies race away from each other. Neither space nor time as we know them exist outside the universe.[6]

To add to the weirdness, scientists demonstrated that two photons or electrons emitted from the same atom remain linked, even miles apart from each other. Whatever is done to one photon or electron, such as measuring its polar orientation, immediately affects its partner the same way. There is zero time involved in the transmission of information from entity to the other, even if they are on opposite sides of the universe. Although Einstein predicted the phenomenon, it was too much for him to believe.[7]

To make matters more interesting, tachyon particles, if they exist as theorized, move faster than the speed of light, and travel forwards and backwards through time. The future and past seem to exist simultaneously with the present. If it were possible for an object of mass to travel faster than the speed of light like tachyon particles, then we could literally travel through time.

By any objective measure, our linear experience of time does not give us an accurate perception of reality. To discover the universe as it really is, we must transcend our limited perceptions of time. We must acknowledge that time exists, since that is our normal day-to-day experience, but if we mentally put ourselves outside the universe then it is also true that time does not exist, so time both does and does not exist. And, if we start talking about tachyons moving forward and backwards through time, then we are basically treading on fundamental questions about the nature of our own lives in terms of fate or free will.

Previously, we discussed the observer effect and the concept of creating our own realities. There are some constraints in terms of the collective definition of reality, but within that definition we have a lot of room to choose. We can literally collapse our own reality into existence. On the other hand, the idea that particles can move forwards or backwards through time seems to imply that the future has already happened. Is it possible that everything you will ever do has already been done, and that you are fated to live your life the way it already happened? Is it possible that if you tried to cheat fate by doing exactly the opposite of what you might normally do, that you are still doing exactly what you were fated to do?

If you imagine becoming an observer from outside the universe where time does not exist, then you might say that there is no sequential past, present, or future, but that everything is happening all at the same time, which is hard to even describe without evoking the use of time as a description. To come to grips with the paradoxical nature of time, it helps to have a quick overview of parallel universe theory.

Roadmap to Reality

Parallel Universe Theory

Parallel universe theory grew out of wave particle-duality and the observer effect in quantum physics. Subatomic particles exist in a state of flux, existing in an infinite number of possible locations all at the same time. When the scientist collapses a wave of possibilities down to a single location, parallel universe theory proposes that the experiment is simultaneously carried out by identical copies of the scientist in an infinite number of parallel universes. The wave of infinite possibilities collapses into an infinite number of parallel universes where every possible version of reality plays out. Parallel universe theory is extremely counterintuitive, because it suggests that the universe is constantly being copied into an infinite number of nearly duplicate versions. Science fiction often depicts parallel universes where characters somehow jump from one universe to another and discover slightly different versions of the same thing. Life typically sucks in every other possible version of reality, except the one the actors came from.

Imagine driving down the highway from point A to point B and every possible outcome happens along the way. We successfully arrive at our destination in an infinite number of parallel universes, although with slightly different experiences along the way. However, there are also an infinite number of parallel universes where something goes wrong, and we crash at an infinite number of points, for an infinite number of reasons, in an infinite number of variations where we either walk away unscathed or get smeared on the pavement. With an infinite number of favorable universes and an infinite number of unfavorable universes, we have only a fifty-fifty chance of arriving at our destination unscathed. We might get lucky and last a week or two, but the odds are greatly stacked against the likelihood of existing in a universe where we beat the odds and die of old age.

I was pondering parallel universe theory while on a road trip with my family. We were driving around considering different campsites near Yellowstone National Park. Based on parallel universe theory, it could be suggested that we chose all of the campsites, each in a different version of reality. However, I realized that we were not impartial observers, and that we had specific criteria for selecting a suitable campsite. In each parallel universe, if they existed, I would use the same process and therefore tend to choose the same campsite or at most two or three other possible sites to collapse into reality.

The culmination of this insight came on a walkabout, while survival camping with some friends without any sleeping bags or blankets. We were sleeping around a fire in the mountains to stay warm, and I slept with my head on my arm, which was stretched out towards the fire. I could see the light of the fire through my closed eyelids, and I awoke in the middle of the night to the sensation that my hand was on fire and my fingers were charred to the bone. I couldn't feel them at all.

208

In a panicked fraction of a second I reached over and thrust my hand into a five-gallon bucket of water we had for fire control. My companions were also stirred into action. Jeff didn't know what was going on, but he was about to unleash a karate move on something or someone, while Dustin was about to dowse me with the entire bucket of water. As I thrust my hand into the water, I had the experience of two different versions of reality at the same time: one where my hand was charred to the bone, and the other where my hand was fine and I was plunging it into a bucket of water. It was obvious an instant later that my arm had merely fallen asleep from lack of blood flow, and the whole delusion about being on fire was the result of seeing the flames through my eyelids.

I felt stupid sitting there with my hand in a bucket of water, although I was greatly relieved that it was intact. However, I was struck by the feeling of duality, as if both realities had the potential to exist, but the one I collapsed into existence was the one where my hand was merely asleep and not charred. I'm not suggesting that was the case, but that's what it felt like, and the experience collapsed into existence a new metaphor for thinking about parallel universe theory. In other words, what if there are an infinite number of parallel *possible* universes, but we only collapse one into existence? We are not impartial observers. Through the process of deciding, we collapse an infinite number of parallel possible universes into a single reality.

On the same camping trip, Dustin told us about his rock climbing adventures and described some interesting experiences. One time he and some friends were headed out rock climbing, but Dustin had a bad feeling about the trip and finally managed to turn the group back to a restaurant before they went out. Upon returning to the site later that day, they discovered that an avalanche had swept through the area. Premonitions are pretty common, but difficult to either prove or explain by conventional means. Maybe you have had a similar experience, even if not as dramatic, such as thinking about someone moments before they call on the phone.

Intuitive feelings about the future suggest that some kind of a future has already happened, which contradicts our linear sense of time. But in terms of parallel possible universes, we could say that an infinite number of possible realities exist in limbo prior to a moment of decision. Some possible versions of reality are more likely than others, and we collapse only one into existence. In Dustin's case, there was a high probability of collapsing a reality into existence where the group was buried under an avalanche. But Dustin intuited something from that parallel possible universe and collapsed a different reality into existence.

In a similar story with a different outcome, sailor Debbie Kiley reluctantly joined a trip to deliver a yacht from Maine to Florida. She had a bad feeling about the trip, but was pressured into going along. As retold by Laurence Gonzales in his book *Deep Survival*, the crew of five sailed into a hurricane, the ship sank, and their life raft blew away, leaving them without any survival supplies in an inflatable dinghy in the ocean surrounded by sharks. Before being rescued five days later, one woman died of injuries and was given overboard to the sharks. Two of the men were physically fine, but so delirious that they hopped out of the dinghy "to get cigarettes," only to be eaten alive. Looking back on the situation, Kiley offered the sensible advice, "Trust your gut." The situation could have been avoided.[8]

The notion that future events could alter the present might seem like crank science on my part, but the idea is consistent with quantum physics theory. According to physicist Fred Allan Wolf, Ph.D., *"[The present moment] requires feedback from the future as well as what I call "feedforward" from the past. Feedback from the future appears to the mind as intuition and thought. Feedforward from the past appears as feelings and perceptions of senses."*[9] In his book *The Yoga of Time Travel*, Wolf describes something very similar to parallel possible universes, theorizing that possibility waves from the past and future merge to form probability curves in the present. These probability curves predict what will most likely happen in any event.[10]

Intuitively, the idea that the future could affect the present makes more sense than many other theories of reality. It raises some intriguing possibilities and is a plausible "explanation" for intuitive experiences. It also raises the possibility of nonlinear cause and effect, where events in a possible future alter the past, without actually messing up the time line. In the avalanche story, a bad feeling about the future led to a change in behavior in the present, which is the past from a future perspective. It is surprising how many events seem to fit nonlinear cause and effect.

For example, Olympic gold medalists often describe how they entered their particular sport, such as skating. In many cases they seemed to know from childhood that they would compete at the Olympics. Is it possible that winning a gold medal in a possible future reality was the whole reason they were inspired to start skating in the first place? Or is it possible that both events caused each other, that they started skating because they won the gold medal in a possible future reality, and they ultimately won the gold because they started skating and trained extensively to make it happen? This kind of paradox is the essence of nonlinear processing.

My first experience with nonlinear cause and effect came about ten years before the burnt hand incident. Grandma Josie had a favorite glass that she always liked to talk about. Our family enjoyed hunting for treasures like antique bottles around old mining camps in the mountains, and Grandma's sister had found this glass on an outing. It wasn't an antique, but it brought back fond memories for Grandma, and she talked about the old days every time she used it. But this time was different.

The glass perched on the edge of the sink, and it seemed like our minds merged on the possibility that the glass was in danger. I experienced an intuitive moment that I can only describe as something like a focal point of our minds on the glass. The glass was safe for the moment, but when I returned a few days later, Grandma told me with great distress that the glass was broken. She was carrying it across the room and it felt *"almost as if someone had yanked it"* out of her hand. That would be the end of the story for most people. The broken pieces are swept into the garbage and the incident is written off to Newtonian physics. But it was such a bizarre coincidence that the glass broke a couple days after we became worried about it that I reflected more on the situation.

Could it have been a subconscious suggestion, that our concern over the glass caused Grandma to drop it? Or did we sense some sort of echo of the glass breaking in a possible future? The glass was in danger, not because it was sitting on the edge of the counter, but because it would be dropped in a few days. Or did our fear that the glass could break merge with the possibility that it would break in the near future in nonlinear cause and effect? Each incident triggered the other. Questions like this are easy to ask and hard to answer, but that event started me wondering about the possibility of nonlinear cause and effect. I prefer to avoid collapsing any specific opinion into reality, but try to acknowledge an entire wave of possibilities. It could have been a case of classical physics at work, or a subconscious thought, or nonlinear cause and effect, or something else altogether, or perhaps a combination of the above.

Fate, Free Will, and Special Destiny

Has the future been pre-determined, such that our lives have already been lived and we are just going through the motions to do what was fated for us? Or do we have free will to determine our own destiny? As we discovered in chapter three, free will is largely an illusion. That would seem to mesh with astrologers who believe that each of us has a destiny that can be divined from the arrangement of the stars and planets.

From a sequential standpoint, I cannot imagine any logical basis for astrology to work. How could fate be determined by the positions of stars and planets at the time of birth? What would happen if we were born on a different planet or on a space ship? On the other hand, I find that everything tends to be true in it's own way and it is just a matter of finding the proper context. If fate is fixed then it wouldn't matter whether we knew our horoscope or not, since the knowledge wouldn't change anything. But it has been suggested that life might consist of 80 percent fate and 20 percent free choice. What an interesting thought, that we could have both at the same time.

In recalling shared realities from the previous chapter, we could consider the collective reality as our fate and our individual experiences as free will. Eighty percent of our existence (or some other arbitrary number) is governed by the opportunities and limitations of the collective reality. Twenty percent of our existence is governed by free will, allowing us to collapse individual choices into reality. Within that twenty percent, we have the wiggle room to choose whether we live in a tipi in the woods or start a multi-billion dollar fast food chain. However, if free will is an illusion, then our choices may be subconsciously dictated by other influences. Some individuals seem subconsciously drawn towards special destinies.

In the book *Three Cups of Tea*, mountain climber Greg Mortenson described his efforts to build schools for poor villages in Pakistan. Mortenson went to Pakistan to honor his deceased sister by leaving her bracelet on top of K2, but the expedition was aborted due to an emergency. Mortenson, nearly delirious with exhaustion, missed the trail back to town. He was the *first* Westerner to ever wander into the village of Korphe. The villagers nursed him back to health with the meager resources they had. Before leaving, Mortensen asked to see their school, and was shocked to discover the children sitting on frosty ground without books, using sticks to write in the mud. It cost a dollar a day to hire a teacher, which was more than the combined wealth of the village could afford, so they shared a teacher with a nearby village. Half the time they had no teacher at all. Although he lacked fundraising or building skills, Mortenson vowed to return and build them a school. The project led to his life's mission. Mortenson founded the Central Asia Institute and built additional schools all over Pakistan and Afghanistan.

Mortenson told how one woman joined the CAI. Julia Bergman knew her cousin Jean Hoerni donated funds for a school in the Himalayas, but didn't know the details. While touring in Pakistan, she joined a helicopter tour in the hopes of seeing K2. On a whim, the pilot volunteered to show the group a typical village. On the ground, the village children eagerly took the tourists to see their new school, which included a plaque recognizing Bergman's cousin as the donor. Out of a thousand-mile range of mountains, Bergman accidentally landed at the only village that had a school funded by her cousin. When Jean Hoerni endowed the CAI with a million dollars to expand its work, Bergman volunteered to serve on the board.[11] Ordinary people experience these extraordinary coincidences all the time.

Serendipitous Moments and Grand Coincidences

Hunter-gatherer cultures called it "magic." In mythical cultures it is said that, "God works his miracles in mysterious ways." Sequential culture denies that serendipitous moments or coincidences are anything more than coincidences. People who talk of higher consciousness seem to invoke the magical/mythical again, saying, "The universe works in mysterious ways." The inability to provide a palatable sequential explanation for life's simple miracles may be one of the primary reasons we continue to hang onto our mythical heritage. Personally, I have experienced enough improbable and serendipitous coincidences in my own life that I find it difficult to deny some kind of cosmic connection.

In higher consciousness circles, serendipity is often described as the result of casting one's desires out into the universe. Consciously and subconsciously, we ask for whatever we seek, and somehow the universe arranges a coincidence to make it happen. It seems as if there is some kind of subconscious behind-the-scenes negotiation across time and space.

Given the universality of serendipitous phenomenon, I wonder if there are forces beyond the present reach of science to explain. If the future exists as an infinite wave of possibilities, then it appears that our desires shape the specific realties we collapse into existence. We broadcast our thoughts and desires into the universe, and reap whatever we sow. Our subconscious desires and deep beliefs are probably bigger factors than our conscious wishes. Whether positive or negative, we manage to negotiate across time and space to be in the right place at the right time to fulfill those desires, even if it results in our own fatality.

Consider Lawrence Grodsky, a nationally known motorcycle safety expert who was killed in a 2006 collision with a deer. In his articles and classes on motorcycle safety he often said that deer were the greatest hazard on the road. Shortly before his death he told his girlfriend, *"That's how I'm going to go, it's going to be a deer."*[12] Sequentially speaking, we tend to dismiss stories like this as mere coincidences. We could argue that millions of people go through their lives predicting how they will die, but we only notice the one-in-a-million person that predicts it correctly. However, while deer are a significant hazard, the odds of being *the* motorcyclist that crashes and dies due to deer is statistically very low. There must be a very large number of people who incorrectly predict that they will die in a collision with a deer. Instead they are ultimately done in by something else: trains, planes, cars, electrocution, old age, cancer, falling off a cliff, etc.

I don't intend to be macabre, but stories like Grodsky's are remarkably common, as if some people just *know*. For example, Steve Irwin, a.k.a. the "Crocodile Hunter" always knew he would die young. He died at the age of forty-four while swimming with stingrays, when a ray flicked its barbed tail up at him and pierced his heart.[13] It is arguable that Irwin lived a dangerous lifestyle, but the odds of fatal strike by the stingray were actually fairly low. He could have been severely injured instead. What do stories like this tell us about the nature of reality?

In searching for the simplest answer, let's disregard nonlinear explanations for the moment. Lawrence Grodsky's belief that he would die in a collision with a deer could have risen from a tendency to ride in places where deer are abundant. Alternatively, his prediction could have led to a subconscious suggestion that affected his reflexes, allowing a fatal crash when the situation arose by chance. We could also say that Grodsky's belief led him to subconsciously collapse his own self-fulfilling prophecy into existence. I live in a rural area where deer are insanely abundant on the highways. Collisions with deer are virtually guaranteed for drivers traveling more than 50 mph at night, so these interpretations are entirely plausible. On the other hand, Grodsky could have been injured rather than killed, but he *knew* he would die.

Nonlinear processing enables us to consider the accident from a fresh perspective with several possible interpretations: 1) Grodsky intuited a possible reality that he would die in a collision with a deer and was unable to collapse a different reality into existence, 2) he intuited his possible demise by deer, then focused on and manifested that reality into existence by prophesizing his own accident and preaching that deer were dangerous, or 3) Grodsky's obsession with the threat of deer on the highway created a possible future reality where he died in collision with one, which he subsequently intuited and finally succumbed to. From a nonlinear worldview, these are all valid possibilities.

While this crank-scientific reasoning provides some satisfying quasi-explanations for situations such as Grodsky's, I don't claim that it is an accurate perception of reality, only that it might be a less distorted version than the sequential worldview. There are still a number of loose ends, such as the volitions of the deer. Did the deer go through life believing that motorcycles were the greatest threat, ultimately collapsing a reality into existence where it arranged to meet with Grodsky on a dark night? Not likely. In hunter-gatherer cultures, it is commonly believed that animals sometimes gift themselves to be hunted. Many of my wilderness survival associates have described similar experiences. Prey animals seemed to offer themselves, "like a gift from the Great Spirit."

I sometimes practice "trust stalking" with wild animals, showing that I am non-threatening so they won't run away. Contrary to expectations, wild animals are not necessarily scared of people because we are people, but only because we act like people. For example, I once ate breakfast with three moose. Instead of hiding when they saw me, I slowly moved my head like I was nibbling on tree branches. I gradually animated my browsing as they became accustomed to my presence, until it was obvious that I was a person peacefully grazing like my moose friends. I wonder if, as preconscious beings, wild animals are as subject to suggestion as a fully hypnotized person. More than hypnotism, could a deer be swayed to give itself up by the intent of a hunter? Is it possible that Grodsky's deer was summoned by his vision of his demise, such that it walked itself onto the road at his unconscious will?

Recall that we may not qualify as a sentient species either, and our perception of free will is largely an illusion. While our conscious attention is focused on one thing, our subconscious deals with everything else. If a deer could be summoned into an encounter with either a hunter or a motorcycle, then any person could just as easily be summoned into a "coincidence." For example, if you desire to learn paragliding, you may "accidentally" bump into someone who is knowledgeable about the sport, because the two of you negotiated your movements across time and space until you met. All of this assumes that some kind of subconscious communication is possible between people and across time. We have traded crank science for wild speculation, but there is no harm in imagining such scenarios in the continuing quest to grasp reality. Who knows what might come of it? At the very least, it gives us the opportunity to try out new and interesting neural connections.

Whether or not the deer was summoned onto the highway, at least Grodsky was in the right place at the right time to hit it. Nonlinear processing provides possible explanations for that and thousands of similar incidents. It is a bigger challenge to apply nonlinear thinking to large-scale disasters such as an airplane crash.

First of all, every plane crash has survivors; they are the people who miss a fatal flight because they purchase different tickets, or are late getting to the airport, or have a last-minute change of plans. We could speculate that these individuals intuit an impending crash, without necessarily being aware of it, and "accidentally" choose alternate realities.

We can also speculate that some crash victims consciously or subconsciously know it is their time to die and willingly participate in an accident. Other participants might feel uneasy about the flight but proceed anyway. Some people are required by duty or prior obligations to keep their flight plans, even if they have a bad feeling about it. If life is eighty percent fate and twenty percent free choice, perhaps there are unavoidable tragedies like a plane crash, the Holocaust, Hiroshima, Pompeii, or Iraq, when the wave of possible future realities has narrowed down to few, if any, alternatives. On the other hand, having previously dissolved all personal identity, we can say that there is no such thing as a personal tragedy. We share a common identity with all dust and microbes and other people. When some of us are lost, the identity still exists and carries on.

Changing the Past

We speculated that it might be possible to intuit an echo from parallel possible futures, which influences the reality we collapse into existence in the present. The idea meshes neatly with the idea that we exist in the present, while the past is fixed behind us, and the future remains a wave of possibilities. But what if it were possible to change the past? In the words of Fred Alan Wolf, *"Albert Einstein and Richard Tolman showed that if quantum mechanics describes events, then even the past is as uncertain as the future. So how do we have any past at all? The answer is that we create them! Yes. What we call the past only exists in the windmills of our mind. We in the present are responsible for our pasts, not the other way around. We are the creators of history."*[14]

History is constantly in flux, at least in our interpretation of it. For example, as a child I learned about the 1876 Battle of Little Bighorn in south central Montana, also known as "Custer's Last Stand." General Custer was a hero who was unmercifully slaughtered by wild Indians, along with every man in his company. But history gradually changed, and Custer is now remembered as a reckless, bloodthirsty glory hound who irresponsibly led his troops into a trap. The "wild Indians" from the Sioux and Cheyenne tribes that "slaughtered" Custer are now recognized as Native Americans who were defending their homeland. History is constantly reassessed in this way, in terms of our understanding of human events, as well as our understanding of natural history through evolution, geology, and astronomy. We have also substantially revised history through the pages of this book. Before reading this text, you may have assumed that our ancestors had the same basic thoughts and motivations that we do today, but now you are aware of magical and mythical worldviews and the different perceptions of reality associated with them.

Interestingly, the past also becomes less distant as we grow older. I remember the Battle of the Little Bighorn as old history when I was a child in the mid-1970s. It was an event that happened ten lifetimes ago from my perspective as a ten-year old. However, time shrank during the following thirty years. From my perspective as a forty-year old, the battle took place barely over three lifetimes ago. My Crow friend Alma Snell's grandfather was an Indian scout for General Custer, which places me three handshakes across time from Custer. I perceive the battle as recent history.

Whether or not we can physically alter the past may be a matter of perspective. Based on our normal day-to-day experience, the past seems fixed and the future open to possibilities, but from a perspective outside the universe, and therefore outside of time, it might be more accurate to say that the past, present, and future exist simultaneously in a wave of parallel possible realities that are negotiated forwards and backwards through time. All past and future history exists simultaneously as a wave of possibilities and as realities that have been collapsed into existence.

Parallel Possible Universes

There are six key numbers that govern the make-up of our universe, and if any one of these numbers were a little bit skewed, then the universe wouldn't work the way it does. Imagine a safe with six dials on it, and every dial has to be set to the right place to open it. The six key numbers are measures of 1) gravity, 2) atomic attraction, 3) the mass of the universe, 4) the amount of dark energy in the universe, 5) the degree of turbulence, and 6) the number of spatial dimensions. If one of the dials were off by a little bit, it would have greatly altered the universe.

For example: 1) If gravity were stronger than it is, then stars would form at smaller scales and burn out before life could form. 2) If the strong force that holds atomic nuclei together were weaker than it is, then hydrogen atoms could not fuse together to form other elements. If the force were too strong, then all hydrogen would have fused already, leaving none to form water or fuel the stars. 3) If the universe contained more matter, then mutual gravitational attraction would have already collapsed everything into a Big Crunch. If there were less matter in the universe, then the blast of the Big Bang would have scattered it before it condensed into stars and galaxies. 4) Similarly, although the expansion of the universe is apparently accelerating due to "dark energy," the presence of more dark energy could have accelerated the universe too fast for galaxies to form. 5) Galaxy formation is also dependent on just the right amount of turbulence in the initial Big Bang. Without turbulence, matter would have dispersed without clumping, but with too much turbulence, it would have coalesced into black holes the size of galactic clusters. 6) and finally, life as we know it would be impossible if we had more or less than three spatial dimensions. The only obvious reason why all these dials are set precisely where they need to be is that we wouldn't be here to notice if they weren't.[15]

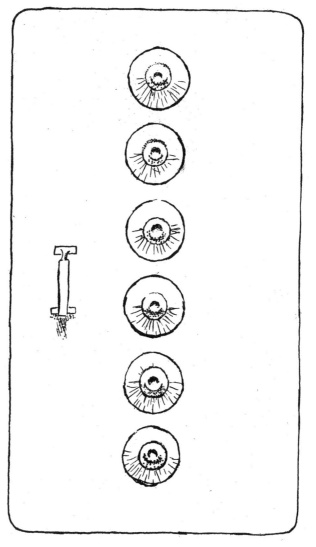

One could argue for intelligent design, that God created the universe, either with the intent of creating life and humanity through evolution, or as an interesting experiment in complexity to see what formed of its own. On the other hand, based on parallel universe theory, some physicists have suggested that there is a multiverse consisting of an infinite number of slightly different universes that are all messed up because the numbers came out wrong. While it seems highly improbable that we should have all the right conditions in our universe, the other perspective is that only the right version of the universe could spawn living beings capable of noticing this improbability. To phrase it another way, only a universe conducive to life can spawn beings capable of noticing that the probability of creating such a universe is extremely small. Statistically, we have a 100 percent probability of existing in a favorable universe.

It might be more accurate to say that there are an infinite number of parallel possible universes where the numbers are messed up, and the only universes that come into existence are the ones with future observers to collapse them into reality. In other words, for the past to exist, it must be collapsed into existence from the future. The past may be collapsed into existence by our presumably more-sentient descendents, or if life should perish on our planet, then perhaps by some other sentient species. In quantum physics, such thinking is not bizarre; it is crucial to the effort to understand the true nature of reality. In essence, time exists and we live our lives by the clock, but as far as we know, time does not exist outside the universe. If we detach from our normal perception of time, then we can say that both perspectives are equally true. Time both does and does not exist, and it could be argued that the entire past and future history of the universe has and has not happened. Paradox is the nature of nonlinear processing.

Interestingly, paradoxical questions or "koans" are essential tools in Zen Buddism, used in the quest for higher levels of consciousness. *"What is the sound of one hand clapping?" "If a tree falls in the forest and no one is there to hear it, does it make a sound?" "What is your face before your parents were born?"* To that I would add one of my own, *"Does time exist if there is no one around to measure it?"* People meditate on koans and ultimately re-wire the brain to process paradox. According to Roshi Philip Kapleau in *The Three Pillars of Zen, "koans appear bewildering, for in their phrasing koans deliberately throw sand into the eyes of the intellect to open our Mind's eye and see the world and everything in it undistorted by our concepts and judgments... By wheedling the intellect into attempting solutions impossible for it, koans reveal to us the inherent limitations of the logical mind as an instrument for realizing ultimate Truth."[16]* In our attempt to transcend time, the final stumbling block appears to be our own intellectual minds.

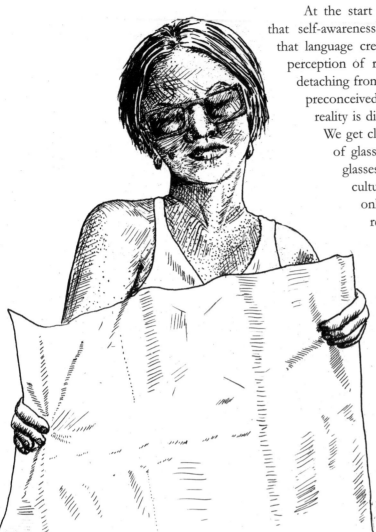

At the start of this journey we found evidence revealing that self-awareness and free will are illusions. We discovered that language creates our sensation of mind and distorts our perception of reality. Since then we have been systematically detaching from our cultural programming and deconstructing preconceived notions of reality. It seems as if our view of reality is distorted by a thousand pairs of colored glasses. We get closer to the truth every time we take off a pair of glasses, but then discover that we still wearing other glasses. Having transcended our personal identity and culture, matter and time, we seem to be left with only one obstacle in the way of determining what reality really is. The mind itself is an obstacle, an artificial by-product of language. The only way to discover the nature of reality is to lose one's mind.

Living in the Present

According to many Eastern traditions the path to enlightenment is to let go of all thoughts and live fully in the present moment. If you are eating dinner, then be absorbed in savoring your food. Be aware of your body and your place, without such distractions as reading the news or thinking about something else. Practice letting go of the inner dialogue, the chatter of the dissatisfied ego that always wants something better in the future. In other words, learn to exist in the Now and appreciate it fully, even if you are having dinner in a foxhole with bullets whizzing overhead. As Eckhart Tolle writes in *The Power of Now*, *"Ask yourself what "problem" you have right this moment, not next year, tomorrow, or five minutes from now. What is wrong with this moment? You can always cope with the Now, but you can never cope with the future—nor do you have to."*[7]

Our ancestors lived completely fused with the present, unable to reminisce over the past or imagine the future. But with metaphorical language and self-awareness we learned to reflect on our past experiences and imagine future possibilities. The problem is that we spend most of our lives worrying about the future or dreaming that it will somehow be better than the present, or we wish for or regret the past. But if we spend today imagining that tomorrow might be better or worse, then we miss today. And if we do the same tomorrow, then we miss that today as well. Most of us spend our entire lives this way, so wrapped up in what was or could be that we seldom experience the present.

From a pragmatic standpoint, existing entirely in the present might seem like a poor way to accomplish anything. If we decide to be content in the moment and don't long for a better future, then we may be satisfied to accept our situation as is, even if that means living under an oppressive government or allowing our community to be contaminated with toxic waste. But living in the Now isn't about being resigned to accept things as they are. We can imagine a better future and work towards it without being trapped by the illusion that we will only be happy when we get everything just right at the end. With a clear vision in mind, embrace the present situation as it is.

In a nonlinear sense, it is a matter of existing concurrently in all todays as if the past and future exist simultaneously with the present. There may be a specific goal at the end of the trail, but the journey consists of present moments, which is the only place we can act. If we live fully engaged in the present moment every day, then we are cohesively orchestrating with ourselves as if there is only one Now. We operate in the present moment today. We operate in the present moment tomorrow and the next day, and from that perspective, we operate in the present moment in the past. A person who applies a thousand days of present-minded effort towards a vision or goal is functionally like a thousand people working together within the single, expansive Now. None of those thousand people would get anything done if they were stressed out about what the others did in the past or might do in the future. To function together, they must each accept their own slice of the present and engage it fully.

Operating in the present is not only a means to achieve goals, it is also the path to enlightenment. In the words of Eckhart Tolle, *"Your mind is telling you that you cannot get there from here. Something needs to happen, or you need to become this or that before you can be free and fulfilled. It is saying, in fact, that you need time — that you need to find, sort out, do, achieve, acquire, become, or understand something before you can be free or complete. You see time as the means to salvation, whereas in truth it is the greatest obstacle to salvation. You think that you can't get there from where or who you are at this moment because you are not yet complete or good enough, but the truth is that here and now is the only point from where you can get there. You "get" there by realizing that you are there already."*[18]

If we have transcended our concept of self and dissolved our personal identity; if we have transcended the concept of matter to see that reality is something we create; and if we have transcended the concept of time, to see the entire past and future history of the universe as a simultaneous event within an expansive sense of now, then we may be at risk of losing our minds. This state of "no mind" is the gateway to universal processing, which we pick up in the next chapter.

Suggested Reading

Matrix Energetics by Richard Bartlett, D.C., N.D.: *Matrix Energetics* is written from the observer and nonlinear worldviews with a touch of mythical-level faith healing. Bartlett cites quantum physics and the observer effect as the conceptual foundation for his healing work. In essence, since we create reality, we can imagine healing to shift our perceptions and instantly achieve a new state. Bartlett facilitates the process with some anchor-collapse techniques borrowed from Neuro-Linguistic Programming. To heal injuries, Bartlett often practices "time travel" by regressing patients into the past before the injuries occurred. The experience of being whole is collapsed into the present to heal the injury.

—Seventeen—

Universal Processing

Reality Beyond the Mind

"Though biologically and psychically nature has been his womb and mother, spiritually, man harkens from a different source. His identity is not to be found in nature alone, but within himself in relationship to that Source. It is one of the traditions of the esoteric wisdoms that humanity needed to be separate from the powerful forces of instinctive, unconscious energies of nature and that the mechanism used to this end was the promotion of the experience of selfhood."

—*The Findhorn Garden*[1]

The practice of Zen Buddhism cultivates three attitudes known as *great faith*, *great doubt*, and *great courage*. Great faith is an unshakable belief in enlightenment. Great doubt is the need to question everything, including that which is already known. Great courage is the determination to stay the course at any cost.

The parallels with our own quest are intriguing. We proceeded with a measure of faith that we might be able to determine, or become enlightened to, the true nature of reality. We cast doubt on our most basic assumptions about reality, shattering illusion after illusion in search of the real thing. And we proceeded with great courage even when the path challenged our values, beliefs, and identity. We paid the price for an enlightened perspective with our own dying egos.

Snapshot: Universal Processing

Technology: All and none.

Origin: Buddhism.

Logic: Nature is perfect.

Perspective: One with the universe, nonjudgmental.

Culture: Unknown.

Social-Political Structure: Unknown.

Notable People: Jesus, Gautama Buddha, Jiddu Krishnamurti, U.G. Krishnamurti, Masanobu Fukuoka, Peace Pilgrim.

Television/Movies: *Peaceful Warrior, Powder, The Thirteenth Floor, The Celestine Prophecy.*

The quest to define reality forced us to systematically deconstruct, or detach from our preconceived ideas about it. In other words, defining reality is largely a process of letting go of our definitions. Reality itself remains unchanged; we only need to learn to see it without judging it. The irony is that, while we are learning to detach from our preconceived notions of reality, our preconscious, prelingual ancestors apparently never had any such notions to begin with. Like children, our ancestors saw reality without judgment, existing in complete fusion with the universe. In this chapter we come full circle, reconnecting with the universe, but from the perspective of conscious awareness of that connection.

A Universe Aware of Itself

Our preconscious ancestors were fused with the natural world in such a way that they were not aware they existed. They were part of nature and lived their lives as automatically as a colony of ants, following an evolved script of behaviors that worked, going through the motions of living without being aware of their own existence. They were not merely in the Garden of Eden; they were part of the ecosystem like any other plant or animal. But with knowledge they discovered their own existence, their individuality, and with it a separate identity from the Garden. It was both a gift and a curse.

It was a gift, because without self-awareness, there is no existence, no self-experience. But it was a curse because with self-awareness comes the potential for self-doubt, self-pity, and apprehension over the potential to cease existing. Along with skills like tool-making and social organization, this self-awareness became part of the cultural heritage that was passed down through the ages, mimicked from one generation to the next, condemning all future generations to be locked out of the Garden. Our ancestors operated efficiently without purpose, but we are left floundering, searching for meaning in life. Why are we here? What is our purpose? What is our destiny? Now we return full circle to the bosom of nature, to once again become part of the Garden and be one with everything, but from the unique perspective of total awareness of that connection.

Through the course of this book we have tested our senses and assumptions about reality, and found them lacking. Our probing reveals that we are not yet a sentient species, and our sense of free will is an illusion. The evidence indicates that our ancestors lived their entire lives in a preconscious state until the Cultural Revolution. As life became increasingly complex, mimicked behaviors and accumulated experience were no longer sufficient to deal with problems. Metaphorical language enabled new ways of thinking and led to glimmers of self-awareness. The reflective mind was born and our ancestors recognized their existence.

With the rise of the Stone Age, people lived in a bubble of first-person individuality, aware of their wants and needs, but not fully capable of connecting with the wants and needs of other people. It was a symbolic, magical, and often hypnotic world, where any bird that flew by could be a sign of something important, and any event could be considered the work of magic. Music and chanting helped people return to a hypnotic state much of the time, especially while processing food, going to war, or dancing around the fire.

Over time our ancestors learned to detach from their personal identities enough to shift into second person, to see the world through the eyes of other people of similar backgrounds. It became a mythical world, where honoring the gods helped to ensure rain and fertility for the crops. However, it was also a black-and-white world where the people of a culture stood united in a single worldview against other cultures. It became a world of conquest, with people driven to convert or eliminate people who were different.

As the world became increasingly complex and new technologies evolved, foreign cultures begin to mingle and meld together. People met foreigners with strange beliefs, made friends anyway, and learned to detach from their own cultural identities enough to shift into third person and compare backgrounds and beliefs, revealing that these foreigners were not so strange or wrong after all, just different. It became a sequential world, where everything was driven by linear cause and effect and everything had an answer, although such answers often proved to be shortsighted. This sequential processing became part of the cultural wisdom that is mimicked and passed down from generation to generation and is still integrating into the collective consciousness.

The world is changing again, becoming increasingly complex, increasingly interconnected, where linear solutions are no longer adequate to resolve social or technological problems, nor sufficient to stay competitive in business. It is becoming a world of systems, where even a small business might include employees in multiple countries creatively tackling complex issues from every angle via teleconferencing. It is becoming a world where the mind and body are viewed as systems, where we can detach from our personal identity and reshape it at will. It is the mark of sentience, the ability to consciously act, instead of merely reacting to the world around us.

But even systems thinking is unable to tackle our biggest problems in the world today, problems like desertification, global warming, and worldwide poverty. These are problems that require a greater level of detachment, the ability to step back and see ourselves holistically as part of the greater web of life, where everything comes full circle. Every action impacts everything else and ultimately comes back to affect ourselves and future generations. Only by seeing the bigger picture will we be able to learn to prosper on this planet without destroying it and ultimately ourselves.

When we have learned to live in harmony with our world and each other, then we will be able to focus directly on the spiritual journey where we learn to completely detach from and ultimately dissolve our personal identities, to see that we are not merely part of nature, but that we are nature. When we dissolve our identities, we become free to identify with any rock or tree or bird or the entire planet, connecting with them as fully as if we were looking at ourselves in a mirror. We begin to focus on the roadmap, seeking a view of reality without the distortions of mimicked cultural beliefs about the nature of the universe.

As we continue to correct for distortions in our view of reality, we learn to see the physical world not as solid matter, but as largely empty space and fields of energy, more holographic than physical. We learn to detach from our preconceptions about reality at the most basic levels, discovering that reality isn't merely something we are faced with; it is something we help create. It is a world that is nearly magical, where one's thoughts ripple out and alter the world in subtle ways. It is a world where we hold the power of creation, and yet it is a world that is still distorted, confined by false perceptions of time.

However, if we detach from our preconceived notions of time then we realize that time is neither fixed nor unidirectional. We learn to see time as something that both exists and does not exist, where events in the past and the future potentially merge to cause each other, and paradox is the norm rather than the exception. It is a universe where our past and future history both have and have not happened. We learn to live in the eternal present moment.

It is at this instant that we must reconsider the nature of the universe. Upon closer examination we discover that matter is even more illusionary than we thought: everything in the universe was formed from absolutely nothing. In the words if physicist Stephen Hawking, *"particles can be created out of energy in the form of particle/antiparticle pairs. But that just raises the question of where the energy came from. The answer is that the total energy of the universe is exactly zero."*[2] According to Einstein's Theory of Relativity, the energy of a gravitational field is negative, while the energy of matter is positive. Observations and calculations totaling all gravity and matter within the observable universe indicate that the two values are precisely counter-balanced. Based on this mathematical accounting, the universe could come from nothing because the opposite values cancel each other. The universe was formed from nothing at all.[3]

At the beginning of this quest we wondered if we could be plugged into some kind of a virtual reality simulation. Now we discover that reality is made from nothing. Quantum physics reveals that matter and antimatter spontaneously pop into existence in the vacuum of "empty" space. Matter has a positively charged nucleus surrounded by negatively charged electrons, while antimatter has a negatively charged nucleus surrounded by positively charged positrons. Matter and antimatter instantly annihilate each other, causing it to disappear as quickly as it appears. The universe itself may be the result of a type of vacuum fluctuation that didn't annihilate itself.[4]

The universe is theorized to have started from a false vacuum, which is characterized by a powerful repulsive gravitational field. A false vacuum does not thin out during expansion, so the energy density remains constant even as the size of the false vacuum grows. Based on this theory, expansion of the false vacuum accelerated exponentially, compounding its repulsive force and creating vast quantities of ever-doubling energy from nothing. The initial size of the false vacuum that turned into the universe could have been unimaginably small before doubling, only about one-billionth the size of a proton.[5]

When matter and anti-matter collide, there is a 100 percent conversion of matter into energy, 143 times as efficient as an exploding H-bomb. Presumably, the Big Bang should have created an equal amount of matter and antimatter, which then would have annihilated each other to produce nothing.[6] However, physicists studying the unstable K° particle in 1964 observed that the particle and its antiparticle were not mirror images of each other, but decayed at slightly different rates. If a similar asymmetry existed between quarks and antiquarks in the initial cooling of the universe, then a small portion of matter could have been leftover without any antimatter to annihilate it. Calculations of the amount of background radiation in the universe, leftover from the annihilation of matter and antimatter, in comparison to the amount of matter in the universe, indicates that about one particle of matter survived for every billion that were annihilated.[7]

The bottom line is that the universe materialized itself into existence from nothing 13.7 billion years ago. Yet, from a perspective outside of time, there is no distinction between the past and present. The entire past and future history of the universe exists as a wave of possibilities simultaneously being collapsed into existence. There is only one vast, continuous "now," and from that perspective, there is no distinction between the Big Bang and our own burst into universal consciousness.

If we transcend our cultural beliefs, dissolve our personal identities, and revise our notions of matter and time, then we can identify with the entire universe across all time. We begin to see our existence from a new perspective where the universe is our identity. From the beginning to the end of time, the universe is us, and we are the universe. As we let go of the mind and look around we find that we are the soil, we are the sky, we are the litter blowing down the road; we are the dinosaurs, the solar system, the stardust, and all stars that have ever existed. We are one with everything. We are the universe becoming aware of itself.

We believed we were kicked out of the Garden of Eden, and yet we never really left. Only our perceptions have changed. The Garden itself is bigger than we ever imagined, stretching out across the cosmos. When we peer through our telescopes looking billions of years back in time, we ultimately see our own reflection. We see the echoes of the birth of the universe, which is our birth, our beginning. And when we imagine detaching from the universe, stepping beyond space or time, we see that it is all happening at once. There is no separation between the Big Bang and our awakening. When we look in the mirror and see the universe looking back, perhaps we collapse reality itself into existence. In other words, we are not *in* some kind of virtual reality simulation; we *are* the virtual reality. We are the program and the programmers.

Asking the Question

Imagine that you are the universe and that you have asked a question, a very simple question, "What am I?" And that question was the Big Bang itself bringing forth an infinite number of parallel possible realities of which the only ones that could collapse into existence were the ones that could ask and potentially answer the question. This reality began with a universe of helium and hydrogen fusing inside the stars to form heavier elements, but none were able to answer the question. The stars exploded, blasting heavier, more complex atoms across the cosmos to form new stars and new planets, some of which evolved the self-replicating units we call "life." But none of these life forms were able to answer the question.

With simple cells evolving into complex multi-cellular organisms, there were soon salamanders and lizards walking the land. But a lizard basking in the sun on a rock is not able to bring forth this question from its subconscious and couldn't answer the question even if it could ask it. However, time continued on, and new life forms emerged with more complex nervous systems. They operated on autopilot at first, but eventually recognized their existence and asked questions like "Where did we come from?" and "What am I?" Maybe we will be able to answer this question if we bask in the sun like the lizard and meditate on it long enough.

If it seems far-fetched to think that we might be the universe asking what we are, then consider that some scientists have described the universe as being like a massive computer where each transfer of energy is equivalent to processing one bit of information. Is it possible that the universe is ultimately a program trying to answer the question, "What am I?" Are we as individuals merely subprograms, subroutines processing what the universe is, contributing to the asking and the defining of reality, all of us collectively deciding what kind of universe we collapse into existence?

In this universe-as-computer analogy, one cannot help but notice that it isn't very efficient. For example, if the universe is processing concepts of life and death, then surely there has been enough murder, wars, and genocide on this planet alone to arrive at some kind of a conclusion. However, the computer is no more self-aware than we are. As individuals, we tend to operate as automatons, acting without thinking, and the universe-as-computer is nothing more than our own collective subconscious/conscious existence. The universe assembled itself from nothing and is processing information through every galaxy, every star, every chunk of rock and life form. That is why many mystics say that good and evil come from the same source. Unaware of itself or its actions, the universe simply acts without thinking. Generation by generation, however, random bits of code are self-assembling into a program of self-awareness, which we see in the levels of consciousness acted out across cultures.

Peace and Enlightenment

How would it alter human behavior to perceive ourselves as the universe becoming self-aware, or that we are the universe capable of collapsing reality into existence? How would it alter the way we interact with people at work or on the street? Try to conceive of living with no separation from the universe. See and feel yourself as the universe and every person, place, and thing within it. When you talk to someone, you are the universe talking to yourself. You are the news you watch on TV. You are the rainforests and the oceans, the politicians, the wars, and the celebrations. You are the sound of one hand clapping. Universal processing is not merely an intellectual exercise, but a deep and profound spiritual connection with everything and everyone. It is enlightenment.

One of the central themes of Buddhist philosophy is that the path to world peace and environmental sustainability is to seek enlightenment. Rather than trying to change the world outside, Buddhists first seek to change the world inside. By meditating and introspecting deeply, they learn to transcend the ego and perceive reality from a universal perspective. With enlightenment comes a deep compassion and reverence for all animate and inanimate things. It changes the way they interact with the world, and they seek to mentor others in achieving a similar perspective. In this way, enlightenment is not just an intellectual exercise, but an emotional and spiritual journey as well.

Peace Pilgrim (1908–1981) recognized a similar connection between inner peace and world peace. She abandoned all possessions, including her given name, to walk for peace. She wrote, *"We can work on inner peace and world peace at the same time. On one hand, people have found inner peace by losing themselves in a cause larger than themselves, like the cause of world peace, because finding inner peace means coming from the self-centered life into the life centered in the good of the whole. On the other hand, one of the ways of working for world peace is to work for more inner peace, because world peace will never be stable until enough of us find inner peace to stabilize it."*[8]

Starting in 1953, with only the clothes on her back, plus a comb, toothbrush, ballpoint pen, copies of her message and current correspondence, Peace walked 25,000 miles back and forth across North America for the cause of peace… then stopped counting the miles. With the words "Peace Pilgrim" lettered on the front of her tunic, and a statement about walking for peace on the back, Peace spoke with individuals and the media, as well as civic and school groups. She neither carried money, nor accepted it. She had no food, and never asked for any, eating only when she was offered food. She had neither a blanket nor sleeping bag and never asked for shelter. She accepted a bed when it was offered, but otherwise found contentment sleeping under bridges, in haystacks and farm fields, or nestled into a pile of leaves in the forest. She found enlightenment in her journey.

In describing the enlightened self, Peace Pilgrim wrote, *"The real you is that divine spark. Some call this the God-centered nature, others the divine nature and the Kingdom of God within. Hindus know it as nirvana; the Buddhists refer to it as the awakened soul; the Quakers see it as the Inner Light. In other places it is known as the Christ in you, the Christ Consciousness, the hope of glory, or the indwelling spirit. Even some psychologists have a name for it, the superconscious. But it is all the same thing dressed in different words. The important thing to remember is that it dwells within you!"[9]*

Processing your life experience from a universal perspective has the potential to change everything. Imagine identifying with every person you meet, with every animal, every mouse and spider, every blade of grass and every material thing you encounter. If all things in the universe are different aspects of your being, how do you interact with them? Do you squash a spider under your shoe merely because it is in your way, or do find a deep level of compassion and avoid the spider, or move it out of harms way? Do you move through life callously using and discarding resources, or do you treat everything, even a scrap of paper, with reverence?

As a teenager I found a mentor in the writings of Tom Brown Jr., a wilderness survival and tracking instructor from New Jersey. In his book *The Search*, Brown described oneness with everything, writing *"There is a place I know where everything lives in harmony. Nothing is envied, stolen, or killed. Instead, everything is shared. The land is everyone's and no one's. Life is sacred there. A dweller in this place thinks highly of human life because he lives so close to the earth. He understands his part in the scheme of nature and is not lost searching for himself. In this place, man sleeps easily, without fear, and rises to greet the day with praises instead of curses… There is serenity for man in this place and a oneness with all of creation… Where is this place? Does it really exist? Yes. It is within me and can be within you. It is a state of mind; it is an awareness; it is an appreciation; it is an understanding; it is a commitment to life."[10]*

In experiencing life from this universal perspective, you may find yourself alone at times, but never lonely. In his book *Mirror by the Road* author Peter Oppenheimer told of his spiritual quest in India, writing, *"the student of Indian wisdom is led away from the habitual perspective of seeing oneself in the world to the more expansive vision of seeing the world in one's self… One practical effect of such vision of the self is that it converts the contracted feeling of loneliness into the expansive feeling of aloneness. In this sense, loneliness implies a projection of some "other(s)" and then further posits an exclusion of oneself from the other selves. If we break down the word "alone," on the other hand, to see its derivation, it reveals itself to be an abbreviated form of "all one" and thus refers to the highest state of all inclusive union in which nothing remains outside. In aloneness there is no other to which to relate or from which to feel estranged."[11]*

The Patriarchal/Mythical Paradox

As we have observed throughout this book, cultural perceptions of reality are driven by technology. Therefore, it seems contradictory that universal processing should be connected with 2,500 year old Buddhist philosophy, which was born in an agricultural and clearly patriarchal/mythical culture.

The mythical imprint on Buddhism is obvious. As in Christianity, monasteries are traditionally male-only clubs of celibate monks. Earthly and bodily desires are perceived as temptations to be overcome in a black-and-white code of conduct. These temptations or impulses are perceived as the work of the devil in some forms of Christianity, and as the Mind or Ego in some versions of Buddhism, temptations that must be crushed or overwhelmed through intensive meditation and self-discipline. In some Zen Buddhist practices it is common to beat disciples with sticks as they meditate, to either snap them back to attention or to distract them so they have to concentrate more fully to sustain their focus. How could an enlightened perspective emerge from such mythical practices?

Technology drives worldviews across entire cultures, but deeply introspective individuals can transcend the viewpoints of any culture at any time to attain higher levels of consciousness. Many people consider the original teachings of Jesus as similar to that of Buddha, before organized religion reinterpreted His work within a mythical context, imposing patriarchal values and order. However, churches should not bear the full blame for altering Jesus' message, because it wasn't possible for the culture to absorb his teachings in any other way.

While Buddhism seems to have survived more intact, the self-control is mythical in its approach, and those who eventually attained an enlightened, universal perspective never succeeded in altering their own patriarchal society. It is only with the diffusion of industrial technology and sequential processing that women are gaining equal rights to meditate at temples. It is only recently that the Dali Lama, the enlightened leader of the Tibetan people, has speculated that a future Dali Lama could possibly be a woman.[12]

Attaining Enlightenment

Those who become enlightened typically agree on two key points, 1) that we are "there" already and just have to wake up to enlightenment, and 2) that the experience of enlightenment cannot be described in words. These points are logical, given that language alters our perception of reality. The mind itself is a fabrication of language, along with our sense of self-identity. It is only by silencing the mind that we can experience undistorted reality. As U. G. Krishnamurti (1918–2007) once said, *"The so called self-realization is the discovery for yourself and by yourself that there is no self to discover. That will be a very shocking thing because it's going to blast every nerve, every cell, even the cells in the marrow of your bones."*[13] This awakening does not necessarily require years of intensive meditation and mental discipline.

226

According to J. Krishnamurti (1895–1986) in his book *The Light In Oneself*, a forced approach is self-limiting. Trying to control our thoughts creates a duality between the controller and the controlled. We do not achieve an enlightened state until that duality ceases to exist. Krishnamurti considered true meditation to be a quiet state achieved without force. *"When there is no movement of any kind in the mind, then naturally the mind is still, without effort, without compulsion, without will. It is naturally still; it is not cultivated stillness because that is mechanical, which is not stillness but just an illusion of stillness."*[14]

Achieving this state of inner stillness does not necessarily require sitting and meditating, but merely casting off our many layers of thought. Just as we have distinguished universal truths from cultural truths, Kishnamurti wrote, *"When the churches with their pictures, their music and their beliefs, their rituals, their dogmas, are all understood and discarded completely, when there is no priest, no guru, no follower, then in that tremendous quality of silence there may come something that is not touched by thought, because that silence is not created by thought."*[15] According to Krishnamurti, *"meditation is this, not sitting cross-legged, or standing on your head, or doing whatever one does, but having the feeling of complete wholeness and unity of life."*[16] Similarly, Peace Pilgrim wrote, *"I did not learn meditation. I just walked, receptive and silent, amid the beauty of nature—and put the wonderful insights that came to me into practice."*[17]

Nature is Perfect

By deconstructing preconceived notions of reality, we ultimately return to something akin to the innocence of childhood, before such notions were conceived in the first place. In that preconscious existence there is no judgment as to how things should or should not be. Reality is what it is, and creatures of nature accept it as it is. Regardless of conditions, nature is perfect, as suggested by Masanobu Fukuoka in his book *The Natural Way of Farming*, *"Although high and low temperatures exist in nature, the notions of hot and cold do not... Heat and cold do exist, and yet do not exist in nature. One will never be wrong in starting with the assumption that the temperature and humidity are everywhere and at all times just right."*[18]

We believe that farmers grow crops. Pests, diseases, and weeds are perceived as problems that must be controlled. But from Fukuoka's perspective, this is a discriminating viewpoint that did not exist prior to human awareness. *"These are only distinctions invented by man. Nature maintained a great harmony without such notions, and brought forth the grasses and trees without the 'helping' hand of man."*[19] By acknowledging that nature is perfect, Fukuoka perceived that all problems, such as insect infestations, are the result of human error. He wrote, *"One never blames nature, but begins by blaming oneself."*[20] He started experimenting with natural farming after World War II and gradually refined his approach to letting nature grow his crops. Fukuoka farmed from a universal perspective, practicing a no-plowing, no fertilizing, no-weeding, no pesticides, "do-nothing method" of natural farming.

Fukuoka recognized that the amount of sunlight hitting rice plants in his field ultimately dictated the maximum possible yield. To the degree that nature is in balance, his fields would produce the most rice. By this logic, neither scientific nor organic farming could ever achieve higher yields than that possible by nature itself. The best that can ever be achieved with the aid of plowing, fertilizing, and pesticides is to match what can be accomplished by nature without all that work.

It would be incorrect, however, to believe that Fukuoka merely cast seeds out into a field to grow wild. Fukuoka's approach is easier to explain using holistic language regarding natural succession in the ecosystem. A typical plot of bare ground will naturally be colonized by short-lived annual plants, followed by perennials, followed by bushes and deciduous trees, climaxing with a thick forest canopy. Since rice is an annual plant, Fukuoka tilted succession in favor of annuals. He encased rice seed in clay pellets to prevent them from being eaten by

animals then broadcast the seed over the surface of the ground, covered only by rice straw from the previous crop. He scattered clover seed among the young rice seedlings to capture nitrogen from the air to fertilize the soil. He did not keep his fields flooded all the time like most rice paddies, but only long enough to weaken the clover and any other competing plants to start the cycle again.

In his orchards, Fukuoka rejected conventional pruning, recognizing that nature invented the perfect form for every tree. In *The One Straw Revolution* he wrote, *"When growing according to the natural form, branches spread alternately from the trunk and the leaves receive sunlight uniformly. If this sequence is disrupted the branches come into conflict, lie one upon another and become tangled, and the leaves wither in the places where the sun cannot penetrate. Insect damage develops. If the tree is not pruned the following year, more withered branches appear."[21]*

Apple and orange trees naturally have a single, straight trunk, but horticulturalists prune the "central leader" out at an early age. Lacking a central leader, the top horizontal branches turn upward to form multiple trunks. Deforming the tree with multiple trunks results in a dead space that doesn't get proper lighting. Pruning the tree thus requires more pruning. Furthermore, those multiple trunks frequently fracture, requiring more work to keep them propped up. Fukuoka preferred to allow his fruit trees to take on their natural form, which is not the same as letting them grow wild. He recognized that injuries could occur to a tree at any age and used careful pruning to reconstruct the natural form as closely as possible. For example, a tree could be grazed off by a passing deer, causing multiple trunks to form. Fukuoka would preserve one of these substitute trunks, while removing the others to recreate something close to the natural form.

Fukuoka's farming isn't just a means to produce food with less work, but is equally a spiritual path of enlightenment. According to him, *"The ultimate goal of farming is not the growing of crops, but the cultivation and perfection of human beings."[22]*

People are Perfect

I remember waiting for my kids at the bottom of the stairs at school one day, just as the kids were dismissed from class. All grades, K-12 are combined under one roof in our small town. The elementary grades streamed downstairs first, all happy and bubbling over with energy and life. Seconds later, the high school kids poured down from the upper levels, and the contrast was startling. Every one of those kids looked stressed and preoccupied. My gut reaction was, *"My God, what are we doing to our kids?!"* I don't intend to imply that school was the problem, but rather my impression was that, as a society, we socialize our kids to become adults. They wore the expressions of adults on their faces, and it seemed so tragic.

Adults are mostly consumed with issues that are only real from within a cultural perspective. They live perpetually preoccupied with desires for things that society values as important, consumed with the type of car they drive, the clothes they wear, the style of their hair, or the dandelions in their lawn. They talk about things that are not real, such as celebrity gossip or the latest fashions. They feel the need to get a good job and endure work to buy expensive toys so they can have fun after work. Adults are so preoccupied that they can no longer see or experience the universe around them. They exist oblivious to birds that flee in front of them, unique flowers beside the path, and spider webs in the bushes. They often walk with heads down, absorbed in thought about a world that is not real. It is no wonder people need to escape it with drugs, alcohol, distractions, and pick-me-ups from coffee to candy.

Illegal drug use is particularly troubling. More than twenty-two million Americans were classified as having substance abuse or dependence problems in 2005. Every day, nearly 8,000 more people try drugs for the first time, and most of them are under the age of eighteen. With only 4 percent of the world's population, Americans consume two-thirds of the world's illegal drugs.[23] What happened to the innocence of childhood? What happened to the joy in simple things like playing in the creek or the street gutter, or exploring the woods or a vacant lot? What happened to the wonderment at discovering a caterpillar or a moth? What happened to the fun in running in circles for no reason at all?

In the same sense that nature and trees are perfect in their natural form, we might wonder if people are inherently perfect in their natural form. In other words, children might be perfect before we accidentally or intentionally prune them into something they are not. In the words of Fukuoka, *"The ones who live peacefully in a world of no contradictions and no distinctions are infants. They perceive light and dark, strong and weak, but make no judgments. Even though the snake and the frog exist, the child has no understanding of strong and weak. The original joy of life is there, but the fear of death is yet to appear."*[24]

Children begin with wide-eyed wonder and nearly every moment is magical. They know nothing about the evils of the world. They don't know about swear words, racism, sexism, hate, or addictions. They have no concept of social status or whether they are rich or poor. They live with a sparkle of delight and idealism, as if life is fundamentally good and anything is possible. In a sense, they see the world as it is, without preconceived notions. However, through various traumas and socialization, kids learn about the "real world" of grown-ups and the sparkle begins to fade. They mimic viewpoints from parents, teachers, media, and peers. They learn to judge the world. They learn fear, insecurity, and the need to conform, or the need to control other people. Children typically lose the sparkle in their eyes somewhere between the ages of fifteen and twenty-five. They learn that life is about conforming to the mold, to complete tasks and jump through hoops.

The most powerful forces in shaping a person's life are the events of childhood. Even traumas experienced inside the womb, such as the emotional distress of the mother, likely have powerful impacts on the baby. At birth there are other potential traumas large and small, such as abandonment by the mother or the bright lights and needles of hospital rooms. Later traumas might include witnessing alcoholic or abusive parents, or being forced to read aloud in front of the classroom when a child is not yet ready. Consider the character Jenny in the movie, *Forrest Gump*. Traumatized from growing up in an abusive household, Jenny proceeded to make poor choices all the way to her grave. Happiness was staring her in the face, but she didn't recognize or seize it in time. Traumatized in her childhood, she fell victim to the worst aspects of socialization until she was consumed by it.

Renee and I visit with many people while running our bookstore and post office, and we have been astonished to meet scores of traumatized parents who have unleashed eighteen year-old kids into the world. As one customer said, *"These kids don't know how to handle unlimited freedom; they just go crazy."* Our culture glorifies partying. On television and in real life, people pretend to have a good time being drunk. Kids mimic what they see and hurt themselves while believing they are having fun. I didn't understand it when I was a teenager. Young adults went partying, got drunk and crashed perfectly good cars, or were arrested for driving under the influence, or were impregnated from some encounter they couldn't remember, or got a broken nose in a bar fight. To the extent that partying is "fun," it is only a conditioned response cultivated by our culture.

Our daughters have similarly witnessed many personal tragedies among their friends. Two boys died in a car wreck after swerving to miss a deer while driving 100 mph at night without seatbelts. In another case, we all felt helpless as one of their best friends slowly descended into chaos through her teenage years. A sweet girl with immense promise, she was consumed by socialization. Starting with caffeine and all night sessions on the Internet with questionable contacts, she started changing her identity, looking like a different person every time we saw her. She had a passion for movies and acting. She got lost in drugs. Other kids started chewing tobacco, smoking cigarettes or marijuana, and drinking. Some of the sweetest kids among them turned into hardcore party animals. In the blink of an eye, these kids lost the innocence and joy of childhood to be consumed by society. They were closer to being themselves before they were socialized.

How can we as a culture watch our children go down in flames and accept it as normal? How is it that life is so insufferable that getting wasted seems like an appealing alternative? To most kids the only other option seems to be to walk the straight and narrow, to go to school, to get a job, to be responsible, and to die of boredom. I don't blame them for seeking an escape. The future isn't worth reaching for. As a society, we need to introspect and reconsider what is important in life. We need to find a more holistic way to socialize our children, so that they will always feel the wonder and merriment of childhood, even as they pursue their dreams as adults. It is a path worth searching for.

From this perspective, raising our young people is not so much a matter of molding them, but rather of limiting how much damage we do to them. As a parent I have learned that most of the time my children are exceptionally reasonable, and our well-intentioned efforts to guide them are sometimes the equivalent of pruning away their natural form. The challenge is that children can make bad choices driven by deeply imbedded programming acquired from past traumas or negative socialization. It is difficult to determine if our children's desires and actions are part of their natural form or the result of some negative pruning. For example, is it a natural part of a child's development to listen to music with hypnotic messages about killing one's mother? How do we respond? Is the answer the same for every child? Could we cause more harm than good by using corrective pruning?

Back to Nature

When my daughters were in elementary school I made it a goal to take their classes out for a field trip every year to do wilderness survival and nature awareness skills. We built shelters from sticks and bark, started campfires with flint and steel or by rubbing sticks together with the bow and drill. We played stalking games, harvested herbs for tea, and cooked marshmallows and ashcakes on the campfire. When they entered junior high we started doing overnight camping trips. It rained 1.3 inches on our first camping trip, but we kept reasonably dry in shelters built of sticks and bark. The camping trip was such a success that I have continued to take the seventh and eighth grade classes out every year since, even though my daughters are now graduating from high school.

It is shocking that some of the students have never been camping before, even though we live in Montana surrounded by farms and ranches and millions of acres of public land. There are spectacular lakes in the mountains just a few miles from town that many of the students have never hiked to. The disconnect I see here is part of a nationwide trend. Starting with the rise of video games in the 1980s, outdoor activities such as fishing, hunting, and visiting or camping in National Parks has dropped by 18 to 25 percent, according to statistics reported in the Proceedings of the National Academy of Sciences. The authors stated that, *"The replacement of vigorous outdoor activities by sedentary, indoor videophilia has far-reaching consequences for physical and mental health, especially in children."*[25] Completely socialized by our culture, most kids recognize more brands of beer than birds, even if the birds are in the neighborhood every day.

In the past when kids had little else to do, they created their own recreation, playing hide-and-seek, exploring, fishing, and building forts. But now kids spend time engaged in mental recreation, watching movies, playing video games, or surfing the internet. Our educational institutions focus on mental engagement, teaching kids to regurgitate facts and figures and perform complex calculations. It is easy to measure this kind of learning progress through written tests, but none of it means anything if not connected it back to physical reality. In a culture where people are increasingly detached from the natural world, it is increasingly common to see printed warnings and instructions for things that should be obvious, such as coffee cups that say "Caution: Contents may be hot."

I've seen it in kids and adults who wonder why a big stick won't ignite with the flame of a single match. They have no concept of physical reality. Like the tourist who asked where they put all the animals at night in Yellowstone National Park, they have no tangible concept of how the world works. As a society, how can we function that way? How can voters make sound choices at the polls when they are not connected to the most basic things, such as where the electricity really comes from when they flip on a light switch?

My friend Jeff has a Ph.D. in agricultural economics. Although he has a good paying job as an economist, he has expressed repeatedly how useless his formal education seems, because he didn't know how to do anything with his hands. It is like having a brain in a box on a shelf; what good is a brain if it isn't wired to the body in a way that enables us to interact with the physical world? How can we claim to understand the world by reading about it?

It is amazing to see the students come alive on the junior high camping trips. They are enthusiastic about learning and experiencing. We start fires by rubbing sticks together. We cook stir-fry on a slab of bark, using hot rocks from the fire. We bake bread in a stone oven. We stalk through the woods in our bare feet to observe wildlife. We wade into the swamps to gather cattail roots and shoots for food. We practice hunting techniques with throwing sticks and spear throwers. According to Linda, the teacher I work with, the junior high camping trip is anticipated by seventh and eighth graders all year long, and referred to in some way almost every week.

I don't care if the students master any survival skills. I simply know that a person can learn more about the world by living in it for a few days than by reading every book that has ever been written about it. For example, it is only by collecting firewood and keeping a fire going that a person can truly grasp energy policy proposals. It doesn't matter what the fuel source is. The numbers are meaningless without an experiential concept of energy.

We have refined the camping trips over time, weeding out junk food and distractions the kids bring with them, while fine-tuning the skills and teaching methods. It is obvious that many of these kids have never really played outside before, and sometimes the best educational experience is to give them free time to throw rocks in the river. These kids come from a world of nonstop television, radio, and Internet media. Many of them are used to eating potato chips drinking sodas with every meal. On our outings, however, we live in huts and eat healthy dinners with slabs of bark for plates and twigs for chopsticks. It is like taking them to a different universe. Granted, they bring our culture with them, mimicking characters from movies and television, but in between acts, they come alive. Two days of living in the woods is the closest many of these kids will ever come to detaching from culture to experience unfiltered reality.

Some students seem especially engaged in the activities and might pursue wilderness skills, awareness, or natural sciences in greater depth if they had the opportunity. But it isn't part of the culture they go home to. The camping trip belongs to a different reality that they have no way of returning to once they leave it. So they talk about current movies and participate in popular extra-curricular activities because that is what everyone else does. They get bored, drive sixty miles to the mall when they can, and learn to accept a way of life that was originally meaningless to them. It is tragic that some kids have said upon graduating from high school that the junior high camping trip was the most memorable experience of their lives. They deserve more opportunities to connect with the natural world.

Through our business, Hollowtop Outdoor Primitive School, we are expanding our programs for public schools, and it is my hope to eventually take every grade out for a field trip every year. I am also writing a curriculum guide for teachers anywhere to be able to engage their students in the outdoors. Kids have an innate hunger to connect with nature. It just isn't part of the culture they grow up in.

Contradictions, Purpose, and Divine Paths

Enlightenment is considered a timeless, harmonious experience without thoughts, words, or self-identity. The universe is perceived as a single entity lacking individuality or differentiation between good and evil. It remains in a preconscious state, with random bits of code self-assembling into a program consciousness. While the thought of being "one with everything" conveys a deep sense of harmony, those who have become enlightened often contradict each other and themselves when they try to interpret additional meaning.

It is the language problem all over again. In attempting to translate feelings and sensory input into words, the speaker focuses on one aspect of reality, disconnecting it from everything else. Communicating fractures reality into something it is not, leading to conflicting viewpoints about right and wrong, self-defense, and the need to make a difference in the world. The problem is magnified by participation, or lack of it, from the enlightened observer. If the observer is passive, pondering his relationship to the universe from a totally detached perspective, then he may conclude, *"The universe is becoming self-aware on its own. Wars and violence are part of the natural unfolding of consciousness, so there is no need to change society, nor to defend myself or my country from harm. Everything is as it should be. There is no specific purpose or meaning to life other than to live. I am no more or less valuable than any thug or murderer, and if confronted, the best defense is none."* This observer may decide, like U. G. Krishnamurti that it is unnecessary or counterproductive to mentor others in enlightenment, since language itself is a barrier to becoming it.

On the other hand, if the observer is active, pondering his relationship to the universe as a participant, he might conclude, *"The universe is becoming self-aware, and I can help the process along by actively promoting peace, harmony, and sustainability. My life is no more or less valuable than any thug or murderer, but with peace in my heart, I will defend myself, my family, and my country. If necessary, I will offer my life for peace."* This observer may be driven by an intuitive sense of mission and purpose in life, as if participating in some kind of cosmic plan. For example, Peace Pilgrim wrote, *"Those who have overcome self-will and become instruments to do God's work can accomplish tasks which are seemingly impossible, but they experience no feeling of self-achievement. I now know myself to be a part of the infinite cosmos, not separate from other souls' or God. My illusory self is dead; the real self controls the garment of clay and uses it for God's work."*[26]

Enlightened or not, many people intuitively follow a path, either by divine guidance or perhaps by sensing a possible future where they did something, which they then collapse into reality. As Sharon Wegscheider-Cruse wrote in *Dancing with Destiny*, *"Just as there are crossroads when we drive, so, too there are choices we must make on the path that has been laid out for each of us. We can cooperate with that path and make it a wonderful journey or we can resist the path and make our own way. Sometimes the path is frightening or painful, sometimes it is bizarre and difficult to fathom. However, if we cooperate with what the universe gives us and follow the road that beckons, we will most often find the gifts, insights and talents required to proceed with strength and courage. At the time, the destination may be far over the horizon and we are mystified and easily turned back. The ultimate purpose is not always revealed so quickly. The journey may take years."*[27]

Sometimes the path is fatal, such as in Burma in 2007 when thousands of protesters and hundreds of monks were executed for non-violent protests against the military government.[28] This was undisputedly a great human tragedy, yet, from a universal perspective it could be said that no individuals were lost. As U. G. Krishnamurti said, *"In nature there is no death or destruction at all. What occurs is the reshuffling of atoms."*[29] If we are all one entity, then individual lives have no meaning, but their sacrifice might lead to democracy and higher consciousness for Burma. As one monk said while envisioning the next demonstration, *"This time we will demonstrate - the government dare not kill all the people. So maybe 10,000 people - if 10,000 people were killed - will be killed, we will get democracy. Surely, we hope so. If necessary I'm ready to sacrifice my life, really. Me, including other monks, same."*[30]

My personal experience of consciousness is ironic, as I find myself moving *away* from enlightenment. For most of the first thirty-some years of my life I drifted in and out of mildly subconscious states. In vague memories seemingly held over from some preconscious experience, I recall a primal connection to every rock and plant and animal. I suspect it to be a real memory, although I acknowledge it could be a creation of my own imagination. In essence, I remember existing as one mind, connected to all other beings, but incapable of expression. That preconscious unity is my answer to the Zen koan, *"What is your face before your parents were born?"*

I felt it was my duty to leave that preconscious existence in order to speak for it. It felt as if I went to live among people to figure out what makes them tick, to learn if it was possible to create a sustainable civilization, and if so, how to implement it. In other words, I was powerless as a hawk or a tree, but in human form, I could enter the world of people and achieve my mission from inside, provided I could hang onto enough of the preconscious experience to remember the mission. In a scenario reminiscent of the virtual reality game from chapter one, it was as if I was given a mission, but had most of my memory wiped to enter this existence and pursue it.

The experience was like seeing the world from the bottom of a swimming pool. I would dive deep into the water and there felt connected to everything, like being in a pool of raw information. But I could not return to the surface and verbally express that which made sense down below. At best, it seemed like I could retrieve intuitive feelings or a sense of light or darkness regarding ideas I was pondering. Having never entirely left the preconscious experience of reality, I approached life from an almost universal perspective. My greatest desire was to contribute to the betterment of humanity and all life on earth. I was a bit like the autistics that spend countless hours in trance-like states memorizing calendars. Although not autistic, I latched onto questions about ecology, economics, consciousness, educational reform, and foreign policy and processed them continuously for days or weeks at a time. Unfortunately, writing did not come naturally, and I was often frustrated at my inability to express myself. I could stare at a blank page all day long, bobbing up and down between my conscious and subconscious perceptions. As I learned to express my intuitions in words, I spent less and less time in trance-like states.

I was always somewhat detached from human culture. I was the ultimate outsider, trying to understand humanity without ever becoming fully human. I was most comfortable operating in second and third person perspectives, while my sense of first person perspective was underdeveloped. In a sense, I remained fused with the universe as if I had never been born. My birth unfolded later, over a period of years that culminated with this writing project. Today I find myself consumed with first-person needs and desires I never felt before. I encountered my personal demons and ego. While the path to enlightenment is to be free of wants and needs, I find myself willingly tortured by them. It might be easier to let go of the ego and acknowledge the great beauty and good fortunes of my world at this moment. Yet, I don't want to be free.

My present situation is mostly the result of too much work and not enough play. Being intellectually oriented, I previously found balance through intense physical stimulation such as twenty-mile hikes, freezing and starving on survival trips, and swimming in ice-cold lakes. Over the last few years, however, I have spent too much time staring at a computer screen, trapped in a mental existence without the balance of physical stimulation. I know it is time to unplug the family from computers and television, to home-school our boys, to go camping and climb trees and wade in swamps again. I cannot change the world without reconnecting with the ultimate source.

Yet, I realize that I cannot change the world from a detached, outside perspective. A strong first person viewpoint is required to passionately call for a rapid transition towards global peace and balance. As noted by Fred Alan Wolf, *"Ego has a very important place in the universe; otherwise, it would have never arisen. Ego provides a deep sense of self and other and an awareness of life and death as well as a basis for experiencing the material world. It enables all of the wonderful individual expressions of life we find in other people different from ourselves. Because it anchors us in time and space, it provides us with the opportunity for deep appreciation of the world. It also enables despair and longing to arise when our needs are not met."*[81] Someday I may tire of listening to the whine of my ego, but not this day. For now I wish to embrace this first-person perspective, to solidify my existence as an individual with wants and needs. I wish to find a voice that is mine. I wish to stand up with opinionated confidence and passion to emphasize the need for a new way of living and being.

Continuing the Quest

The effort to define reality through the pages of this book doesn't involve microscopes or telescopes, but is based on sorting the collective knowledge and mythology of our species. The great danger is in believing we have found the answer. In the words of Thomas Campbell, *"Learning should not stop because a conclusion is reached. If the process continues, the conclusions can always change. To be effective, seeking the Big Truth should be an iterative process that lasts a lifetime. Conclusions should, for the most part, remain tentative. Such is the nature of open mindedness."*[32] To have a hope of learning anything, we must remain open-minded, neither believing nor disbelieving, while questioning everything, especially our most basic assumptions. We must strive to detach from our perceptions, to identify which box we are in now, and to step outside of it, to perceive reality in new and astonishing ways.

Our quest began on solid ground as we examined tangible evidence in human history, behavior, and psychology to learn that there are many different perceptions of reality, which can be thought of as layers of consciousness. People naturally shift through these layers as they mature, at least up to the level of their own culture. The magical, mythical, and sequential layers are easiest to understand, since they directly reflect our personal and historical experience. And although they are new and not yet fully familiar, the systems and holistic layers also make logical sense as well. We can see these versions of reality emerging into the collective consciousness.

However, as we progress into mystical, observer, nonlinear, and universal processing, we shift so far beyond our habitual worldviews that the concepts can be challenging to identify with. These layers of consciousness also exceed the grasp of scientific understanding. Science remains ambiguous in quantum physical realms, making this discussion on consciousness increasingly speculative. Like hunter-gatherers imagining that the stars are campfires of their ancestors, we lack the knowledge and experience to be able to define the universe precisely. We have identified and transcended many distortions in our perceptions of reality, but it would be naïve to claim that we have figured it all out.

We know that up to five percent of the universe consists of "normal" matter, like the stuff we are made of. The other ninety-five percent consists of unidentified "dark matter" and

"dark energy." While we understand many of the physical laws of the universe, we have yet to link them into a cohesive theory of everything. We don't even know how many dimensions there are, though theoretical speculation runs as high as eleven. Moreover, if we come to understand the physical laws of our universe, we might not understand why those laws exist in the first place, how many other universes exist, how the laws of physics might work in those universes, or what laws exist beyond the universes that would allow any of them to come into existence at all. In the years ahead we may discover new truths about our existence, or understand old truths in a whole new light. We may find, for example, that everything is true, that the stars are indeed the campfires of our ancestors, since after all, we are all born from the remains of interstellar material. Perhaps our own speculations about the nature of reality will one day be viewed similarly, as approximations of the truth, quaintly expressed within the limits of our knowledge and language.

Similarly, the danger in drafting a map of reality is that someone might try following the map too closely or turn it into a degree or a religion. Imagine the horror of a future with standardized tests or ceremonies and rites of passage to track our progress from one level of consciousness to another. Imagine the horror of having school administrators or priests and gurus tell us whether we have transcended or not. Anyone who considers himself a prophet or guru is at risk of leading us astray. Worse, we lead ourselves astray when we place them on a pedestal ourselves.

We cannot find our truth by blindly following the gospel of other people. We can read, listen, and consider what others have to say, but then we must transcend them to find our own meaning. Zen master Lin Chi emphasized this point in the ninth century when he said, *"If you meet the Buddha, kill the Buddha. If you meet a Patriarch, kill the Patriarch."* I have killed many Buddhas in my time, through the process of assimilating, doubting, and transcending the works of other writers. I know I have learned something when I can see holes in their work. I only ask that you do the same. Refrain from putting *me* on a pedestal. Assume the roadmap is flawed. Search for the holes and you may find the truth you seek.

—Eighteen—

The Awakening

Becoming Sentient

"this higher level of body/mind consciousness takes me around six weeks of wilderness trekking to achieve. But this is when magical things begin to happen. Wild animals start losing their fear of me; often I find myself approaching them closely, and they, me. My sense of smell becomes acute, and I can use it to become more aware of animals and people in my vicinity, and of the surrounding landscape. For example I can smell where someone had camped hidden in the brush a hundred yards off the trail. Beyond that I begin sensing things that cannot be known by ordinary means. I sense when other hikers are approaching - still at a distance - and even what kind of people they are, whether they are friendly or not. I begin to sense what the weather will do, and to know in advance when I should descend to more protected terrain to wait out an approaching storm. The landscape begins speaking to me, telling of the forces that shaped it thus, whether it is healthy or declining in vitality, and why."

—Ray Jardine, "Shortcuts to Wilderness Connection"

Do we qualify as a sentient species? No, not by any reasonable standard. Since the moment I first realized we behaved as if we were not sentient, my assessment of our status as such has steadily lowered. We are so dependent on socialization to teach us how to think and act, that I once suggested to a friend that it may be possible to live an entire lifetime without ever having an original thought. He assumed I was joking, but I wasn't so sure. I wonder if we are not so different from Oxana, the Ukrainian girl who grew up with a pack of dogs, running on all fours and barking. Socialization or enculturation is so deeply a part of who we are that it is impossible to tell where mimicry ends and originality begins. We merely run with a different pack and bark a different language, but do we ever say or do anything other than what we have copied from somewhere else?

There are glimmers of awareness, as if we have looked in the mirror and recognized *something*. But we still live as automatons. Our beliefs, our worldviews, our actions and our reactions, are driven by cultural scripts mimicked and passed down through the generations. We react to situations as if our thoughts and actions are controlled by other people. We believe that we go to the polls to vote on the issues, and yet, too often the values we vote by were themselves mimicked without questioning where they came from. Even our desires are determined for us, from the shape of the house we want, to the clothes we wear and how we cut our hair. In blissful ignorance, we walk through life totally unaware as we buy products

237

made by children in slavery, consume the last meals from the ocean, and fund terrorists with oil and gas money. To any outside observer, we would seem completely unaware of our actions.

Fortunately, the path to self-awareness is simple, at least in principle. It is a matter of becoming an outside observer and living with great consciousness. By mentally stepping outside of ourselves and our culture, we can observe our actions and question our motivations. In relationships, we can transcend our own narrow viewpoints to see how the issues look through another person's eyes or from a neutral perspective. We can learn to notice how we automatically react to other people and outside circumstances, and in doing so we can generate a broader menu of choices, to choose our own actions.

As observers, we can question everything, especially our most basic assumptions, to distinguish cultural truths from universal truths. By doing so, we can transcend beliefs and values that seem normal within our cultural context, but which are damaging to other people or the environment we live in. As observers, we can become aware of the impacts of our decisions, and we can learn to make more sustainable choices. We can begin to see how we shape reality, and we can decide what kind of reality we want to create. In this chapter we transition from purely intellectual musings about reality and consciousness towards practical steps a person can take along the journey.

The Path to Higher Consciousness

In the quest to determine what reality really is, we discovered that our preconceived notions about reality are seriously limited and distorted. While reality is what it is, our ideas about it make it impossible to recognize what is right in front of us. In the effort to correct for distortions, we shattered old illusions and learned to see reality in a new light. We not only redefined what reality is, we transcended old ways of thinking and started up the path to higher levels of consciousness. The quest to become enlightened about reality became a quest for enlightenment itself.

While this book is a roadmap to higher consciousness, it is only a map. Just as a roadmap enables us to see relationships between places like New York, Chicago, and Los Angeles, this guide provides a broad perspective of reality and consciousness. The map can guide us to the ends of the universe and back, but it is just a map. We gain a more expansive view of the universe on this intellectual tour of reality and consciousness, but reading about reality isn't the same as experiencing it. It is only by changing our lives that we begin the journey towards enlightenment.

Some authors suggest that there is no journey, no map, and no destination. There is nothing to change, grow, or mature into. We need only let go of the mind and live in the present moment. They say that enlightenment isn't about going anywhere. It is about being here now. All of that may be true, and yet it is easier said than done. Eckart Tolle was depressed and suicidal before he experienced a sudden flash of insight, jumping immediately to higher levels of consciousness. Other people have meditated for years or decades before experiencing similar insights. Unfortunately, enlightened individuals often struggle in their attempt to assist others in attaining a similar state, because they don't fully understand how they achieved it themselves.

"It is not about achieving anything," they might say, *"just let go of the mind and be here now."* That mantra might trigger enlightenment in the rare individual primed to embrace it, but it is meaningless babble to the 99.9 percent of us who are not yet poised to grasp it's meaning. Enlightenment cannot be understood nor achieved through words, but words can help a person shift through the layers of consciousness to become more primed to one day *"understand that there is nothing to understand."* The path to enlightenment is real, and the map is a legitimate

guide, although it would be foolish to take it too seriously. The map is best acknowledged and passed along to friends, rather than quibbling over the details. The real work is in making an effort to live more conscientiously every day of our lives. If we focus on that, the spark of enlightenment will come when the timing is right. It cannot be forced before we are ready.

Journey Beyond

When an anthropologist visits a primitive culture, she comes as an outside observer, able to notice patterns of behavior so deeply ingrained in the culture that the people are oblivious to it. In a similar way, we can journey beyond our own culture to see it from a new perspective. For example, by rediscovering our hunter-gather heritage we can detach from our culture to see it from the outside. It seems ironic, since hunter-gatherer cultures are associated with a first-person existence, virtually lacking an outside perspective of themselves. Yet, the most sentient people I know wear buckskin clothing and practice the skills of our hunter-gatherer ancestors. Unlike our ancestors, who were able to mimic all the skills they would need in life without consciously thinking about it, the new hunter-gatherer is a person who consciously steps outside of our culture to learn to live more intimately with nature.

Like Moses or Jesus on a forty-day quest, the wilderness experience—with or without primitive skills—is one of soul-searching and awakening. In the words of John Muir, *"The clearest way into the Universe is through a forest wilderness."*[2] It takes us beyond our comfort zone and pushes our buttons, transforming us into outside observers of our behaviors and our cultural notions. The wilderness experience becomes a means for getting out of the box, to see the world from a new perspective.

The more we detach from our own culture to live in a hut in the woods, the more bizarre our cultural customs and traditions seem. Why do we eat the things we do and disdain other foods? Why do we live by the clock, with millions of people stuck in traffic because everybody drives at exactly the same time every day? Why do humans spend so much time working to pay for land that would exist whether we paid for it or not? Why are we so self-conscious about our physical bodies when half the population has similar anatomy, and our ancestors were perfectly

239

comfortable wearing nothing at all? Why do people try so hard to be cool, when they are just mimicking other people who are also trying to be cool? When we detach from our culture to go live in the woods, we connect more directly with reality, and we start to question our assumptions about how the world works. We start to see the world more objectively.

As I wrote in *Participating in Nature*, life in the wilderness is simplified down to the bare essentials such as physical and mental well-being, shelter, warmth, clothing, water, and food. We go on an expedition to meet those needs with little more than our bare hands. In the quest to meet those needs, we are faced with new and challenging situations that push our buttons and force us to set aside old, mimicked beliefs and behaviors to try new and more resourceful ones. We build up our personal strengths and interact with the world around us. We journey into nature with little more than our bare hands, and we return with knowledge, wisdom, and strength to enrich our lives in contemporary society.

In wilderness therapy programs for troubled teenagers, urban kids are brought outdoors where they are completely out of their element. With only a blanket, a poncho, and simple foods like rice and beans, these kids have to start their own fires with flint & steel or by rubbing sticks together with a bowdrill kit. They have to pack their own gear and walk from camp to camp. It pushes all their buttons, and in responding they find that familiar coping strategies have no effect. A kid might drop down on the ground halfway between campsites and give up, but what good does it do? They mope, they cry, they swear and yell, but in the end they are still sitting there in the middle of nowhere. Nature doesn't care. The rocks and the trees and the sky have no sympathy. The only way to change the situation is to get up and do something positive about it. A person cannot go on that kind of a journey and come back unchanged. He begins to see himself and the world from new perspectives. He learns to generate a menu of more constructive choices.

The wilderness journey is a highly spiritual experience. It jars a person out of ingrained habits to experience reality on its own terms. In an intimate and physical way, I've experienced every level of consciousness out-lined in this book at some time or another on wilderness outings, especially on survival trips. Partly it is a matter of faith. It is one thing to say we have faith when we go to church, but we say it without ever leaving our safety net. Faith takes on a whole new meaning when we go camping in the wilderness with little or no gear. If we have no tent, no sleeping bag, and no blanket when a storm rolls in, then yes, survival skills are going to keep us alive, but it is always a matter of faith that everything will work out okay. It is a matter of tuning into our intuition to sense where we need to go and what we need to do. When I am camping I find that everything is just a little bit clearer. There are no distractions, no temptations, just reality in the raw.

As human society becomes increasingly immersed in virtual reality, the wilderness experience becomes ever more essential to reconnect people with real reality. In the words of Henry David Thoreau, *"In wildness is the salvation of the world."* It is for this reason, among others, that we need to conserve our remaining wild places to ensure that all generations can have the opportunity to experience their own quest, to discover reality on its own terms.

I do not intend to imply that wilderness survival living is the only route towards higher consciousness, but rather, that it is simply one of the most effective pathways. My friend Jeff has joined me on numerous survival outings and finds that it predictably jars him out of his patterns and addictions to comfort, sugar, and routines. By day two he regrets coming and longs for the comforts of home. On day three he crashes in an emotional release of energy and then lets it all go, becoming totally free in spirit and ready for the adventure. At the end of our adventures he goes home feeling completely recharged.

The process of becoming more sentient is about stepping beyond the boundaries of the world we know to challenge our preconceived notions and broaden our horizons. Learning nature skills is one way to do that, but so is traveling abroad and living with people that have different background and customs than our own. We can even journey beyond our cultural perspective in our community, by seeking out a different social scene than we are accustomed to. We can spend time on the other side of town, or with people that we would not normally hang out with. Such actions might push us out of our comfort zone, but that is exactly the point. Our familiar habits and viewpoints no longer work, so we learn to detach from old perspectives and embrace more expansive worldviews. In the process we become more compassionate.

Great Compassion

Living with great compassion is the process of learning to care deeply about everyone and everything. Achieving a deep level of compassion is challenging. It is hard to feel compassion for a nasty customer or sales clerk. It is challenging to feel compassion for someone who has cut you off on the highway, or taken advantage of you either physically, emotionally, or financially. That's okay. Try feeling compassion for ordinary people you meet on the street. Try feeling compassion for people in emotional turmoil, or who are experiencing a difficult illness or financial hardship. Try feeling compassion for every dog that does not get out for a walk, for the bugs splattered on the windshield, or for landscapes that are littered and neglected. Try feeling compassion for every plant and animal that gives up its life to sustain our own. The more compassion you feel for the world around you, the more the world will change for the better.

There is no need to achieve a high level of compassion all at once. If you bleed your heart out over every little thing, you may lose yourself in despair and depression. However, by starting with a little compassion where you can give it, you may find yourself naturally feeling more and more compassion as you go along. Most of the time you will keep that compassion to yourself and merely experience it in your heart, but you may also feel a great desire to help. Even a genuine smile and good cheer can be uplifting to a stranger in need. You may also find yourself helping out in volunteer organizations, writing letters to politicians, or taking charge to clean up and plant a vacant lot. The important thing is to direct your actions through genuine love and compassion at all times.

Also keep in mind that there can be misplaced compassion. Many of the dramas people fall into are self-inflicted and habitual. Giving money to a drug addict to buy food isn't very compassionate if he uses it to buy more drugs. Bailing out a friend with gambling debts may only provide him the means to make poor choices all over again. Buying a meal and spending time together may be more helpful. Taking time to listen to a troubled teen may be more helpful than condemning his present choices. Compassion must come in a form that truly addresses the issues. Sometimes heartfelt compassion may be all the only gift we can offer, and that is enough.

Honesty

In this quest to become enlightened about reality we searched for the truth by stripping away the illusions layer by layer. In a similar way, we can only be enlightened as individuals if we live with impeccable honesty. If we lie to other people or sneak around with covert habits, such as gambling or smoking cigarettes, then we ultimately lie to ourselves. It is only through absolute honesty that we can learn to trust each other and find peace in this world. In a world of temptations, being honest is far more important than attempting to be totally virtuous.

It has always astonished me how many married couples go through life hiding things from each other. People hide things like bad habits, extramarital affairs, purchases, secret bank accounts, and what they do when they are out with their friends. Yet, people who lie about even the smallest things must live under a constant shadow of suspicion about everything else. I don't know how anyone could call that a relationship. It is only by being totally honest about trivial things that couples can build the necessary trust to discuss more serious issues. I feel especially fortunate and secure in my own marriage because of that deep level of trust, and I know I can talk openly with Renee about absolutely anything.

Some people believe that dishonesty naturally begins with childhood and it is something that people have to unlearn as they mature. However, lying is so deeply embedded in our culture that children inevitably mimic it themselves. Lying is encouraged at the family level by the strict father model of the mythical worldview. Kids are punished for misbehaving, but only if they get caught, so there is an incentive to lie. Our justice system works on a similar model of right and wrong. Even worse, when criminals are brought before a court of "truth and justice," we actively encourage them to lie about their actions by pleading "not guilty." They will not be punished for what they did wrong, only for what can be proven against them. Thus, the individuals who most need to learn about honesty are actively taught to lie even more. In this environment we socialize our young people to become great liars.

Dishonesty is common even among individuals who strive for higher levels of consciousness. For example, many environmentally minded people perceive corporations as evil, and therefore perceive shoplifting as retributive justice. The corporation is perceived as so big that "nobody is going to miss it anyway." This kind of thinking is so deeply engrained that it is difficult to mingle with environmentally-minded, semi-mystical thinkers without being affected by it. I struggled with this philosophical dilemma for years, and only overcame it after I received a duplicate check for book sales from a corporate bookstore. I deposited the first check and knowingly deposited the duplicate check. I rationalized that I could put the free money to good use to help make the world a better place. I was greatly relieved when the bank returned the check uncashed. I realized that I could never make the world a better place while emulating behaviors that make the world so screwed up to begin with.

Impeccable honesty is essential for achieving a more enlightened world, yet there is also such a thing as excessive honesty. For example, I have at times been too honest with my children, describing my needs and frustrations in ways that they were not mentally or emotionally equipped to handle. Honesty should be tempered when the truth has the potential to do more harm than good.

Let go of the Ego

This entire text has been about detaching from the ego, but primarily in an intellectual sense, to see what reality looks like from the outside. Truly detaching from the ego requires letting go of the desire for power and control over other people. The ego thrives in the desire to be better than other people, to be smarter, faster, braver or more skilled than they are. We gain prestige and elevate our status by impressing others. But the trouble with inflating the ego is that it has a tendency to pop unexpectedly. I am astonished at how quickly and unexpectedly my own ego rises out of nowhere. For example, in demonstrating a skill, such as starting a fire by rubbing sticks together, it is easy to impress people, and in so doing, to impress myself. But I also know that it is dangerous to get caught up in that feeling, because downfall and embarrassment are waiting just around the corner.

The beauty of letting go is that without an ego there is nothing left to protect or defend. It is a wonderful feeling not to be embarrassed by poor performance, since there is no ego to be embarrassed by. It is a wonderful feeling to follow the leadership of a ten-year old without discomfort, when she is a knowledgeable authority on a subject. It is a wonderful feeling to be able to be honest about one's shortcomings, because there is nothing to hide or protect.

Detaching from the ego goes hand-in-hand with becoming honest, because it is the desire to protect one's ego that leads to lies. As long as there is an ego to protect, then a person must live in fear. It is only by letting go of the ego that we can risk speaking openly about our shortcomings and know that everything will be okay. It is only by letting go of the ego that we can experience true freedom.

Many people go through life spinning half-truths in a vain attempt to protect the ego, but the only person who truly suffers from such delusions is one's own self. Being honest and letting go of the ego implicitly leads to self-acceptance. In other words, we all have our shortcomings, and the path towards healing and betterment is to start by accepting where we are right now. Just as alcoholics learn to admit their addictions in Alcoholics Anonymous, we can all learn to accept ourselves and admit our additions, desires, and cravings, whatever they may be. As said by Sharon Wegscheider-Cruse in *Dancing with Destiny*, *"Every person is a miracle, a never-to-be repeated, irreplaceable being with astounding capacity to both endure and transcend pain to fulfill his or her unique potential. Like the caterpillar who becomes the butterfly, we must undergo transformation to become our true selves. But unlike the caterpillar's unconscious metamorphosis, we must choose to let go of the past and test our frail new wings in an unknown and often frightening future."*[8]

There is nothing to be gained on this path of metamorphosis by berating ourselves for failing. If, for example, we fail to be virtuous in a moment of impulse, then we need not berate ourselves for the fall from grace. We need only accept that we are human, learn to let go of the ego, and talk openly and honestly about our shortcomings in order to move forward more successfully in the future. The point isn't merely to accept oneself as flawed, but to embrace one's shortcomings as part of the journey. For example, in spite of my efforts to lead an enlightened existence, there are events that trigger deep feelings of anger and resentment. But rather than beat myself up for being so shallow, I have learned to say, *"Okay, today I am going to get nothing done. My ego is going on the rampage. I am just a passenger along for the ride. Let's see where it goes. Then I can put my life back together."* By accepting that my ego is on the loose, I can let it go that much faster, and hopefully not be haunted by it again so soon.

Similarly, I have learned to embrace being sick as my body's way of saying *"Time out."* Rather than fighting against it, I embrace it and find that I seem to get sick less often. I have learned to embrace moments of despair as a resourceful state to question everything and consider completely new pathways in life. In other words, accepting oneself is about living in the moment, and acknowledging that, *"This is where I am right now."* Only then can we move forward.

Build Relationships

No matter where our journey into higher consciousness takes us, the path always returns home to the day-to-day reality of co-existing with other people, raising a family, working a job, and paying the bills. In the effort to form healthy and sustainable relationships we must be courageous and willing to step outside of our viewpoints to admit when we might be wrong, even when it requires apologizing to a four-year old. We have to learn to consider carefully the advice of others, regardless of whether they might be far older or far younger, and regardless of their credentials, or lack of them.

It would be nice to be resourceful all the time, but it is a great challenge when faced with screaming kids, a messy house, bills to pay, or a stressful work situation. We shouldn't feel like we have failed when we have a bad day. Each new moment is an opportunity to try again. Choosing a positive response to a situation is not a matter of suppressing undesirable emotions and behaviors, but rather of acknowledging them and letting them go. The challenge is that we are controlled by reactive behaviors, triggered by the reptilian part of our brain. We react to situations before we think.

It is helpful to take time out after an incident, such as an argument, to review the situation and envision how it could have been handled more resourcefully. We can rewind and observe the mind, body, and emotions in turmoil. Is there a recurring pattern? Is it like a theatre production where we act out the same roles to the same frustrating conclusion every time? By detaching from the situation to become an observer, we can notice patterns and become empowered to try a new approach.

Unfortunately, in the heat of an argument, we may forget our positive intentions and react again with preprogrammed behaviors. We may not realize the apparent failure to alter our behavior until hours or days later. But we can keep imagining a different outcome for the situation. The next time, even if we fail again, we might at least become aware of the lack of success sooner. We may even become aware of our behaviors while acting them out. We can mentally shift into the perspective of an outside observer, watching the self like a movie: *"Hey, there I am totally red in the face, stomping mad, and what good is it going to come to?"* We may not alter our behavior at that moment, but we bring the awareness ahead in time, until one day we realize somebody is pushing our buttons. That is the moment when we can test an alternative program to hopefully achieve a different result. The situation may go badly, but each time through the loop, we learn new things and strengthen the new neural pathway. Over time, we not only grow new neural pathways to change a specific behavior, we also increase our ability to try other programs. We learn to recognize our reactive patterns and try alternative programs.

If we cannot mentally detach from a situation, we can physically detach from it to calm down. Peace Pilgrim described a number of people who used physical exertion to work through their anger. One man pushed a manual lawn mower around his yard. Another saved his marriage by taking up jogging. He ran until he exhausted his angry energy. One couple resolved their differences by walking around the block in opposite directions, passing each other until they could meet amicably and talk through the issues together.[4]

Conscientious Actions

Living conscientiously is a matter of thinking about every decision we make and how it affects other people, our environment, and other species. In the words of Roshi Philip Kapleau in *The Three Pillars of Zen*, *"To treat things with reverence and gratitude, according to their nature and purpose, is to affirm their value and life, a life in which we are all equally rooted. Wastefulness is a measure of our egocentricity and thence of our alienation from things, from their Buddha-nature, from their essential unity with us. Further, it is an act of indifference to the absolute worth of the wasted object, however humble. Thus, breaking a glass heedlessly at any time, leaving a light burning when it is no longer needed, using more water than is required for a particular task, permitting a book to remain overturned after it has been read—these are all wanton acts in the deepest religious sense..."*[5]

The path to higher consciousness includes paying attention to the pattern of resource consumption in our lives, and how our choices impact the rest of the universe. We can hunt down air leaks with a caulk gun, switch to more efficient lightbulbs, and install solar water heaters and better insulation. It is a matter of learning where our products come from, and making an effort to buy locally, or from ethical and sustainable sources, while re-using and recycling everything. Every conscious decision is an act of sentience, of being aware of ourselves and our actions.

Taking control of your energy security may seem daunting at first, but it can turn into a satisfying sport and lead to greater consciousness. If you make a goal to do one energy efficiency project every year, you can quickly get caught up in the vision of drastically reducing your power bill, or even becoming your own energy provider. It isn't that difficult to do if you tackle the easiest challenges first, things like changing the lightbulbs or installing a more efficient washing machine or refrigerator. Gradually you become attuned to the patterns of energy use, aware of approximately how much energy you use for everything from running a microwave to heating the house. In terms of transportation, it is a matter of eliminating unnecessary trips, walking, driving, or car-pooling when possible, and upgrading to more efficient vehicles and using sustainable fuels where available.

Living with awareness includes getting in touch with our food supply. Even a tiny yard can grow an amazing amount of nourishing food, and those who don't have time for gardening can plant fruit and nut trees to provide food year after year with little maintenance. It is immensely satisfying to share a harvest with one's family, friends, and neighbors. Even if you don't happen to utilize the bounty yourself, at least you know it is there, an investment that produces a steady crop of dividends, should you ever want them. Perhaps most importantly, by planting fruiting bushes and trees near the sidewalk, you can enrich the world of our children, helping to create a new Garden of Eden, where children can enjoy the abundance as they play around the neighborhood.

At the community level, we can participate in grassroots groups to help out with social or environmental causes. Even small projects make a difference, such as setting up a neighborhood composting heap, organizing an annual block-wide garage sale for recycling and re-using materials, or providing job training for disadvantaged people. Taking ownership of the vision is one of the best ways to ensure we successfully create a better world.

We can become increasingly aware of how we make a living in this world. We can take steps to ensure that our work is making a difference, not merely extracting money or resources, but enriching the lives and sustainability of our clientele. It is about starting or greening businesses to close the loop on wasted energy and resources, increasing prosperity while reducing consumption. Living conscientiously is about envisioning a reality of green prosperity and actively collapsing it into existence through innovation and entrepreneuring. It is about making the world a better place for all, including for people in distant countries whom we may never meet in person.

Positive Speech

In making a better world, it is vital that we carefully consider our contribution every time we open our mouths to speak. As Jesus said in Matthew 15, it is not what goes into a mouth that defiles a man, but what can come out of his mouth.[6] Speaking derisively of others is not good for anyone, whether it is our next-door neighbor or the President of the United States. We can disagree on worldviews and matters of substance without putting other people down. Our words speak louder if we treat all people with respect and participate in the change we hope to see.

Swearing and derogatory jokes also darken the world. As prudish as it sounds, I have always found that people who swear tend to have a more pessimistic worldview. By talking positively, we can bring more light into the world and create a better reality for all.

Our thoughts even have the potential to brighten or darken the world. In the words of Peace Pilgrim, *"If you realized how powerful your thoughts are, you would never think a negative thought. They can be a powerful influence for good when they're on the positive side, and they can and do make you physically ill when they're on the negative side. I don't eat junk foods and I don't think junk thoughts! Let me tell you, junk thoughts can destroy you even more quickly than junk food."* Over the years, Peace helped a number of people with physical illnesses achieve healing by releasing their negative thoughts.

Rediscover Your Inner Child

If I had one wish I could give to my own kids, it would be the ability to set free their inner child, so they could experience their adult lives with the wonderment and joy they knew as children. I simply wish for them what I wish for every person on earth, the freedom to go hopping and skipping down the road of life, celebrating dandelions and butterflies, or climbing trees simply because they are there for the climbing.

As Anthony deMello Wrote in *Awareness*, *"We do have to fall from a stage of innocence and be thrown out of paradise; we do have to develop an "I" and a "me" through these concepts. But then we need to return to paradise... When we start off in life, we look at reality with wonder, but it isn't the intelligent wonder of the mystics; it's the formless wonder of the child. Then wonder dies and is replaced by boredom, as we develop language and words and concepts. Then hopefully, if we're lucky, we'll return to the wonder again."*[8] I simply wish that all people could be free to follow their dreams, to live a life of discovery and fulfillment, rather than being pressured into jumping through hoops to meet the expectations of parents, teachers, employers, and culture. I wish for my children and every person on earth the freedom to simply become who they are, without being socialized into something they are not. Remembering how to play is a big part of that.

As adults it is easy to forget that it is okay to play. We act as if there is a rulebook that says adults are not allowed to climb trees or splash in mud puddles or wrestle in the yard. We are supposed to act mature and sit and talk about nothing. I say, *"Forget the rules!"* Let's have a pillow fight. Let's sample fruit trees along the sidewalks wherever we go. Let's not be afraid to get wet or dirty. Big deal if we destroy some good clothes for a bit of fun climbing trees or navigating through the brush. Let's play.

These thoughts of living like a child might seem strange coming from me, when I seem to carry the weight of the world upon my shoulders. But it is only as an adult that my life's work feels like a burden. When I experience my life as a child then I know no burdens, although I work just as hard to make a difference. Strangely, I am frequently frustrated in my hopes of finding playmates. I live in an adult world, and it is rare to encounter other people who desire to go skipping down the path, hopping over rocks and bushes, roaring like lions, wrestling in the grass, and laughing. As anthropologist Colin Turnbull wrote in *The Forest People* after living with the African Pygmies:

> *One night in particular will always live for me, because that night I think I learned just how far away we civilized human beings have drifted from reality. The moon was full... [and] there, in the tiny clearing, splashed with silver, was the sophisticated Kenge, clad in bark cloth, adorned with leaves, with a flower stuck in his hair. He was all alone, dancing around and singing softly to himself as he gazed up at the treetops.*
>
> *Now, Kenge was the biggest flirt for miles, so after watching a while, I came into the clearing and asked, jokingly, why he was dancing alone. He stopped, turned slowly around and looked at me as though I was the biggest fool he had ever seen; and he was plainly surprised by my stupidity. "But I'm not dancing alone," he said. "I am dancing with the forest, dancing with the moon." Then, with the utmost unconcern, he ignored me and continued his dance of love and life.*[9]

Fortunately, it is never too late to set free our inner child. We can all be children again, and the world will be better because of it. It might seem risky, or scary, or like a violation of the rules for an adult to splash in a mud puddle or dance in the moonlight, but true freedom is to be found only by making the leap. It is by casting off the shackles of adult roles and expectations that we can free the inner child and rediscover our humanity.

Follow A Path With Heart

In fusion with the universe there is no distinction between self and other. Life flows naturally and harmoniously with clarity in the absence of thought. There is no struggle, no worry, no regrets or longing. But when we fall into existence we create a duality. We become separate and alone. We go through life facing challenges and overcoming obstacles. We create our own dramas. We act as if there were something to struggle against. We toil and strive to achieve something, to get somewhere. We may be successful or unsuccessful. We beat, or are beaten by, opponents of our own making. But the chasm that separates us from our true nature is both immense and imaginary. We never are separate from the universe except in our own minds. In recalling the example of Jenny in the movie Forrest Gump, we can embrace peace and contentment at any moment if we can only recognize what has been staring us in the face all along.

As Masanobu Fukuoka wrote in *The One Straw Revolution*, *"Originally human beings had no purpose. Now, dreaming up some purpose or other, they struggle away trying to find the meaning of life. It is a one-man wrestling match. There is no purpose one has to think about, or go in search of. You would do well to ask children whether or not a life without purpose is meaningless."*[10] Children experience the world without conjuring purpose or meaning, and they do not flounder or doubt. They are driven to act by innate inspiration.

Ultimately, the only path we can follow is our own. We must reach inside to find an intuitive direction, a path we are passionate about. As noted in Carlos Castaneda's book, *The Teachings of Don Juan*, *"Does this path have a heart? All paths are the same: they lead nowhere. They are paths going through the bush, or into the bush. In my own life I could say I have traversed long, long paths, but I am not now anywhere. My benefactor's question has meaning now. Does this path have a heart? If it does, the path is good; if it doesn't, it is of no use. Both paths lead nowhere; but one has a heart. The other doesn't. One makes for a joyful journey; as long as you follow it you are one with it. The other will make you curse your life. One makes you strong; the other weakens you."*[11]

The Roadmap

We are the universe assembled from pure nothingness. We are the stardust of the cosmos, the living pond muck of this planet. We are communities of single-celled organisms; we are the reptiles, the mammals, the apes, and the cavemen. In seeing the universe in ourselves, we become aware of our true nature.

As human beings we have a natural tendency to self-actualize towards our potential. We are unlike any other species on earth, as noted by Yatri in *Unknown Man*, *"A cow is a cow is a cow; she does cow-ish things. She gives no indication that she ever yearns to be a butterfly… human beings are unique in this way. In the animal kingdom we are eternal pilgrims on our unending quest for ourselves and more than ourselves."[2]* We have an innate desire to learn, to grow, to improve ourselves.

The roadmap to reality outlined in the pages of this book is a beginner's guide to consciousness. The awareness you now have about the many layers of consciousness is something you will carry with you always. Even when you are not thinking about it directly, it will continue to percolate through the subconscious recesses of your mind, re-interpreting old ideas, and wiring in the potential for new worldviews.

Once you have seen the map, it is difficult to ignore it completely. Even if you forget the map, you will still be following it, still following suggestions from your subconscious mind to continue expanding your horizons, learning new ways of thinking and new ways of being. And if you should find yourself agitated or irate about something, but not sure what it is, it may be your own subconscious poking at you to remind you to modify your actions on the outside to match your continued growth on the inside. It may be your intuition telling you it is time for a change in life, a time to try something new and challenging, more fulfilling and holistic. It is a journey that once you have begun, you can never leave. Pass it on.

Help refine this book!

You are invited to treat this book as if it were your own: Write it the way you would write it, and submit your input to improve future editions of *Roadmap to Reality*. This deeper processing of the material will help you connect with the layers of consciousness more fully, and you may journey in directions I never considered. I make no promises as to whether or not I will include your input in future editions. However, I will do what I can to consider every comment. Please submit suggestions, corrections, and comments via our website.

The more detailed and documented your material is, referenced to reasonably reputable sources, the more likely I will use it. Wikipedia is okay, provided that 1) the topic is non-controversial and unlikely to be skewed by biased agendas, and 2) the text accurately reflects other reputable sources on the Internet. Additional references are appreciated.

I will acknowledge you as the source if I quote or reference your original text in the book. Do not expect acknowledgement for edits, comments, or leads, although your input will be greatly appreciated. I retain the copyright on the content of *Roadmap to Reality*. Please check the website for information on the most up-to-date edition of the book. Special discount pricing is available for readers who wish to upgrade to the latest version.

Thomas J. Elpel
Pony, Montana
March 9, 2008

www.RoadmapToReality.com

Acknowledgements

Tom,

> *"Just read the Universal chapter. Attached are some edits. I must say that I found the chapter a bit of a disaster, or like walking into a construction site. Little pieces of stuff everywhere, with only the writer knowing how to connect them. I did not feel like that chapter tied up anything—it was disorganized. It is part parenting handbook, part physics, part other stuff that seems to be a discussion about universal processing as opposed to giving people any map or tips on how to process universally."*

—Jeff Blend

This is the most complex book I have ever written, and it could not have been completed without extensive editing and discussion among friends and family members. Thanks especially to my best friend and wife Renee for twenty years together exploring life and the universe. Thanks to my sister Cherie for transcribing sixteen hours of videotaped ramblings. It is daunting to write a book starting from a blank page; your draft made all the difference.

Thanks to my mother Jan Elpel for insightful comments and influence. Your numerous years of graduate school psychology subtly influenced my path and the development of this book. Thanks to my sister Jeanne Elpel for line-by-line editing, and for keeping the business rolling whenever I am "distracted." Thanks to my friend Jeff Blend for extensive editing and blunt honesty every step of the way. Thanks to Lisa and Bonnie Andrich and Kris Reed for extensive editing and input, and thanks Bonnie for the fantastic artwork. Thanks also for input and examples by my kids Felicia, Cassie, Donny, and Edwin and from friends Sholei Morrow and Norm Grondin.

End Notes

1. Quest for the Real Reality
   1. William Harmon. <u>Global Mind Change</u>. Berrett-Koehler Publishers, Inc. 1998. Page 14.
   2. Elizabeth Grice. *"Cry of an enfant sauvage."* Telegraph. http://www.telegraph.co.uk/arts/main.jhtml?xml=/arts/2006/07/17/ftdog17.xml. June 7, 2006. Accessed February 24, 2008.
   3. _____. *"Hello mutter, hello Fido."* DogsInTheNews.com. http://dogsinthenews.com/stories/060925b.php. September 25, 2006. Accessed February 24, 2008.
   4. _____. *"Major Religions of the World Ranked by Number of Adherents."* Adherents.com. http://www.adherents.com/Religions_By_Adherents.html. Accessed December 17, 2006.
   5. _____. Adherents.com. http://www.adherents.com. December 17, 2006.
   6. Jamie Sarns & David Carson. <u>Medicine Cards.</u> Bear & Company: Santa Fe, NM. 1951, 1988. Pages 100 – 103.
   7. Jim Baggott. <u>A Beginner's Guide to Reality.</u> Pegasus Books, LLC: New York. 2005. Page 97.
   8. Antonion Damasio. *"In the Beginning Was… Emotion."* Science & Spirit. http://www.science-spirit.org/article_detail.php?article_id=360. Accessed February 13, 2008.
   9. _____. *"Squirrels have two very interesting relationships with fungi."* Illinois Mycological Association. http://www.ilmyco.gen.chicago.il.us/Terms/acorn73.html. Accessed August 28, 2007.
   10. Joseph Lemasolai Lekuton. <u>Facing the Lion.</u> National Geographic: Washington, DC. 2003.
   11. William Harmon. <u>Global Mind Change.</u> Berrett-Koehler Publishers, Inc. 1998. Pages 57 - 58.

2. Are We a Sentient Species?
   1. Lewis Cotlow. <u>In Search of the Primitive</u>. Little, Brown & Co.: Boston. 1942, 1966. Page 75.
   2. _____. <u>Random House Webster's College Dictionary</u>. Random House: New York. 1999. Page 1196.
   3. Peter Miller. "Jane Goodall." <u>National Geographic</u>. Volume 188, No. 6. December 1995. Pages 102 - 128.
   4. _____. "Chimpanzees 'hunt using spears.'" <u>BBC News</u>. http://news.bbc.co.uk/2/hi/science/nature/6387611.stm. February 22, 2007. Accessed February 22, 2007.
   5. Rowan Hooper. "Dolphins teach their children to use sponges." <u>New Scientist</u>. June 6, 2005. http://www.newscientist.com/article.ns?id=dn7475. Accessed February 22, 2007.
   6. Alison Jolly. "A new science that sees animals as conscious beings." <u>Smithsonian</u>. March 1985.
   7. Alison Jolly. "A new science that sees animals as conscious beings." <u>Smithsonian</u>. March 1985.
   8. Joel Achenbach. "Monkey See, Monkey Recognize." <u>National Geographic</u>. January 2004.
   9. Sue Savage-Rumbaugh. "Kanzi Understands Spoken Language." Video. The Great Ape Trust of Iowa. http://www.greatapetrust.org. Accessed February 22, 2007.
   10. Alison Jolly. "A new science that sees animals as conscious beings." <u>Smithsonian</u>. March 1985.
   11. AP. "Language of Prairie Dogs Includes Words for Humans." <u>Live Science</u>. December 6, 2004. http://www.livescience.com/animalworld/prairie_dogs_041206.html. Accessed February 22, 2007.
   12. _____. "Dolphins 'have their own names'." <u>BBC News</u>. May 8, 2006. http://news.bbc.co.uk/2/hi/uk_news/scotland/edinburgh_and_east/4750471.stm. Accessed February 22, 2007.
   13. Peter Miller. "Jane Goodall." <u>National Geographic</u>. Volume 188, No. 6. December 1995. Pages 102 – 128.
   14. Alison Jolly. "A new science that sees animals as conscious beings." <u>Smithsonian</u>. March 1985.
   15. _____. "Eyes Wide Open: The Sleepwalking Story." <u>Dental and Health Articles</u>. http://www.dentalplans.com/Dental-Health-Articles/Eyes-Wide-Open-The-Sleepwalking-Story.asp. Accessed December 27, 2007.
   16. _____. "Eyes Wide Open: The Sleepwalking Story." <u>Dental and Health Articles</u>. http://www.dentalplans.com/Dental-Health-Articles/Eyes-Wide-Open-The-Sleepwalking-Story.asp. Accessed December 27, 2007.
   17. Alan Park. "Sleepwalking out of Jail." <u>Now Toronto</u>. APRIL 13 - 19, 2006. VOL. 25, NO. 33. http://www.nowtoronto.com/issues/2006-04-13/news_story5.php. Accessed December 27, 2007.
   18. Rachel Nowak. "Sleepwalking woman had sex with strangers." <u>New Scientist</u>. October 15, 2004. http://www.newscientist.com/article.ns?id=dn6540. Accessed December 27, 2007.
   19. _____. "Eyes Wide Open: The Sleepwalking Story." <u>Dental and Health Articles</u>. http://www.dentalplans.com/Dental-Health-Articles/Eyes-Wide-Open-The-Sleepwalking-Story.asp. 2005, Healthology, Inc. Accessed December 27, 2007.
   20. John Boslough. "The Enigma of Time." <u>National Geographic</u>. March 1990. Pages 109 – 132.
   21. Jeff Warren. "Sleeping Like a Hunter-Gatherer." <u>Discover</u>. December 2007. Pages 66 – 67.
   22. Malcom Gladwell. <u>The Tipping Point</u>. Little, Brown and Co: New York. 2000, 2002. Pages 216 - 224.
   23. Ann Savours. <u>The Search for the North West Passage</u>. St. Martin's Press: New York. 1999. Pages 51 – 52.
   24. Margot Adler. "Behind the Ever-Expanding American Dream House." <u>NPR</u>. http://www.npr.org/templates/story/story.php?storyId=5525283. July 4, 2006. Accessed November 14, 2007.
   25. U.S. Census Bureau, "Statistical Abstract of the United States: 2003. No. HS-12. Households by Type and Size: 1900 to 2002."
   26. Elise Kleeman. "Biodiversity—It's What's for Dinner." <u>Discover</u>. February 2006. Volume 27, Number 2. Page 10.
   27. Richard Black. "'Only 50 years left' for sea fish." <u>BBC News</u>. http://news.bbc.co.uk/2/hi/science/nature/6108414.stm. November 2, 2006. Accessed November 14, 2007.
   28. Edward O. Wilson. <u>Nature Revealed: Selected Writings, 1949-2006</u>. The Johns Hopkins University Press: Baltimore, MD. 2006. Page 13.
   29. Thomas Campbell. <u>My Big TOE</u>. Lightning Strike Books. 2003. Book 1. Page 220.
   30. Julian Jaynes. <u>The Origin of Consciousness</u>. Houghton Mifflin Company: Boston. 1976.
   31. Julian Jaynes. <u>The Origin of Consciousness</u>. Houghton Mifflin Company: Boston. 1976. Page 24.
   32. Paul Raffaele. "In John They Trust." <u>Smithsonian</u>. http://www.smithsonianmag.com/people-places/john.html. February 2006. Accessed February 12, 2008.

33. _____. "Cargo Cults." H2g2. http://www.bbc.co.uk/dna/h2g2/A2267426. April 27, 2004. Accessed February 12, 2008.
34. Marvin Harris. Cows, Pigs, Wars, and Witches. Vintage Books/Random House: New York, NY. 1974, 1989. Pages 133 – 152.
35. _____. "Cargo cult." Wikipedia. http://en.wikipedia.org/wiki/Cargo_cult. Accessed December 6, 2006.
36. Richard B. Lee. The Dobe !Kung. Holt, Rinehart and Winston, Inc. 1979. Pages 47-48.

3. The Illusion of Free Will

1. Dennis Overbye. "Free Will: Now You Have It, Now You Don't." New York Times. http://www.nytimes.com/2007/01/02/science/02free.html. January 2, 2007. Accessed January 7, 2007.
2. Edward T. Hall. The Silent Language. Fawcett Publications, Inc.: Greenwich, CT. 1959, 1966. Pages 111 - 112.
3. _____. "Joan of Arc." Wikipedia. http://en.wikipedia.org/wiki/Joan_of_Arc. Accessed August 22, 2007.
4. _____. "Joseph Smith, Jr." Wikipedia. http://en.wikipedia.org/wiki/Joseph_Smith,_Jr. Accessed August 22, 2007.
5. _____. "Muhammad." Wikipedia. http://en.wikipedia.org/wiki/Muhammad. Accessed August 22, 2007.
6. Ivan Leudar and Philip Thomas. Voices of Reason, Voices of Insanity. Taylor & Francis, Inc: Philadelphia, PA. 2000, 2001.
7. Marcel Kuijsten. "Consciousness, Hallucinations, and the Bicameral Mind." Reflections on the Dawn of Consciousness. Julian Jaynes Society. Henderson, Nevada. 2006. Page 122.
8. Julian Jaynes. The Origin of Consciousness. Houghton Mifflin Company: Boston. 1976. Pages 95 – 96.
9. Julian Jaynes. The Origin of Consciousness. Houghton Mifflin Company: Boston. 1976. Pages 88 – 89.
10. Julian Jaynes. The Origin of Consciousness. Houghton Mifflin Company: Boston. 1976. Pages 72 – 73.
11. Ivan Leudar and Philip Thomas. Voices of Reason, Voices of Insanity. Taylor & Francis, Inc: Philadelphia, PA. 2000, 2001. Pages 28 – 51.
12. Ivan Leudar and Philip Thomas. Voices of Reason, Voices of Insanity. Taylor & Francis, Inc: Philadelphia, PA. 2000, 2001.
13. Bible, King James Version. BibleGateway.com Accessed October 29, 2007.
14. Dennis Overbye. "Free Will: Now You Have It, Now You Don't." New York Times. http://www.nytimes.com/2007/01/02/science/02free.html. January 2, 2007. Accessed January 7, 2007.
15. Susan Blackmore. Consciousness. Oxford University Press: Oxford & New York. 2004. Pages 104 – 105.
16. Jared Diamond. The Third Chimpanzee. Harper Perennial: New York. 1993, 2006.
17. _____. "Physical, Verbal Aggression Linked to Gene." WebMD. http://www.webmd.com/balance/news/20050307/physical-verbal-aggression-linked-to-gene. March 7, 2005. Accessed February 5, 2008.
18. Malcom Gladwell. The Tipping Point. Little, Brown and Co: New York. 2000, 2002. Pages 77 - 78.
19. Malcom Gladwell. The Tipping Point. Little, Brown and Co: New York. 2000, 2002. Pages 74 - 76.
20. Marvin Harris. The Sacred Cow and the Abominable Pig. Touch Stone Books/Simon & Schuster, Inc.: New York. 1985/1987.
21. Jeff Koinange. "Living off rats to survive in Zimbabwe." CNN.com. http://www.cnn.com/2006/WORLD/africa/12/19/koinange.zimbabwe/index.html. December 19, 2006. Accessed December 19, 2006.
22. Edward T. Hall. The Silent Language. Fawcett Publications, Inc.: Greenwich, CT. 1959, 1966. Page 39.
23. Peter Farb. Man's Rise to Civilization. Avon Books: New York. 1968. Page 33.
24. Peter Farb. Man's Rise to Civilization. Avon Books: New York. 1968. Page 33.
25. Henry David Thoreau. Life Without Principle. 1863. http://www.4literature.net/Henry_David_Thoreau/Life_Without_Principle/. Accessed February 5, 2008.
26. David Burnham. "Misuse of the I.R.S.: The Abuse of Power." September 3, 1989. http://query.nytimes.com/gst/fullpage.html?res=950DE3DA1E31F930A3575AC0A96F948260. Accessed February 5, 2008.
27. _____. "Compliance Costs & Tax Complexity." Tax Foundation. http://www.taxfoundation.org/research/topic/96.html. Accessed March 12, 2008.
28. Anthony deMello. Awareness. Image Books/Doubleday: New York. 1990. Page 68.

4. Language and Metaphor

1. Julian Jaynes. The Origin of Consciousness. Houghton Mifflin Company: Boston. 1976. Page 55.
2. William H. Calvin. A Brief History of the Mind. Oxford University Press: Oxford and New York. 2004. Page 45.
3. William H. Calvin. A Brief History of the Mind. Oxford University Press: Oxford and New York. 2004. Page 67.
4. _____. "Human evolution." Wikipedia. http://en.wikipedia.org/wiki/Human_evolution. Accessed April 24, 2007.
5. Terrence W. Deacon. The Symbolic Species. W. W. Norton & Co.: New York. 1997. Page 58.
6. Jared Diamond. The Third Chimpanzee. Harper Perennial: New York. 1993, 2006. Pages 156-159.
7. Robbins Burling. The Talking Ape. Oxford University Press Inc: New York. 2005. Page 117.
8. Marisa Brook. "The Birth of a Language." DamnInteresting.com. http://www.damninteresting.com/?p=708. November 3, 2006. Accessed February 4, 2008.
9. William H. Calvin. A Brief History of the Mind. Oxford University Press: Oxford and New York. 2004. Page 78.
10. Temple Grandin. Thinking in Pictures. Vintage Books / Random House: New York. 1995, 2006. Pages 33 - 57.
11. Michael D. Lemonick. "Babies Vs. Chimps: Who's Smarter?" Time.com http://www.time.com/time/health/article/0,8599,1659611,00.html. September 6th, 2007. Accessed September 6, 2007.
12. Jared Diamond. "Why Did Human History Unfold Differently On Different Continents For The Last 13,000 Years?" The Third Culture: www.edge.org. http://www.edge.org/3rd_culture/diamond/diamond_p5.html. April 23, 1997. Accessed February 4, 2007.
12. Jared Diamond. The Third Chimpanzee. Harper Perennial: New York. 1993, 2006. Page 157.
14. _____. "Brassiere." Wikipedia. http://en.wikipedia.org/wiki/Brassiere. Accessed February 20, 2008.
15. Paul Raffaele. "Speaking Bonobo." Smithsonian. November 2006. Volume 37, No. 8. Page 74.
16. George Lakoff and Mark Johnson. Metaphors We Live By. The University of Chicago Press: Chicago and London. 1980.

[17.] George Lakoff and Mark Johnson. Metaphors We Live By. The University of Chicago Press: Chicago and London. 1980.

[18.] Reuters. "Jungle tribe says 'no' to numbers." News in Science. http://www.abc.net.au/science/news/health/ HealthRepublish_1181286.htm. August 20, 2004. Accessed February 19, 2008.

[19.] Robert Lado. Linguistics across Cultures. Ann Arbor/University of Michigan Press. 1957, 1960. Pages 65 – 66.

[20.] John Boslough. *"The Enigma of Time."* National Geographic. March 1990. Pages 109 - 132.

[21.] Carol R. Ember & Melvin Ember. Cultural Anthropology. Appleton-Century-Crofts: New York. 1973. Page 80.

[22.] Sam D. Gill. Beyond The Primitive. Prentice-Hall Inc.: Englewood Cliffs, New Jersey. 1982. Page 17.

[23.] Daniel Tammet. Born on a Blue Day. Free Press. New York. 2006. Page 163.

[24.] Daniel Tammet. Born on a Blue Day. Free Press. New York. 2006. Page 76.

[25.] Temple Grandin. Animals in Translation. Harcourt, Inc.: Orlando, FL. 2005. Page 17.

[26.] Julian Jaynes. The Origin of Consciousness. Houghton Mifflin Company: Boston. 1976. Page 50.

[27.] Edward T. Hall. The Silent Language. Fawcett Publications, Inc.: Greenwich, CT. 1959, 1966. Page 96.

[28.] Jim Baggott. A Beginner's Guide to Reality. Pegasus Books, LLC: New York. 2005. Page 21.

[29.] Carol R. Ember & Melvin Ember. Cultural Anthropology. Appleton-Century-Crofts: New York. 1973. Page 80.

5. Growing Up

[1.] Danah Zohar. The Quantum Self. Quill/William Morrow: New York. 1990. Page 65.

[2.] Jean Gebser. The Ever Present Origin. Ohio University Press: Athens, OH. English Translation 1985.

[3.] ____. *"Theory of cognitive development."* Wikipedia. http://en.wikipedia.org/wiki/Theory_of_cognitive_development. Accessed March 27, 2007.

[4.] Ken Wilber. A Brief History of Everything. Shambala: Boston & London. 1996. Page 162.

[5.] Colin M. Turnbull. The Forest People. Touchstone/Simon & Schuster: New York, NY. 1968. Page 252.

[6.] Ken Wilber. A Brief History of Everything. Shambala: Boston & London. 1996. Page 165.

[7.] Robert Kegan. The Evolving Self. Harvard University Press: Cambridge, MA. Pages 27 – 28.

[8.] Ken Wilber. A Brief History of Everything. Shambala: Boston & London. 1996. Page 175.

[9.] ____. *"Theory of cognitive development."* Wikipedia http://en.wikipedia.org/wiki/Theory_of_cognitive_development. Accessed March 27, 2007.

[10.] ____. *"Prohibition in the United States."* Wikipedia. http://en.wikipedia.org/wiki/Prohibition_in_the_United_States. Accessed April 23, 2007.

[11.] William H. Calvin. A Brief History of the Mind. Oxford University Press: Oxford, New York. 2004. Page 71.

[12.] ____. *"Theory of cognitive development."* http://en.wikipedia.org/wiki/Theory_of_cognitive_development. Accessed March 27, 2007.

[13.] Ken Wilber. A Brief History of Everything. Shambala: Boston & London. 1996. Pages 176.

[14.] Ken Wilber. A Brief History of Everything. Shambala: Boston & London. 1996. Pages 148.

[15.] AP. *"Boyfriend: Phobia caused woman's 2-year bathroom stay."* Cnn.com. http://www.cnn.com/2008/US/03/13/ woman.in.bathroom.ap/index.html. March 13, 2008. Accessed March 13, 2008.

[16.] Ken Wilber. A Brief History of Everything. Shambala: Boston & London. 1996. Pages 183-184.

[17.] Danah Zohar. The Quantum Self. Quill/William Morrow: New York. 1990. Page 116.

6. Cultural Evolution

[1.] William Harmon. Global Mind Change. Berrett-Koehler Publishers, Inc. 1998. Pages 7 – 8.

[2.] Ken Wilber. A Brief History of Everything. Shambala: Boston & London. 1996.

[3.] Ken Wilber. A Brief History of Everything. Shambala: Boston & London. 1996. Page 52.

[4.] Peter Farb. Man's Rise to Civilization. Avon Books: New York. 1968.

[5.] Peter Farb. Man's Rise to Civilization. Avon Books: New York. 1968.

[6.] Peter Farb. Man's Rise to Civilization. Avon Books: New York. 1968.

[7.] Paul R. Ehrlich. Human Natures: Genes, Cultures, and the Human Prospect. Penguin Group: New York, NY. 2002. Page 206.

[8.] Frank B. Linderman. Pretty-shield. Bison Books/University of Nebraska Press: Lincoln, Nebraska. 2003. Page 44.

[9.] John Tanner. The Falcon. Penguin Books: New York. 2003. Pages 197 – 200. Originally published in 1830.

[10.] Peter Farb. Man's Rise to Civilization. Avon Books: New York. 1968.

[11.] Peter Farb. Man's Rise to Civilization. Avon Books: New York. 1968. Pages 192 -196.

[12.] Robert J. Sharer with Loa P. Traxler. The Ancient Maya, Sixth Edition. Stanford University Press: Stanford, CA. 2006. Page 89.

[13.] Ken Wilber. Up from Eden. Quest Books: Wheaton, IL. 1981, 1996. Page 177.

[14.] Julian Jaynes. The Origin of Consciousness. Houghton Mifflin Company: Boston. 1976. Page 174.

[15.] Michael D. Coe & Rex Koontz. Mexico: From the Olmecs to the Aztecs. Thames & Hudson Ltd.: London. Fifth Edition. 2002. Page 193.

[16.] Julian Jaynes. The Origin of Consciousness. Houghton Mifflin Company: Boston. 1976. Page 173.

[17.] Julian Jaynes. The Origin of Consciousness. Houghton Mifflin Company: Boston. 1976. Page 174.

[18.] Julian Jaynes. The Origin of Consciousness. Houghton Mifflin Company: Boston. 1976. Page 174.

[19.] Julian Jaynes. The Origin of Consciousness. Houghton Mifflin Company: Boston. 1976. Page 179 - 180.

[20.] Julian Jaynes. The Origin of Consciousness. Houghton Mifflin Company: Boston. 1976. Page 182 - 183.

[21.] Julian Jaynes. The Origin of Consciousness. Houghton Mifflin Company: Boston. 1976. Page 161.

[22.] Julian Jaynes. The Origin of Consciousness. Houghton Mifflin Company: Boston. 1976. Page 161.

[23.] Lewis Cotlow. In Search of the Primitive. Little, Brown & Co.: Boston. 1942, 1966. Pages 367- 369.

[24.] Phil Mercer. *"Vanuatu cargo cult marks 50 years."* BBC News. http://news.bbc.co.uk/2/hi/asia-pacific/6363843.stm February 15, 2007. Accessed February 15, 2007.

[25.] Lewis Cotlow. In Search of the Primitive. Little, Brown & Co.: Boston. 1942, 1966. Page 73.

[26.] Andrew Quinn. *"Bushman hero of 'Gods Must Be Crazy' dead."* Sify movies. http://sify.com/movies/hollywood/fullstory.p

hp?id=13190694. July 5, 2003. Accessed February 13, 2008.

27. Lewis Cotlow. In Search of the Primitive. Little, Brown & Co.: Boston. 1942, 1966. Page 55.

28. Richard B. Lee. The Dobe !Kung. Holt, Rinehart and Winston, Inc. 1979. Page 85.

29. John Tanner. The Falcon. Penguin Books: New York. 2003. Page 89.

30. Neelesh Misra, AP. "Reading waves may have saved ancient Indian island tribes." Helena Independent Record. http://
www.helenair.com/articles/2005/01/05/national/a03010505_01.txt. January 5, 2005. Accessed March 17, 2007.

31. Neelesh Misra and Rupak Sanyal. "Ancient Tribe Survives Tsunami." CBS News. http://www.cbsnews.com/stories/2005/
01/04/world/main664729.shtml. January 6, 2005. Accessed March 17, 2007.

32. _____. "During Tsunami Remote Viewing primitive tribes in Andaman Nicobar Islands of India moved to higher grounds – so did most
animals." India Daily. http://www.indiadaily.com/editorial/01-02-05.asp. January 2, 2005. Accessed March 17, 2007.

33. John Leo. "The North American Conquest." U.S. News & World Report. May 13, 1991. Page 25.

7. Preconscious Processing

1. Helen Keller. The World I Live In. New York: Century. 1904, 1908. Pages 113-14.

2. Temple Grandin. Animals in Translation. Harcourt, Inc.: Orlando, FL. 2005.

3. Jane Goodall. My Life with the Chimpanzees. Byron Priess/Pocketbooks/Simon & Schuster, Inc.: New York. 1988,
1996. Pages 3 - 5.

4. Temple Grandin. Animals in Translation. Harcourt, Inc.: Orlando, FL. 2005.

5. Temple Grandin. Animals in Translation. Harcourt, Inc.: Orlando, FL. 2005.Pages 155-161.

6. Temple Grandin. Animals in Translation. Harcourt, Inc.: Orlando, FL. 2005. Page 105.

7. Peter Farb. Humankind. Houghton Mifflin Company: Boston. 1978. Page 8.

8. Elizabeth Grice. "Cry of an enfant sauvage." Telegraph. http://www.telegraph.co.uk/arts/main.jhtml?xml=/arts/2006/
07/17/ftdog17.xml. June 7, 2006. Accessed February 24, 2008.

9. _____. "Secret of the Wild Child." PBS Nova. Airdate: March 4, 1997. http://www.pbs.org/wgbh/nova/transcripts/
2112gchild.html. Accessed July 1, 2007.

10. _____. "The Story of Genie." FeralChildren.com. http://www.feralchildren.com/en/showchild.php?ch=genie. Accessed
July 1, 2007.

1. _____. "Secret of the Wild Child." PBS Nova. Airdate: March 4, 1997. http://www.pbs.org/wgbh/nova/transcripts/
2112gchild.html. Accessed July 1, 2007.

2. _____. "Kenyan baby girl 'rescued by dog.'" BBC News. http://news.bbc.co.uk/2/hi/africa/4530423.stm. May 9, 2005.
Accessed March 17, 2007. Accessed July 1, 2007.

3. _____. "The Saharan Gazelle Boy." FeralChildren.com http://www.feralchildren.com/en/showchild.php?ch=sahara.
Accessed July 3, 2007.

4. _____. "Kamala and Amala, the Wolf Girls of Midnapore." FeralChildren.com http://www.feralchildren.com/en/
showchild.php?ch=kamala. Accessed July 2, 2007.

5. Anne Merwood. "Plants of the Apes." Wildlife Conservation. March-April 1991. Pages 54 – 59.

6. Carl Rogers. Freedom to Learn For the 80's. Charles E. Merrill Publishing Co. Columbus, OH. 1983. Page 258.

7. Laurence Gonzales. Deep Survival. W. W. Norton & Company: New York. 2003. Pages 161-162.

8. Barry Holstum Lopez. Of Wolves and Men. Charles Scribner's Sons/ Macmillan Publishing: New York. 1978. Page 62.

9. Barry Holstum Lopez. Of Wolves and Men. Charles Scribner's Sons/ Macmillan Publishing: New York. 1978. Page 58.

20. Michael J. Roads. Talking With Nature. HJ Kramer Inc.: Tiburon, California. 1985,1987. Pages 27 –30.

2. Alma Hogan Snell. Grandmother's Grandchild. Bison Books/University of Nebraska Press: Lincoln, NE. 2001. Page
37.

22. Derrick Jensen. A Language Older Than Words. Context Books: New York. 2000. Page 64.

23. Derrick Jensen. A Language Older Than Words. Context Books: New York. 2000. Page 2.

24. Daniel Tammet. Born on a Blue Day. Free Press. New York. 2006. Pages 79 - 80.

25. Daniel Tammet. Born on a Blue Day. Free Press. New York. 2006. Page 44.

26. Daniel Tammet. Born on a Blue Day. Free Press. New York. 2006. Page 80.

27. Temple Grandin. Thinking in Pictures. Vintage Books / Random House: New York. 1995, 2006. Page 21.

28. _____. "René Descartes." Wikipedia. http://en.wikipedia.org/wiki/René_Descartes. Accessed February 10, 2008.

29. Temple Grandin. Animals in Translation. Harcourt, Inc.: Orlando, FL. 2005. Pages 179 – 240.

30. Daniel Tammet. Born on a Blue Day. Free Press. New York. 2006. Page 103.

3. _____. "Unlocking the brain's potential" BBC News. http://news.bbc.co.uk/1/hi/health/1211299.stm. March 10, 2001.
Accessed February 22, 2008.

32. Temple Grandin. Animals in Translation. Harcourt, Inc.: Orlando, Florida. 2005. Page 25.

33. _____. "Unlocking the brain's potential." BBC News. http://news.bbc.co.uk/1/hi/health/1211299.stm. March 10, 2001.
Accessed February 22, 2008.

34. Temple Grandin. Animals in Translation. Harcourt, Inc.: Orlando, FL. 2005. Page 63.

35. Temple Grandin. Animals in Translation. Harcourt, Inc.: Orlando, FL. 2005. Pages 63 – 64.

8. Magical Processing

1. Lewis Cotlow. In Search of the Primitive. Little, Brown & Co.: Boston. 1942, 1966. Page 197.

2. Sir James George Frazer. The Golden Bough. Touchstone: New York. 1996. Pages 23 – 24.

3. Lewis Cotlow. In Search of the Primitive. Little, Brown & Co.: Boston. 1942, 1966. Page 228 - 236.

4. _____. "Voodoo head found in air luggage." BBC News. http://news.bbc.co.uk/1/hi/world/americas/4703328.stm.
February 11, 2006. Accessed February 11, 2006.

5. Rick Mikula. The Family Butterfly Book. Storey Publishing. 2000. Page 5.

6. D. H. Lawrence. "Self-Pity." http://www.poemhunter.com/poem/self-pity/." Accessed September 19, 2007.

7. Ken Wilber. Up from Eden. Quest Books: Wheaton, IL. 1981, 1996. Page 68.

8. John Tanner. The Falcon. Penguin Books: New York. 2003. Page 23. Originally published in 1830.

9. _____. "Grizzly Bear Recovery." U.S. Fish and Wildlife Service. http://www.fws.gov/mountain%2Dprairie/species/

mammals/grizzly/. Accessed February 24, 2008.

10. Lewis Cotlow. In Search of the Primitive. Little, Brown & Co.: Boston. 1942, 1966. Page 109 - 110.

11. Joseph Lemasolai Lekuton. Facing the Lion. National Geographic: Washington, DC. 2003.

12. Frank B. Linderman. Pretty-shield. Bison Books/University of Nebraska Press: Lincoln, Nebraska. 2003.

13. John (Fire) Lame Deer and Richard Erdoes. Lame Deer: Seeker of Visions. Washington Square Press / Pocket Books: New York. 1972. Page 124.

14. Ivan Leudar and Philip Thomas. Voices of Reason, Voices of Insanity. Taylor & Francis, Inc: Philadelphia, PA. 2000, 2001.

15. Jon Young. "Learning the Language of the Birds." Audio Tape. OWLink Media.

16. Jared Diamond. The Third Chimpanzee. Harper / Perennial: New York. 1992. Pages 223 – 234.

17. Joseph Bruchac. Native Plant Stories. Fulcrum Publishing: Golden, Colorado. 1995. Pages 87 – 101.

18. Pierre Berton. The Arctic Grail. Viking/Penguin: New York. 1988. Pages 116 - 117.

19. Pierre Berton. The Arctic Grail. Viking/Penguin: New York. 1988. Page 58.

20. Mark J. Plotkin, Ph.D. Tales of a Shaman's Apprentice. Penguin Books. 1993. Pages 1, 101, 102.

21. Alma Hogan Snell. Grandmother's Grandchild. University of Nebraska Press: Lincoln and London. 2000. Page 27.

22. Stephen E. Ambrose. Undaunted Courage. Touchstone/Simon & Schuster: New York. 1997. Page 197.

9. Mythical Processing

1. Ken Wilber. Up from Eden. Quest Books: Wheaton, IL. 1981, 1996. Page 94.

2. Bible, King James Version. BibleGateway.com. Accessed October 29, 2007.

3. Daniel Quinn. Ishmael. Bantam/Turner: New York. 1993. Pages 71 - 72.

4. Ken Wilber. Up from Eden. Quest Books: Wheaton, IL. 1981, 1996. Page 183.

5. _____. "Heaven's Gate (cult)." Wikipedia. http://en.wikipedia.org/wiki/Heaven's_Gate_(cult) Accessed December 12, 2006.

6. _____. "Cult Suicide." Wikipedia. http://en.wikipedia.org/wiki/Cult_Suicide. Accessed December 12, 2006.

7. Yatri. Unknown Man. Fireside Books/Simon & Schuster, Inc.: New York. 1988. Page 126.

8. Andrew Sullivan. "When Not Seeing Is Believing." Time. http://www.time.com/time/magazine/article/0,9171,1541466-1,00.html. October 2, 2006. Accessed October 2, 2006.

9. Todd Pitock. "Science and Islam." Discover. July 2007. Pages 36 – 45.

10. Robert Kegan. The Evolving Self. Harvard University Press: Cambridge, MA. Page 113.

11. George Lakoff. "Metaphor, Morality, and Politics." http://www.wwcd.org/issues/Lakoff.html 1995. Accessed August 31, 2007.

12. George Lakoff. "Metaphor, Morality, and Politics." http://www.wwcd.org/issues/Lakoff.html 1995. Accessed August 31, 2007.

13. Joseph Lemasolai Lekuton. Facing the Lion. National Geographic: Washington, DC. 2003.

14. Anthony Stevens. The Roots of War and Terror. Continuum International Publishing Group: 2005. Page 194.

15. Pedro de Cieza de León. The Discovery and Conquest of Peru. Duke University Press: Durham and London. 1998. Page 122.

16. _____. "Zion's Christian Soldiers." CBS News: 60 Minutes. http://www.cbsnews.com/stories/2002/10/03/60minutes/main524268.shtml. June 8, 2003. Accessed September 4, 2007.

17. Abraham Odeke. "Ugandans flock to concrete cross." BBC News. http://news.bbc.co.uk/2/hi/africa/6181427.stm. December 15, 2006.

10. Sequential Processing

1. Stephan Shennan. Genes, Memes, and Human History. Thames & Hudson: New York. 2002. Page 264.

2. _____. "Nicolaus Copernicus." Wikipedia. http://en.wikipedia.org/wiki/Copernicus. Accessed November 1, 2006.

3. Richard Hooker. "World Civilizations: The European Enlightenment." http://www.wsu.edu/~dee/ENLIGHT/SCIREV.HTM. 1996. Updated 6-6-1999. Accessed February 10, 2008.

4. David Burne. Get a Grip on Evolution. Time Life Books. 1999. Page 44.

5. David Burne. Get a Grip on Evolution. Time Life Books. 1999. Pages 48 – 49.

6. David Burne. Get a Grip on Evolution. Time Life Books. 1999. Page 42.

7. David Burne. Get a Grip on Evolution. Time Life Books. 1999. Pages 40 – 41.

8. David Burne. Get a Grip on Evolution. Time Life Books. 1999. Pages 46 – 47.

9. David Burne. Get a Grip on Evolution. Time Life Books. 1999. Pages 50 – 51.

10. David Burne. Get a Grip on Evolution. Time Life Books. 1999. Pages 52 – 55.

11. David Burne. Get a Grip on Evolution. Time Life Books. 1999. Pages 62 – 63.

12. David Burne. Get a Grip on Evolution. Time Life Books. 1999. Page 70.

13. _____. "Interchangeable parts." Wikipedia. http://en.wikipedia.org/wiki/Interchangeable_parts. Accessed November 8, 2006.

14. Wolfgang Schivelbusch. The Railway Journey. The University of California Press: Berkeley, CA. 1977, 1986.

15. Richard Hooker. "World Civilizations: The European Enlightenment: René Descartes." http://www.wsu.edu/~dee/ENLIGHT/DESCARTE.HTM. 1996. Updated 6-6-1999. Accessed February 10, 2008.

16. Henry David Thoreau. Walden, Or, Life in the Woods. Dover Publications. 1995. Page 37.

17. _____. "New Study Of The Literacy Of College Students Finds Some Are Graduating With Only Basic Skills." American Institutes for Research. http://www.air.org/news/documents/Release200601pew.htm. January 19, 2006. Accessed February 3, 2008.

18. Barbara Kingsolver. "Stalking the Vegetannual." Orion Magazine. March/April 2007. http://www.orionmagazine.org/index.php/articles/article/239/. Accessed February 3, 2008.

19. George Lakoff. "Metaphor, Morality, and Politics." http://www.wwcd.org/issues/Lakoff.html 1995. August 31, 2007.

20. Richard Louv. Last Child in the Woods. Algonquin Books: Chapel Hill, NC. 2005. Page 20.

21. George Lakoff. "Metaphor, Morality, and Politics." http://www.wwcd.org/issues/Lakoff.html 1995. Accessed August 31,

2007.

22. Nader Khalili. <u>Sidewalks on the Moon</u>. Cal-Earth Press: Hesperia, CA. 1994. Pages 80 -81.

23. Pope John Paul II. *"Truth Cannot Contradict Truth."* <u>New Advent</u>. http://www.newadvent.org/library/docs_jp02tc.htm. October 22, 1996. Accessed March 4, 2007.

24. Pat Feldsien, editor. <u>I Drink the Living Water</u>. Trafford Publishing: Victoria, British Columbia. 2006.

25. Thomas S. Kuhn. <u>The Structure of Scientific Revolutions, 3rd Edition</u>. University of Chicago Press: Chicago and London. 1996. Page 24.

11. Systems Processing

1. Amory Lovins. *"Imagine a World..."* Rocky Mountain Institute 25th Celebration Speech. August 2007.

2. Steven Johnson. *"Your Brain on Video Games."* <u>Discover</u>. July 2005. Volume 26, No. 7. Pages 39 – 43.

3. Rocky Mountain Institute. *"Systems Thinking."* http://www.rmi.org/sitepages/pid62.php. Accessed February 10, 2008.

4. Eckart Tolle. <u>The Power of Now</u>. Namaste Publishing / New World Library: Novato California. 1999, 2004. Page 193.

5. Jocelyn Voo. *"Why do unmarried couples opt out of wedlock?"* CNN.com. http://beta.cnn.com/2007/LIVING/personal/09/19/unmarried.couples/index.html. September 19, 2007. Accessed September 19, 2007.

6. Carl Rogers. <u>Carl Rogers on Personal Power</u>. Delacorte Press: New York. 1977. Page 30.

7. Carl Rogers. <u>Carl Rogers on Personal Power</u>. Delacorte Press: New York. 1977. Pages 135 – 136.

8. Carl Rogers. <u>Freedom to Learn For the 80's</u>. Charles E. Merrill Publishing Co. Columbus, OH. 1983. Page 26.

12. Holistic Processing

. *"Great Aviation Quotes: Space."* http://www.skygod.com/quotes/space.html. Accessed June 14, 2007.

2. Emily Eakin. *"Study Finds a Nation of Polarized Readers."* The New York Times. http://www.nytimes.com/2004/03/13/arts/13BOOK.html. March 13, 2004. Accessed October 31,2006.

3. Valdis Krebs. *"Perpetually Polarized?"* Orgnet.com. http://www.orgnet.com/divided2.html. Accessed October 31, 2006.

4. Valdis Krebs. *"Perpetually Polarized?"* Orgnet.com. http://www.orgnet.com/divided.html. Accessed October 31, 2006.

5. Jo Robinson. <u>Pasture Perfect</u>. Vashon Island Press: Vashon, WA. 2004. Page 27.

6. _____. *"The Soil Carbon Manifesto."* http://www.carboncoalition.com.au/. Accessed November 6, 2007.

7. Jim Scott. "Arid Australian interior linked to landscape burning by ancient humans." http://www.eurekalert.org/pub_releases/2005-01/uoca-aai012505.php. January 25, 2005. Accessed November 6, 2007.

8. Ron Gluckman, Fengning, and Langtougou. *"Beijing's Desert Storm."* http://www.gluckman.com/ChinaDesert.html. Accessed December 18, 2007.

9. Rohr, Dixon. *"Too Much, Too Fast."* <u>Newsweek</u>. June 1, 1992. Pg. 34.

10. Allan Savory with Jody Butterfield. <u>Holistic Management</u>. Island Press: Washington, D.C. 1988, 1999. Pages 41 – 42.

1. Wayne Burleson. *"Our Fences are Shrinking."* <u>The Whole Approach</u>. Belgrade, MT. Vol. 1, No. 1. Page 7 – 8.

2. _____. *"The other side of global warming."* ManagingWholes.net. http://managingwholes.net/?p=22. Accessed October 24th, 2007.

13. Christopher Cooper. *"In Katrina's Wake: Where Is the Money?"* CREW. http://www.citizensforethics.org/node/19906. January 27, 2007. Accessed February 12, 2008.

4. _____. *"Audits: Millions of dollars in Katrina aid wasted."* MSNBC. http://www.msnbc.msn.com/id/11326973. February 3, 2006. Accessed February 12, 2008.

13. Transcendence

. Eckart Tolle. <u>The Power of Now</u>. Namaste Publishing / New World Library: Novato California. 1999, 2004. Page 181.

2. _____. Random House Webster's College Dictionary. Random House: New York. 1999. Page 1385.

3. Yatri. <u>Unknown Man</u>. Fireside Books/Simon & Schuster, Inc.: New York. 1988. Page 71.

4. Ken Wilber. <u>A Brief History of Everything</u>. Shambala: Boston & London. 1996.

5. Leona Evans and Carol Keefer. *"A New Paradigm for the 21st Century."* <u>Unity Magazine</u>. January 2000. Pages 14 – 22.

6. Jared Diamond. *"The Golden Age That Never Was."* <u>Discover</u>. December 1988. Pages 71 – 79.

7. Jared Diamond. *"The Golden Age That Never Was."* <u>Discover</u>. December 1988. Pages 71 – 79.

8. Alma Hogan Snell. <u>Grandmother's Grandchild</u>. University of Nebraska Press: Lincoln and London. 2000. Page 8.

9. Lewis Cotlow. <u>In Search of the Primitive</u>. Little, Brown & Co.: Boston. 1942, 1966. Page 49.

0. Duane Champagne. <u>Social Change and Cultural Continuity Among Native Nations</u>. Altamira Press: Lanham, MD. 2006. Page 304.

1. Jared Diamond. *"Playing Dice With Megadeath."* <u>Discover</u>. April 1990. Pages 55 - 59.

2. Jared Diamond. *"Playing Dice With Megadeath."* <u>Discover</u>. April 1990. Pages 55 - 59.

3. _____. *"The Industrial Symbiosis at Kalundborg, Denmark."* Indigo Development. http://www.indigodev.com/Kal.html. Last modified June 12, 2003. Accessed February 24, 2008.

4. Marion Long. *"The Discover Interview."* <u>Discover</u>. March 2008. Pages 64 – 67.

5. Megha Bahree. *"Child Labor."* <u>Forbes</u>. http://www.forbes.com/forbes/2008/0225/072_print.html. February 25, 2008. Accessed February 25, 2008.

6. _____. *"Child protection from violence, exploitation and abuse."* <u>Unicef</u>. http://www.unicef.org/protection/index_childlabour.html. Accessed February 25, 2008.

14. Mystical Processing

. Eckart Tolle. <u>The Power of Now</u>. Namaste Publishing / New World Library: Novato California. 1999, 2004. Pages 99-100.

2. James Lovelock. <u>Healing Gaia</u>. Harmony Books: New York, NY. 1991.

3. Joel Achenbach. *"Fire and Ice."* <u>National Geographic</u>. April 2003. Page 3. Rick Gore. "The Rise of Mammals." National Geographic. April 2003. Pages 4 – 37. _____.

4. *"Cretaceous-Tertiary extinction event."* Wikipedia. http://en.wikipedia.org/wiki/Cretaceous_extinction. Accessed October 25, 2006.

5. Joel Achenbach. *"Fire and Ice."* <u>National Geographic</u>. April 2003. Page 3.

6. Rick Gore. *"The Rise of Mammals."* National Geographic. April 2003. Pages 4 – 37.
7. _____. *"Cretaceous-Tertiary extinction event."* Wikipedia. http://en.wikipedia.org/wiki/Cretaceous_extinction. October 25, 2006.
8. Richard Louv. Last Child in the Woods. Algonquin Books: Chapel Hill, NC. 2005. Pages 22 - 23.
9. Josie Glausiusz. *"Your Body is a Planet."* Discover. June 2007. Pages 44-45.
10. _____. *"Gut flora."* Wikipedia. http://en.wikipedia.org/wiki/Microflora. December 17th, 2006.
11. Sarah Richardson. *"Tongue Bugs."* Discover. October 1995. http://findarticles.com/p/articles/mi_m1511/is_n10_v16/ai_17449585. Accessed January 31, 2008.
12. David R. Caprette. *"Cellular 'Slime Molds:' Dictyostelium and relatives."* Experimental Biosciences. http://www.ruf.rice.edu/~bioslabs/studies/invertebrates/dicty.html. June 27, 1996. Accessed February 24, 2008.
13. Carl Zimmer. Parasite Rex. The Free Press: New York. 2000. Pages 79 -117.
14. Pat Feldsien, editor. I Drink the Living Water. Trafford Publishing: Victoria, British Columbia. 2006.
15. Roshi Philip Kapleau. The Three Pillars of Zen, 25th Anniversary Edition. Anchor Books/Doubleday: New York, NY. 1980, 1989. Page 62.
16. Ken Wilber. A Brief History of Everything. Shambala: Boston & London. 1996. Page 204.
17. Daniel Greenberg. *"And 'Rithmetic."* http://www.mountainlaurelsudbury.org/Rithmetic.asp. Accessed January 31, 2008.
18. Hanna Greenberg. *"The Art of Doing Nothing."* http://www.sudval.org/05_underlyingideas.html#03. Accessed January 31, 2008.
19. Hara Estroff Marano. *"Education: Class Dismissed."* Psychology Today. May/June 2006. http://www.psychologytoday.com/articles/index.php?term=20060424-000004. Accessed January 31, 2008.
20. Barry Holstum Lopez. Of Wolves and Men. Charles Scribner's Sons/ Macmillan Publishing: New York. 1978. Page 204.
21. Barry Holstum Lopez. Of Wolves and Men. Charles Scribner's Sons/ Macmillan Publishing: New York. 1978. Page 5.
22. Barry Holstum Lopez. Of Wolves and Men. Charles Scribner's Sons/ Macmillan Publishing: New York. 1978. Pages 144 – 145.
23. Barry Holstum Lopez. Of Wolves and Men. Charles Scribner's Sons/ Macmillan Publishing: New York. 1978. Page 150.
24. Barry Holstum Lopez. Of Wolves and Men. Charles Scribner's Sons/ Macmillan Publishing: New York. 1978. Page 239.
25. Barry Holstum Lopez. Of Wolves and Men. Charles Scribner's Sons/ Macmillan Publishing: New York. 1978. Page 179.
26. Barry Holstum Lopez. Of Wolves and Men. Charles Scribner's Sons/ Macmillan Publishing: New York. 1978. Page 180.
27. Barry Holstum Lopez. Of Wolves and Men. Charles Scribner's Sons/ Macmillan Publishing: New York. 1978. Page 139.
28. Masanobu Fukuoka. The Natural Way of Farming. Japan Publications, Inc.: Tokyo & New York. 1985. Pages 30 - 31.
29. *"Las Vegas to Build World's First 30 Story Vertical Farm."* Next Energy News. http://www.nextenergynews.com/news1/next-energy-news-las-vegas-vertical-farm-1.2b.html. Accessed January 10, 2008.
30. Lisa Chamberlain. *"Skyfarming."* New York News & Features. http://nymag.com/news/features/30020/. Accessed January 10, 2008.
31. Fraser Cain. *"Artificial Meat Could be Grown on a Large Scale."* Universe Today. http://www.universetoday.com/2005/07/06/artificial-meat-could-be-grown-on-a-large-scale/. July 6, 2005. Accessed February 25, 2008.
32. Bruno Maddox. *"Blinded by Science: The Way of All Flesh."* Discover. http://discovermagazine.com/2006/jul/blinded/ Accessed January 10, 2008.
33. Tim Folger. *"Patently Absurd."* Discover. March 2008. Pages 55 – 57.

15. Observer Processing

1. Mike Dooley. *"Thoughts Become Things."* http://www.tut.com/beliefnet/thoughts_become_things.htm. January 28, 2002. Accessed January 31, 2008.
2. Jack Lucentini. *"Hydra of My Heart."* Discover. December 2003. Page 14.
3. Thomas Bass. *"Robot, Build Thyself."* Discover. October 1995. Pages 64 – 72.
4. Eric Drexler. The Engines of Creation. Bantam Doubleday Dell. 1986.
5. Susan Blackmore. Consciousness. Oxford University Press: Oxford & New York. 2004. Page 222.
6. Bob Berman. *"Much Ado About Nothing."* Discover. July 2002. Page 28.
7. David Barry. *"The (Long and Winding) Road to Reality."* Discover. June 2005. Pages 27 - 35.
8. William Harmon. Global Mind Change. Berrett-Koehler Publishers, Inc. 1998. Page 59.
9. Richard Rabkin, M.D., *"The Indian Rope Trick: The Cultural Creation of Reality."* Whole Earth Review, Summer 1987.
10. Susan Kruglinski. *"Who Moved The Earth?"* Discover. October 2004. Volume 25, Number 10. Page 12.
11. Jeanne Lenzer. *"Citizen, HEAL Thyself."* Discover. September 2007. Pages 54 – 59, 73.
12. Jeanne Lenzer. *"Citizen, HEAL Thyself."* Discover. September 2007. Pages 54 – 59, 73.
13. Jeanne Lenzer. *"Citizen, HEAL Thyself."* Discover. September 2007. Pages 54 – 59, 73.
14. Jeanne Lenzer. *"Citizen, HEAL Thyself."* Discover. September 2007. Pages 54 – 59, 73.
15. John (Fire) Lame Deer and Richard Erdoes. Lame Deer: Seeker of Visions. Washington Square Press / Pocket Books: New York. 1972. Page 124.
16. Carlos Castaneda. A Separate Reality. Washington Square Press/Pocket Books: New York. 1971, 1972. Pages 144 - 148.

16. Nonlinear Processing

1. Thomas Campbell. My Big TOE. Lightning Strike Books. 2003. Book 1. Pages 120 – 121.
2. Stephen Ambrose. Nothing Like it in the World. Simon & Schuster: New York, NY. 2001. Page 57.
3. Michio Kaku. *"Through the Wormhole."* Discover. March 2008. Pages 38 – 42.
4. John Boslough. *"The Enigma of Time."* National Geographic. March 1990. Pages 109 - 132.

5. Martin Rees. Just Six Numbers. Basic Books: New York. 2000. Page 38.

6. Tim Folger. "In No Time." Discover. June 2007. Pages 78-79.

7. Tim Folger. "Patently Absurd." Discover. March 2008. Pages 55 – 57.

8. Laurence Gonzales. Deep Survival. W. W. Norton & Company: New York. 2003. Pages 183 - 204.

9. Fred Alan Wolf, Ph.D. Dr. Quantum's Little Book of Big Ideas. Moment Point Press: Needham, MA. 2005. Page 60.

10. Fred Alan Wolf, Ph.D. The Yoga of Time Travel. Quest Books: Wheaton, IL. 2004.

1. Greg Mortenson, David Oliver Relin. Three Cups of Tea. Viking / Penguin: New York. 2006. Pages 185–186.

12. Sally Kalson. "Obituary: Lawrence Grodsky / Top American expert on motorcycle safety." Pittsburgh Post-Gazette.com. http://www.post-gazette.com/pg/06101/681096-122.stm. Tuesday, April 11, 2006.

3. _____. "Croc Hunter Irwin Predicted Early Death." Sky News. http://news.sky.com/skynews/article/0,,30200-1290606,00.html. October 29, 2007. Accessed October 29, 2007.

4. Fred Alan Wolf, Ph.D. Dr. Quantums' Little Book of Big Ideas. Moment Point Press: Needham, Massachusetts. 2005. Page 54.

5. Martin Rees. Just Six Numbers. Basic Books: New York. 2000.

6. Roshi Philip Kapleau. The Three Pillars of Zen, 25th Anniversary Edition. Anchor Books/Doubleday: New York, NY. 1980, 1989. Page 70.

7. Eckart Tolle. The Power of Now. Namaste Publishing / New World Library: Novato California. 1999, 2004. Page 85.

8. Eckart Tolle. The Power of Now. Namaste Publishing / New World Library: Novato California. 1999, 2004. Pages 146 – 147.

17. Universal Processing

. The Findhorn Community. The Findhorn Garden. Harper Colophon Books/Harper & Row Publishers: New York. 1975. Page 145.

2. Stephen Hawking. A Brief History of Time. Bantam Books: New York. 1988. Page 129.

3. Brad Lemley. "Guth's Grand Guess." Discover. April 2002. Volume 204, Number 2. Pages 32 – 38.

4. Brad Lemley. "Guth's Grand Guess." Discover. April 2002. Volume 204, Number 2. Pages 32 – 38.

5. Brad Lemley. "Guth's Grand Guess." Discover. April 2002. Volume 204, Number 2. Pages 32 – 38.

6. Bob Berman. "What's the Antimatter?" Discover. October 2005. Volume 26, Number 10. Page 22.

7. Martin Rees. Just Six Numbers. Basic Books: New York. 2000. Pages 95 – 96.

8. Peace Pilgrim. Peace Pilgrim. Ocean Tree Books: Santa Fe, NM. 1982, 1989. Pages 98 - 99.

9. Peace Pilgrim. Peace Pilgrim. Ocean Tree Books: Santa Fe, NM. 1982, 1989. Page 129.

0. Tom Brown Jr. with William Owen. The Search. Berkley Books: New York. 1980. Pages xvii – xviii.

1. Peter Oppenheimer. Mirror by the Road. Inner Wealth Press: Forest Knolls, CA. 1988. Page 114.

2. Richard Spencer. "Dalai Lama says successor could be a woman." Telegraph.co.uk. July 12, 2007. http://www.telegraph.co.uk/news/main.jhtml?xml=/news/2007/12/07/wlama107.xml. Accessed January 31, 2008.

3. U. G. Krishnamurti. Quotes and Photos. http://www.ugkrishnamurti.org/ug/quotes_and_photos/album01/page07.html. Accessed February 19th, 2008.

4. J. Krishnamurti. The Light in Oneself. Krishnamurti Foundation Trust, Ltd.: Bramdean, England. 1999. Page 83.

5. J. Krishnamurti. The Light in Oneself. Krishnamurti Foundation Trust, Ltd.: Bramdean, England. 1999. Page 62.

6. J. Krishnamurti. The Light in Oneself. Krishnamurti Foundation Trust, Ltd.: Bramdean, England. 1999. Page 50.

7. Peace Pilgrim. Peace Pilgrim. Ocean Tree Books: Santa Fe, NM. 1982, 1989. Page 141.

8. Masanobu Fukuoka. The Natural Way of Farming. Japan Publications, Inc.: Tokyo & New York. 1985. 132.

9. Masanobu Fukuoka. The Natural Way of Farming. Japan Publications, Inc.: Tokyo & New York. 1985. Pages 16 – 17.

20. Masanobu Fukuoka. The Natural Way of Farming. Japan Publications, Inc.: Tokyo & New York. 1985. Page 122.

2. Masanobu Fukuoka. The One Straw Revolution. Bantam Books: New York. 1985. Page 16.

22. Masanobu Fukuoka. The One Straw Revolution. Bantam Books: New York. 1985. Page 103.

23. Lou Dobbs. "The war within: killing ourselves." CNN.com. http://www.cnn.com/2007/US/02/13/Dobbs.Feb14/index.html. February 1, 2007. Accessed February 1, 2007.

24. Masanobu Fukuoka. The One Straw Revolution. Bantam Books: New York. 1985. Page 151.

25. AP. "Communing without nature." CNN.com. http://www.cnn.com/2008/TECH/science/02/05/nature.interest.ap/index.html. February 5, 2008. Accessed February 5, 2008.

26. Peace Pilgrim. Peace Pilgrim. Ocean Tree Books: Santa Fe, NM. 1982, 1989. Page 128.

27. Sharon Wegscheider-Cruse. Dancing with Destiny. Health Communications, Inc.: Deerfield Beach, Florida. 1989. Page xiv.

28. _____. "Burma: Thousands Dead in Massacre of the Monks Dumped in the Jungle." This is London. http://www.thisislondon.co.uk/news/article-23414471-details/Burma:+Thousands+dead+in+the+massacre+of+the+monks+dumped+in+the+jungle/article.do. Updated January 10, 2008. Accessed February 22, 2008.

29. U. G. Krishnamurti. Quotes and Photos. http://www.ugkrishnamurti.org/ug/quotes_and_photos/album01/page06.html. Accessed February 19th, 2008.

30. Rory Byrne. "Crackdown Against Buddhist Monks Shakes Burmese Society." Voice of America. http://www.voanews.com/english/archive/2008-01/2008-01-02-voa22.cfm. January 2, 2008. Accessed February 22, 2008.

3. Fred Alan Wolf, Ph.D. The Yoga of Time Travel. Quest Books: Wheaton, IL. 2004. Page 199.

32. Thomas Campbell. My Big TOE. Lightning Strike Books. Book 2, Page 119.

18. The Awakening

. Ray Jardine. "Shortcuts to Wilderness Connection." TGO Magazine, January 2000.

2. John Muir. BrainyQuote.com. http://www.brainyquote.com/quotes/authors/j/john_muir.html. Accessed August 9, 2007.

3. Sharon Wegscheider-Cruse. Dancing with Destiny. Health Communications, Inc.: Deerfield Beach, Florida. 1989. Page 148.

4. Peace Pilgrim. Peace Pilgrim. Ocean Tree Books: Santa Fe, NM. 1982, 1989. Pages 64 - 65.

5. Roshi Philip Kapleau. The Three Pillars of Zen, 25th Anniversary Edition. Anchor Books/Doubleday: New York, NY. 1980, 1989. Page 210.

6. Matthew 15. Bible, King James Version. BibleGateway.com. February 15, 2008.

7. Peace Pilgrim. Peace Pilgrim. Ocean Tree Books: Santa Fe, NM. 1982, 1989. Page 15.

8. Anthony deMello. Awareness. Image Books/Doubleday: New York. 1990. Page 126.

9. Colin M. Turnbull. The Forest People. Touchstone/Simon & Schuster: New York, NY. 1968. Page 272.

0. Masanobu Fukuoka. The One Straw Revolution. Bantam Books: New York. 1985. Page 141.

1. Carlos Castaneda. The Teachings of Don Juan. Ballantine Books: New York. 1969 – 1973. Page 106.

2. Yatri. Unknown Man. Fireside Books/Simon & Schuster, Inc.: New York. 1988. Page 253.

Index

Ever dream of building your own low-cost, energy efficient home?

Living Homes
Integrated Design & Construction
by Thomas J. Elpel

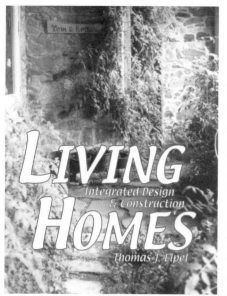

The house of your Dreams does not have to be expensive. The key is all in the planning. How much a house costs, how it looks, how comfortable it is, how energy-efficient it is—all these things occur on paper before you pick up even one tool. A little extra time in the planning process can save you tens of thousands of dollars in construction and maintenance. That is time well spent!

Living Homes takes you through the planning process to design an energy and resource efficient home that won't break the bank. Thomas J. Elpel guides you through the nuts and bolts of construction from the footings on up to the roof. You will learn how to do slip-form stone masonry, log home construction, building with strawbales, making your own "terra tile" floors, windows & doors, solar water systems, masonry heaters, framing, plumbing, greywater, septic systems, swamp filters, painting and more!

The fifth edition includes new material covering concrete-fly ash countertops, the latest stone masonry tips, plus revised and expanded tips and techniques throughout the book. 5th Edition. 2005. ISBN: 1-892784-18-1. 233 pages, with 300+ drawings and photos. Printed on 100% recycled paper. $30.

Slipform Stone Masonry DVD
With Builder and Author Thomas J. Elpel

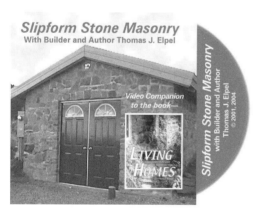

Want to build a stone house? *Slipform Stone Masonry* brings to life the nuts-and-bolts of the slipforming process featured in Thomas J. Elpel's book *Living Homes.*

Slipforming is the process of using forms as guides for the stonework. The forms are filled with stone and concrete, then "slipped" up the walls to form the subsequent levels. Slipforming makes stone work easy even for a novice.

In this unique video, Thomas J. Elpel and Robert Taylor build an insulated workshop of stone, demonstrating the building process from site excavation right through to putting the roof on and finishing the inside. This video is intended as a companion to *Living Homes.* The principles of design and construction are outlined in the book, enabling the reader to create dwellings customized to their own unique situations. In this video you will see just one application of those principles, but in vivid detail from start to finish. With both the book and the video you too will be able to design and build in a way that is completely unique to your Vision. DVD. ISBN: 1-892784-17-3. 2001. 1 hr. 50 min. $25.

Browse the bookshelf at **www.GrannysStore.com** for additional titles.

Looking for an easier way to learn to identify plants?

Shanleya's Quest
A Botany Adventure for Kids Ages 9 to 99
By Thomas J. Elpel Illustrated by Gloria Brown

In a world where time is a liquid that falls as rain upon the land, young Shanleya paddles her canoe out to the Tree Islands to learn the plant traditions of her people. Each island is home to a separate family of plants and an unforgettable Guardian with lessons to teach about the identification and uses of those plants. *Shanleya's Quest* is a truly unique educational book that presents botanical concepts and plant identification skills in an easy and fun metaphorical format for children, as well as for adults who are young at heart.

Read the book. Play the game!
Book: 2005. ISBN: 1-892784-16-5. 32 pages. $12.50
Game: 2006. ISBN: 1-892784-23-8. 52 cards. $12.50

Botany in a Day
The Patterns Method of Plant Identification
Thomas J. Elpel's Herbal Field Guide to Plant Families of North America

Botany in a Day is changed the way people learn about plants! Elpel's book has gained a nationwide audience almost exclusively by word-of-mouth. It is now used as a text and recommended by herbal schools and universities across North America. Instead of presenting individual plants, *Botany in a Day* unveils the patterns of identification and uses among related plants, giving readers simple tools to rapidly unlock the mysteries of new species they encounter throughout North America.

Too often people try to learn plants one-at-a-time without rhyme or reason, but now you can cut years off the process of learning about plants and their uses. *Botany in a Day* takes you beyond the piecemeal approach to botany and herbalism towards a "whole" approach. Within 1 1/2 hours you can understand the big picture of botany and herbalism. Learn how related plants have similar features for identification. Discover how they often have similar properties and similar uses.

Tom's book takes you beyond the details towards a greater understanding of the patterns among plants. By mid-morning you can be in the field, matching flowers to the patterns in the book. Instead of learning plants one-at-a-time, you will discover that you can learn them by the dozens—just by looking for patterns. Most plant books cover only one or two hundred species. *Botany in a Day* includes more than 100 plant families and over 700 genera—applicable to many thousands of species. Four indexes. 5th Edition. 2004. ISBN: 1-892784-15-7. 221 pages. 100% recycled paper. $30.

Browse the bookshelf at **www.GrannysStore.com** for additional titles.

Ever desire to get closer to nature and go camping with little or nothing?

Participating in Nature
Thomas J. Elpel's Field Guide to Primitive Living Skills

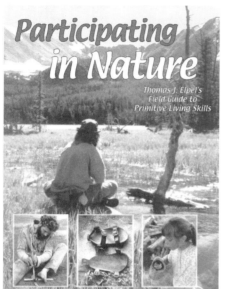

Get in touch with your wild side! Primitive living is a way of learning about nature by participating in it. Instead of merely camping in the wilderness or passing through it, you become part of the process. You learn about nature by using it to meet your needs for shelter, fire, water, and food. Set aside the trappings of modern culture and step directly into nature with little or nothing, to experience nature on its own terms.

This book is the source for in-depth coverage of primitive shelters, butchering road kill deer, making braintan buckskin, tire sandals, bedroll packs and pack frames, felting with wool, quick bows and bone arrowheads, sinews, hide glue, cooking, fishing by hand, water purification, primitive pottery, wooden containers, cordage, twig deer, stalking skills, simple knives, flint & steel, bowdrill and handdrill fire-starting, and much more. Tom publishes unique new information that is not found in any other source. 5th Edition. 2002. ISBN: 1-892784-12-2. 198 pages. 100% recycled paper. $30.

The Art of Nothing
Wilderness Survival Video Series on DVD
with Thomas J. Elpel and special guests

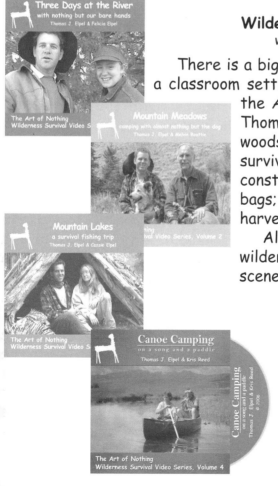

There is a big difference between learning wilderness skills in a classroom setting, versus applying them in the real world. In the *Art of Nothing Wilderness Survival Video Series*, Thomas J. Elpel and special guests journey into the woods and demonstrate all the skills they need to survive, including: making knives and tools; shelter construction to stay warm without blankets or sleeping bags; primitive fire starting; water purification; plus harvesting and cooking wild plant and animal foods.

Also included in the videos are wild mushrooms, wilderness cooking techniques, unique tools, great scenery and wildlife footage.

Each video documents completely different skills to meet the same basic needs for shelter, fire, water, and food, as well as wilderness philosophy and conservation. DVDs are $25 each or buy all four for $75 (save $25).

1 - Three Days at the River: 1-892784-20-3
2 - Mountain Meadows: 1-892784-21-1
3 - Mountain Lakes: 1-892784-22-X
4 - Canoe Camping: 978-1-892784-24-7

Hundreds more wilderness survival, nature, and house-building books on-line!